Commanders of
Dutch East India Ships
in the Eighteenth Century

1. Jakobus Ariesz Arkenbout (1766–1834). The son of VOC commander Arie Arkenbout, he was born in Enkhuizen and entered Company service at the age of thirteen. In 1792, after he had just been appointed commander, he had this porcelain statuette of fired clay made in Canton. Arkenbout is dressed in a long coat, wears a wig and has a tricorn hat folded under his arm. He made another voyage as commander in 1794. Shortly afterwards, he entered service in the Navy of the Batavian Republic and in 1815 he was appointed Deputy-Superintendent of the Naval Dockyard in Medemblik. A small dish bearing the family coat-of-arms is the companion piece to the statuette.

Commanders of Dutch East India Ships in the Eighteenth Century

Jaap R. Bruijn

Translated by
R. L. Robson-McKillop
and Prof. R. W. Unger

THE BOYDELL PRESS

Originally published in Dutch as *'Schippers van de VOC
in de achttiende eeuw aan de wal en op zee'*
First published 2008
De Bataafsche Leeuw, Amsterdam

© Jaap R. Bruijn 2011
English Edition © The Boydell Press 2011

All Rights Reserved. Except as permitted under current legislation
no part of this work may be photocopied, stored in a retrieval system,
published, performed in public, adapted, broadcast,
transmitted, recorded or reproduced in any form or by any means,
without the prior permission of the copyright owner

The right of Jaap R. Bruijn to be identified as
the author of this work has been asserted in accordance with
sections 77 and 78 of the Copyright, Designs and Patents Act 1988

First published 2011
The Boydell Press, Woodbridge

ISBN 978 1 84383 622 3

The Boydell Press is an imprint of Boydell & Brewer Ltd
PO Box 9, Woodbridge, Suffolk IP12 3DF, UK
and of Boydell & Brewer Inc.
668 Mount Hope Ave, Rochester, NY 14620, USA
website: www.boydellandbrewer.com

A catalogue record for this book is available
from the British Library

The publisher has no responsibility for the continued existence or accuracy of URLs
for external or third-party internet websites referred to in this book, and does not
guarantee that any content on such websites is, or will remain, accurate or appropriate.

Papers used by Boydell & Brewer Ltd are natural, recyclable products
made from wood grown in sustainable forests

Printed and bound in the United States of America

Contents

List of Illustrations	viii
Preface to the English Edition	xi
List of Abbreviations	xiii
Introduction	1

Part One: Commanders at Home Ashore

Introduction to Part One	13

1. Enkhuizen — 17
   The city – Some commanders' families – Commanders and retired commanders home from the sea – Retired Commander Klaas Goedhoen and his financial dealings in the port area – Changes in the second half of the century – More commanders from outside Enkhuizen – The often sedate retirement of former commanders

2. Hoorn — 40
   The city – The characteristics of Hoorn commanders – Two seafaring families – Two dignified gentlemen – The final days of the Hoorn Chamber

3. Middelburg — 55
   The city – The majority of commanders from the city of Middelburg – From Company to Navy – Making a fortune at the Cape – Two very different men – Changes in geographical origins

4. Delft — 74
   Delft and Delfshaven – Commanders' families in Delfshaven – Commanders and retired commanders in the city of Delft – Former commanders living off their investments – Two unfortunate men

5. Rotterdam — 90
   The Chamber and the population of the city – Humble beginnings – Sailing to riches – The trade of the Van Brattem brothers – Rogge and Smalt: portents of different times ahead

6. Amsterdam — 105
   Almost no commanders resident in exclusive neighbourhoods – The city – The Company in the city – Foreigners also appointed

commander – Characteristics of the commanders – Jan de Marre: theatre director and playwright – Jan de Marre in his role as examiner – The last commanders of the Amsterdam Chamber

7. Commanders from Outside the Six Chamber Towns   127
   Vlaardingen and Maassluis – Katwijk-aan-Zee – Texel – Two whaling fleet commanders to the East

8. Naval Officers Employed by the Company   140
   Changes in 1742 – Van Imhoff's favourites – Back and forth between the Navy and the Company – Naval ranks after all

Part Two: Commanders at Sea

Introduction to Part Two   157

9. Appointment as Commander   159
   By rotation and drawing lots – Did a commander pay for his position? – Asking around

10. Examinations, Ranks and Training   172
    Examinations – '1742' – The return to the old system – The commander becomes a captain after all – The *Académie de Marine* in Batavia – The usual course of instruction and the changes introduced

11. Normal Income   188
    Monthly wages – Bonuses and gratuities – Personal cargo – Rising incomes – The actual payment – An incomplete cargo – Amounts withheld from stipends – Benevolent Fund

12. Private Income   204
    Regulations for the outward voyage – A glimpse of private trade on the voyage out – Regulations for the voyage home – Transfers of money from Asia to the Republic – Caught and punished – Earning money in Asia and a few big earners

13. On Board   225
    In the roads – A box brimming with instructions and regulations – The commander's cabin – Slaves in the commander's cabin – Social life on board – The ship's business – Arrival overseas – Going home

14. Their Ships   249
    Problems with the ships and the commanders – The commanders of the Zealand Chamber as champions of a different East Indiaman – Ships lost without trace – Reaction of the *Hoge Regering* to the shipping disasters

15. Striking Differences in Personalities 264
    'Humane heads of ships' – Brutal and drunken commanders –
    Authors and victims of tensions – 'A horrible man': Jan Hokkeling
    – No new command after the loss of a ship? – No longer
    admissible

16. Professionals in a Conservative Company 282
    Knowledge and experience of navigation – Commanders and
    their navigational instruments – Stagnation in charting the sea
    – Innovations in navigation around 1790 – A closer look at the
    route to China – Towards another type of commander: the 1780s
    and 1790s

17. The English East India Company and Other Companies: 300
    Dutch Commanders in a Broader Perspective
    The English East India Company – The French *Compagnie des
    Indes* – The *Dansk-Asiatisk Compagnie* and the *Svenska Ostindiska
    Kompani* – VOC commanders in comparison

Conclusion: Commanders in Retrospect 310

Bibliography 317
Index of Names 329
Index of Ship Names 335

Illustrations

1. Jakobus Ariesz Arkenbout (Amsterdam, Scheepvaartmuseum, 2003.1378) — ii
2. Roelof Blok (The Hague, Iconographisch Bureau, private ownership) — 31
3. Provisions on board (Hoorn, West-Fries Archief, oud-archief Enkhuizen 423, no. 1576) — 49
4. Extra supplies for the captain's cabin and the sick bay (Hoorn, West-Fries Archief, oud-archief Enkhuizen 423, no. 1576) — 50
5. A silver loving cup dating from 1795 (Amsterdam, Scheepvaartmuseum, 1993.3289) — 57
6. Maarten Haringman (The Hague, Iconographisch Bureau, private ownership) — 61
7. In the roads of Rammekens (Middelburg, Zeeuws Archief) — 65
8. An anonymous mate (Amsterdam, Rijksmuseum, NG-1985-7-1-41) — 80
9. Gold commodore's medallion (Amsterdam, Scheepvaartmuseum, 4a 4077) — 96
10. East Indiaman, the *Blijdorp* (Rotterdam, Scheepvaart- en Haven Museum, M201) — 101
11. Jakobus van Dam (Amsterdam, Scheepvaartmuseum, 2004.5707) — 106
12. Flower boat (Sneek, Fries Scheepvaartmuseum, 2004.362) — 110
13. Jan de Marre (The Hague, Iconographisch Bureau, private ownership) — 121
14. Dirk Muller (Amsterdam, Scheepvaartmuseum, S 1277/01.0031) — 125
15. The *Wezenputten* on Texel (Oudeschild, Maritiem & Juttersmuseum) — 133
16. Uilke Barends (Sneek, Fries Scheepvaartmuseum, G-100) — 138
17. Jan Zacharias Nauwman (Amsterdam, Scheepvaartmuseum, A 3146.01) — 146
18. Mrs Nauwman, born Rebecca Schuller (Amsterdam, Scheepvaartmuseum, A 3146.02) — 147
19. Damiaan Hugo Staring (private ownership) — 152
20. Voting in a meeting of directors in 1741 (Hoorn, West-Fries Archief, oud-archief Enkhuizen 423, no. 1575) — 161
21. List of appointments on the recommendation of directors in 1773–1774 (Middelburg, Zeeuws Archief, archief Mathias-Pous-Tak van Poortvliet 227) — 163
22. Octant (Amsterdam, Scheepvaartmusum) — 176
23. Sea chests (Harlingen, Het Hannemahuis) — 195

24.	Sea chests (Harlingen, Het Hannemahuis)	195
25.	A silver ducatoon (Utrecht, Geldmuseum)	210
26.	Clavichord (private ownership)	237
27.	Ventilator or air pump (Amsterdam, Rijksmuseum, MC 569)	239
28.	Cooling sail (Amsterdam, Rijksmuseum, MC 570)	239
29.	Gustaaf Willem, Baron Van Imhoff (The Hague, Iconographisch Bureau, private ownership)	252
30.	East Indiaman, the *Gerechtigheid* (Amsterdam, Scheepvaartmuseum)	258
31.	The wreck of the *Woestduin* in 1779 (Middelburg, Zeeuws Archief, Collectie *Zelandia Illustrata* III, 0233)	260
32.	A diver at work (in A. Pol, *Schepen met geld*, The Hague 1989, 24)	262
33.	The quarterdeck of the *Stavenisse* (Amsterdam, Rijksmuseum, NG-1985-7-1-3)	267
34.	The surgeon's cabin (Amsterdam, Rijksmuseum, NG-1785-7-1-4)	272
35.	The *Vrijburg* (Middelburg, Zeeuws Museum, AB1259 1756)	296
36.	The Reverend Brandes' cockatoo (Amsterdam, Rijksmuseum, NG-1785-7-1-51)	307

Maps

1.	The Dutch Republic in the eighteenth century	12
2.	Shipping routes to and from Asia	156

Tables

5.1	Wages and financial transactions of Kornelis and Teunis van Bratten	100
6.1	Geographical origins of sailors of the Amsterdam Chamber	114
14.1	Losses of ships in the period 1721–1740	251
14.2	Average duration of voyages between the Republic and Batavia/Ceylon	254

Preface to the English Edition

In the early modern era commanders of East Indiamen were men of considerable importance. They commanded big ships which carried expensive commodities from Asia to European markets, ships mostly crewed by impressive numbers of seafarers, and soldiers too. Their journeys were long. From the beginning of the seventeenth century until well into the eighteenth the Dutch East India Company was the largest organization in European-Asian trade. From 1602 to 1795, many thousands of voyages took place under its aegis. Most voyages were in the eighteenth century: 2,957 times to Asia and 2,369 times back to the Dutch Republic. Hundreds of men were in command on board these ships, some making a voyage only once but others on two or even more occasions. The commanders were men about whom we know very little, perhaps almost nothing. The ordinary seaman is in several respects perhaps better known.

A solid study of commanders of Dutch East Indiamen has to be founded upon research into their individual lives and careers. This research was done by forty-four students in three consecutive seminars in Maritime History at Leiden University. Inspired by Ms Els van Eyck van Heslinga, Ms Els Jacobs and myself the students wrote 'biographies' of commanders assigned to them by selective random sampling. The biographies were mainly based upon documents available in national, provincial and municipal archives. These reports became the starting point for this book. The focus is on the eighteenth century, chosen because it was then that the Company deployed its greatest shipping activity. That meant that more consistent and archival material with few breaks exists for the period. Last but not least, the all-important ship's pay-ledgers survive, covering the whole period from 1700 to 1794. They include 655,000 names, probably 95 per cent of the total of all the men who sailed on board Company ships.

The book is divided into two parts. The lives of commanders – in Dutch they were called *schippers* – are not described in chronological order. In Part One the home front is the centre of attention. This home front mainly consisted of the six Chambers which formed the Company, which were located in the cities of Amsterdam, Middelburg, Enkhuizen, Hoorn, Delft and Rotterdam. The commanders' social background and origins are discussed as well as their lives ashore. The economies of most cities in which the majority of the commanders lived could be characterized as stagnant or in decay, sometimes an advantage and sometimes a disadvantage for the men who sailed for the Company. Part Two offers studies of the commanders as professional seamen. How they got their appointments, their qualifications, their incomes and extra earnings and their ships are the focus. In the final chapter, the commanders of the Dutch East

India Company are compared with their opposite numbers in other East India Companies.

The book was first published in a Dutch version by De Bataafsche Leeuw in Amsterdam in 2008, with the title *Schippers van de VOC in de achttiende eeuw aan de wal en op zee*. Mrs Rosemary Robson-McKillop (Leiden) and Prof. R.W. Unger (Vancouver) did the translation. I am very grateful to both of them, as I am to Wietse Veenstra, who has drawn the maps. My thanks go as well to three Maritime Funds whose grants made this all possible: Directie der Oostersche Handel en Reederijen, Stichting Vaderlandsch Fonds ter Aanmoediging van 's-Lands Zeedienst and Stichting Admiraal Van Kinsbergenfonds. My thanks also go to Prof. H.V. Bowen who suggested bringing out this English edition which varies on a number of points and has a supplementary final chapter.

Jaap R. Bruijn
Oegstgeest, June 2010

List of Abbreviations

AA	Admiraliteits Archieven (Admiralty Archives)
C. of P.	Council of Policy
DAS	*Dutch-Asiatic Shipping*
DTB	Doop-, Trouw- en Begraafboeken (Baptismal, Marriage and Burial Registers)
GA	Gemeente Archief (Municipal Archive)
NA	Nationaal Archief (National Archive, The Hague)
Not. Arch.	Notariële Archieven (Notarial Records)
OBP	Overgekomen Brieven en Papieren (Letters and Papers Dispatched)
VOC	Verenigde Oost-Indische Compagnie (East India Company)
WA	West-Fries Archief, Hoorn
WIC	West-Indische Compagnie
ZA	Zeeuws Archief, Middelburg

Introduction

Around 1600, two companies were set up in early modern Europe expressly to trade with and ship goods to and from Europe and Asia. They were the English East India Company (EIC) in 1600 and the Dutch (United) East India Company (*Verenigde Oost-Indische Compagnie*, abbreviated to VOC) two years later in 1602. Both companies eventually grew into enormous businesses. Most of the growth in the English Company was in the eighteenth century. In contrast, the Dutch Company grew exponentially almost immediately after its foundation in the seventeenth century. Both Companies have attracted considerable attention in modern historiography. By and large, historians of the Dutch Company have concentrated on the seventeenth century as this was the period in which the Dutch Republic played a prominent role in both Europe and the rest of the world. Naturally, in their work, historians have not neglected the all-important maritime history of this century. The VOC or the Company – as the Dutch Company will be referred to throughout the rest of this book – falls into this category. The gradual establishment of a huge overseas business in Asia and South Africa throughout the course of the century is a spectacular story, thrown into even sharper relief when the triumphs of the VOC are compared to the activities of the EIC and other East India companies in France, Sweden and Denmark.

Despite its spectacular growth and power in the seventeenth century, the VOC only really reached its peak as a trading and shipping company in the following century. During the eighteenth century, a total of 2,957 outward-bound voyages to Asia were made against 2,369 homeward-bound voyages to the Dutch Republic. Many hundreds of different commanders were put in charge of these voyages. In the eighteenth century the quantities of gold and silver dispatched to Asia for the purchase of wares tripled and the value of the Asian goods bought for the European market rose by 250 per cent. The conspicuous growth in the shipping sector would have been obvious to any contemporary inhabitant of the port cities. Although at most twenty ships sailed to Asia per year in the seventeenth century, in the period 1720–1740 this number rose to as many as thirty-seven or thirty-eight, almost double that in the seventeenth century. These eighteenth-century ships, which were purpose-built East Indiamen, were, on average, larger. A great deal of attention has quite rightly been paid to the VOC, in particular to its shipping business, during the eighteenth century, but this is a book about the people intimately involved in the shipping business of the Company, specifically the commanders of the great East Indiamen.[1]

In the midst of all the other maritime activities which predominated in the Dutch Republic in that period, the VOC immediately stands out because of the massive numbers of sailors it employed. Besides mariners, it also needed to recruit large numbers of soldiers. Consequently, in each year throughout the eighteenth century it required between 5,000 and 8,000 men and boys to undertake either maritime activities or military duties. From the beginning of the seventeenth century recruitment occurred at set times. In the months of December/January, April and September, the Christmas, Easter and Fair Fleets set sail. The last derived its name from the great fair which had been held in Amsterdam in that month since 1306. It was the highlight of the year for most of the people of Amsterdam. In the course of the eighteenth century, to ensure that the big ships were used more efficiently, departures were more frequent and the recruitment campaigns needed to find the men to crew them were run in all the other months of the year as well.

Given the circumstances, those men who sailed on the ships were withdrawn from the Dutch labour market for very long periods of time, a great many of them for ever. Deaths on board and overseas took a huge toll and many men never saw the Republic again. Those who did return had not only survived the protracted voyages to Asia and back, but had also spent at least three to five years in Asia as well. These risks were known and recognized and the Company openly committed its personnel to these conditions when they signed on. Fortunately, a constant stream of foreigners, in more modern terms economic migrants, in search of employment in the thriving Republic meant that there were always enough men willing to accept the challenge. Amsterdam in particular, which was experiencing a dramatic period of growth, acted as a magnet to attract many unemployed Scandinavians and Germans from the patchwork of small German states looking for labour opportunities away from their relatively impoverished homelands.

Ships and Shipping in the Eighteenth-Century Netherlands

The favourable labour market, continuously supplied by this stream of immigrants, ensured that the other three branches of sea-faring in the Republic did not lack personnel in the eighteenth century. Unquestionably one of the most obvious reasons for this was that these branches paid better than the VOC

---

[1] For background information and numerical data about the VOC, see F.S. Gaastra, *De geschiedenis van de VOC* (Zutphen, 2002); and J.R. Bruijn, F.S. Gaastra and I. Schöffer (eds), *Dutch-Asiatic Shipping in the 17th and 18th Centuries*, 3 vols, Rijks Geschiedkundige Publicatiën, Grote Serie 165–167 (The Hague, 1979–87), abbreviated as *DAS* and the number of the volume.

INTRODUCTION 3

and there was plenty of work on offer. The ordinary merchant navy was busily employed in Europe, West Africa and in the rest of the Western hemisphere. It employed ships of all types and tonnages, from small boyers to frigates and fluyts. Their exact numbers are unknown but probably ranged from well below 2,000 to a somewhat higher figure. Calculations of the number of sailors employed in the merchant navy fleet suggest there were well over 20,000 men.[2] By tradition, merchant navy crew members were signed on for the length of the agreed voyage. This was one difference from the VOC practice in which enlistment was for a fixed period of five years. The length of a period of service in the whaling or deep-sea fishing fleets depended on the duration of the hunting and catching seasons.

The second branch of maritime activity, whaling – now largely forgotten – was seasonal. It needed men around March and laid them off again after their arrival home in August/September. Until around 1745, anywhere between 180 and 250 ships, manned by between 7,000 and 10,000 men, annually set sail for Arctic waters. After 1745, the enthusiasm for the fitting-out of whalers dropped and the number of ships was only just above 100 by 1779. After 1780 this fell again to sixty or seventy a year as the catches gradually decreased. By the 1780s, there were only approximately 2,000 to 3,000 men still working in whaling.

The size of the sea fishery, the third branch of maritime activity, had already shrunk. The principal reason was the drastic losses suffered by the herring fleet around 1700 as a consequence of the persistent wars first against England and then against France, and the privateering which was an integral part of the conflicts. There was no recovery for the herring fishery. By contrast, catches of cod and flatfish increased. Probably somewhere in the region of 4,000 to 5,000 fishermen worked on fishing boats during the eighteenth century. This short catalogue demonstrates that, as an employer, the VOC far surpassed the various other commercial fleets in sheer size.

The maritime business of the Republic took place in the many harbours strung out along the seaboards of the maritime provinces of Zealand, Holland and Friesland. These harbours were linked either to the North Sea or the Zuiderzee (nowadays the IJsselmeer). There were nearly fifty harbours, some of them small, some even tiny. However, at about this point in time an economic process was evolving in the Republic which was to reinforce the growing importance of Amsterdam as a trading and shipping hub. More modest Rotterdam had also begun to realize its potential as a port city in this period. As they expanded, trade and shipping gradually tended to be more concentrated in these

---

[2] J.R. Bruijn, 'Zeevarenden', *Maritieme Geschiedenis der Nederlanden* III (Bussum, 1977), pp. 147–90, see p. 147; J.V. Th. Knoppers, 'De vaart in Europa', *Ibid.*, pp. 226–61, see p. 227; J. van Lottum and J. Lucassen, 'Six Cross-Sections of the Dutch Maritime Labour Market': A Preliminary Reconstruction and its Implications (1607–1850)', in R. Gorski (ed.), *Maritime Labour in the Northern Hemisphere c. 1600–1950* (Amsterdam, 2007), pp. 13–42.

two cities, which are still among the biggest harbours in the world today. Paradoxically, their expansion set in motion a process of contraction. Their growth was at the expense of the other port cities which had once been bustling hubs of maritime activity. Their former prominence is indisputable. To give just one piece of evidence to support this, in around 1600 there were no murmurs of doubt when it was proposed that Chambers of the VOC should be established in the cities of Enkhuizen, Hoorn, Delfshaven (Delft) and Middelburg. At that time, as in Amsterdam, the citizens of these smaller cities were able to assemble enough capital to invest in the newly founded VOC. Awareness of the prevailing financial situation meant that in 1602 the VOC had deliberately been constructed with a federal structure, with six establishments, or Chambers, in the provinces of Holland and Zealand: Enkhuizen and Hoorn in the northern part of Holland, Amsterdam, Rotterdam and Delft in the southern part. As the province of Zealand still also played a very prominent role in contemporary trade and maintained its own Admiralty, Middelburg in Zealand was also given a Chamber. The central policy was determined by the *Heren Zeventien* (Gentlemen Seventeen) with representatives of the six Chambers, meeting twice a year. (There were eight representatives from Amsterdam, four from Zealand, one from each of the smaller Chambers, and one appointed by one of the Chambers other than Amsterdam, thus preventing an Amsterdam majority.) A hundred or a hundred and fifty years later, as the two major harbours grew in importance and the other, once bustling harbours and cities suffered a remarkable economic eclipse, there would have been no reason to establish Chambers in the cities of Enkhuizen, Hoorn, Delft or Middelburg.

As this general process of contraction continued, to the benefit of Amsterdam and Rotterdam, and there was a concomitant draining away of trade and shipping business from the other port cities, the position of the Company in the economic life of the latter four small towns changed. As other trade dried up, its importance became even stronger. In stark contrast to the marked general economic and maritime slump which affected these cities, the Company and its business experienced a strong growth spurt, especially in the first half of the eighteenth century. Locally the VOC assumed the role of the largest employer and was the source of all the principal economic activity in the city. It was not just the periodic auctions of the Eastern wares held there when the fleet returned, but also the shipyards, kept busy constructing new ships and repairing old ones, along with the requisite regular fittings-out, which provided many citizens with employment. It has to be said that not all six Chambers were able to profit equally from all this economic activity, and this disparity is attributable to the simple fact that they were not all of equal size. Each of the Chambers of Enkhuizen, Hoorn, Delft and Rotterdam was responsible for one-sixteenth of all the fittings-out of ships. The Chamber of Zealand, situated in Middelburg, was allocated a quarter of this work, that is as much as all the four smaller Chambers put together. In the sixteenth century, the economic significance of the island of Walcheren on which Middelburg is located was still derived from its strategic location near the mouth of the Westerschelde on the direct shipping route to the commercial metropolis of Antwerp. This position had ensured that it was possible to argue a strong case for Zealand when the VOC was founded in 1602. Riding on an economic boom, the rapidly expanding city of Amsterdam, the last of the six, assumed responsibility for one-half of all the Company business and consequently assumed a leading role in management of the VOC.

The one remaining part of the maritime structure of the Republic yet to be discussed is the Navy. During the eighteenth century, its establishments in Amsterdam and Rotterdam suffered little from the fact that the Navy shrank drastically from its strength in its heyday a century earlier. The same cannot be said for the other three of the five Admiralties. Like the VOC, the Navy maintained a number of establishments in the three coastal provinces of Zealand, Holland and Friesland. Dating from the end of the sixteenth century, there had been a total of five Admiralties responsible for the fitting-out of the war fleet. With one exception, these Admiralties were all located in the same cities as the Chambers of the VOC. Only Delft did not become an Admiralty headquarters. The smaller cities of Hoorn and Enkhuizen shared one, the Admiralty of the Northern Quarter. The fifth Admiralty was located in Harlingen in Friesland from 1645. All five had once seen a great deal of action as the Dutch Republic was repeatedly embroiled in naval wars to defend its trade and its territory in the course of the seventeenth century. The Admiralties regularly participated in the fitting-out of an enormous fleet. Naval warfare was so intense and such a financial drain that, by the end of the War of the Spanish Succession (1702–1713), the finances of all the Admiralties had been completely exhausted. Only the boards in Amsterdam and Rotterdam managed to stage something of a recovery from the massive expenditures which had been expected of them. The other three slid inexorably into a deep decline. The financing of the naval set-up was unquestionably one of the reasons for this eclipse. To supply their daily requirements the Admiralties were invariably dependent on the income derived from taxes on trade and shipping in their headquarters towns and in the regions around those towns. Because of the process of contraction, this income had dropped drastically in Middelburg, Hoorn/Enkhuizen and Harlingen. The economic decline had huge detrimental knock-on effects for the finances of the Admiralties and for business in the local naval dockyards and their warehouses.[3]

During the War of the Austrian Succession (1740–1748), the only large-scale fittings-out of the fleet took place in 1744 and 1747–1748. This same level of activity was reached one last time during the Fourth Anglo-Dutch War (1780–1784). Apart from these wartime peaks, fitting-out of the naval fleet was restricted to equipping convoys. These were regularly required to patrol the White Sea, the Mediterranean and the West Indies. Furthermore, every summer

---

[3] Jaap R. Bruijn, *The Dutch Navy of the Seventeenth and Eighteenth Centuries* (Columbia, SC, 1993), Part 3.

four warships put to sea to escort the homeward-bound VOC fleet for the last part of its voyage to harbours in the Republic. Under the circumstances, the Navy did not require a large number of personnel, no more than 2,000 to 3,000 men per year, and often only for short-haul voyages. Only the officers were given permanent commissions and even they did not have much opportunity to see active service. This explains why, in the course of the eighteenth century, various naval officers tried to enlist to sail with the VOC.

In some periods during the eighteenth century, the Company directors, who formed the local administration in each Chamber, showed an interest in these naval officers when they solicited employment. In 1742 and the years thereafter, this happened in all the Chambers, but in the Zealand Chamber it was almost constant. It is important to bear in mind that the directors were usually members of the local gentry or prominent merchants of the city in which their Chamber was located. Often they had more affinity with the naval officers than they had with their own commanders and ship's officers (*schippers* and *stuurlieden*), whose origins were, as this book shows, largely more humble. Many naval officers were men from their own circles. As in the merchant navy, the Company invariably called the officers on its ships 'commanders' and 'mates'. It was only in 1784 that the more prestigious title of 'captain' and other naval ranks such as 'lieutenant' were given to VOC commanders and ship's officers.

From 1784, a number of changes, some large and some small, were introduced in the Company's shipping business. The Fourth Anglo-Dutch War proved disastrous for the VOC, depleting it of money, goods and ships. The position of the Company overseas in Asia was severely undermined. A number of trading posts were lost to the EIC and the enmity of the British continued unabated. In 1783, for the first time in its history, Dutch warships were sent to Asia in order to restore the tottering authority of the Company by a display of military might. Three small squadrons in total were dispatched to the East. However, the Company had no opportunity to enjoy any benefit from the improvements in its shipping business. In 1795 the Dutch Republic was rocked to its foundations. The Republic was abolished by invading French revolutionary armies. This political transformation had far-reaching consequences for the political and economic structure of the country and for Dutch society at large. The sovereignty of the Seven Provinces was revoked and the administration of the government centralized in The Hague. The former political leaders, the regents, were replaced by new leaders recruited from classes other than those of the traditional ruling elite. The Batavian Republic was inaugurated as a satellite state of revolutionary France. The VOC disappeared. All the directors of the six Chambers were dismissed as of 1 March 1796. Their place was taken by a Committee for Matters pertaining to the East Indian Trade and Possessions (*Comitté tot de zaken van de Oostindische Handel en Bezittingen*), which was composed of twenty-one members and had its headquarters in Amsterdam. The VOC business was not actually dismantled but nationalized. As of 31 December 1799, the Company monopoly was rescinded. The change was irrelevant since direct shipping to and from Asia was virtually impossible. Great Britain at that point firmly ruled the waves.

The Commander

Great responsibility rested on the shoulders of a man with the rank of commander. It was only after he had proceeded through a series of ranks – third mate (also known as third watch), second and first mates – that a man could aspire to the rank of commander. The duty of the commander was to sail his ship safely to the East and, besides this display of nautical skill, perhaps his most weighty responsibility was to ensure that the silver and gold, stored in chests and bags in his own quarters, were delivered intact and undamaged to the *Hoge Regering* (High Government) in Batavia. This body was the highest authority overseas, headed by the Governor-General and the Council of the Indies. On the homeward-bound voyage, the commander's job was to ensure that the highly prized Asian products were safely delivered to the home ports in the Republic. It was a long voyage. In the eighteenth century, the average length of a journey to Batavia was 245 days, to Ceylon 250 days – a little over eight months. The distance from the Channel to Batavia was nearly 15,000 nautical miles, to which 300 miles could be added if the fleet took the alternative route, usually chosen in wartime, and sailed around the north of Scotland. If Ceylon was the destination, an extra 300 miles was added to the length of the voyage. On average, the return trip from Batavia lasted 237 days and from Ceylon 277 days. The respective distances were 13,400 and 13,000 nautical miles.[4] The courses were strictly dictated by the pattern of the winds and currents. A rough estimate gives an average speed of 2.6 knots (about 4.8 km per hour) for a VOC voyage, which includes the obligatory time spent at the Cape. In other words, the speed was no more than walking pace.

On board, the commander was by no stretch of the imagination a first among equals, a *primus inter pares*. He was the highest authority on board. Everybody on the ship had to obey him. In the early years this had not always been the case. In the seventeenth century, under certain meticulously defined circumstances, if a Chief Merchant (*opperkoopman*) happened to be on board, he held supreme authority. In theory, this situation did not change until 1742, but in practice the role of the Chief Merchant had long since been eroded. Despite what was really happening, it was only in 1742 that the Company actually officially decreed that, no matter what the circumstances were, supreme power on board was vested in the commander and any Chief Merchant who happened to be on board his ship was only a passenger. As far as the six Chambers were concerned, the commander bore the unchallenged responsibility for the fortunes of the ship

---

[4] *DAS* I, chs 4 and 5.

and her cargo. He was assisted in his task by the ship's officers, the mates. In 1775, in a personal note, Commander Willem Ferret said that he carried out all his duties scrupulously, 'so that he would have the freedom to reprimand and reprove others. He spurred on those of his officers who required it so that each of them would perform his functions with a similar steadfast devotion to duty. He made certain that his officers enjoyed the respect of and exercised authority over the crew.'[5]

Of course, the picture that Ferret painted of himself did not always tally with the daily reality among the many hundreds of commanders the Company employed over a period of almost 200 years. The quotation gives an indication of how many commanders saw themselves. A commander never lost sight of the fact that the directors of the Company both at home and abroad could always demand from him a detailed explanation of everything that had happened on a voyage. He had to abide by a multitude of rules and regulations and his obedience to these was subsequently checked. At the time at which it began sailing to Asia, around 1600, the Company had already begun to record all kinds of prescriptions to do with life on board. All of these were assiduously recorded in what was known as the Article Book (*Artikelbrief*). It was the duty of the commander to see that the rules were scrupulously obeyed. Moreover, at the outset of a voyage he was handed the ship's box, filled with a large assortment of specific instructions relating to all kinds of business. If one or more of these instructions was not obeyed, the commander could be faced with a series of punitive measures, which ranged from a fine, to demotion, suspension, or even dismissal for life. The directors of the Company were particularly harsh in their judgements concerning any irregularities which affected the cargo.

In the eighteenth century, more than 1,000 commanders made the voyage out or home in charge of an East Indiaman two or more times. At least 600 others made just one voyage, either homeward- or outward-bound. A commander in the service of the VOC enjoyed a position which was highly respected in merchant navy circles. The records and the careers, or sometimes only one or the other, of nearly one-fifth of these men have been examined in detail. This proportion is fairly constant for all six Chambers of the Company.[6] Inevitably, the accessibility and availability of source material has often been a crucial factor in making decisions about whether or not to pursue the study of the career of a particular commander.

---

[5] H. Bonke, *De zeven reizen van de Jonge Lieve. Biografie van een VOC-schip, 1760–1781* (Nijmegen, 1999), p. 69.

[6] The count is based upon the index of persons in volume III of *DAS* from the numbers 1823 and 6032 onwards. At the start of the research the sample was very broad and not selective, but later on it concentrated on those commanders for whom opportunities were available for more thorough investigation in archival material. The spelling of names is modern and according to the system used in *DAS*.

This book begins with an account of the lives of the commanders at home, on land. The organization is derived from the way in which this book evolved, which has been described in the Preface. There is a reason for this unconventional sequence in a study of maritime history. Almost invariably in past studies, the sea-faring lives of the commanders have claimed the most attention. However, seafarers also have lives at home on land, sometimes only for short periods and sometimes perhaps for longer spells. The influence of their earlier lives as sailors often left indelible traces on their later careers. This trend is particularly conspicuous in the paths pursued by the VOC commanders, because their positions gave them the chance to earn large amounts of money which in turn opened the door to upward social mobility. Consequently, they were often able to move out of the class into which they had been born. These aspects are dealt with in Part One; their work on board and their seamanship are the main themes of Part Two.

PART ONE

COMMANDERS AT HOME ASHORE

Map 1. The Dutch Republic in the eighteenth century

Introduction to Part One

A VOC commander earned a high income. Back at home after the completion of a voyage to Asia, his earnings could be counted in many hundreds, but more usually in thousands, of guilders, whereas an ordinary seaman in his crew had a monthly wage of 10 or 11 guilders. Obviously, this large discrepancy meant that the commanders lived a very different life ashore than that of their crew members. The research has revealed that the vast majority of commanders lived in towns, especially the six towns in which the Chambers of the Company were established. In order to get some sense of early modern Dutch society and the place of the commanders in this society it is important to look at the social stratification in the towns of the provinces of Holland and Zealand. To get an idea of this it is necessary to draw up a list of the many outward signs of prosperity which had very real significance for people at the time.

The commanders, especially retired commanders, were among the better-off citizens of a town. Generally speaking they could be categorized as members of the bourgeoisie (*brede burgerij*), not the lower middle class (*smalle burgerij*). This is the terminology used in modern historical writing to describe social stratification during the Republic. The bourgeoisie consisted of small entrepreneurs and well-to-do shopkeepers, successful craftsmen, municipal officials and low-ranking officers in the Army or Navy. Lower-ranking administrative officials, small shopkeepers and craftsmen, schoolmasters and skippers of small boats were reckoned to belong to the lower middle class. Above the bourgeoisie was the group known as the *grote burgerij* (the upper middle class), composed of rich merchants and shipowners, naval captains and flag officers, high-ranking officials, and university graduates such as doctors, lawyers and ministers of religion in the town. The gentry (*patriciaat*) consisted of the governing families of the towns, the regents. In towns, large and small, the groups with higher social status lived in houses built along the canals and at the harbours and in the more prestigious streets and areas. The dwellings of the craftsmen, workmen and ordinary sailors were located in the narrower streets, depending on their daily or weekly wages. Those who owned no property, the masses (*grauw*), lived in the innumerable alleyways and back streets in single rooms, basements and hovels.[1]

---

[1] P. Knevel, 'Een kwestie van overleven. De kunst van het samenleven', in T. de Nijs and E. Beukers (eds), *Geschiedenis van Holland* II (1572 tot 1795) (Hilversum, 2002), pp. 217–54, see pp. 220–3.

Certainly, the location and size of a house was a significant external sign of prosperity, but these were not the only clues to a person's financial position and the social class of a household. The social position of those involved could also always be deduced from the status of witnesses at weddings and christenings. An even more significant marker was the fee (*impost*) which had to be paid to the government on the occasion of a wedding or a funeral. Throughout the whole province of Holland these amounts remained unchanged from 1695 on. Finally, prosperity could also be heard in the length of time the bells were rung at a wedding or funeral, or could be seen from the number of pallbearers at a funeral. Everything depended on the income a person received or, even more importantly, the value of a person's goods and chattels and real estate. Everybody knew their place in the urban societies of the Republic.

One very good example of this important distinction was the burial fee. This was called the tax on the Means of Burial and it had to be paid in order to get permission to hold a funeral. The highest sum was ƒ. 30, which meant that the deceased had property worth more than ƒ. 12,000 or enjoyed an annual income of ƒ. 800 or higher. This highest rate also had to be paid by university-trained physicians and lawyers. The second level was ƒ. 15 and had to be paid by people with assets worth between ƒ. 6,000 and ƒ. 12,000 and by notaries, procurers, bailiffs and bureaucrats with an annual income estimated to be between ƒ. 400 and ƒ. 800. The third level, f. 6, had to be paid by those who had means of ƒ. 2,000 to ƒ. 6,000 or a professional income of ƒ. 200 to ƒ. 400. If anyone owned less than ƒ. 2,000, the fee was ƒ. 3. Property which was valued at less than approximately ƒ. 500 formed the cut-off point for qualifying for a charitable or 'pauper' burial, for which no licence fees or taxes had to be paid. In Delft, research has shown that deceased commanders could be found in all of these categories with the exception of the last, and some were certainly in the highest which required payment of ƒ. 30.[2] This burial fee was payable immediately and sometimes an inventory of the deceased's estate was drawn up at the same time. Everything which the deceased possessed in the house at the time of his or her death was described. All the objects were noted room by room, from furniture and jewellery to handkerchiefs and jam pots.

Another criterion by which an eighteenth-century town-dweller could measure his or her social standing was the tax register (*kohier*) of the two-hundredth penny. This was another yardstick by which to measure affluence. In essence it was the record of the tax assessments for indirect taxation. Anyone who had assets worth more than ƒ. 1,000 was noted in the register.

The amount of money a person had at his or her disposal was usually the principal criterion by which his or her social standing was measured. The eighteenth century appears to have been a time of economic decline which gave rise

---

[2] Th. Wijsenbeek-Olthuis, *Achter de gevels van Delft. Bezit en bestaan van rijk en arm in een periode van achteruitgang (1700–1800)* (Hilversum, 1987), pp. 104–5 and 114–15.

to talk of wage stagnation in various sectors of economic life. There was certainly no question of any conspicuous increases in salaries. During the second half of the century real purchasing power actually declined as a consequence of rising prices of food and various other goods. In Amsterdam, the town with the highest cost of living, an average household would have been living at an absolute subsistence level if it had an annual income of ƒ. 200, and half the households in Amsterdam had to make do with less than ƒ. 300. This sort of sum was earned by rope-makers, unskilled workers in the textile industry and other branches of manufacturing, porters and the men who worked on the wharves. There is no comparison between the stipends of VOC commanders and the income of manual workers since the former earned between ƒ. 60 and ƒ. 80 a month. A quotation from 1776 describes the generally worsening standard of living of the lowest groups in society: 'In the meantime, the commons, who are by far the great majority of the inhabitants, live in the direst poverty and see no chance whatsoever to earn their bread by some other means or to better themselves.' On account of their stipends, commanders in Amsterdam were typically classified in the 10 per cent of households which had an annual income of between ƒ. 600 and ƒ. 1,000.[3]

This brief introduction to Part One is intended to serve as a background to the following eight chapters which contain descriptions of the circumstances in which the commanders from the various parts of Holland and Zealand lived. An attempt has been made to make a thorough investigation of their place in society. Individual commanders will be focused on one by one. There is a description of the six Chamber towns in which the Company was represented. The socio-economic situation in each town will be briefly described. During the eighteenth century, the economic situation in most of them was pretty gloomy, which meant that locally the Company was often a prominent source of employment and at least ensured that there was some action on the economic front. Moving from Chamber to Chamber, different aspects of the commanders' lives and of the Company business will be examined. These descriptions commence with the two small Chambers in the north of Holland, Enkhuizen and Hoorn, followed by the Zealand Chamber in Middelburg, then Delft and Rotterdam and, finally, the most prominent, the Amsterdam Chamber. In most of these six towns the VOC loomed very large. As the degree of attention paid to the six Chamber towns does not do justice to the commanders who came from other parts of Holland and continued to live in their places of birth after they had become commanders, the seventh chapter is devoted to the stories of these men. The eighth chapter takes a look at some of the naval officers who chose to transfer temporarily from the Navy to make a career with the Company.

---

[3] J. de Vries and A. van der Woude, *The First Modern Economy. Success, Failure, and Perseverance of the Dutch Economy, 1500–1815* (Cambridge, 1997), pp. 607–27; W. Frijhoff and M. Prak (eds), *Geschiedenis van Amsterdam 1650–1813. Zelfbewuste stadstaat* II, 2 (Amsterdam, 2005), pp. 258–62.

1

Enkhuizen

Enkhuizen had once been a busy herring port on the Zuiderzee, but in the eighteenth century it was only the shipping business of the VOC that left an indelible mark on the city. The town was thronged with sailors who lived in the city while they waited for the new crew musters of the Company, and many others left their families behind there when they sailed. Old VOC hands, among them commanders, also lived and worked in the town. Some were still hoping for a new command, while others had settled down and left their maritime careers behind them. Enkhuizen fitted out no more than one-sixteenth of all the Company ships, which meant that two or three a year were equipped and manned in the town for the long voyage to Asia. The shipping business of the Company had expanded enormously in the first half of the eighteenth century and Enkhuizen had profited from the growth. A century earlier it had often sent out only a single ship. Now far more crew members were required, and naturally more commanders and officers. The great majority of these officers lived in their own native town, as they also did in neighbouring Hoorn.[1]

Every Company ship had a ship's council of four: the commander and three other officers. When they returned, these men would have been away from Enkhuizen for approximately two years, often for far longer periods. Many never returned because they died on board during the voyage out or while they were participating in intra-Asia trade or on the return voyage. Malaria claimed the most victims. Often any time spent in Batavia was tantamount to running a fatal risk. A very small number of mariners actually chose to settle overseas. If men survived as commander or as an officer, they often signed on voyage after voyage. In the course of the eighteenth century, the number of ships annually fitted out by the VOC began to decline and, as a consequence, the need for commanders and officers also fell. Usually the Enkhuizen Chamber showed a preference for appointing Enkhuizen men. In the period 1725–1765, two times out of three it was an Enkhuizen man who was commissioned as commander.[2]

---

[1] J.K. Beers and C. Bakker, *Westfriezen naar de Oost. De kamers der VOC te Hoorn en Enkhuizen en hun recruteringsgebied, 1700–1800* (Hoorn, 1990), pp. 57–9 and 79–80.

[2] Statement by Mr H. de Vos in Schoorl. De Vos generously placed his transcripts of VOC archivalia in the Westfries Archief at my disposal, and gave me the benefit of his insights

The City

For Enkhuizen as a city it was of immeasurable importance that, in the first half of the eighteenth century, the VOC offered more people employment than it had in earlier years. Around 1700 the town was struggling with economic problems. The economic boom of the previous century had now faded to little more than a memory. Both the herring fishery and the carrying trades were facing severe problems. Commercial voyages from the town, even those to the Baltic, had virtually ceased. A modest coastal traffic to Hamburg did continue though. Fishing for herring – three of which were emblazoned on the town's coat-of-arms – was waning. In the period around 1670, about 100 Enkhuizen men worked as skippers of herring busses. By 1718 the number had dwindled to sixteen and a few years later they could be counted on the fingers of one hand. In this climate, the growing VOC demand for seafaring men was welcomed.[3]

The consequences of this precarious economic situation could be clearly seen throughout the town. Signs of stagnation and decline were inescapable. Houses and business premises stood vacant. The total number of houses dropped from 3,615 in 1632 to 2,605 in 1730. Within the confines of the walled town, which had been laid out on generous lines, there was an increasing number of vacant allotments where vegetables or other crops could be grown. In 1727, part of the oldest harbour area, the Noorderhavendijk, was filled in with debris from demolition work. By around 1730 the population had halved compared to a century earlier. There were only 9,000 to 10,000 people, compared to 19,000 earlier. In the first half of the eighteenth century, the annual death rate exceeded the birth rate by 100. In 1727 and 1728 an epidemic of dysentery doubled the death rate. This scenario was repeated in 1779 and again in 1780. One of the few positive changes in town life in Enkhuizen was the placing of lanterns along the canals and streets. However, for financial reasons these could only be lit in the seven darkest months of the year and even then not for the whole night.[4]

---

into the way Company business worked. People from outside Enkhuizen often settled in the town. One in five of the commanders appointed came from Scandinavia or Germany. The commanders who have been examined in greater detail are: Arie Pietersz Arkenbout (1721–1771), Jacobus Ariesz Arkenbout (1766–1834), Roelof Blok (1712–1776), Steven Booms (1734–1795), Gerrit Bruijn (1740–c.1807), Jakob Bruijn (1737–1807), Kornelis de Boer (c.1700–1736), Anthonie Chef (?–1725), Dirk Dol (c.1695–1738), Hero Dol (c.1669–1721), Jan Everwijn Drillinger (1748–1807), Ype Engelsman (1692–1730), Klaas Goedhoen (?), Kornelis van der Hoeven (1690–1741), Karel Lavia (?–1712), Pieter van Loosen (1690–1743), Willem van Mensburg (1704–1776), Dirk Pomp (1704–1741), Jan Pomp (?–1741), Simon Pomp (1701–1737), Adriaan Pool (1709–1759), Sieuwert Pool (1684–1732), Jan Russeplukker (1685–1762), Lucas Semeyns (?–1736), Jakob Sombeek (?–1767) and Jochem Aldertsz Tarncke (?–1760).

[3] R. Willemsen, *Enkhuizen tijdens de Republiek. Een economisch-historisch onderzoek naar stad en samenleving van de 16ᵉ tot de 19ᵉ eeuw* (Hilversum, 1988), pp. 57, 65, 80–1, 93–5 and 171.

[4] Willemsen, *Enkhuizen*, pp. 32–4, 114–18 and 177–81. See also R.J. de Vries, *Enkhuizen 1650–1850, bloei en achteruitgang van een Zuiderzeestad* (Amsterdam, 1987), pp. 72–5.

In 1732, the retired commander Jan Russeplukker was still able to profit from the darkness which enshrouded the town at night. One winter evening he stole into the house of First Mate Kornelis de Boer on the Breedstraat. The head of the household was then in the East but his wife, Bregje Schaap, was at home. That afternoon, Russeplukker and a merchant from Amsterdam had visited her to view a collection of Japanese porcelain. On the second visit the commander did not leave until the middle of the night, and it may not have been his first nocturnal call on the lady. Both Bregje and Russeplukker enjoyed a dubious reputation in the town. Bregje, who was the daughter of the late town physician and chairman of the town's council of aldermen, Michiel Schaap, had been married in 1728. It was a marriage at the highest tariff paid for a marriage licence. Bregje was plagued by loneliness when her husband was at sea. Matters had grown steadily more difficult for her, especially since Kornelis' latest departure to the East in July, 1731. She now behaved in an 'exasperating, scandalous and argumentative' fashion. She began to drink heavily and on many nights she received male visitors, one of whom was Jan Russeplukker. These visits were often accompanied by plenty of 'noise, cursing and swearing, and hubbub'. This disturbed the nocturnal peace of the Breedstraat. Neighbours and acquaintances discussed the problem with one another. One said that Bregje had told her that she 'had made a bad marriage and that she needed a husband who could be with her constantly, because she was unable to manage without a husband'. Another said that she had asked him 'to make a baby with her' and she had promised him 'a guilder for every night'. In the spring of 1732, Bregje's behaviour had become so scandalous that a small group of acquaintances and neighbours went to a notary. At the request of her mother and one of her husband's cousins, they had a record compiled of what had happened. This was the usual procedure to permit further steps or action to be taken, and notaries were frequently asked to assist in such matters. At that time there were no fewer than fourteen of them in the town.[5] What happened in Bregje's case is unknown. After his return, First Mate De Boer was promoted to commander, but died during his first command. His death occurred in July 1736 when he was sailing in Asian waters.[6]

The arrival of street lighting did not alleviate the sort of problems with which Bregje wrestled. Mariners were often away from home for a long time, especially those who worked for the VOC. They were often absent for years at a time.

---

[5] C.M. Lesger, *Hoorn als stedelijk knooppunt. Stedensystemen tijdens de late middeleeuwen en vroegmoderne tijd* (Hilversum, 1990), p. 226.

[6] To set up a practice, notaries had to have permission from the States of Holland and from the municipal council. If their offices were in their own homes, they hung out signboards. They also held sessions in inns. When a notary died or closed down his practice, the local authorities preserved the records of his deeds. For more, see Hoorn, Westfries archief (WA), Notarieel Archief (Not. Arch.) 1263, akte 19, 5 and 7.4.1732. See also D. Haks, *Huwelijk en gezin in Holland in de 17de en 18de eeuw. Processtukken en moralisten over aspecten van het laat 17de- en 18de-eeuwse gezinsleven* (Assen, 1982), pp. 59–62; and A. Verburg, 'De Vlaardingse notarissen vóór 1811 en hun archieven', *Historisch Jaarboek Vlaardingen*, 2004, pp. 36–61.

Those they left behind did not know whether they were dead or alive or when they would return. As a general rule, officers married after their twenty-fifth birthday when they had made the rank of third or second mate. De Boer had been twenty-eight when he married Bregje, who was twenty-four. Jan Russeplukker had been born in 1685 and was divorced. Usually the families of commanders and officers did not cause the people in their vicinity any trouble, and probably First Mate De Boer's wife was an exception. Notaries were not often required to record such goings-on in such detail.

In Enkhuizen, commanders, and certainly retired commanders, belonged to the upper crust and lived scattered throughout the town. The streets in which they lived were those considered the most fashionable and were the most sought after.[7] Their houses, like all the best houses in Enkhuizen, had high but narrow façades and were deep, extending a long way back from the street. Commanders were apparently comfortable enough financially to be able to afford prestigious addresses. Life at sea may have lost its charm for the retired but it had provided them with a good income.

Some Commanders' Families

By the first decade of the eighteenth century, sailing with the Company had become an established pattern in several families. The men had already sailed to the East as boys. The same pattern was regularly reproduced in the world of herring fishing as well. The Pools, father and son, were by no means an exception. Dirk Dol's uncle, Hero, had also been a commander. Two sons and a son-in-law of the seafaring man Jan Pomp had also earned their keep with the VOC. The pattern was repeated with Ype Engelsman and with the children of Master Surgeon Maarten Ramas. Disentangling the networks of work and close family ties is an interesting exercise. Engelsman (1692) was the oldest. In 1716 he had married Grietje Ramas, the surgeon's daughter. From 1723 Engelsman made three voyages as commander and during those voyages he welcomed two Pomp brothers and a brother-in-law on board as officers: Simon (1701) and Dirk (1704) Pomp and Jan Ramas (1700). Dirk Pomp became Engelsman's brother-in-law in 1729 when he married another of the surgeon's daughters. In 1731, the Pomp brothers saw their sister, Jeltje, marry the officer, later commander, Willem van Mensburg (1704). Life on board in the tropics wrought havoc among these men. Engelsman died in 1730, Simon Pomp and Jan Ramas in 1737 and Dirk Pomp in 1741. Van Mensburg survived his brothers-in-law. Like the others, he had only one child who survived to adulthood. Engelsman never knew that his wife had predeceased him. Years later the Pomp widows remarried.[8]

---

[7] I am very grateful to Mr P.J. de Vries in Schellinkhout for his information about Enkhuizen in the eighteenth century.
[8] Data about the dates of commanders and their relatives are based on research done on

Van Mensburg was the only one to enjoy the life of a retired commander, but their work with the VOC made it possible for all of them to advance financially and socially. They exchanged tiny, one-room houses for larger ones closer to the centre of town. The monthly salaries and the extra income which could be earned made such moves possible. The change was not as great for Ramas' daughters because before they had married they had already lived in fashionable streets. In those days a surgeon was considered an artisan and a member of the bourgeoisie and was not categorized among the people who worked for wages, which is why when Suzanna married Dirk Pomp she had the security of a prenuptial agreement. After all, she brought bonds and obligations worth 3,000 guilders and some expensive pieces of jewellery into the marriage.[9]

For many sailors' families it was extremely important that the VOC also offered them two possible ways to earn an income during the absence of the male bread-winner. These provisions were what were known as monthly letters (*maandbrieven*) and transfer letters (*transportbrieven*), which functioned more or less like letters of credit. Commanders and officers also made regular use of these facilities, which meant they did not have to leave their families behind penniless. By means of a monthly letter, to a maximum of three months' salary each year, the family of each man on board could claim a month's salary, but no third party had access to the funds – a limitation on distribution that was introduced in 1682. Once every year, three months' wages could be collected at the pay office of one of the Chambers upon presentation of the monthly letter. To make financial matters on the home front even easier, there was also the transfer letter. This was a pre-printed bond form on which the seaman concerned, 'at the present moment on the point of departure … to sail to the East-Indies on the ship the …', declared that he owed a particular sum to the person whom he named by name. The total sum could range from 150 to 300 guilders. Commanders and officers could choose the highest sum. When family members were the beneficiaries of the sum required, the pay office did not deduct any administrative costs, from 1671 on. And the sum could be taken out in instalments. Commanders also made use of these facilities, especially during their maiden voyages. These letters occasionally appear in the inventories of the estates of deceased wives of commanders who were overseas. The Company pay offices administered these withdrawals of money scrupulously and, when the accounts were closed, any amount that had been paid out was deducted from the total sum earned. All the transactions for every single crew member from the time he was mustered on each ship to the time he was signed off were recorded in the ship's pay books, and nearly all are there for the researcher to find.[10]

---

the baptismal, marriage and burial registers (in Dutch abbreviated DTB) in the towns and villages concerned.

[9] Hoorn, WA, Not. Arch. 1282, akte 112, 2.3.1729.

[10] D. van den Heuvel, '*Bij uijtlandigheijt van haer man*'. *Echtgenotes van VOC-zeelieden, aangemonsterd voor de kamer Enkhuizen (1700–1750)* (Amsterdam, 2005), pp. 20–8 and 65–6; J.R.

Many of the retired commanders were able to live a comfortable life on land. They had earned plenty from their salaries, emoluments and from trading overseas. They were no longer obliged to wend their way to the East India House on the Wierdijk, with a splendid view over the Zuiderzee, because all that was owed them had been paid. Sometimes the process of payment took more time if the money had to come via another Chamber or from an overseas factory in Asia. This sort of situation arose when a commander had made his voyage home in a ship which was not the property of the Enkhuizen Chamber. Sometimes the contents of the chests of trade goods he was permitted to bring back were auctioned in another place. The money which the commander had earned in the East from his own private trade was paid by a bill of exchange from Batavia. Occasionally payment might not come until years later, and the sums in the bills of exchange could be substantial. In Chapter 12, payments of this type will be discussed in more depth. Occasionally notarial deeds offer a clue as to what the commanders did with their money.

The *Oost-Indisch Huis* (East India House) was the most important building belonging to the Chamber. It was a large building in Dutch Renaissance style with a large inner courtyard and warehouses at the rear. The directors met there, and the pay office as well as the other administrative departments were housed there. The House burned to the ground in 1816.[11]

Commanders and Retired Commanders Home from the Sea

Before a commander reached the highest post in the VOC, he had to pass through all, or nearly all, the ranks, from ship's boy to ordinary seaman, from petty officer to third mate and then second and first. It took some people longer than others to achieve promotion, but all of them, no matter how rapid their rise through the ranks, were frequently away from home for very long periods. For a number of them it is possible to say something about the lives they led after they finally left their seafaring days behind them. For others there is information about the reputation they enjoyed and what administrative positions they held in Enkhuizen.

After his final voyage in 1732, Dirk Dol, who was a bachelor, had the chance to enjoy his prosperity for another six years. He employed a housemaid. He had begun his career in 1709 as a ship's boy, on board his uncle Hero's ship. On a number of occasions when he was overseas his illiterate mother had visited the pay office to withdraw three months' wages to cover her living costs, and in 1721 she had also inherited some money from her brother Hero. When she died, she left Dirk Dol bonds worth *f.* 8,500. When Dol died, he was able to leave only

---

Bruijn and J. Lucassen (eds), *Op de schepen der Oost-Indische Compagnie. Vijf artikelen van J. de Hullu* (Groningen, 1980), p. 51.

[11] R. van Gelder and L. Wagenaar, *Sporen van de Compagnie. De VOC in Nederland* (Amsterdam, 1988), pp. 28–9.

some 4,000 guilders to third parties. His maid inherited the contents of his house plus the sum of 1,000 guilders.[12] It seems that working for the Company had not made Dol a rich man.

Adriaan Pool was more successful as a commander. He made better use of the opportunities available to him in the East. One voyage as commander was sufficient to allow him to retire in 1739 at the age of thirty. At that point he was financially comfortable. In 1732 he had already inherited a considerable sum from his father. He had enough resources to purchase bonds worth $f.$ 21,800 within a few weeks. Not long afterwards, he bought and sold some more. As a further investment, he purchased a house in a main street, once the residence of a retired alderman, for $f.$ 5,300. Shortly afterwards, in 1740, he married. His bride was the daughter of a merchant in Grootebroek, a village a few hours' walk west of Enkhuizen. Along with the villages of Bovenkarspel, Lutjesbroek and Hoogkarspel, Grootebroek formed the municipality of the same name. Each village supplied a director for the orphanage and a mayor for the municipal administration. Pool held both these offices in Grootebroek. It was common practice in the West Friesland countryside for captains in the merchant marine to be on town councils and to be mayors, an indication that they were among the richest inhabitants.[13] Shortly before his death in 1759, Pool was mayor in Bovenkarspel, the village between Grootebroek and Enkhuizen. Since his marriage he had owned a country estate there called *Nooit Gedagt*.[14]

In those days money could be invested in houses and estates, in shares, in parts of ships, in personal loans and very commonly in debentures, redeemable bonds and life annuities (*losrenten and lijfrenten*). Most of the bonds were issued by the provinces, cities and towns and the Generality which was the fiscal and administrative division of the States-General in The Hague. Until 1788, bonds were a very safe investment. Their market price was often higher than the original face value. Holland bonds paid 4 per cent interest; those issued by the Generality stood mostly around 3 per cent circa 1730. The interest was always paid on time. After the deduction of the hundredth or two-hundredth penny tax, this left a return equal to 2.5 per cent of the value of the Holland bonds. After coming back from Asia there was nothing unusual in the way Pool invested his money. There were no very high rates of return to be had. A bond worth $f.$ 1,000 paid $f.$ 25. That was equal to twenty days' pay for a master carpenter in the town, assuming an average day wage of 25 *stuivers*.[15]

---

[12] Hoorn, WA, Not. Arch. 1293, akte 32, 7.4.1734 and 1306, akte 34, 29.9.1738.
[13] P.A. Boon, *Bouwers van de zee: zeevarenden van het Westfriese platteland, c. 1680–1720* (The Hague, 1996), pp. 165–6 and 183–4.
[14] Hoorn, WA, Not. Arch. 1291, akte 5a, 12.5.1732; 1306, akte 138, 7.10.1739, akte 140, 8.10.1739 and akte 143, 21.10.1739; 1336, akte 28, 1.5.1745 and 1371, akte 19, 23.1.1758. Dr P.A. Boon drew my attention to this country seat which was later converted into a farmhouse.
[15] K.W.J.M. Bossaers, '*Van kintsbeen aan ten staatkunde opgewassen*'. *Bestuur en bestuurders van*

After he had retired from seafaring, Pool rose high through the ranks of the administration, but, generally speaking, in the first half of the eighteenth century VOC commanders and retired commanders in Enkhuizen did not enjoy any particular esteem. In contrast to naval officers, they did not move in the highest circles. Naval officers were often the sons of regents and highly placed officials or were aristocrats by birth. Such people were few and far between in Enkhuizen, however. During the seventeenth century, the Admiralty of the Northern Quarter had enjoyed some prosperity, but it had become mired in enormous financial difficulties during the War of the Spanish Succession (1702–1713). After that, it fitted out few ships and any it did fit out had to be shared with Hoorn, so there were few commissions available for officers.

The retired commander Pieter van Loosen was one man who did enjoy some local fame. He was distantly related to the circle of the Enkhuizen regents. As well as being a merchant and a ship-owner/director of the WIC, his namesake and second cousin was also a bailiff. This probably helped Pieter in procuring several appointments in the town. He married late. When he did marry in 1731 he was already forty. This meant that he had to pay the highest marriage licence fee of f. 30. In the same year the directors of the Enkhuizen Chamber appointed him Examiner of Ship's Officers of the Company, a position which required him to examine and certify the professional knowledge of his colleagues as well as advise on matters relating to shipping. He was also one of the two customs and excise officers in the town. They were the men from the Admiralty who checked the loading and unloading of ships and carts and kept an eye out for tax evasion. The appointment generated a permanent annual income, which was always highly desirable because it also offered security. Nevertheless, Van Loosen never made a fortune from all his official positions. He was buried in the Westerkerk in 1743. His funeral was second-class, because death duties of only f. 15 guilders had to be paid on his estate. Shortly before his death Van Loosen had been the subject of some controversy. When somebody came to the door to complain about the behaviour of his young son, Jan, his wife abused the man and Van Loosen followed suit. Thereupon the man grabbed the retired commander, who stumbled down onto the pavement, which caused 'his hat and his wig to fall off his head'. Van Loosen's sister Joosje, the widow of former commander Kornelis van der Hoeven, did not live particularly comfortably – she kept a shop. The widow of Dirk Pomp had a similar fate; she had a haberdashery and clothes shop in the same street.[16]

A few of the commanders had a bad reputation. Kornelis van der Hoeven was most certainly one of them. A nephew of Burgomaster (mayor) Dirk Haak, a

---

het Noorderkwartier in de achttiende eeuw (The Hague, 1996), p. 176; Wijsenbeek-Olthuis, *Achter de gevels*, pp. 124–6; L. Noordegraaf, *Daglonen in Alkmaar 1500–1800* (Oostvoorne, 1980), pp. 37–8, 45 and 58.

[16] Hoorn, WA, Not. Arch. 1309, akte 4, 22.1.1748 and 1335, akte 100, dec. 1741. Rotterdam, Gemeentearchief (GA), Oud Stadsarchief 4169.

director of the Company at the time, complained to his uncle about 'this lummox Van der Hoeve' and his 'brutish [way of] life and unbelievably vicious behaviour' during the voyage of the *Geertruid* to Batavia in 1731. As a junior merchant on board, the nephew had had personal experience of the commander's conduct. This sort of behaviour and complaints about it did not stop Van der Hoeven being appointed to another two consecutive commands.[17]

Former commander Jan Russeplukker had a reputation as a womanizer, not as a rush-cutter as his name would imply. His visit to Bregje Schaap in 1732 was not an isolated incident. In 1715 he had married Meinoutje Popman, with a third-class licence (*f.* 6). It was not a happy marriage. Russeplukker did not take his marriage vows seriously, to such an extent in fact that he 'had even … forgotten himself so far as to have had voluptuous congress with other women, so much so that he was reduced to such a condition, by the diseases he had picked up, his only recourse was to seek a cure from the surgeon'. In other words he had to undergo a smear or fume cure using mercury or a decoction of the guaiacum plant to deal with venereal disease. This sort of work was undertaken by the surgeon, not the town physician.[18] This took place just prior to Russeplukker's next departure for the Indies in May 1720. When he returned in September 1722 he found Meinoutje with a four-month-old baby. As was usual in this sort of situation, just before the delivery the midwife had made Meinoutje confess who the father was.[19] Such a procedure meant that Russeplukker was not the legal father. In April 1723 he applied for and was granted a divorce. Meinoutje appealed, but in vain, and she ended up in the poor house. Twenty years later, then fifty-eight, Russeplukker remarried, this time a widow. Her daughter pleased the former commander so much he made her his heir, cutting out all the other members of the family. This meant that on the death of her step-father in 1762 she inherited Russeplukker's house as well as bonds and life annuities valued at *f.* 20,000 guilders. In 1742 the commander had been taxed on an annual income of no more than *f.* 1,000 guilders a year.[20]

All commanders had been born into Protestant families. Ministers of the Westerkerk or the Zuiderkerk presided over their betrothal and wedding ceremonies. They did not have large families. Some of them died childless. Others left one or at the very most two children.[21] This was the norm for urban families. The interiors of their houses often clearly showed that the breadwinner was in Company service. For instance, Ype Engelsman imported a large quantity of

---

[17] Manuscript De Vos, icoon I, fols 34–5.
[18] A.E. Leuftink, *Harde heelmeesters. Zeelieden en hun dokters in de 18e eeuw* (Zutphen, 1991), pp. 106–9.
[19] Haks, *Huwelijk*, pp. 57, 90–1 and 207–9.
[20] The Hague, Nationaal Archief (NA), Hof van Holland 942; Hoorn, WA, Not. Arch. 1384, akte A 72,17.7.1762.
[21] Haks, *Huwelijk*, ch. 5; J. Lucassen, 'Holland, een open gewest. Immigratie en bevolkingsontwikkeling', in De Nijs and Beukers, *Geschiedenis van Holland*, pp. 180–216, see p. 186.

porcelain, some Chinese but the bulk of it Japanese. Such goods were often not for private enjoyment but intended as merchandise to be sold at a profit. In the period around 1730, having trade goods in the house was still not as usual as it was to become in houses later in the century.[22] Engelsman had a fine assortment of porcelain objects: small brown Japanese pots with lids, Japanese and Chinese butter-dishes, small Japanese bottles and beakers, small East Indian tea-pots and deep saucers, or tea-cups. In total there were many hundreds of different items. An East Indian chest, an East Indian sewing cushion and three East Indian rugs proclaimed their place of origin. Besides these souvenirs, there was a large quantity of gold and silver jewellery and utensils in the house.

Twenty years later, Dirk Pomp's widow had considerably less porcelain in her possession, but she did possess a series of small Japanese fruit-plates 'two of which were glued', some enamelled plates and brown enamelled coffee cups. Enamelled pieces were a novelty. These were the kinds of ceramics which usually had a dark background over which a special glaze had been poured. In the post mortem inventories of both Engelsman's and Pomp's widows there is mention of a golden *hoofdijzer*, a sort of golden headgear which was worn under a cambric cap. Engelsman had been at sea when his wife died. She left two small children, and interestingly in the inventory of possessions there were two children's piggy-banks and a child's chair. There was *f.* 42 in one piggy-bank and *f.* 23 in the other. Both of them included 'some foreign coins'. In the main front section of the house there were two small bags, one containing *f.* 275 and the other *f.* 225 in cash. There was also a monthly letter for three months of a commander's salary.[23]

Retired Commander Klaas Goedhoen and His Financial Dealings in the Port Area

After he retired from the sea, commander Klaas Goedhoen did what probably very few of his colleagues ever did. He invested his money in buying up transfer letters (*transportbrieven*). In this case, these were debt bonds of seamen who were not from Enkhuizen and had had to seek board and lodging before they were mustered. They made their landlords beneficiaries of the transfer of funds when they entered service, covering any debt they owed with what became in effect a promissory note, based on their forthcoming earnings on board. Goedhoen started his financial business in 1734, six years after his final voyage, purchasing debt. As a buyer of those debts he became closely involved in the welfare and woes of the sailors and soldiers of the VOC. It follows from this that he was also deeply involved in everything that took place in the port area. His activities require more detailed explanation.

---

[22] Wijsenbeek-Olthuis, *Achter de gevels*, pp. 100–1, 219 and 243.
[23] Hoorn, WA, Not. Arch. 1238, akte 75, 1.11.1729 and 1309, fols 1–23, 22.1.1748.

In the port towns and cities, lodging-house keepers offered the men and boys looking for work on the East Indiamen board and lodgings and also supplied them with the kit they needed for the voyage. They also lent their services during recruitment and signing on. In the first quarter of the eighteenth century, there were about ten of them working in the port of Enkhuizen. Of course they did not perform their services for nothing. The bounty which a seaman or a soldier was paid as an advance was never sufficient to settle the bill with the lodging-house keeper. It was two months' wages, that is, *f.* 20 to *f.* 25 at the most. To cover the remainder of their debts, guests signed their transfer letters over to the lodging-house keepers. The standard sum signed over by sailors or soldiers was 150 guilders, but the amounts could be higher. The lodging-house keepers could convert the transfers into cash, but only when the debtor had earned enough to cover the debt. At a monthly wage of roughly *f.* 12 that would take one and a half year or longer. In addition there was the time required for the bookkeeping records to arrive at one of the six Chambers from Asia. Moreover, the indebted crew members might die or desert not long after they had sailed and so never earn enough to cover the face value of the transfer letter. In short, lodging-house keepers might have to wait a very long time for their money, while in the meantime the costs of running their businesses continued. They needed ready money. So the debt bonds, made out in the name of, or to, the bearer, were sold – not, of course, for their nominal value, but at a discount. The purchaser then had to wait to see a return on his money and assumed all the risk of loss due to the death or desertion of the debtor. Discount rates fluctuated and were inevitably influenced by reports from the East and news of fast voyages, delays and maritime disasters. In practice, it was usually five years before any debt could be discharged and even then it might not be for its nominal value. Even if all went well, it would take a minimum of two years.

Speculators in sailors' debt were occasionally mentioned in tax registers. It was not a job with any great prestige. They preferred to see themselves noted as merchants in the tax registers. Klaas Goedhoen chose to be registered as *rentenier*, that is a man of independent means. The services of such people were extremely useful because they kept work in the land-based hospitality industry functioning. Of course, in doing so they were motivated not by altruism but by the hope of profit. Goedhoen did not require much start-up capital and his last credit received from Batavia did not amount to much – it was a bill of exchange worth *f.* 1,156.[24] At that time it was common practice to borrow money from money-lenders, so a bundle of transfer letters could be handed over to a money-lender as collateral. The discounts at which letters changed hands fluctuated. Usually they were around 50 per cent, but might be less, even as low as 30 per

---

[24] The Hague, NA, VOC 2209, fol. 3196. Data about the exchange of transfer letters are borrowed from the filing cards made by G. Wolvers during his research for his MA thesis, 'Het wisselverkeer van het maritieme personeel van de Verenigde Oostindische Compagnie vanuit Azië naar Nederland in de 18ᵉ eeuw' (Leiden University, 1988).

cent. Often the traffic in such debts was a lively one. If the purchaser did not wish to visit the boarding houses himself to buy up transfer letters, he could obtain them through an agent.

This trade was one of those in the harbour which, comparatively speaking, a substantial number of women, some even the wives of commanders, took up. However, most of them were of a somewhat dubious character. In Middelburg in 1730, almost the entire trade in debt was run by women. Around 1720, Maria van Dijkhuizen, a former prostitute from Amsterdam, dominated the trade in transfer letters drawn on the Chambers of Enkhuizen and Hoorn. She had taken up residence with a man in one of the main streets in Enkhuizen in 1695 and the following year she opened a boarding house, soon the biggest in the town. She also launched a trade in oriental wares from the front room of her house. Not long after starting this business she also began to deal in sailors' and soldiers' debts. She had a large number of affairs and the lodging house was the scene of a great deal of rowdiness. All of these activities rewarded her handsomely. After her death in 1724, Maria van Dijkhuizen's four grandchildren inherited, between them, a total of ƒ. 40,000.[25]

Klaas Goedhoen never made a fortune from dealing in debt, but in 1742 his direct tax assessment was for an annual income of ƒ. 1,500 guilders, twice as much as he had earned from his salary as a commander. He continued his work until 1760. For instance, his name is noted in the ships' pay books for Enkhuizen between the years 1749 and 1756, when he came to collect what was owed him. He also lent money to commanders, the loans recorded as promissory notes. In the notarial deeds in which these were registered he described himself as a retired chief commander (*groot-schipper*) of the VOC. With the money they had borrowed, the commanders bought private trade goods in the East. They had to pay back the sums borrowed either in Batavia or when they returned home.

In these ventures, Goedhoen was always running the risk that he would not see his money again. That fate befell him with the money he lent to Commander Jochem Aldertsz Tarncke. Initially he got on well with this commander of the Enkhuizen Chamber who had been born in Stralsund, in what is now Mecklenburg-West Pommerania. In 1749, Goedhoen authorized Tarncke to pick up money for him from someone in Batavia. At the end of 1750, Goedhoen lent Tarncke ƒ. 2,630 guilders for trading purposes during the latter's second voyage as commander. He, in his turn, was Tarncke's business proxy in the Republic. For example, Goedhoen collected all outstanding debts owed to Tarncke. However,

---

[25] M.A. van Alphen, 'The Female Side of Dutch Shipping: Financial Bonds of Seamen Ashore in the 17th and 18th Centuries', in J.R. Bruijn and W.F.J. Mörzer Bruyns (eds), *Anglo-Dutch Mercantile Marine Relations 1700–1850* (Amsterdam/Leiden, 1991), pp. 125–32. See also the same author's extensive MA thesis entitled 'Handel en wandel van de transportkoper. Opkopers van VOC-transportbrieven in Enkhuizen (1700–1725)' (Amsterdam University, 1988). M. van der Heijden and D. van den Heuvel, 'Sailors' Families and the Urban Institutional Framework in Early Modern Holland', *History of the Family* 12 (2007), pp. 296–309.

in 1754 Goedhoen loaned Tarncke *f.* 2,550 but he never saw the money again. Tarncke ran into trouble in Batavia, relating to problems to do with a transaction in Bengal cloth, and so his voyage turned out to be a financial disaster. He had to pay a heavy fine of *f.* 3,788 to the Company because of a shortfall in his cargo, and on his return home the Chamber of Enkhuizen confiscated his personal sea-chests because they did not have the required brand marks. The upshot was that Tarncke had earned less than Goedhoen had assumed he would. Matters went from bad to worse for Tarncke. In 1757, on the homeward-bound voyage, his ship had got into difficulties near the Cape because his crew was drunk and incapacitated. This situation led to violent quarrels with his officers. Tarncke's creditors, among them Klaas Goedhoen, now attacked him from all sides. They tried to retrieve their money by taking him to court. Goedhoen's sympathy for Tarncke had reached the point of no return. Goedhoen was still waiting for the money he had lent in 1754 so he issued an official claim for the amount in Batavia, plus half a per cent interest per month, starting from October 1754. How the matter ended is a mystery. Tarncke died during his fourth voyage out to the East in 1760.[26] Most likely, Goedhoen had to bid his money good-bye.

In the 1770s the trade in VOC mariners' debts tailed off. Women had already been forced out of the trade by men with more capital behind them. The probable reason for problems with the trade in debt was the rising death rate among crew members. Interest in buying the letters melted away. Consequently, from 1772 the Company office was forced to purchase them. In Enkhuizen this was the task of the chief bookkeeper. After all, the service provided by the boarding-house keepers was essential to staff the ships, and so essential to the operations of the Company. All Chambers had to contend with the problem in the late eighteenth century.

The port area of Enkhuizen stretched out on the eastern and especially on the southern side of the town. There were plenty of diversions on offer in the narrow alleys between the Oude and the Nieuwe Buishaven.[27] Given his business in transfer letters, Goedhoen must have been very much at home here. It was thronged with people around the times of the sailings and the arrivals home of the East Indiamen. The fishermen's boats and the ships of the merchant marine aroused far less interest. In their case, the cargoes, not the crews, were the centre of interest. It was rare for the departures and the arrivals home of the Company ships to coincide. The greatest chance of this occurring was in September because of the late arrival of a ship of the return fleet. The departing

---

[26] Hoorn, WA, Not. Arch. 1328, akte 3, 23.1.1749, akte 43a, 10.10.1750 and akte 59a, 15.12.1750, 1309, akte 86, 17.12.1750, 1367, akte 86a, 4.10.1754 and 88a, 5.10.1754 and 1372, akte 11, 11.4.1759; D. van den Heuvel, 'Bij uijtlandigheijt', p. 105.

[27] For illustrations of the ports see J.P. Sigmond, *Nederlandse zeehavens tussen 1500 en 1800* (Amsterdam, 1989), pp. 134–5 and pp. 218–19; P.J. de Vries, *De plattegronden van Enkhuizen. Van ganzenveer tot cd-rom* (Enkhuizen, 2004).

ships needed between 150 and 200 men to crew them; fluyts needed about fifty fewer men, but after 1732 fluyts were hardly ever used.

Commanders and officers were not among the clients of the lodging-house keepers because, unlike the majority of the ordinary crew members, nearly all of them were already resident in the town or its environs. Three-fifths of the petty officers as well as the craftsmen required on board came from elsewhere. The percentage was even higher among the ordinary seamen and the soldiers.[28]

Changes in the Second Half of the Century

As the eighteenth century progressed, much in Enkhuizen changed for the worse. During the second half of the century, as a town and seaport as well as a Company seat Enkhuizen was victim to an accelerated process of decay. The number of citizens continued to fall, even though from around 1750 such declines had begun to abate in most Holland towns. The demolition of houses and warehouses was a constant feature of Enkhuizen life. By 1751 only two herring skippers were still living in the town. In the 1720s, various sons of herring fishers' families, for example those of Hamer and Lub, had gone over to the VOC. They reached the rank of officer or even that of commander after several voyages, as did Reinder Lub in 1729.[29] Later on in the century, as a consequence of the cutting back in its business, the VOC had to reduce the number of ships setting sail annually. From 1788, often only one single ship was fitted out in Enkhuizen in a year. Of course, this decline was reflected in the composition of the urban population and in the chances of finding a berth on a Company ship. The numbers of commanders and retired commanders living in the town fell. There was no longer any question of there being whole families in which all the boys and men joined the VOC as a matter of course. The diminished supply of townspeople freed the way for another type of commander, one not recruited from one of the seafaring Enkhuizen families.

Willem van Mensburg was still one of the old school. In 1731 he married a sister of Simon and Dirk Pomp. He was still a boy, under fifteen years of age, when he made his maiden voyage with the VOC in 1719. He carried on for thirty-five years, after 1745 as a commander. After three voyages in this rank, in 1755 he called it a day and retired. No traces of business or official positions which he might have filled can be found. Van Mensburg and his wife outlived all their relations. As a consequence, she in particular was named in various wills on a number of occasions, inheriting both moveable property and real estate. The Van Mensburgs' prosperity increased considerably. In 1740, their possessions were estimated to be worth no less than ƒ. 4,000. In the 1760s, the couple moved

---

[28] Manuscript De Vos, icoon I, fol. 21ff.; Beers and Bakker, *Westfriezen*, pp. 1–93 and 106.

[29] D. de Wolf-Smoes, 'De Enkhuizer haringvisserij en de rol van het stadsbestuur tijdens de oorlogen in de periode 1670–1720' (MA thesis, Leiden University, 1998), pp. 36–41.

2. Roelof Blok (1712–1776). This son of an Enkhuizen glass-blower enjoyed an impressive career with the VOC at sea as a commander and later on land as an administrator. He went to sea at the age of eleven. He retired to Enkhuizen in 1762 and became a member of the local gentry. He was fabulously rich. This 1762 portrait is by an unknown painter.

to a house in a very fashionable street. There was even enough money to have a portrait painted of the former commander. The highest tariff for a burial licence was paid for each of their funerals, in 1776 and 1786 respectively. Their only child, Jan, had sailed to the East with his father in 1748 as a *cadet de marine* and had returned with him in 1751. Jan never married. He made his way up, rising in the municipal administration to become commissioner of petty sessions, one of the more humble posts in the town's government. His task was to deal with minor misdemeanours. As Jan was a member of the Reformed Church, to which he donated the sum of *f.* 2,000, he was able to stipulate that his parents' grave, in which he was later laid himself, 'would be sealed forever'. The epitaph states that his father had sailed for the VOC as commander and captain.[30]

Among those who represented the totally new type of commander were such men as Roelof Blok, Jakob Bruijn, Jan Everwijn Drillinger, Arie Arkenbout and Steven Booms. Although their career paths to commander were normal, their origins and the courses their lives took were certainly very different. To begin with Blok, when he finally returned from Asia, of all of his colleagues he had by far the most remarkable career behind him. He had risen very high indeed. His maiden voyage had been in 1723 as an eleven-year-old boy sailing under Commander Russeplukker. His father was a glazier, a craftsman, who was also involved in the Reformed Church as a deacon and an elder. Roelof Blok's career was meteoric as he was a commander by 1741. His appointment as captain by the Admiralty of the Northern Quarter was also remarkable. It was shortly before he was due to embark on a voyage for the VOC. He was immediately granted leave by the Admiralty to take up his new post. Blok's star rose even higher in the East. He developed obvious talents for the shipping business and for trade. After his second outward-bound voyage as commander, in 1745, he remained in Asia, where he was appointed to increasingly more important positions. He only returned home in 1762 and then as admiral of the returning fleet. By that time he was truly rich. He brought with him bills of exchange worth more than *f.* 88,615 and before his departure he had already sent over the bulk of his wealth in ten bills worth *f.* 36,000 each. His three marriages illustrate his social ascendancy. In 1737 he married a woman from his own social circle, and in Batavia he married a woman who was the widow of an extra-ordinary member of the *Hoge Regering* (the ruling body of the VOC in the East). Again a widower, shortly after his return to Enkhuizen in 1763 he married the much younger daughter of a patrician family from The Hague. His money and his third marriage directly assured Blok of a position which happened to be open on the town council of Enkhuizen.

In the Northern Quarter of the province of Holland, this was not an unusual story throughout the eighteenth century. In many of the villages and towns there

---

[30] Hoorn, WA, Not. Arch. 1273, akte 89, 27.2.1758, 1310, akte 115, 18.12.1754; 1368, akte 19, 11.4.1755; 1371, akte 20, 24.1.1758 and 1514, akte 174, 30.5. 1808. The use of the rank of captain is discussed in Chapter 8.

were regularly too few candidates from the local gentry available to fill municipal offices. The reason for this was the dying out of the patrician families. The obvious solution was to look for replacements beyond the local circle. In terms of social prestige, a place on the municipal council was the highest that could be achieved. After all, the council was the source of political power, initially only locally but later far more wide-reaching. Such a position was for life. The most important office on the council was that of mayor, or burgomaster. Four burgomasters were elected from among the councillors each year, and Blok received the honour immediately. In 1764 he was already one of the burgomasters of Enkhuizen and he was selected on another three occasions. In 1772 and 1773 he was also elected to the Board of the Admiralty of the Northern Quarter.

After his retirement, Blok lived in an extremely expensive residence worth ƒ. 15,000, with its own stables and coach-house. When he died in 1776, he left nearly ƒ. 240,000 to be divided among his four children. They also inherited two highly profitable shares in the Amfioen Society, the lucrative private company involved in the opium trade, which was founded in 1745. In the main front rooms of his house he had seventeen portraits of members of the House of Orange (later the Dutch royal family), in black frames.[31] No other commander could compete with Roelof Blok's achievements. He was the only citizen to have begun as a ship's boy and risen to the position of burgomaster. He was almost in the same league as his fellow-townsman, Jakob Mossel, who started out as an ordinary seaman and rose in 1750 to the rank of Governor-General in Batavia. Blok had profited from his patronage. Blok was no flash in the pan. His son, Anthonie, certainly equalled his father in his administrative achievements. He was a burgomaster and a member of the Admiralty board, and also a member of the States-General and a director of the Company.

Jakob Bruijn was a newcomer to the town when he was married before the commissioners for marital affairs in 1766. His family belonged to the Reformed Church, but his bride did not. She was an Old Catholic and had been christened in the Old Catholic church in Enkhuizen. A mixed marriage had to be solemnized before the magistrates. The sum of only ƒ. 3 was paid for a licence for this wedding. Nevertheless, Bruijn was a scion of those circles in which it was customary to pay the highest fee. He was the son of Dr Gerrit Bruijn, who had been a member of the town council of nearby Monnickendam and a burgomaster from 1728 until his death in 1740. He had obtained his doctorate in medicine from the University of Harderwijk. However, there was something not quite right about the 1725 marriage of Jakob's parents. It was undoubtedly a

---

[31] Y. Prins, 'Van scheepsjongen tot admiraal van de retourvloot. Het leven van VOC-dienaar Roelof Blok (1712–1776)', *Jaarboek Centraal Bureau voor Genealogie 1998*, vol. 52 (The Hague, 1998), pp. 156–99. Bossaers, 'Van kintsbeen', pp. 85–110, 152 and 201; E.M. Jacobs, *Merchant in Asia. The Trade of the Dutch East India Company during the Eighteenth Century* (Leiden, 2006), pp. 127–33; F.S. Gaastra, *Particuliere geldstromen binnen het VOC-bedrijf 1640–1795* (Leiden, 2002), p. 27.

forced marriage because a baby was born only four weeks after it took place. This child was followed by six others. It is possible that Dr Gerrit Bruijn had married far beneath him and his family. His widow was shunned by the gentry in Monnickendam. She died in 1748 leaving young children and having taken a brother in as a lodger. The amount paid for her funeral was a trifling *f.* 3. There are no records of what happened to the children after this. Employment with the VOC was sought for Jakob who had been born in 1737 and Gerrit who was born posthumously in 1740, and this was found in the Chamber of Enkhuizen. In 1753 Jakob sailed to the East as constable's mate. His brother Gerrit held the same position five years later. Both their careers prospered. They were appointed commanders in 1768. Gerrit especially had risen very rapidly through the ranks.

After he had made one voyage as commander and had sailed to the East ten times in total, Jakob retired from the sea in 1770. He became superintendent (*equipagemeester*) of the Company shipyard, which was situated between the Wierdijk and the Oosterhaven, north of East India House. Its terrain had been enlarged in 1751. Superintendent of the Shipyard was a splendid position, one of the highest positions available in a Chamber, and it came with an annual salary of nearly *f.* 3,000 plus various emoluments. Jakob Bruijn was responsible for the construction, maintenance and fitting out of all the ships and other vessels which were the property of the Enkhuizen Chamber. Among the benefits that came with the position was being able to claim reimbursement for the expenses incurred when he sailed to the Texel Roads on the Company yacht to inspect the outgoing and incoming ships. In 1786 Jakob was kept exceptionally busy when the ship the *Voorberg* lost all her rigging during a very severe storm in the Channel on New Year's Eve and could barely limp into Dartmouth Harbour. She had to be fully re-rigged. The superintendent went to inspect the damage for himself and spent more than a month in England. When the *Voorberg* returned to Texel Roads in the autumn of 1786, Jakob had to visit her on a number of occasions because the rigging was faulty and the ship revealed all kinds of defects and leaked badly. This was evidence that the repair work had been faulty.

According to a 1791 report, besides a bookkeeper and a master ship's carpenter, Superintendent Bruijn had about 150 people working under him, including carpenters, sawyers, smiths and coopers.[32] Nevertheless, the position of Superintendent in Enkhuizen cannot have kept its occupant constantly busy, since Jakob also had time to make himself available for the municipal position of commissioner of petty sessions. It is possible that these positions came to Jakob because of his patrician background and the influence exerted on his behalf by his cousin Nikolaas Bruijn, alderman and burgomaster of the town in which he was born and on many occasions a member of the Executive Board of the Northern Quarter.

---

[32] H. Bonke and K. Bossaers, *Heren investeren. De bewindhebbers van de West-Friese Kamers van de VOC* (Enkhuizen, 2002), pp. 33–7; see also a log of the '*Voorberg*' kept by J. Arkenbout in the Maritiem Museum, Rotterdam.

Jakob Bruijn was soon a trusted figure in the town. He was well acquainted with the risks and opportunities which sailing with the Company offered. Before his own final voyage in 1768, he had bought wine and tobacco worth at least ƒ. 7,000 on credit advanced to him by a merchant and former alderman. He had to pay the lender back in Batavia at half a per cent interest per month, the going rate at the time. In later years, various commanders and crew members authorized him to carry out financial transactions on their behalf and appointed him executor of their wills. The Company shipyard closed in 1795, but Bruijn did not have to join the ranks of the unemployed because in 1797 he became an alderman of the town of Enkhuizen under the regime of the new Batavian Republic, and this was only one of his many positions. He was definitely well-to-do. When his wife died, he had to pay the highest tariff for a burial licence. When he died in 1807, the tax on burials had just been abolished. He was survived by four children. His son Jan, born in 1778, was a lieutenant in the navy of the Batavian Republic. His brother, Gerrit Bruijn, continued to sail for a much longer period. He stopped in 1785 and in the same year was appointed alderman and mayor of Monnickendam. Shortly afterwards he married a lady of some standing and they subsequently had two sons.[33]

More Commanders from Outside Enkhuizen

Despite the fact that the Enkhuizen Chamber was gradually forced to cut back on the number of ships it fitted out, it became increasingly difficult to find men among the townspeople seeking employment as an officer or commander. In the case of Jakob Bruijn, who was from nearby Monnickendam, his particular background might have played a role, but there were other appointments which give a hint of the flattening out of the supply of suitable candidates from the town itself. A growing number of appointments as officer or commander were of men recruited from other places but who in the long run settled in the town. One such man was Steven Booms. He was a native of Mandal in southern Norway. In 1760 he married the daughter of an Enkhuizen coppersmith. He had been living in the town since his appointment as third mate in 1757. His climb up the ladder was swift but, during his fourth voyage home as commander in 1771 he had to remain behind at the Cape because of a 'severe indisposition'. When he had recovered, he travelled home as a passenger. After this Booms put an end to his sailing career. Nevertheless, he showed signs of restlessness because he was constantly moving house. In 1769 he finally bought a house worth ƒ. 1,900 from his father-in-law,[34] where he died at the end of 1795 from a 'debili-

---

[33] Hoorn, WA, Not. Arch. with various notarial deeds, for instance 1368, 14.12. 1768 and 1459, 3.5.1797.
[34] S. Messchaert-Heering, *Van koopmansstraat tot Nieuwmarktspijp* (Enkhuizen, 2001), p. 95. P.J. de Vries pointed this out to me.

tation in strength', childless but worth more than ƒ. 12,000. Booms was a good businessman who exploited the chances for trade which came his way to the best of his ability. In the periods in which he was not at sea, he regularly bought debentures and, in partnership with the merchant Pancras de Wit, provided all those who sailed with the Company with consignments of various kinds of wares which they could use for their own private trade. A year after his death, Booms' widow bought a bond worth ƒ. 150, issued by the *Sociëteit Fonds voor Weduwen en Ongehuwde Vrouwspersonen* (Social Fund for Widows and Spinsters), from a third party. This society had been founded in 1755 under the motto 'a person reflects on his ways'. Social funds such as these were not unusual and were intended to provide widows with some support. The entry fees and annual contributions were invested in bonds.[35]

Booms only just lived to see the political changes of 1795 but he was spared the accelerated economic and social decline of Enkhuizen. This cost Bruijn his job as Superintendent of the Shipyard. All the Company establishments were closed. In Enkhuizen approximately 275 jobs were lost. In 1796 Bruijn and the chief bookkeeper compiled a list of these. By that time the Chamber still owned just two East Indiamen. The Admiralty was also abolished, and its headquarters and dockyard were closed. Only the naval hospital, which had been opened in 1784, was spared for the town. In many years the herring fishing fleet lay idle. There was hardly any work to be had for net-makers or in the ropewalks. Enkhuizen sank rapidly into poverty. In 1801, 1,188 people were given assistance by the poor relief and this number rose to 1,645 in the winter. Enkhuizen was one of the hardest hit towns in the whole country. In the winter months one-third of the population earned their living by begging. The desertion and dilapidation of houses was a never-ending problem. Of the 1,980 parcels of land which still existed in the town in 1796, 315 were empty, forty-seven were demolished and forty-six simply disappeared from the records. Many warehouses stood empty too. Fences or walls hid the vacant lots in the streets. Demolition work and clearing away the rubble assumed a new importance. Enkhuizen increasingly began to take on the character of a village. The western part of the town consisted of pastures, orchards and vegetable gardens and farms were also established there.[36]

Confronted with these altered conditions on his return from having been a prisoner-of-war of the British, Commander Jan Everwijn Drillinger became morose. There was little for him to do. On his homeward-bound voyage in

---

[35] Hoorn, WA, Not. Arch. 1458, akte 174, 30.7.1796; The Hague, NA, VOC 4265, 18–19, 81. See also A. Schmidt, *Overleven na de dood. Weduwen in Leiden in de Gouden Eeuw* (Amsterdam, 2001), p. 207.

[36] Willemsen, *Enkhuizen*, pp. 149–56, 177 and 201. R. de Vries, 'Crisis en sociale politiek in Enkhuizen, 1650–1850', in R.P. Zijp et al. (eds), *Barre tijden. Crisis en sociale politiek rondom de Zuiderzee, 1650–1850* (Zutphen, 1989), pp. 36–57, see pp. 45–6; J. Jas et al., *Het Peperhuis te Enkhuizen* (Zwolle, 1996), pp. 24–6.

October 1794 he had been escorted into Plymouth by British warships. He probably did not have much income. As time passed he repeatedly insisted on being paid an annual allowance to which he thought he had a right as a former naval officer, but his pleas went unheard. It seems the money he had earned as commander and from his own 'permitted' private trade had been spent. In 1807 he was buried in the Westerkerk where he was joined soon after by his only daughter. Drillinger was not a native of Enkhuizen. In 1748, he had been born in Vollenhove in the eastern part of the Republic, where his father was bailiff, a position he also held in nearby Blokzijl. He started his maritime career as a seventeen-year-old in Enkhuizen where he signed on as third mate. He was later appointed commander in 1774. He continued to sail until the liquidation of the Company, with an interruption, from 1782 to 1786, when he sailed as a captain for the Admiralty. For a short period before this appointment, he had also been commissioner of petty sessions.[37]

Jacobus Arkenbout was the last Enkhuizen man to sail out as a VOC commander, in 1794. We still know what he looked like because he had his likeness fashioned in a small polychrome statuette of unbaked clay in Canton in China in 1792. He had just been placed in charge of his ship following the death of the previous commander. During the eighteenth century, a number of commanders had had similar statuettes of themselves fashioned by Cantonese 'face-makers' during the long wait in Canton. Often they are depicted sitting on a Chinese chair. Arkenbout is shown standing, wearing a long coat, with a wig on his head and a stick tucked under his left arm. The statuette and a dinner service survived the stranding of Arkenbout's ship in the vicinity of the Cape of Good Hope on 20 May 1793. The commander had just been married in Cape Town and had his wife on board with him. Arkenbout's father had also been a VOC commander and had died at sea in 1771. Like Drillinger, Jacobus was captured by the British in 1795 but he was not held captive for long. After his release, he entered the service of the navy of the Batavian Republic and sailed in charge of a number of smaller warships. After the French left in 1813, it took him almost two years to find a job, as Deputy-Superintendent of the Naval Dockyard in Medemblik. He retired in 1831 on an annual pension of *f.* 1,500. He died three years later in Enkhuizen, and his wife followed him to the grave in 1837. The fire which totally ravaged the former East India House in the Wierdijk in 1816, the building having been used as a hospital since 1810, perhaps awakened memories of his Company past in Arkenbout.[38]

---

[37] Hoorn , WA, Not. Arch. 1471, 19.5. and 15.9.1806.
[38] G.C. Arkenbout and A.A. Arkenbout, *Arkenbout op zee. Leden van een bekende familie op Voorne-Putten in dienst van de Verenigde Oost-Indische Compagnie en de Nederlandse marine, 1721–1834* (Bernisse, 2001); J.C. Overvoorde and P. de Roo de la Faille (eds), *De gebouwen van de Oost-Indische Compagnie en van de West-Indische Compagnie in Nederland* (Utrecht, 1928), pp. 114–16. J.C.A. Schokkenbroek, 'Versteend verleden. Chinese portretbeeldjes in de collectie

The Often Sedate Retirement of Former Commanders

During their lives as mariners in Company service, the Enkhuizen commanders made a considerable contribution to the economic welfare of the town. Most of their salaries and the other income they earned were spent there. Their private trade, which will be more discussed in more detail in later chapters, brought in many thousands of guilders. The money was used to buy household utensils and consumer goods for the Company personnel in the East and at the Cape. Moreover, a large number of Asian products, from textiles to porcelain, which the commanders brought with them when they returned, found a home with friends and local merchants, or were sold at auctions held in the town. The inventory compiled for the estate of Ype Engelsman lists great quantities and types of porcelain. The afternoon call paid to Bregje Schaap in 1732 was to view porcelain which was for sale. This sort of business came to an abrupt end when the commander died at sea or abroad and his affairs were settled from Batavia. The same winding up of business operations was common when a commander retired.

It is possible to follow the lives of a number of Enkhuizen commanders after they retired from seafaring. A few were appointed to official positions, among them Pieter van Loosen as a customs and excise officer at the Admiralty and Jakob Bruijn as Shipyard Superintendent for the Company. A few others were appointed commissioners of petty sessions, a much sought after municipal position. In 1795 Arkenbout had been able to transfer to the Admirality just in time. Drillinger on the other hand was too late. However, very little information is available about other retired commanders. They did not become merchants and even Goedhoen preferred to call himself a man of independent means rather than a trader in debts. Notarial deeds are the only source in which it is possible to trace some of the commanders' economic activities, albeit on a modest scale. Steven Booms was the most engaged, although Goedhoen ran him a fairly close second. Everything they undertook was in fact an extension of their former position as a Company employee. They lent money, helped others in purchasing private trade goods and supplied financing for business in the port. By preference they invested their money in bonds. None of them bought shares in the merchant marine or herring fishing vessels. Sometimes they were able to move house thanks to one or even more bequests. Roelof Blok, the son of a glazier, won his way into the ranks of the town gentry. Earlier Adriaan Pool had achieved the same status in the neighbouring villages.

One of the most striking facts which emerges from the first half of the eighteenth century is that many commanders came from true seafaring families. It was usual for them to be linked by close kinship ties. Later in the century this

van het Nederlands Scheepvaartmuseum Amsterdam', *Vormen uit Vuur* 203 (2008/4), pp. 2–13.

pattern changed. It was customary to retire from the sea at the age of around forty or even younger. Living in a house in one of the more respectable streets was generally a matter of course for a retired commander. A first-class burial was also customary. However, when a commander married he could not always afford a first-class wedding licence. The great majority of the commanders could very soon count themselves among the bourgeoisie (*brede burgerij*), but only a few of them could claim to belong to the gentry. As the century drew to a close, the domination of the rank of commander by men who had been born in Enkhuizen waned. This made room for people from other places, among them Booms and Drillinger.

2

Hoorn

Like Enkhuizen, the city of Hoorn was situated on the Zuiderzee, just a little further from the entrance to the sea at Texel where ships sailed on their way in to and out from the inland sea. Also like Enkhuizen, Hoorn was one of the four small chambers of the VOC. The starting capital it put up in 1602 was only half as much as that of Enkhuizen, but nevertheless Hoorn provided one-sixteenth of the total turnover of the Company's business. This had been agreed in the charter which the States-General had granted the new company in 1602. The Chamber of Hoorn also had seven directors, most of them nominated by the Hoorn municipal council from among prominent local people. A director of such a small chamber would not have had a lot of work to do. The few ships which were on the high seas or were expected in the harbour, the shipyard occupied with some new construction or repair work and the annual auctions were certainly not enough to keep the directors busy every day. The appointment of a commander and his officers appeared on the agenda of the weekly meeting of the directors only two or three times a year.

In each chamber the usual practice was that each director took upon himself certain sections of the business. There were three or four committees: (1) fitting out, for supervision of the building, maintenance and fitting out of the ships and the recruitment of sailors and soldiers, (2) warehouse, for the supervision of the administration of goods, (3) receipts, for the supervision of all monetary matters, and (4) pay office, for the supervision of the bookkeeping and the administration of the shares. Only Amsterdam had a pay office committee. At least two directors sat on each committee. If he was a member of the fitting out committee, a Hoorn director had to be prepared to travel to the Texel Roads one or more times a year to carry out inspections. He travelled there on the admirably furnished Company yacht, occasionally accompanied by the Superintendent of the Shipyard or the master ship's carpenter. He could be away from home for some days, but the length of his visit was never long – the per diem of *f.* 6 was paid for only six days. Other directors made the journey to Amsterdam or Middelburg, when the general board of the Company, the *Heren Zeventien* (Gentlemen Seventeen), met, and occasionally to The Hague for consultations with the States-General. A director of one of the smaller chambers received a remuneration of *f.* 1,200 per annum. This sum was raised slightly by interest paid at the rate of 5 per cent, amounting to an additional *f.* 60; directors were only paid at the end of the year. Needless to say, there were also a number of emoluments.[1]

As elsewhere, in Hoorn the VOC owned its own real estate. The main building was the *Oost-Indisch Huis*, situated on the northern side of the town just past the administrative centre. For a person coming from the shipyard, it was an easy quarter of an hour's walk. A commander would go to the *Oost-Indisch Huis* to apply for a new post or to pick up his instructions. The building, of which the outside shell is still extant, on the Muntstraat, was first occupied in 1670. It consisted of two buildings with one entrance. In 1776 an anonymous observer described the building: 'it has a double flight of steps and looks like an ordinary gentleman's residence'. Just around the corner were two warehouses. The shipyard and the stores were situated on the eastern side of the Kielhaven. In the first half of the eighteenth century everything exuded prosperity and growth. A third warehouse, dating from 1670, was expanded extensively in 1727. In 1723 two houses were built in the shipyard, one for the superintendent and the other for the master ship's carpenter. In 1732 a new storehouse was built. As late as 1767 the area of the shipyard was extended to provide more storage space. In 1744 between 200 and 250 people were employed there. The Company ensured that there was 'a great deal of hustle and bustle in the town', as someone remarked in the same year.[2]

The City

In the eighteenth century, as with Enkhuizen, Hoorn was not prosperous. A decline in trade and shipping had been experienced as early as the third quarter of the previous century. The enormous outer harbour, which was protected with palisades, was needed less and less for putting up the merchant fleet during the winter months. In the course of the eighteenth century, the town surrendered the western part to the Zuiderzee and let the area of the eastern part shrink, as a result of sedimentation. It was an uphill job to keep the inner harbours and the route to Texel deep enough for navigation. Adjusting the flow of water was not enough and dredging became increasingly expensive. The virtual disappearance of direct import and export of goods across the North Sea meant it was necessary to keep the harbours open only for the East Indiamen and warships. Around 1750, there was 'scarcely a hand's breadth of water' in the Kielhaven; 'the crows and the ravens come there daily to search for carrion'. Hoorn was no longer

---

[1] Gaastra, *The Dutch East India Company*, pp. 149–64; H. den Heijer, *De geoctrooieerde compagnie. De VOC en de WIC als voorlopers van de naamloze vennootschap* (Deventer, 2005), pp. 59–61 and 135–40; Bonke and Bossaers, *Heren investeren*, pp. 25–7 and 66–82.

[2] Van Gelder and Wagenaar, *Sporen van de Compagnie*, pp. 42–55; Lesger, *Hoorn*, p. 147; Bonke and Bossaers, *Heren investeren*, pp. 38–43.

a desirable harbour for the import of goods. The bulk of its shipping traffic was intraregional, largely confined to the Zuiderzee area.

The economic contraction hit hard. By the mid-eighteenth century foreign wares did not reach the town directly but via Amsterdam. The once sizeable salt and timber trade and whaling had all but disappeared. At the end of the century, there were no private shipyards left in the town. By around 1790, the number of merchant ships in Hoorn had dropped to only eleven ships, against 145 a century earlier and about fifty between 1710 and 1720.

The Hoorn commanders were more fortunate in the environment in which they lived than their colleagues in Enkhuizen. Here perhaps fewer houses stood vacant and there was less razing of buildings than in Enkhuizen because the population density had never been as high as in the nearby port. Around 1660, Hoorn reached its greatest number of inhabitants, a good 14,000. After that the number declined slowly, but the drop was less dramatic than in Enkhuizen. The death rate was particularly high in the period 1700–1740, a period in which the number of baptisms and marriages was low. By 1795 the number of inhabitants in Hoorn had fallen to 9,500. In that same year, the three West Frisian towns of Hoorn, Enkhuizen and Medemblik had 18,400 inhabitants all together, a decline of more than half compared to the number reported in a 1622 survey. In the total area of the West Frisian countryside at that time there were about 27,300 people, a decline of more than 40 per cent over 173 years. These figures were to drop even lower in the period of the Batavian Republic and during the French occupation.[3]

In the eighteenth century, the Company was the only large business which offered business and employment of any significance in Hoorn. The weekly cheese market held every Thursday at the Red Stone (*Rode Steen*) provided only a limited amount of business and in fact served to emphasize the regional function of the town. After the War of the Spanish Succession, the Admiralty did keep a more or less fixed number of people in service but their numbers were often higher than the real requirements in numbers of personnel. Because the seat of the *College van Gecommitteerde Raden* – the body which managed the day-to-day affairs of the northern section of the province of Holland – was in Hoorn, the town did fulfil the function of political capital of Holland north of the IJ. The need to repair the sea dikes unexpectedly brought in temporary extra employment opportunities in the 1730s. In 1731, within a short period of time, shipworm destroyed the wooden pilings of the dikes and sluices. An inspection in 1732 revealed that 47 kilometres of timber frameworks had been completely destroyed and another 21 kilometres had been affected. The long-term solution was to replace the wooden pilings with stone (*keien*). For a few years after the discovery of the effects of shipworm tens of thousands of loads of stone were

---

[3] Lesger, *Hoorn*, pp. 137, 140–51, 156–72 and 220; L. Kooijmans, *Onder regenten. De elite in een Hollandse stad. Hoorn 1700–1780* (Amsterdam, 1985), pp. 17–19.

imported into Hoorn and Enkhuizen, largely from Norway. The repairs were completed in 1740, but after that most of the work on the sea defences faded away.[4]

In fact, it was the Company and the Company alone which provided large-scale and long-term job opportunities with its annual dispatch of one, two or three ships, the shipyard, the administration and the auctions of the goods brought in by the returning ships. Moreover, twice in three years, a new ship was launched from the Company shipyard. Many suppliers delivered materials required in the shipyard or profited from the provisioning of the ships. Scores of bakers were required to provision one ship alone. The character and fate of the boarding-house keepers were just the same as in the other Company towns. In the alleys of Hoorn, among the lodging houses the *Willem in de Lantaarn* was particularly notorious.[5]

Every year the Hoorn Chamber recruited several hundred sailors, soldiers and craftsmen. This number dropped somewhat as the century wore on. A total of approximately 5,000 men from the town signed on with the Company in the eighteenth century, almost as many as in Enkhuizen. But that meant the town itself did not even provide half of all the Company's maritime personnel. The majority came from the rest of the Republic, especially from the city of Amsterdam, and from Germany. Most of the commanders and officers were residents of Hoorn but even so they dominated the officer corps to a lesser extent than did the townspeople of Enkhuizen. A random sample of the commanders of the Hoorn Chamber found a total of twenty-five. Twelve of them came originally from outside the town, including two foreigners from northern Germany. On his ill-fated 1763 voyage on the *Nijenburg*, which culminated in a mutiny, Commander Ketel, who was from Husum in Schleswig, had a first mate and a third mate from Hoorn and a second mate from Amsterdam. The other foreign commander was Klaas Stuiver from Spaden near Bremerhaven. In 1756 he sailed with a whole complement of officers who were not men from Hoorn, but on a subsequent voyage five years later all of his officers were Hoorn men. This shows that the local character of the ship's officers could fluctuate quite remarkably.[6]

---

[4] Lesger, *Hoorn*, pp. 157–8. See also P. Boon, *Een dijk van een kaart* (Hoorn, 1991), p. 8.
[5] DAS I, 53.
[6] The commanders who have been investigated are: Hendrik Jurriaansz Ben (c.1665–1752), Jan Jurriaansz Ben (1669–1718), Arend Dirksz Bent (1684–1726), Daniël Arendsz Bent (1685–after 1723), Daniël Dirksz Bent (1683–1722), Daniël Jakobsz Bent (1688–1722), Dirk Daniëlsz Bent (c.1658–1709), Gerrit Bruijn (see Enkhuizen), Adriaan de Graaf (?–1765), Gerrit van der Gracht (1714–1778), Leendert van Koopstad (1734–1780), Gerrit Jansz Kuit (1696–1755), Jan Peereboom (1709–1782), Lukas Rozeboom (?–1741), Gerrit Scheler (?–1802), Volkert Schellinger (1708–1746), Daniël van Staden (1687–1738), Dirk de Veth (1689–1741) and Klaas Zeeridder (?–1732). Besides the random sample, a count of all the commanders appointed in Hoorn and Enkhuizen shows that in Enkhuizen nearly twice as many townspeople were given a command as in Hoorn. I am very grateful for the assistance of Th. van Velzen of the Nationaal Archief in The Hague for his help in counting

The Characteristics of Hoorn Commanders

In 1742 tax collectors in the town recorded a total of six retired commanders, of whom two had an annual income of *f.* 600, two of *f.* 1,000 and two of *f.* 1,200. In Enkhuizen there were seven; six with an annual income of *f.* 600 and one with *f.* 700, plus one first mate with *f.* 600.[7] The sum of 600 guilders was the lowest taxable income, which meant that only the wealthy were taxed, so probably there were commanders who were below this limit. Unfortunately, the opportunities for investigating the backgrounds of the commanders in the town and their lives on shore are not as good as they are for Enkhuizen. The Hoorn Archive does not contain many documents that can be browsed to discover facts about the lives of commanders. For instance, the notarial archives are not indexed which means they are very difficult to access. Another problem is that proportionately a greater number of commanders from Hoorn died on board or overseas during their service with the Company. The result is there are fewer traces of them in the local archives.

Dirk de Veth was one who grew accustomed to a life both under sail and in the tropics. Nevertheless, he died not at home but in Batavia in 1741, shortly after his arrival there on his tenth voyage. De Veth, and by far the majority of his colleagues in the random sample, remained loyal to the Hoorn Chamber, year in, year out. They began their careers with this Chamber. De Veth had been born in Leiden and had started his career in 1708 as a sailor in Hoorn where he went to live and where he later married. He climbed the promotion ladder and by 1724 he had already been appointed commander. After achieving this rank he made voyages as commander in 1726, 1729, 1732, 1737 and 1740. His second wife died in 1743. She was not terribly wealthy but her estate was nevertheless assessed at *f.* 4,000. Her husband's most recent earnings from trade in Batavia, which brought him *f.* 3,600, had not yet reached her when she died.

Daniël van Staden, who had been born in Batavia in 1687, made eight voyages. On his first voyage in command he had taken his wife with him. Perhaps it was for this reason that he borrowed *f.*1,000 shortly before their departure in January 1718. Twenty years later, Van Staden died during his fifth voyage home as commander, on the way from the Cape to Hoorn.[8] Adriaan de Graaf sailed to the East at least ten times and on five of these voyages he was the commander. He also died on a voyage home, in 1765 after leaving the Cape. Gerrit van der

---

the numbers of signings on of the inhabitants of Enkhuizen and Hoorn. See also http//VOCopvarenden.nationaalarchief.nl/; and J.C. Mollema, *Een muiterij in de achttiende eeuw. Het afloopen van het Oost-Indisch Compagnieschip Nijenborg in 1763* (Haarlem, 1933), pp. 15–30.

[7] W.F.H. Oldewelt, 'De beroepsstructuur van de bevolking der Hollandse stemhebbende steden volgens de kohieren van de Familiegelden van 1674, 1715 en 1742', *Economisch-Historisch Jaarboek* 25 (1951), pp. 167–248, see pp. 182, 184 and 214.

[8] Hoorn, WA, Not. Arch. 2373, akte 68, 25.11.1717; The Hague, NA, VOC 14368.

Gracht had had enough of sea life in 1766, having sailed on at least eight voyages. He had himself honourably discharged in Batavia and received an annuity which he used to buy into a house for elderly people in Semarang on Java. Individuals could buy a share in such houses as accommodation for their retirement (a *proveniershuis*). He was then sixty-two and it is highly likely that back home in the Netherlands his wife and only son had already died.[9] At the time, most other Hoorn commanders had completed fewer voyages in charge. However, in the Hoorn Chamber it was no exception for a commander to have sailed past the Cape in both directions ten or more times during his seafaring career.

There was no question of conspicuous wealth among the Hoorn commanders. Many a widow must have been relieved when she received the final bill of exchange from Batavia. After tidying up her husband's financial affairs, Van Staden's widow received ƒ. 4,190 in 1743. De Graaf's widow received ƒ. 4,589 in 1766. Lukas Rozenboom left a widow and six children when he died in Ambon in 1741; two years later his family was informed that a bill of exchange worth ƒ. 12,813 had arrived. De Veth's wife was less fortunate. She had to contend with the administrative precision of the Company. In 1738, after the completion of De Veth's second to last voyage, it had been discovered that there was less tea in the cargo than had been registered on the ship's papers. This was an instance of 'less weight' for which the commanders and their officers were held responsible. It was designated 'malversing' (*minwicht*) and the sum at stake was ƒ. 2,366. In 1743 the full amount was debited from De Veth's outstanding earnings. However, the bill of exchange worth the ƒ. 3,600 he was owed arrived too late for his widow.[10]

Just as in Enkhuizen, most of the commanders were married and they had one or more children, but never many. Once a man had been promoted to first or second mate, marriage was apparently considered a responsible step. Gerrit Bruijn was someone who only took this step very late in life. He was married in 1790, not in Hoorn but in his birthplace of Monnickendam, five years after he had completed his final voyage from the Cape to Hoorn. He paid the highest licence fee of ƒ. 30, but, like his brother Jakob (see Chapter 1), by birth he was not a run-of-the-mill commander. For their first marriages, their colleagues who had beaten them to the altar had paid no more than 3 or 6 guilders for the licence fee. They came from families of tradesmen and seafarers. Dirk De Veth's father was a hatter in Leiden and he and his colleagues tended to live on the periphery of Hoorn or near the harbour, rather than in the more expensive streets in the centre.[11]

In Hoorn, it was not taken for granted that the directors would appoint commanders and officers only from Dutch Reformed families, and who actually

---

[9] The Hague, NA, VOC 833, rubriek G, 22.11.1776.
[10] The Hague, NA, VOC 222, 14.11.1743.
[11] Kooijmans, *Onder regenten*, pp. 24 and 326. For a very clear ground plan of all the streets and alleys see B. van Tartwijk *et al.* (eds), *Hoorn en de zee* (Hoorn, 2002), p. 16.

went to church regularly. Roman Catholics and Mennonites formed large minorities in the town, and Remonstrants and Lutherans also lived there. There were ten churches in total in the town. Van der Gracht came from a Roman Catholic family and had been baptized into that church in 1714. However, both his marriage in 1754 and the baptism of his son took place in the Reformed Church. Dirk Bent had his first child baptized in the Remonstant church in 1683 but his last in the Roman Catholic in 1701. By that time he was already a commander. The children of his son Daniël, who had been baptized in the Remonstrant church, were both baptized in the Roman Catholic church, in 1708 and 1711 respectively. By that time Daniël too was a commander. After this there were two branches in the Bent family, one Roman Catholic, the other Remonstrant.[12] There was an official rule which stated that Company personnel should belong to the Reformed religion but in practice this was honoured more often in the breach than the observance. One only has to think of the stream of people who came to the Republic in search of work with the VOC from countries in which the chief Christian denomination was Lutheranism. After the appointment of the Lutheran Gustaaf Willem Baron Van Imhoff as Governor-General in 1742, Lutheran churches were built in both Batavia and Cape Town.

Probably it depended on the personal attitude of a director whether or not the religious affiliation of a prospective commander played any role in the latter's appointment. In formal terms, membership of a deviant Christian sect could be grounds for not appointing a man. In 1754 there was some lack of clarity in the Hoorn Chamber about the appointment of First Mate Pieter de Bok as commander. De Bok had 'Romish inclinations'. One of the directors made enquiries with a lawyer to find out whether the Company regulations contained a rule which would forbid such an appointment. The lawyer was unable to find any such rule. Nevertheless, De Bok was not promoted to commander and a few years later he sailed again as first mate.

There were a great many Lutheran commanders sailing for the Company in the eighteenth century and, as time passed, Roman Catholics such as Benjamin van der Spek, appointed by the Amsterdam Chamber in 1775, were also found in its service. In that same year, Director Jakob van der Heim of the Delft Chamber meticulously noted on the application of Pieter Verkerk for a berth on a ship that this candidate and his parents had been Roman Catholics in Leiden but after they had moved to Rotterdam they had converted to the Reformed religion.[13]

---

[12] A. Smolders, an MA student in history at Leiden University, wrote a very detailed report.
[13] The Hague, NA, Archief Van der Heim 92; P.A. Boon, 'Kerk en schip. Westfriese zeelieden omstreeks 1700 en hun godsdienstige achtergrond', in L. Akveld *et al.* (eds), *In het kielzog. Maritiem-historische studies aangeboden aan Jaap R. Bruijn bij zijn vertrek als hoogleraar zeegeschiedenis aan de Universiteit Leiden* (Amsterdam, 2003), pp. 317–29, see p. 317.

Two Seafaring Families

At the beginning of the eighteenth century there were still true seafaring families in Hoorn who dedicated their lives to sailing for the Company. Examples are the Bent family and the Ben family, who greatly resemble the Pomp and Pool families in Enkhuizen. Towards the close of the seventeenth century and during the first three decades of the eighteenth century, members of these families regularly put to sea for the VOC. Around 1690, Dirk Daniëlszoon Bent was the master of a privately-owned merchant vessel rated at 90 *last* or about 180 tons, on which he sailed to Portugal. In 1693 the Hoorn Chamber took him into its service. He made two long voyages and died a few months after he had left on his third voyage in 1709. Thanks to a legacy of *f.* 8,100 in 1708 and a bill of exchange worth *f.* 7,440 in 1711, his widow had plenty of ready money at her disposal.[14] Her sons Daniël and Arend also joined the Company. They both sailed with their father in 1703. Daniël was appointed commander in 1712, and Arend followed in his footsteps five years later. In notarial deeds, assuming an air of gentility they both referred to themselves as chief commanders (*groot schippers*), though they were only doing what a great many of their colleagues also did. Both the brothers died at sea. It is possible that their father was quite rich because both Daniël and Arend were able to afford an expensive marriage licence, the first in 1707 paying *f.* 15 and the second in 1712 paying *f.* 30. Perhaps the long absence of her father or his early death in 1726 was partly to blame, but some time around 1730 Arend's daughter, Meinoutje, was called the 'famous whore … who has seduced various married and unmarried persons into terrible debaucheries'. After an affair with a regent she was placed in the house of correction. Later, around 1750, Meinoutje was once more in the glare of publicity when, as a widow who had remarried, she openly conducted a relationship with a married Hoorn lawyer and alderman.[15] A nephew of Dirk Bent, Daniël Arendsz, twice sailed for the VOC around 1750, first as a sailor and later as a gunner. There was also a certain Daniël Jacobsz. Bent. He was a commander in 1721 but he was not directly related to the family. His father was a sailmaker.

None of these seafaring Bents enjoyed a long career as a sailor followed by a peaceful retirement on land. It was the same story with the father and son Jan and Barend Ben, although a different fate befell Jan's elder brother Hendrik, whose career began in the seventeenth century. He made his first voyage as commander in 1705 and this was followed by another three. He married in 1695, at which time his assets were assessed at less than *f.* 2,000. His brother Jan had married a year earlier and had had to pay a licence fee of *f.* 3. In 1700 he signed on as a gunner. He became a boatswain's mate in 1705 and finally commander in 1714. Examining the birth dates of his children it seems he did

---

[14] Hoorn, WA, Oud Archief Hoorn 2577, 12.1.1688 and 7.8.1691 and 2267, 23.12.1708.
[15] Kooijmans, *Onder regenten*, pp. 157–8 and 259.

not sail for the Company before 1700, because he was never absent for very long. When he married for a second time in 1704 he paid the same licence fee as he had in 1694. Jan Ben died in Batavia in 1718 from where his widow later received a bill of exchange worth the considerable sum of ƒ. 11,898. An inventory of house contents reveals that his family lived in fairly modest circumstances. His son, Barend, sailed in 1725 as third mate and died two years later overseas.

The life of his uncle Hendrik Ben took another direction. In September 1717, he was dishonourably discharged from his position as commander by the authorities in Batavia and a year later he was 'deported' home as an 'ex-commander'. His salary was confiscated to cover the shortfalls in the cargo. He had been 'dishonest with the victualling', had accepted payment for the transportation of rice and had dealt out punishments without consulting the ship's council. In fact, Ben had had a bad name with the government in Batavia as there had been earlier incidents in which he was involved. In 1713 he had made ill-mannered objections when asked to transport certain passengers. On that occasion he had also been deprived of his command. He did not sail again after 1718. He was declared 'incompetent' and was never recalled by the Company. Hendrik Ben died in his native town at a very advanced age, probably in 1752. A burial licence fee of a mere ƒ. 3 does not seem to indicate any degree of prosperity.[16]

Two Dignified Gentlemen

In contrast to Hendrik Ben, Gerrit Kuit was an exemplary commander who finished off his career at sea in a proper manner and then proceeded to earn himself a good reputation among his fellow townspeople. Kuit set sail to the East as a gunner's mate in 1716 when he was twenty. In 1730 he was a commander. At the end of his second voyage in 1735 he married and gave up seafaring. Kuit could be counted among the wealthier citizens of the town and in 1739 he was appointed as one of the five commissioners of petty sessions. Twice a week this commission met to judge crimes for which the sentence was the imposition of a fine of up to 50 guilders. These misdemeanours included quarrels, brawls and 'deeds such as threatening with intent, fighting and the like'. This commission was the lowest rank in the administrative organization in a town and could be the first step on the way to a career as a regent. However, Kuit climbed no higher, but in 1750 he was appointed an elector (*boonganger*, literally one who goes to get a bean), a position which went back to the late Middle Ages. Every year on Good Friday a number of well-to-do citizens came together in the Great

---

[16] For details about the Ben family the best source is the report by Smolders (see note 12). See also W.Ph. Coolhaas (ed.), *Generale Missiven van Gouverneurs-Generaal en Raden aan Heren XVII der Verenigde Oostindische Compagnie* VII (1713–1725) (The Hague, 1979), pp. 44, 321 and 380 (other editions of the *Generale Missiven* are referred to by the name of the editor, abbreviated title and number of volume).

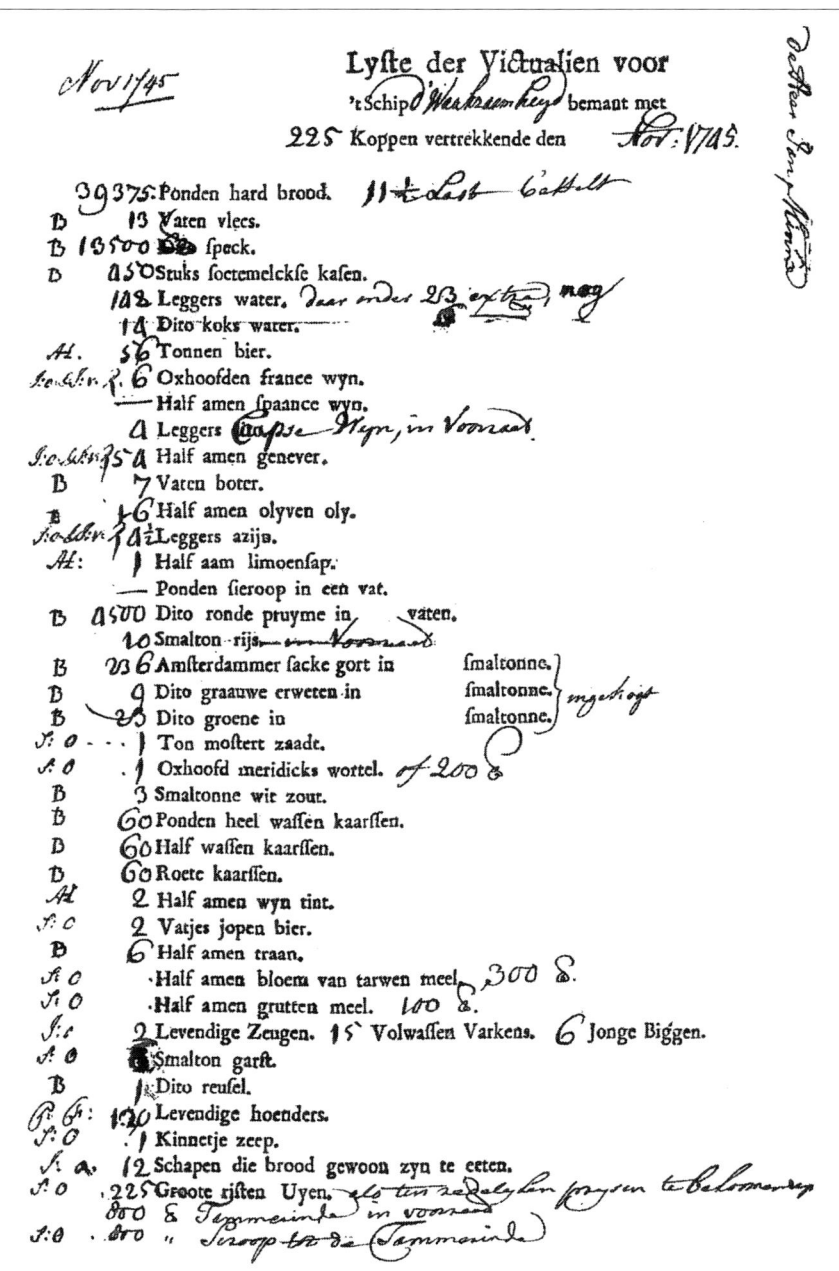

3. Provisions on board. There were printed lists of the components of the ship's provisions and matters pertaining to them. The quantities were filled in by hand according to the size of the crew. In the end more than 225 men sailed because 234 arrived at the Cape on 17 April 1746; ten had died. The *Waakzaamheid* under Roelof Blok enjoyed a healthy voyage. There was a large number of livestock on board: 2 sows, 15 pigs, 6 piglets, 120 chickens and 12 sheep. Director Jan Minne preserved this list among his private papers.

Lyſte voor de Cajuyt
en ſieken.

Kaßkn?	A	Oxhoofden france wyn.
ıst?	4	Half ameſt ſpaanſe wijn
B	6	Vierendeels hollandſe boter.
A:	A	Tonnen goed bier in Pypen.
ſ: o	150	Ponden poeyer ſuyker.
ſ: o	150	Ponden ſieroop.
	16	Stukken gerookt vlees ⎫
	10	Hammen ⎬ in Voorraad
	12	Koe tongen. ⎭
D	9	Komminne kaeſen.
D	9	Goudſe kaeſen.
ſ-o	6	Smalton beſchuyt. 3op 8
D	4	Sack turkſe boonen.
ſ o	50	Ponden lange roſynen.
ſ o	50	Dito corenten.
A o	5	Oncen faſſeraan.
ſ. o	20	Ponden comyn.
ſ. o	20	Dito annijs.
·ſ. o	15	Dito ſpaanſe zeep.
ſ o	6	Dito gember.
	8	Dito Peper ⎫
	3	Dito Noten ⎪
	3	Dito Caneel ⎬ in Voorraat
	9	Dito Nagelen ⎪
	3	Dito Fouly ⎭

4. Extra supplies for the captain's cabin and the sick bay. There were also printed lists of the extra portions of food and drink for the guests in the captain's cabin and the sick. The quantities available to Roelof Blok on his voyage on the *Waakzaamheid* in 1745–1746 have been filled in by hand. The most striking fact is that foodstuffs such as cow's tongues, hams and smoked meats were in stock in the Company warehouse in Enkhuizen.

Church of Hoorn to elect the burgomasters and aldermen. Besides the members of the town council, the election college consisted of certain citizens who met the requirement of possessing a certain degree of wealth. These so-called *boongangers* were appointed by the town council for life. One by one, the *boongangers* picked a bean out of a bag which was held aloft by one of the mayors. There were nine black beans among the white ones and whoever pulled out one of the black ones had a right to elect the four mayors. In turn each of these nine chosen electors (*keurmannen*) proposed a person and then voted for the candidates. They also nominated twenty-one men from among whom the bailiff chose seven aldermen. Kuit went 'to the bean' (*te boon*) three times. He died at the beginning of 1755. His prosperity is evidenced by the fee for the burial licence, which was *f.* 30, the highest possible level.[17]

Besides Gerrit Bruijn, Jan Peereboom is possibly one of the few commanders of the Hoorn Chamber who came from the gentry, though he was from Monnickendam. Peereboom's father had been a member of the town council there since 1695 and was delegated by his town to sit as one of the *Gecommitteerde Raden* in Hoorn in 1705. For reasons which can no longer be discovered, he was rapidly appointed to the position of one of the three messengers (*bodes*) and renounced his position as *Gecommitteerde Raad*. He moved to Hoorn with his family and once there it was not long before he exchanged his position as messenger for that of keeper of the lodgings of the members of the *Gecommitteerde Raden*, a well-paid job. In 1718, Jan Peereboom had one of his three sons, eight-year-old Jan, sign on as a sailor on a ship under the command of Commander Van Staden. Perhaps he had been able to arrange this through his contacts in the higher administrative circles in which Van Staden's family-in-law also moved. In an unbelievably short time, the son, Jan Peereboom, achieved the rank of commander. This appointment came as early as 1729. Luck played some part in it. A fortnight after departure, his commander died and the ship's council appointed him acting-commander. Peereboom was then only twenty and had only held the rank of first mate for just two weeks. His appointment was confirmed in Batavia. After this he made two more voyages, but he stopped in 1736 when he was twenty-seven. In the meantime in 1731 he had married a young daughter from the well-to-do Schellinger family, a merchant family. This family also had connections among legal practitioners in Hoorn. In 1738 Peereboom became a commissioner of petty sessions, a year before Kuit was appointed to the same position. He was also appointed a *boonganger*, but only in 1773.[18]

In 1743 Jan Peereboom was appointed a naval captain in the service of the Admiralty of the Northern Quarter. In his case this was almost certainly a

---

[17] Kooijmans, *Onder regenten*, pp. 30, 34–5 and 38. Dr P.A. Boon (Wijdenes) provided some personal details.
[18] The Hague, NA, VOC 760, 28.7.1730; Bossaers, '"Van Kintsbeen"', pp. 72–4 and 120; Kooijmans, *Onder regenten*, pp. 161 and 354.

sinecure because he probably sailed only once as captain of a warship, in the summer of 1748 on the *Kasteel van Medemblik*, 'designated to meet and escort ships returning from the East Indies'. As captain he received a salary of 30 guilders a month. At the end of his life in 1779 he was even appointed rear admiral, promoted over other colleagues who were naval men. By that time the local Admiralty did not amount to much. For many years its income had been much lower than its expenses. In the eighteenth century the five Admiralties in the Republic received no money from the States-General for years on end, just at a time when income from taxes on maritime and land trade and from shipping had dropped enormously in the areas under their authority. This drop in income was particularly marked in Hoorn and Enkhuizen but the number of people employed by the Admiralty was not adjusted to meet the more straitened circumstances. In part because the whole administration moved back and forth between the two towns every three months, a number of the positions had two incumbents. In 1744 it came to light that the wages of the carpenters and the dock-workers had not been paid for years. In neither Hoorn nor Enkhuizen were there any new ships built in the dockyards. The construction of a new ship was put out to tender, often as cheaply as possible and without the work being supervised. In the 1750s a warship capsized during her maiden voyage even though there was not much wind. Casual carpenters and dock-workers were taken on for repair work and fitting out. In 1749 the Admiralty had no more than four ships. New construction work was not undertaken again until the 1780s. As far as the fitting out of ships was concerned, the War of the Austrian Succession (1740–1748) did suddenly generate some extra activity. Peereboom's 1748 command was one of the rare cases of the Admiralty fitting out a vessel. This was because it was the duty of his Admiralty to send a frigate to sea once every two years to escort the homeward-bound Company fleet. This escort always took place in a convoy with three ships from other admiralties. In the summer months, this was often the only work of the Board of the Admiralty. Despite this fact, Peereboom had eight or nine colleagues in the Admiralty with the rank of captain.[19]

In the circles of Peereboom's family and family-in-law, 'sea fever' was not an unknown phenomenon. His brother-in-law, Volkert Schellinger, was a boatswain with the VOC, and in 1740 his brother Reinier, a lawyer, had married Sijtje Doen, the widow of his colleague, Klaas Zeeridder. She herself was the daughter of a naval captain and the niece of two deceased VOC commanders. There was also a real family drama among the Peerebooms. Jan's twin sister was insane. Until her mother's death in 1743, this sister had remained at home in the lodgings of the *Gecommitteerde Raden*. After her mother died, her three brothers,

---

[19] The Hague, NA, Admiraliteits Archieven (AA) XXXVII, 357, 163ff.; The Hague, KB (Royal Library), Handschriften (Manuscripts) 73D 13C (memorandum by Admiral Cornelis Schrijver); Rotterdam, Maritiem Museum (MM), Notes J.C. de Jonge V, 21; J.R. Bruijn, *De admiraliteit van Amsterdam in rustige jaren 1713–1751. Regenten en financiën, schepen en zeevarenden* (Amsterdam, 1970), pp. 21–2.

Jan, Reinier and François, the last a Reformed minister in Monnickendam, did not want to put their sister in a house of correction but rather to leave her legacy intact so that the interest on it could be used to pay for her care. After a while, when this proved impracticable, their sister was finally put in the house of correction. In 1748, Jan's mother-in-law left him and his wife a legacy worth ƒ. 7,828.[20]

The Final Days of the Hoorn Chamber

Although Peereboom spent the last years of his life in Amsterdam, a few other commanders and ex-commanders did not desert their home town, which in the second half of the eighteenth century, with the exception of a few extremely rich regents and merchants, was inhabited by a growing number of destitute and unemployed people. Here once again vacant houses and demolition were symptomatic of the falling number of inhabitants, though the situation was not as bad as in Enkhuizen. In 1777 three Mennonite merchants took the initiative, setting up a few workshops for the unskilled poor for both spinning and manufacturing wallpaper. This initiative was quite successful. The children of the poor received at least some education. However, an attempt to breathe new life into whaling failed. The reconstruction and refurbishment of the naval dockyard did bring more business and employment to the town in the 1780s.[21]

In the meantime, the Company provided routine work in new construction, repairs, fitting out of ships, and auctions. However, the Fourth Anglo-Dutch War (1780–1784) and the necessity of sailing with chartered private merchant ships instead of its own ships temporarily disturbed this pattern. There were no longer many Hoorn commanders in Company service. The directors showed an increasing tendency to look for their commanders outside the town. Leendert van Koopstad was from Rotterdam. He made his maiden voyage for the Company in 1765 when he was appointed commander. Shortly before he had married in Hoorn. During his fifth command in 1780 he died on the voyage out. The position of Superintendent of the Shipyard in the 1780s did not go to another townsman but went instead to the naval officer Isaak Louis de Bellon, who had sailed for the Amsterdam Chamber for many years. Scandinavians and Danes, from Schleswig-Holstein in particular, had opportunities to be appointed commander. There were five in the years 1782–1787. In itself this was not unusual but it seems there were suddenly more of them even though there were fewer places available. It was similar to the story in Enkhuizen.

---

[20] Hoorn, WA, Not. Arch. 2470, 158, 10. 12.1748; Kooijmans, *Onder regenten*, pp. 61, 260, 310 and 354.
[21] Lesger, *Hoorn*, pp. 136–7; J. Kok, "'t Weldaadig stormtuig". Sociaal-politieke initiatieven in Hoorn, 1770–1850', in Zijp *et al.*, *Barre tijden*, pp. 58–73.

In 1793 two East Indiamen departed from Hoorn for the last time. They completed their voyage as usual and arrived in Batavia. Another Hoorn ship, the *Oosthuizen*, sailed from Texel Roads on 22 December 1794, a few weeks before French troops occupied the Republic. This ship was sailing for the Amsterdam Chamber under Gerrit Scheler, who had also commanded the same ship for the Hoorn Chamber in 1791. This time Scheler did not get very far. His ship was placed under an embargo off the Scilly Isles and more than a year later was auctioned for £9,000. Scheler made another voyage to Java in 1802. This time the English south coast proved fatal to him. He refused a pilot even though a November gale was brewing. He perished with his young son and more than 360 passengers and crew in the surf near a sandbank off Ramsgate.

By 1795 there was scarcely any work to be had in the shipyard in Hoorn or on the Company premises. Those workers who were still there just hung around with time on their hands. Gradually everything was dismantled and closed down. The navy took over the shipyard. The powder magazine was transformed into a hospital. The town of Hoorn bought the *Oost-Indisch Huis* and two warehouses in 1809.[22] By that time there may well no longer have been any ex-commanders still living in the town.

In the second half of the eighteenth century in both Hoorn and Enkhuizen the real seafaring families who had served the Company for generations through thick and thin had completely disappeared. High death rates on board and in Batavia were partly to blame. It was especially bad in the 1730s but the shrinking town population also had an effect. Not many commanders were able to end their seafaring lives on land. A few were appointed to the lower ranks of the town administration, and any roots in the gentry assisted them in this. However, for the widows of some commanders the bills of exchange, sometimes posthumously transferred from Batavia and other places in Asia, were undoubtedly of vital importance. Mostly they contained sums of several thousand guilders, a truly princely sum for an eighteenth-century family. In tranquil Hoorn, the Company disappeared virtually unnoticed in the 1790s. There were no longer commanders or ex-commanders to attract the attention of the researcher.

---

[22] E.S. van Eyck van Heslinga, *Van Compagnie naar koopvaardij. De scheepvaartverbinding van de Bataafse Republiek met de koloniën in Azië 1795–1806* (Amsterdam, 1988), pp. 35, 45 and 194; I.G. Dillo, *De nadagen van de Verenigde Oostindische Compagnie 1783–1795* (Amsterdam, 1992), p. 173; Bonke and Bossaers, *Heren investeren*, pp. 41–3. Data about the Scandinavian commanders are taken from S.W. Aarsbog, *Med Mars og Merkur. En analyse av norsk deltakelse i VOC basert på skipssoldbøker 1633–1794* (Trondheim, 2003), pp. 69–71 and Appendix II.

3

Middelburg

Moving southwards, to the province of Zealand, the seat of the Zealand Chamber was in the city of Middelburg. It was a large Chamber which generated a quarter of the turnover of the Company, in fact as much as that of Enkhuizen, Hoorn, Delft and Rotterdam combined. In contrast to both the previous cities, Middelburg was not situated on open water; nevertheless of all the Company harbours it had the shortest and the best connection with the North Sea. The distance from Middelburg to open water was 7 kilometres. Towed by horses, a ship would travel from Middelburg via a straight canal, dug in 1535, and then by the narrow, somewhat winding canal of Welsinghe, to the Vlacke, the entrance to the Sloe, the waterway between the islands of Walcheren and Zuid Beveland, at Fort Rammekens on the Wester Scheldt. The navigability of this route was constantly deteriorating and in need of maintenance, but it was only in 1792 after repeated complaints by the Zealand Chamber that the canal and the harbour were dredged. In the roads off Rammekens, the additional loading took place and cargo was discharged after a return voyage.

The city was equipped with the usual facilities of a VOC Chamber; these were situated on the harbour in the vicinity of the entrance to the canal. As it was equipped with locks, this was the oldest tidal harbour in the Dutch Republic. The facilities consisted of the *Oost-Indisch Huis*, the shipyard and the warehouses. The ropewalk was just outside the city walls. All these facilities were expanded at the beginning of the eighteenth century. In 1711 the *Oost-Indisch Huis* was considerably enlarged and afterwards extended to the warehouses situated at its rear, reached via three consecutive courtyards. The havoc wreaked by war in 1940 destroyed all the buildings with one exception: the house of the superintendent of the shipyard remained intact.[1]

---

[1] Overvoorde and De Roo de la Faille, *De gebouwen van de Oost-Indische Compagnie*, pp. 56–82; Van Gelder and Wagenaar, *Sporen van de VOC*, pp. 125–38; Sigmond, *Nederlandse zeehavens*, pp. 27–8, 71–2 and 109.

The City

Middelburg was the administrative centre of the province of Zealand. In both the seventeenth and the eighteenth centuries the city had more inhabitants than either Enkhuizen or Hoorn, but there are few reliable population figures. A 1660 estimate gives a number of between 28,000 and 30,000 townspeople, and an estimate in 1700 a slightly lower total. Around 1780 there would have been approximately 18,000 inhabitants. After 1795 the number of people resident in Middelburg shrank drastically, to little more than 10,000. From an economic point of view, Zealand trade in agricultural products, especially wheat and madder, was invariably conducted through Middelburg. Until the end of the War of the Spanish Succession in 1713, in times of war, privateering stirred up a great deal of extra activity in the city. The slave trade and the Atlantic triangular trade offered an additional source of employment. Nevertheless, there can be no doubt that the Company was the local 'economic giant'. Without it, someone remarked as early as 1715, 'the trade in this city would have been meagre'. However, not even the Company was able to prevent a one-third drop in the amount of income tax paid by the citizens between 1710 and 1740 and the city's subsequent slump into impoverishment.

The Company put food in many mouths in the town. In the years of its greatest activity (1720–1740), more than a thousand citizens found employment in the office, shipyard, warehouse and ropewalk. According to a report of 1790, in that year there were still 826 in its employ and in 1796 it still accounted for 433 jobs. Besides these people, there were also those who sailed to the East every year on the ships. For a long time, the population of Middelburg provided half of the Zealanders employed on board. In practical terms this meant that there were always approximately 900 to 1,200 men from Middelburg either at sea or sojourning in the East. In the second half of the century these numbers were even higher. Every year the Company also took some twenty orphan boys into its service. Given the high death rate on board the ships and overseas, this recruitment certainly contributed to the decline in Middelburg's population. Less than half as many ship's crew members came from nearby Flushing (Vlissingen). Among them there were always a number of orphan boys, on average sixteen years of age. Their warrants were often in the name of the parish poor relief board in their native town.[2]

---

[2] M. van der Bijl, *Idee en interest. Voorgeschiedenis, verloop en achtergronden van de politieke twisten in Zeeland en vooral in Middelburg tussen 1702 en 1715* (Groningen, 1981), pp. 200–3; P. Priester, *Geschiedenis van de Zeeuwse landbouw circa 1600–1910*, A.A.G. Bijdragen 37 (Wageningen, 1998), pp. 51–2; J. Francke, *'Utiliteyt voor de gemeene saake'. De Zeeuwse commissievaart en haar achterban tijdens de Negenjarige Oorlog, 1688–1697* (Middelburg, 2001), pp. 380–1 (correction of Priester's figures); V. Enthoven, '"Veel vertier". De Verenigde Oostindische Compagnie in Zeeland, een economische reus op Walcheren', *Archief Koninklijk Zeeuwsch Genootschap der Wetenschappen* 1989 (Middelburg, 1989), pp. 49–127, see

5. A silver loving cup dating from 1795. Since the end of October 1794 six returning ships, seized by the British authorities, had lain anchored in Plymouth for months on end. The VOC correspondent in Plymouth, William Symons, was very helpful in arranging such matters as the payment of the wages of disembarking crew members. In July 1795, the British laid formal claim to the ships and their cargoes. The principal ship's papers were burned in time by the Dutch commanders. The six commanders (captains) showed their appreciation of Symons' efforts by presenting this loving cup, bearing the inscription: 'This cup is presented to Right Honourable W. Symons as a memento by the Sea Captains Drillinger, Westphal, Vanderplas, Molenaar, Van Dyck and Van Wymeren in command of the Dutch East India Company ships *d'Enckhuyer Maagd*, *Scheld*, *Delf*, *Africaan*, *Blitterswyk* and *Nagelboom*, which lay at anchor in the Plymouth Roads for nine months in the years 1794/5.' On the reverse side of the cup are the initials W.S. and a family coat-of-arms.

Nonetheless, Zealanders were always by far the minority on the Zealand ships. For instance, in 1712 they formed 23 per cent of the total, and nearly fifty years later this had dropped to only 12 to 13 per cent. In the course of

pp. 49–50, 91 and 93; A. Tramper, 'Vlissings varend verleden: "uijt het weeshuijs na Oostindiën gevaren voor den armen"', *Den Spiegel* 20, no. 3 (2002), pp. 13–17; Van Gelder and Wagenaar, *Sporen van de VOC*, p. 124. The figure for 1796 in Middelburg, Zeeuws Archief (ZA), Archief Matthias Pous 227.

the century, the proportion of men from the South Netherlands (present-day Belgium) outstripped that of the Zealanders.[3]

The Majority of Commanders from the City of Middelburg

The men of Middelburg were strongly represented among the commanders of the vessels. This is not surprising because, as was the case with every Chamber, this top job on board was open for application, and the fact that nine of the twelve directors were fellow townsmen must have influenced the choices made. Middelburg commanders, along with colleagues from Flushing and Veere, landed the most appointments. Evidence for this is found in two reviews of appointments in the periods 1736–1740 and 1772–1779. In the first period forty-three commanders were appointed. In thirty-five cases, the commander was a native of the island of Walcheren on which Middelburg is situated. Among them fourteen were from Middelburg itself. In the second, somewhat longer period, the corresponding numbers were forty-one, twenty-three and seventeen respectively. This is unmistakable proof of a constant supply of men from Middelburg. The same situation prevailed among the mates; however, the number of candidates for a mate's place from Flushing and Veere dropped sharply. This meant that there were more opportunities for non-Zealanders, even indeed for foreigners.[4] The same development could also be observed in Enkhuizen and Hoorn.

Commanders and their retired colleagues were well-known figures in Middelburg, the city being so inextricably bound up with the business of the Company. It is impossible to find as much information about these men in Middelburg as can be found about their colleagues from other Company cities. The German bombardment on 17 May 1940 destroyed an enormous amount of archival material. Fortunately, thanks to prolonged research into a great diversity of sources by Mr P.F. Poortvliet (Den Helder), a surprising amount of data about the careers of the seafaring Zealanders in the early-modern merchant marine, whaling and fishing fleets and the Navy is available. This data was used to find out something about the Company commanders, but the quest for further information about their lives on land was mostly in vain.[5]

---

[3] Enthoven, 'Veel vertier', pp. 100–5. See also D. Roos, *Zeeuwen en de VOC* (Middelburg, 1987), pp. 12–122; V. Delahaye et al., 'De Vlaeminck en de Zeeuw; 30.000 mensen overzee', in J. Parmentier (ed.), *Uitgevaren voor de Kamer Zeeland* (Zutphen, 2006), pp. 47–87.

[4] E. van der Doe and A. Wiggers, 'Varen voor de kamer Zeeland van de V.O.C. Enige opmerkingen over zeevarenden aan boord van de Zeeuwse schepen in de achttiende eeuw', *Zeeuws Tijdschrift* 37, no. 6 (1987), pp. 209–21, see. pp. 211–13.

[5] The masters who have been investigated in depth are: Jan van den Broek (c.1695–1740), Kornelis van Eps (1759– before 1810), Justinus van Gennep (1744–1801), Hermanus Grindet (1680–1746), Maarten Haringman (1715–1784), Reinier Heijpe (c.1680–1725), Maarten Ingelse (c.1665–?), Jan Kakelaar (c.1715–1754), Michiel de Keizer (1697–1746), Kornelis Pietersz (1727–1780), Johan van der Plas (1762/3–after 1795), Salomon Reynders

Besides Poortvliet's database, the ship's payrolls or pay books, which have been preserved, were of assistance in reconstructing the careers of Zeeland mariners. This data reveals that the majority of the commanders began their seafaring lives as ship's boys or ordinary seamen in the employ of the VOC. Most of the commanders married before or just after their first command. The use of the monthly letters, referred to in Chapter 1, was fairly general. In 1701, the wife of Master Maarten Ingelse withdrew 225 guilders, in 1706 440 guilders and in 1707 320 guilders. In 1703 she did not take advantage of this facility. When he was still a second mate in 1738, another man from Middelburg, Jan Kakelaar, gave his wife permission to withdraw three months' wages, but this permission was withdrawn after he had been promoted to first mate. During the three voyages he made as commander in 1746, 1749 and 1750, permission was once again given and sums amounting to between 198 and 486 guilders were withdrawn.

These are only two examples. A number of orphan boys from Zeeland enjoyed successful careers. In Ceylon, Johan van der Plas, a former inmate of the Municipal Orphanage in Middelburg, was promoted to commander of a ship in the homeward-bound fleet in 1791. His business on the island must have prospered, because after he had returned home his bills of exchange brought him nearly 20,000 guilders. On his second homeward-bound voyage, at the end of October 1794, trapped by bad weather and the war, Commander Van der Plas and five other homeward-bound vessels ended up in Plymouth. After the French occupation of the Dutch Republic in January 1795, the British Government confiscated these ships. Van der Plas' ship was sailed to London where sale of her cargo raised only 550 pounds sterling. The six commanders of the confiscated ships had a difficult time. Their idle crews demanded that their wages be paid or they would jump ship. Punishment drills and large-scale desertions were the consequence. In their hour of need, the commanders probably obtained assistance from a prominent citizen of Plymouth, because in the summer of 1795 they offered this man a silver loving cup (now in the collection of the Scheepvaart Museum at Amsterdam) as a token of their gratitude. This was engraved with their names and those of their ships. Van der Plas was the third master mentioned. First on the list was Drillinger of Enkhuizen. Around about the same time the six commanders travelled home. Van der Plas, the former orphan boy, who had had two younger brothers serving under him at an earlier

(1708–1770), Jakob Rijzik (1723–1792), Jan Siereveld (1742–1788), Karel Sluiter (?–1772), Willem de Smit (?–1732), Johan Splinter Stavorinus (1739–1788), Gerard Stocke (?–1736), Kornelis Vis (1714–1789), Dirk Wagtels (?–1779), Evert Wesseling (1740–1808), Christiaan Zummack (?–?). Mr P.F. Poortvliet in Den Helder generously placed his data pertaining to the careers of the commanders of the Zeeland Chamber at my disposal. This databank is also available in het Rijksarchief in Middelburg and from here on is cited as Verzameling P.F. Poortvliet.

stage of his career, must have envisaged a different end to his career with the VOC.

From Company to Navy

In Middelburg it was not unusual for a commander who had stopped sailing with the VOC to assume other maritime duties or sometimes even to hold two posts at the same time. The commanders concerned transferred to the Admiralty of Zealand, even though for some of them this was no more than a partial change. Peereboom in Hoorn took much the same step, but there are not many other examples.

The Admiralty of Zealand also had its seat in Middelburg. After the three Anglo-Dutch Wars its glory and its purpose had been severely tarnished. From the beginning of the eighteenth century, it had to watch its importance gradually ebb away, mirroring the fate that had befallen the Admiralty of the Northern Quarter. Throughout the whole of the eighteenth century it employed a total of forty-eight different flag officers and captains. It appears that, among them, prior to their commissions as captains, no fewer than fifteen had served as commanders with the VOC. Seven others had served with the Dutch West India Company (WIC) or had worked for private ship owners. In the Navy, a couple of the erstwhile commanders achieved the high flag officer rank of vice admiral: Salomon Reynders from Middelburg in 1766 and Kornelis Vis from Colijnsplaat in 1782. This transfer from Company to Navy did not take place regularly but occurred in two distinct periods: 1720–1739 and 1751–1770. The commissioning of a VOC commander as a captain in the Navy indicates that naval officers in Zealand were not always recruited from the higher echelons of society. One indication of the esteem the profession of naval officer still enjoyed around 1780 is apparent in the following quotation. Hendrik August, Baron Van Kinckel, who came from Heilbronn in Germany and was commissioned as captain by the Admiralty of Zealand in 1777, remarked in 1782 that not 'everybody without discrimination' ought to become a midshipman, 'among them [there] never should be young persons, whose parents keep a shop or pursue a trade or hold some lowly office'.[6]

Perhaps it was precisely this difference in social class which made it attractive for VOC masters to transfer to the Navy, but so far it has proved impossible to investigate this matter thoroughly. In the eighteenth century a captain's place would not have been sought after by those who wanted to enrich themselves. Only if the Board members of the Admiralty favoured a particular captain

---

[6] J.R. Bruijn and P.F. Poortvliet, 'De officieren van de admiraliteit (1714–1795): hun carrières, bemanningen en schepen', in J.R. Bruijn, A.C. Meijer and A.P. van Vliet (eds), *Marinekapiteins uit de achttiende eeuw. Een Zeeuws elftal* (The Hague/Middelburg, 2000), pp. 17–29; pp. 30–3 contains a list of all captains and flag officers from Zealand.

6. Maarten Haringman (1715–1784). Born in Colijnsplaat on the Zealand island of North Beveland, Haringman climbed up through the ranks to become a commander and in this capacity he made four voyages for the Zealand Chamber in 1747, 1749, 1751 and 1754. On his final voyage, he was in command of the returning fleet. Shortly after his return from this voyage, Haringman was appointed captain in the Zealand Admiralty where he held various commands. In 1765, he had himself painted by the otherwise unknown artist A. Ferrero, as did his colleague Bonifacius Cau. In his hand Haringman is probably holding a signal trumpet. In 1766, with the rank of rear-admiral, he was appointed Superintendent of the Naval Dockyard in Flushing, where he lost no time in joining and becoming director of the *Zeeuwsch Genootschap der Wetenschappen* (Zealand Scientific Society).

and gave him more commands than others could he expect to enjoy financial rewards. Money had to be made from the provisioning arrangements and not from the monthly stipend. It was usual for the Admiralty of Zealand to fit out no more than one or two warships a year, and sometimes these were intended only for short-haul voyages. A former commander would have had to have seen to his financial situation during the time he served the Company. Perhaps it was purely a financial question which prompted some commanders to apply to return to Company service shortly after their commissions as captains – applications which were often granted. In 1720, after two voyages as commander, Reinier Heijpe from Middelburg became a naval captain, but within less than a year he had once again voyaged to the East. He died in 1725 shortly after his return. Heijpe had requested permission for this voyage from the Board of the Admiralty and it had been granted. There had been precedents in former years. In contrast, after his transfer, Hermanus Grindet from Flushing remained loyal to the Admiralty. He made the change, which was in fact for him a return to the Navy, in 1720, after having sailed with the VOC for twenty years, including two voyages as commander. He began his naval career in 1689, when he was presumably barely nine years old. He was given regular commands by the Admiralty and in 1734 he was actually promoted to rear admiral.

In 1725, Heijpe's captain's place went to his colleague Gerard Stocke from Veere, who also asked permission to undertake one more voyage to the East Indies. By 1729 he had returned and he then held three consecutive commissions, in 1731, 1733 and 1735, as captain of a naval frigate stationed for three to four of the summer months in the North Sea and the Channel, waiting for and escorting the homeward-bound Company fleet. He died a year later. Willem de Smit is another example. At the time he was given his commission by the Admiralty in 1731 he had been sailing for the Company for some time. His commission formed no impediment to him sailing to the East again as a commander the following year. This was to be his final voyage because his ship, the *Slot ter Hoge*, foundered off one of the Cape Verde islands. De Smit was dishonourably discharged and declared incompetent as the disaster was blamed on the laxity of the commander and his officers.[7]

Kornelis Vis initiated a new series of transfers to the Admiralty in 1751. Vis had been born into the fishing community of Colijnsplaat on the island of North Beveland in 1714. When he was thirty, having first passed through all the usual ranks of ship's officers, he became a commander. During his first command, he remained in the East where he engaged in lucrative private business for an extended period. He was able to transfer nearly 20,000 guilders to Zealand. In 1749 Vis married the daughter of a distinguished merchant in Middelburg. In 1751, a second, much shorter voyage earned him almost the same sum in bills of exchange. Even before his return he was commissioned as a captain by the

---

[7] The Hague, NA, VOC 221, 26.8.1733.

Admiralty. By this time he had settled in Middelburg, where he often changed his address. Towards the end of his life, from 1778 to 1789, he lived in one of the better streets, which was lined with elegant patrician mansions. Vis was highly thought of and was awarded with the command of warships no less than five times, in 1753, 1756, 1759, 1760 and 1764. He was promoted to rear admiral in 1766 and to vice admiral in 1782. Vis was a respected citizen of the city, and he was also held in high regard in naval circles in The Hague because, as late as 1778 and 1780, he was asked to be a member of an investigative commission into the condition of the naval fleet and to sit on a naval court-martial.

Maarten Haringman, who was a year younger, was a fellow villager and in many ways his life ran parallel to that of Vis. He climbed up through the ranks of the Company, married a woman from the village of Saint Annaland on Tholen shortly before he was promoted to commander in 1747, and moved to Middelburg. He made four voyages as commander, in 1747, 1749, 1751 and 1754. After his final return in 1756 he also became a naval captain. Like Vis, Haringman enjoyed great good fortune and was given various commands. Within a decade he had sailed as a captain in the Navy four times. In 1766, he moved to Flushing where he had been appointed Superintendent of the Admiralty Dockyard. He was simultaneously promoted to rear admiral. In 1783 Haringman returned to Middelburg, where he was to die a year later. His opportunities for making money had not been confined to his service with the Company. His four commands in the Navy also proved very profitable. As was the custom, and as was considered general practice, in his rank as captain he was responsible for the provisions on board. For each man on board the commander received an allowance, known as 'provisioning pennies' (*kostpenningen*), which amounted to seven *stuivers* per day. The commander needed no more than four or five *stuivers* per day for victuals and other supplies, so the rest was profit. Depending on the size of the crew and the length of the voyage, this difference could run into many thousands of guilders. A commander's actual monthly stipend was no more than 30 guilders. Haringman was also a prosperous and respected citizen in the town. His annual income was estimated at between 1,000 and 2,000 guilders. At least two to three servants were always employed in his household, and he had several children.[8]

Dirk Wagtels was another who transferred during the second period. By birth he came from The Hague but shortly after his appointment by the Chamber of Zealand in 1754 he had settled in Middelburg, which henceforward became his place of residence. When he was granted his commission as naval captain in 1769 he was living with his family in one of the principal streets, not far from the Abbey. He was happy in his new position and was apparently able to bear the financial brunt of living on this less profitable sinecure. Before he had transferred to the Zealand Chamber, between 1747 and 1752 Wagtels had undertaken

[8] B. Loeve, 'Een matroos uit Colijnsplaat: Cornelis Vis (1714–1789), in Bruijn *et al.*, *Marinekapiteins*, pp. 94–110; T. van Wingen, 'Van konstabelsmaat tot gevierd kapitein: Maarten Haringman (1715–1784)', in *ibid.*, pp. 111–18.

three voyages for the Delft Chamber and had consequently been promoted to commander by the Zeeland Chamber in 1759. On his third homeward-bound voyage in 1769, he commanded the returning fleet. In 1766 and 1767 bills of exchange to the value of *f.* 6,646 and *f.* 30,000 were received for him from the East. Two years later there was yet another to the value of 19,000 guilders. He sailed as captain of a naval vessel on only one occasion, in 1776. Wagtels died in 1779. His son, who bore the same name, joined the Navy directly as an officer and did not first serve with the Company.[9]

Making a Fortune at the Cape

Jacob Rijzik, a native of Brielle, was not in the country when the Admiralty commissioned him as captain in 1759 and he never took up his commission, nor did he ever command a warship. Half a year after his return from his second voyage as commander, Rijzik left again for Asia as usual, eventually to cut his fourth voyage short at the Cape. There he was offered the opportunity to take up the position of Superintendent of the Company Shipyard. His wife joined him in 1767, which was standard practice. Rijzik's private trade in the East had earned him substantial sums of money (*f.* 6,480 in 1754, *f.* 5,243 in 1759, *f.* 7,200 in 1763 and in 1764 *f.* 1,661), but if his financial operations at the Cape were as successful as those of his successor, Damiaan Hugo Staring, he returned home a very rich man indeed.

Staring, who was a native of Doetichem in the province of Guelders, was a naval captain who had spent most of his time unemployed. In 1771 he had asked for a temporary discharge from the Navy, which had been granted. His reason for this request was to serve as a commander with the VOC. On his homeward-bound voyage on a Zeeland ship in 1773 he disembarked at the Cape in order to take up the vacant position of Superintendent. He was to remain there until 1781 and in that period he had no less than 300,000 guilders transferred to his business agents in the Dutch Republic. He made the bulk of his money in the timber trade at the Cape.

The position of superintendent in Cape Town was a much sought after and prominent position, one regularly occupied by a retired commander. When Rijzik was appointed in 1765, his predecessor, the Amsterdam commander Willem Vrucht, had just died. The position required that 'the person-in-charge could place all his confidence in him'. This 'person-in-charge' was the governor, with whom the superintendent was in daily contact. The arrival of Rijzik, the 'States [General] captain', at the Cape was reported in the newspaper the *Middelburgse Courant* on 24 May 1766. At the Cape the new superintendent found he had at his disposal a large official residence at the shipyard as well as coaches, sedan

---

[9] Verzameling P.F. Poortvliet; see also The Hague, NA, AA 2853 and 2854.

7. In the roads of Rammekens. Two ships of the Zeeland Chamber sailing from the roads at Rammekens. The monogram on the rear ship reads VOC M[iddelburg], but the rest of the name is illegible. There is a good view of the windows of the commander's cabin. Engraving by Matthias de Sallieth (1749–1791) after a drawing by the Middelburg maritime artist Engel Hoogerheyden (1740–1807).

chairs and a number of slaves. He was in fact responsible for everything to do with shipping at the Cape, and this included the ships sailing under a foreign flag which visited the 'Indies Sea Hostelry'.[10] After he had spent a good seven years in this post, Rijzik returned to Zealand at the beginning of 1773. For several months he had been 'indisposed'. As the commander of a homeward-bound vessel was forced to remain at the Cape for health reasons, Rijzik returned home not as a passenger but as commander. Consequently he received half of the customary gratuity of 2,000 guilders for having brought the ship safely back to her home port. He had in fact demanded the whole amount.[11]

In the official documents there is no mention of why Rijzik had remained behind at the Cape during his fourth voyage in 1765. The story behind this is told by the VOC servant Jakob Haafner in his *Lotgevallen en vroegere zeereizen*.[12] In 1766 as a young orphan Haafner had been taken into the household of the childless superintendent who had been like a father to him. At this point he

---

[10] A. Staring, *Damiaan Hugo Staring. Een zeeman uit de achttiende eeuw 1736–1783* (Zutphen, 1948), pp. 21, 32–3, 47 and 53–4.
[11] Cape Town Archives Repository, Resolutions Council of Policy of Cape of Good Hope, 9.2.1762, 11.2.1766 and 19.2.1773 (www.tanap.net), abbreviated to Cape Town Archives, resolutions C. of P.; The Hague, NA, VOC 222, 18.10.1774; *Middelburgse Courant*, 24 May 1766.
[12] J.A. de Moor and P.G.E.I.J. van der Velde (eds), *De Werken van Jacob Haafner*, I, Werken Linschoten-Vereeniging XCI (Zutphen, 1982), pp. 55–6 and 95.

remarks that Rijzik's marriage in Middelburg had not been a happy one. When he returned home from his voyages as commander, his wife invariably made his life miserable. He had taken up the position of superintendent at the Cape in order to create 'an unbridgeable space' between him and his wife. However, he made a sad misjudgement because, as soon as his wife heard that he would not return for the foreseeable future, she immediately organized a passage to Cape Town, accompanied by a brother and a cousin. Scarcely had she recovered from the voyage than she immediately set about reorganizing Rijzik's household completely, leaving no stone unturned. The slaves no longer had a moment's rest. The house, 'where once peace and pleasantness had prevailed, now resounded with scolding, shouting and scrubbing'. The wife was too much for Haafner and so he found a home elsewhere.

Eventually Rijzik and his 'domestic tyrant' did return, not to Middelburg, but to Brielle. Rijzik was no longer a naval captain as he had asked for and been granted an honourable discharge from this post in 1771. In his native town, Brielle, he was a prominent man. On his mother's side he was counted among the local worthies. His grandfather had been a burgomaster. As a boy he must have felt the lure of the sea. At the age of sixteen he signed on with the VOC as a ship's boy, and he subsequently passed through all the customary ranks of the Zealand Chamber until in 1755, at the age of thirty-two, he was given his first ship. He sailed for the East on no fewer than nine occasions. China fascinated him, as it did many others. During the time he spent there in 1757, he could not resist the temptation to order porcelain plates decorated with an illustration of his ship, the *Vrijburg*.[13] By the time he returned in 1773 he was unquestionably a man of substance. He immediately bought a house in Brielle worth 2,500 guilders, and four months later, on 13 November, he purchased yet another house in which to live. The new home cost him 4,350 guilders and came complete with stables and a coach-house. Apparently he had grown used to such amenities in Cape Town. In 1774 he bought yet another house (614 guilders) and a warehouse (210 guilders). Besides investing in real estate, Rijzik also put money into fishing. He bought a *gaffelschuit*, a fishing smack rigged fore and aft, from the fishing village of Zwartewaal near Brielle, paying 1,520 guilders for it. He did not lose much time in selling a share of it. As did other worthies, in 1775 he indulged in a country house in Rockanje, surrounded by four hectares of land, for which he paid 13,000 guilders. He called his manor 'Weltevreden' (Contented). As the years passed he extended his landholdings in Rockanje and purchased yet another manor house. He also bought and sold land and farms as well as taking a one-twelfth share in a madder processing factory – a building in which the red madder dye extracted from the roots of a star-shaped plant was processed ('laked') first by drying and then by crushing the roots to extract the

---

[13] L. Wagenaar, *Galle, VOC-vestiging in Ceylon. Beschrijving van een koloniale samenleving aan de vooravond van de Singalese opstand tegen het Nederlandse gezag, 1760* (Amsterdam, 1994), pp. 117 and 211.

dye-stuff. Despite the unhappy marriage, in 1792 an inventory of his possessions still listed the 'old blue and polychrome porcelain' bought in the 1750s.

Rijzik also threw himself into administration. He became an alderman, but was not granted a seat on the municipal council. As he declared that he was a *patriot* and opponent of stadtholder William V of the House of Orange, he was thrust aside during the successful revolt by supporters of the House of Orange in 1788. Both he and his wife felt at home in the strict Calvinist parish which worshipped in the *Catharijnekerk* (St Catherine's). They had the certificate of their membership of the Dutch Reformed Church which they had received in Cape Town registered immediately. In 1787 they presented their beautifully bound copy of the so-called Staten-Bible (the translation as authorized by the States-General in 1637) to the church to be placed on the pulpit. His wife died in 1789, followed three years later by Rijzik himself who succumbed to gout and fever. The tariff for the funerals was the highest that could be paid, 30 guilders. According to the text engraved on the silver medallion on the front of the Bible and in a large number of legal deeds, Rijzik referred to himself as a retired VOC captain, a title to which he had indeed been entitled at the very last moment in 1755, but which had been rescinded just a few months later.[14]

To be appointed superintendent in Cape Town was not an honour to which every commander could aspire. Generally speaking, it was a post which was set aside for commanders from the upper echelons of society and it was in the gift of the Board of Directors of the VOC, the *Heren Zeventien*. Rijzik's successor, Staring, came from extremely well-placed social circles in the Achterhoek region of Guelders and was a naval captain. In 1782 he was succeeded by the son of a *regent* in Gorinchem (sometimes Gorcum), Justinus van Gennep. At the age of twenty this man was appointed a third mate and in 1774 he was given his first independent command by the Chamber of Zealand. This was followed by another two voyages. Homeward bound from China in July 1781, at the Cape he and four other commanders lost their ships, which were riding at anchor, to the British in a raid. The loss of his ship did not prevent Van Gennep from marrying a girl of the Cape two months later. In fact, marriage in Cape Town was a regular occurrence. In February 1782 Van Gennep was appointed superintendent of this Company settlement and he remained in the post until four years later when he and his family and his in-laws left for home, going first to Gorinchem and then later to Rotterdam.

Like his two predecessors, Van Gennep probably owed his lucrative position to a background that was somewhat different from that of the average run of commanders. He too became phenomenally rich. He followed in Rijzik's footsteps and invested only a trifling sum of his money in Zealand itself. Directly upon his return in 1786, he bought a large mansion with stables and a coach-

---

[14] Mr A. van der Berg in Brielle gave me this information. See also J. Kroes, 'Chinees porselein met Nederlandse familiewapens', *Genealogie* 3, no. 1 (1997), pp. 4–7. For the title of captain see Chapter 10.

house in Gorinchem at a cost of 6,000 guilders. Nor could he resist the temptation to buy a country seat. In 1788, the purchase of two manors, Heukelom and Leyenburg in the vicinity of Leerdam, was executed before a notary. Part of the Heukelom estate consisted of the rectangular fortification of Merkenburg, constructed in 1734. This cost him 60,000 guilders. In fact Staring had paid even more, 95,000 guilders, for the manor of Wildenborch near Vorden.[15] Van Gennep purchased more houses in Gorinchem and later in his life he chose to live on the Leuvehaven in Rotterdam. He actively bought shares in public funds and bonds and lent large sums of money to third parties. In 1796 he also invested money in a sugar refinery in Rotterdam. After his death in 1801, his sons had an inheritance of 310,000 guilders to share among them. In the settlement of the legacy, the sole reminders of the seafaring past of their father and the origins of their mother were some financial claims at the Cape of Good Hope.[16]

As time passed, it seems that Jan Siereveld, who had been born and bred in Middelburg, apparently lost his love of the sea. After he had spent two years without a post at the Cape, where he was occasionally asked by the commanders who called there for his advice about problems pertaining to ships, he returned home with his family for a second time. The homeward-bound voyage in the autumn of 1786 was on the naval frigate the *Juno*, which ran aground on rocks on the Isle of Wight and was afterwards smashed to pieces in a storm. Most of those on board were rescued, including the Siereveld family. After he had returned to Middelburg, Siereveld moved to Breda, where he died in December 1788. He was given an expensive funeral, which included burial in a crypt in the *Grote Kerk* (Great Church). Siereveld bequeathed an extensive inheritance, including estates and various goods and chattels in Zealand and elsewhere. He had earned the bulk of his fortune, which amounted to several tens of thousands of guilders, from business dealings in the East. Siereveld only married late in life and so had regularly sent bills of exchange to his father. Finally, on his outward-bound voyage to China, he was married at the Cape in March 1778. During his voyage home, the authorities at the Cape had granted him permission for his wife to be given free passage to Middelburg. She was allowed to take 'the slave-girl Helena van de Caab' with her for her 'personal toilette', but had to pay the usual costs for food and transportation for the slave in advance, both for her passage to Zealand and for her voyage back home. In 1793 Siereveld's eldest son entered the Navy as a midshipman; he died in 1795 on a voyage to the West.[17]

---

[15] Staring, *Damiaan Hugo Staring*, p. 63.
[16] Cape Town Archives, resolutions C.of P. 3.8.1781, 12.2.1782 and 5.3.1782 (www.tanap.net); Rotterdam, Gemeentearchief (GAR), Ambtenboek 810, fol. 280 and 811, fol. 22; GAR, Not. Arch. 3357, 14.6.1796 and 3372, 24.4.1802; Gorinchem, Gemeentearchief, Schepenarchief, Verkoopboek 1786, fol. 47 and Not. Arch. 4273, 21.7.1788; Verzameling P.F. Poortvliet.
[17] L.S. Schuyleman, 'Jan Siereveld, de "manhafte" schipper der V.O.C. en zijn nageslacht', *Van Zeeuwse Stam* 65 and 66 (1989), pp. 115–17 and 182–9; J.C. de Jonge, *Geschiedenis*

Two Very Different Men

Some mariners committed their experiences to paper, but they are very much in the minority. Perhaps for most of them keeping the daily log was enough of a burden. This was a chore which was one of their duties when they were mates. In the eighteenth century, the commanders of the Company seldom reached for the quill. The most famous and also the most widely read was Johan Splinter Stavorinus, whose writings were published by his son Jan in 1793, five years after Stavorinus' death. A second volume was published in 1798. A French translation of the first volume and a complete English translation appeared that same year. The family fully supported the project. The English translator S.H. Wilcocke stated that Stavorinus' writings contained 'much new information respecting the actual and late possessions of the Dutch in India, which in the present situation of affairs [the Batavian Republic was then in a state of war with Great Britain] cannot fail of being extremely interesting'. Stavorinus wrote about the two voyages he had made as commander in the period 1772–1778. This is not the appropriate place to delve into his travel accounts in more depth. It is sufficient to say that these often vividly written texts contain the personal and critical vision of a highly cultivated contemporary who recounted how the overseas business of the Company was conducted. The work transformed this mariner, born in Middelburg in 1739, into an outstanding figure among eighteenth-century commanders. However, his full worth only became apparent after his death.

Even during his lifetime Stavorinus had been a remarkable figure among his fellow townsmen. As his father had done before him, he first served the Admiralty of Zeeland for a period before he began to sail under the flag of the VOC. Both of them were commissioned as captains and eventually returned to the Navy. Johan Splinter obtained his commission in 1766 and in 1788 he was promoted to rear admiral. He died only a few months later after having suffered a stroke. Financially Stavorinus was very comfortably off. In 1756 he had married the daughter of a prominent merchant family in the city. The family, with four children, always lived at one of the better addresses in Middelburg. During the summer they spent their time at their country seat 'Het Park' near West Souburg, near Flushing. Stavorinus was a prominent citizen of Middelburg. Shortly after the *Zeeuwsch Genootschap der Wetenschappen* (the Zealand Scientific Society) had been founded in 1769, he became a member. His rank as a naval captain made him eligible for membership. The goal of this society was to promote virtue and discover solutions to social problems through debates and the setting of competitions. Stavorinus displayed his scientific bent by measuring temperatures during his Asian voyages in order to demonstrate that the state of

van het Nederlandsche zeewezen IV (Haarlem, 1861), pp. 726–7; Cape Town Archives, resolutions C. of P. 13.4.1779 and 5.8.1785 (www.tanap.net); Verzameling P.F. Poortvliet.

health of a place was not related to the prevailing temperatures. He also carried a microscope on board. He was a regular member of the juries which judged the competitions. His former colleagues Vis and Haringman also played an active role in the society from its foundation.

During his commands Stavorinus kept a watchful eye on his financial interests. Twice, in 1777 and 1778, he dispatched bills of exchange for a value of 13,000 guilders to Middelburg, the fruits of his private trade in the East. Shortly after the completion of his three-year voyage to Asia, as captain of a naval squadron (1783–1786) and accompanied by his son Jan, he submitted an itemized declaration of funds due to him from the Admiralty, amounting to approximately 65,000 guilders. There can be no doubt that Stavorinus was a man of standing in Middelburg.[18] The fact that there could be a very different side to the story is shown by vice admiral and former commander Salomon Reynders.

Reynders had been the subject of gossip in the town for years and he was the author of 'scurrilous pamphlets'. His fellow citizens read these avidly. This activity all took place in the years 1755–1762, more than fifteen years after his final voyage for the Company. He was the eponymous son of the successful Middelburg privateer captain during the War of the Spanish Succession.[19] As a boy of twelve Reynders signed on for the Company and, having completed six voyages, he was made a commander in 1737. One final voyage after this proved enough and in 1739 Reynders opted for the Navy in which he was commissioned as a captain. He was given the command of various warships and never returned to the VOC. By 1752 he even reached the rank of rear admiral. His principal sideline was the directorship of the important *Middelburgse Commercie Compagnie* (Middelburg Trading Company), a commercial and shipping business which had been founded in 1720. Towards the end of 1749, he and another former master of this company were elected to the board of directors to rectify 'the dearth of men knowledgeable about the sea'. Reynders' new colleague was Evert Blonkebijle from Flushing, who had now become an employer instead of being an employee. In 1751 Blonkebijle was commissioned as a captain by the Admiralty.

Reynders and Blonkebijle loathed each other and this mutual antipathy erupted into an open quarrel in 1755. They each accused the other of acting in a high-handed manner and of breaking agreements which had been made. In the aftermath, Reynders was said to have failed to accept a challenge to a duel. The quarrel was a very public affair and was openly discussed. Reynders seized his pen as their fellow directors stood helplessly by. The row dragged on

---

[18] M.A.P. Meilink-Roelofsz, 'Johan Splinter Stavorinus (1739–1788)', in L.M. Akveld *et al.* (eds), *Vier eeuwen varen. Kapiteins, kapers, kooplieden en geleerden* (Bussum, 1973), pp. 176–96; J. ten Bokkel Huinink, 'Een vergeten Zeeuwse zeekapitein: Johan Splinter Stavorinus (1739–1788)', in J.R. Bruijn *et al.*, *Marinekapiteins*, pp. 145–56, see also pp. 117–18); Verzameling P.F. Poortvliet.

[19] J.Th.H. Verhees-Van Meer, *De Zeeuwse kaapvaart tijdens de Spaanse Successieoorlog 1702–1713* (Middelburg, 1986), pp. 149, 153 and 190.

and finally it was the superiors of Reynders and Blonkebijle, the Board of the Admiralty, who took action. By then it was 1761. A naval court-martial, which consisted of three flag officers from Holland and four captains from Zealand, including the two former commanders Vis and Haringman, was convened. It seemed that the proceedings would drag on for ever with no prospect of an end in sight. Many, often untrustworthy, witnesses were summoned to give evidence about what had actually occurred in 1755. For instance, Blonkebijle is alleged to have threatened Reynders with: 'I'll give you a taste of my Flushing knuckles'. The judgment which was handed down in 1762 decreed that both men were guilty of 'conduct unbecoming an officer and a gentleman', and each was given a reprimand. They were also fined, Blonkebijle having to pay 2,400 and Reynders 1,200 guilders, which, added up, amounted to the cost of the trial. In fact, the Board of the Admiralty treated its rear admiral mildly, because he was soon given a sinecure which more than covered the cost of his fine. In 1766 Reynders was even promoted to vice admiral. He died at his country seat in 1770 after a long illness.[20] Such was life in Zealand for a former seaman, who had ventured to the East in his younger years.

Changes in Geographical Origins

Both Reynders and Stavorinus were scions of seafaring families and both had also enjoyed brilliant careers on land. In the eyes of their contemporaries, as they grew older, they were seen as distinguished individuals. This was less the case with the other commanders mentioned, but Reynders and Stavorinus nevertheless provide good illustrations of dual careers, which were not found in this form in the other Chambers. What has also emerged from the research is a steady pattern of climbing up through the ranks of the Company, to finally become a commander, with the prospect of a sizeable income. Better social origins were important to those who became superintendent at the Cape.

However, in the course of the eighteenth century, the domination of men from Zealand among commanders began to wane. Only those who came from Middelburg managed to retain their position. Gradually the geographical background of the commanders and mates grew more diverse. Kornelis van Eps from Flushing fits into the traditional pattern. Signing on in 1778, he made his way up through the ranks from seaman to gunner's mate, third mate and so on, and became a commander in 1792. In 1772 Gilles van Laarbeek from Middelburg sailed to the East for the first time, as third surgeon; three years later he was

---

[20] Th. Niemeyer, 'Een strijdbare zeekapitein: Evert Blonkebijle Corneliszoon (1696–1769)', in Bruijn *et al.*, *Marinekapiteins*, pp. 65–82; C. Reinders Folmer-Van Prooijen, *Van goederenhandel naar slavenhandel. De Middelburgse Commercie Compagnie 1720–1755* (Middelburg, 2000), pp. 47 and 50; Verzameling P.F. Poortvliet; *Middelburgse Courant*, 4 October 1770.

gunner's mate, in 1779 third mate and finally in 1787 first mate. However, he never rose higher than this in the Company ranks.[21]

In the meantime, a growing number of foreigners were being appointed commander by the Zealand Chamber. This chapter concludes with four examples of these. The first to become a commander, in 1765, was Karel Sluiter from Karlskrona in Sweden. He was followed by Kornelis Pietersz who was a native of the North Frisian island of Sylt in the duchy of Schleswig-Holstein. After having sailed as third mate in 1750, for a number of years he signed on on a merchantman sailing to the Mediterranean, after which he returned to the Zealand Chamber, where he was appointed commander in 1763. He made three voyages, two of them in what was known as a three-decker, a ship specific to the Zealand Chamber.[22] It was partly because of this experience that he was made a member of the jury of the *Zeeuwsch Genootschap der Wetenschappen*, the organization to which Stavorinus also belonged. Pietersz, who had been married to a woman from Berlin, died in 1780. From 1766 both had been members of the Lutheran congregation in Middelburg.

The third example of a foreigner who made a career in Zealand is Evert Wesseling from Stavanger, appointed commander in 1776. Between 1769 and 1775, Wesseling had risen from third to first mate, after he had first signed on as an ordinary seaman and later was promoted to mate on a Dutch merchantman sailing to Nantes in France. He made good money in private trade abroad. In 1773, 1777 and 1779 he had transferred bills of exchange from Batavia to Middelburg worth 6,646, 13,292 and 13,500 guilders respectively. On his homeward voyage in 1781 he lost his ship to British privateers off the Azores but was able to continue his journey on another homeward-bound ship. Thereafter Wesseling disappeared from Company service. In 1803 he was living in Rotterdam and he died five years later in Stavanger. He made very good use of his lucrative earnings as it is possible that he had a wife in Middelburg as well as one in Stavanger. When in Norway he used his original name, Ivar Gjode Westlye. Two daughters, whom he acknowledged, were born to his Norwegian 'wife', to whom he was not officially married, in 1793 and 1794. One of his brothers had emigrated at the same time as he had, settling in Middelburg and later in Flushing. Upon his death Wesseling left his one surviving daughter a considerable fortune. Besides household effects, which included books in Danish and Norwegian, there were sea charts as well as maps, with a total value of 2,410 guilders. There was also a small island off Stavanger, with a house, stables and a barn, worth 7,500 guilders, and bonds valued at 50,000 guilders.[23]

---

[21] I.D.R. Bruijn, *Ship's Surgeons of the Dutch East India Company. Commerce and the Progress of Medicine in the Eighteenth Century* (Leiden, 2009), pp. 190–1.

[22] See Chapter 14.

[23] Collection P.F. Poortvliet; P. Dekker, 'Zwischen Amsterdam und Batavia. Der Aufstieg des gebürtigen Sylters Nickels Petersen vom Schiffsjungen zum Kommandeur in niederländischen Seediensten', *Nordfriesisches Jahrbuch, Neue Folge* 10 (1974), pp. 133–42.

Finally, the fourth foreigner chosen as an example is Christiaan Zummack from Stettin. Before becoming commander of a chartered East Indiaman in 1785, he too had sailed in the merchant marine. From 1790 to 1792 he was commander of one of the new packet boats, designed to maintain a fast connection with the East. The then rising Rotterdam merchant and ship owner, Anthonie van Hoboken, to whom we shall return in Chapter 5, was extremely interested in the exotic Asian animals which Zummack had on board when he returned to Middelburg. The Rotterdam merchant saw in them an opening for trade: 'I request that you purchase them on my account.' Zummack's final voyage was in 1793 on another chartered ship, which bore the prophetic name the *Surseance*.[24] The deferring of payment to which the name of Zummack's ship referred was but a gentle intimation to the Company. Its end came inexorably shortly after. The consequences for Middelburg were dramatic. The Zealand director Daniel Radermacher had already sketched what these might be around 1790: 'An enormous drop in income and in cargo, the inhabitants forced to move elsewhere, one-third of the houses standing empty....'[25] This is precisely what happened and Middelburg never again played a prominent role in overseas shipping and trade.

None of the commanders of the Chamber of Zealand made such a glorious career as Roelof Blok from Enkhuizen. Although a number of citizens of Zealand did occupy lucrative positions overseas, as F.S. Gaastra has shown, the position of commander was not automatically a foot on the ladder to higher, lucrative jobs on land abroad. Such employment was largely set aside for men equipped with the requisite letters of recommendation from directors, who departed for the East with the rank of senior merchant, or for men who had been able to establish good contacts in the administrative elite in Batavia.[26] The position of superintendent in Batavia, at the Cape or in Ceylon did apparently come within the purview of commanders, as they did have the knowledge essential to do the job. Commanders from Zealand often occupied this post at the Cape, and it paid them handsomely, with sums they would not have dared to dream of as ship's boys or ordinary seamen. Their earnings as commander plus their profits from trade in private goods meant that, thanks to the Company, they were able to join the relatively small social elite of Middelburg. This was particularly true in the second half of the century when Reynders became director of the prestigious *Middelburgse Commercie Compagnie*. Through their employment on the Company ships, Vis, Haringman and Stavorinus all rose to become men of consequence in Middelburg as well as in The Hague. Their financial standing brought the purchase of a country seat or manor house within their reach.

---

[24] P. Moree, '*Met vriend die God geleide*'. *Het Nederlands-Aziatisch postvervoer ten tijde van de Verenigde Oost-Indische Compagnie* (Zutphen, 1998), pp. 133 and 196–7.

[25] Enthoven, 'Veel vertier', p. 50.

[26] F.S. Gaastra, 'Zeeuwen in de VOC in de tweede helft van de achttiende eeuw', in J. Parmentier (ed.), *Noord-Zuid in Oost-Indisch perspectief* (Zutphen, 2005), pp. 99–116.

4

Delft

The Chambers of Delft and Rotterdam were situated in close proximity to one another and the Meuse (Maas) was the home port for the ships of both Chambers. These two Chambers also belonged to what were known as the quartet of smaller chambers. In fact, Delft and Rotterdam were such close neighbours that many sailors switched from one Chamber to the other during their lives. The same can be said of the commanders. Nevertheless, for all their similarities there were differences between the two Chambers, many of which will emerge more clearly in the next chapter about Rotterdam.

The lifestyle of Delft commanders and ship's officers did not differ greatly from that of their colleagues in the West Frisian towns. Delft had always had more inhabitants than either Enkhuizen or Hoorn but the town was situated on a much smaller area of land. Consequently Delft was both more densely populated and busier. The walls were not extended after 1355 but the town reached its largest population – approximately 24,000 – around 1680. After that Delft fell into a decline, dropping to 15,000 inhabitants by 1733 and to some 14,000 in 1749. After that the number remained fairly stable.

At the beginning of the eighteenth century, around 1700, there were still quite a few industries in Delft, such as brewing, textile manufacture and pottery making. Gradually these fell into decline and during the century this decline gained such momentum that many breweries and potteries closed. By the end of the century Delft had been transformed from an industrial town into a market and service centre for the region. The face of the town altered. Factories disappeared from the most important canals and this made way for a greater distinction between rich and poor. The rich lived in the centre, along the most imposing canals and in the large market squares. The poor had their dwellings in the remaining 125 alleyways, small streets and other streets along lesser canals. The more indigent a person was, the closer his or her dwelling was likely to be to the town walls and gates. In the first half of the eighteenth century, the different social groups were still relatively evenly dispersed throughout the town. In 1790, an English visitor described Delft as 'exceedingly dull'. A later historian called it a 'quiet, tidy place'. Presumably, the dilapidated houses, or those which had collapsed altogether further away from the centre, and the large number of people dependent on poor relief – 26 per cent in 1749 – escaped the notice of these observers.[1]

Delft and Delfshaven

A great many VOC commanders and retired commanders lived in the town, but like their colleagues in Enkhuizen and Hoorn they did not witness much economic activity around them. As time passed, even their own employer began to struggle. One important feature of the Delft Chamber was that its activities were divided between Delft and Delfshaven. The latter was the port of the town, situated some 12 to 13 kilometres away on the River Meuse. Unquestionably, in the first half of the eighteenth century the Chamber shared in the flourishing trade and shipping business of the Company but the impact of this economic activity was less direct in Delft than in either Enkhuizen or Hoorn. The construction and fitting-out of the majority of the ships took place, not in the town itself, but in Delfshaven. Delft was purely the seat of administration and the location for the warehouses. The large buildings, the *Oost-Indisch Huis* and the warehouse, were situated on either side of the main canal, the Oude Delft, on the southern side of the town. That position offered direct access to the River Schie, the link between the town and Delfshaven. A ropewalk and a tar kiln provided some skilled work in Delft. In 1749 the Chamber employed around sixty people on a permanent basis, not many for a town of 14,000 inhabitants.[2]

Delfshaven was where the growth in Company shipping could be seen on a daily basis. It was here that the ships were loaded and unloaded, constructed and repaired. The trade goods were transhipped onto inland shipping barges to be transported via the Schie to the warehouses in Delft. After signing on at the *Oost-Indisch Huis* in Delft, the crews assembled there to embark, and returned to the *Huis* in Delft once they had signed off. In Delfshaven there was the storehouse for ship's supplies, the so-called *Zeemagazijn*, an enormous building which stood on the Buizenwaal. When this was completely gutted by fire in 1746 the Company lost no time in rebuilding it completely. It was situated alongside the Company shipyard, which was equipped with three slipways. The *Zeemagazijn* (chandler's store) and the shipyard provided employment for between 150 and 200 people. As was the VOC custom, the complex was under the command of the Superintendent of the Shipyard.

In the smallish community of Delfshaven, with some 2,100 inhabitants in 1733 and slightly more than 2,200 in 1795, the VOC was by far the biggest employer. The herring fishing industry had virtually died out but there was one

---

[1] Wijsenbeek-Olthuis, *Achter de gevels*, pp. 20–2, 61–84, 151–7 and 317–35.
[2] Van Gelder and Wagenaar, *Sporen van de Compagnie*, pp. 84–101; H.L. Houtzager *et al.* (eds), *Delft en de Oostindische Compagnie* (Amsterdam, 1987), pp. 13–36, 119–50.

new business appearing, brandy distilling. In 1716 there were only eight distilleries, but by 1794 there were no fewer than thirty-two. Four grist mills, which were essential to the distilling industry, were built during the century. Eventually these new developments meant that Delft and Delfshaven grew apart, and in 1811 Delfshaven was granted separate status. As early as 1725, the municipal council in Delft had had to give its assent to the establishment of what was called a college of legal commissaries (*college van commissarissen van de wet*), which was empowered to deal with a number of local affairs in Delfshaven. This body could handle matters pertaining to the civil militia, fire prevention, marriages by the magistrate (*van de pui*, literally on the steps) and the inheritances of orphans. There were four commissaries who were drawn from the ranks of the 'wealthiest' and 'most law-abiding' citizens of Delfshaven. The differences in terms of economic activity between Delft and its outport could be clearly seen in the lives of the commanders on land in the two communities, sometimes indeed even in their sailing careers with the Company.[3]

Commanders' Families in Delfshaven

In the first half of the eighteenth century, the small community of Delfshaven mainly revolved around the construction of East Indiamen and their maintenance and sailings. It was only later in the century that the distilling of gin (*korenwijn*) really got off the ground. Most people lived and worked in the area where the Schie flowed into the Voorhaven. The families were closely inter-related. During that period the Company offered more work – in the shipyard, in the storehouse and on the ships – than ever before. Rotterdam was not far away and could be reached by water along the Meuse or by land along two dikes. There was no lack of work for the Van der Poel, Van der Meer, De Wit or Van Heemstee families, certainly if the men chose a life at sea.

The Van der Poels are a good example of a family in which many of the men achieved the rank of commander and many of the women married commanders. The two first cousins Koenraad I and Koenraad II became commanders at an early age; Koenraad I in 1737 when he was thirty-three and Koenraad II in 1742 when he was barely twenty-eight. From 1710 to 1728, Jakob, the father of Koenraad II, was a successful commander. Earlier, both he and his brother, Hendrik, were of sufficiently modest means that they were able to marry without paying a fee. Koenraad I died, unmarried, in Batavia in 1743. Koenraad II followed him a year later, also in Batavia. He had married a girl from Zealand and he was no longer a Delfshaven resident. He lived in Veere and sailed from there for the Zealand Chamber. It is possible that his move to Zealand had something

---

[3] Wijsenbeek-Olthuis, *Achter de gevels*, pp. 21 and 27. J.C. Okkema, 'Het College van Commissarissen van de Weth', in *De Stad Delft, cultuur en maatschappij van 1667 tot 1813* (Delft, 1981), pp. 69–70.

to do with his elder sister, who had lived in Veere ever since her marriage to Michiel de Keizer who was a native. De Keizer was also a Company commander, but for the Zealand Chamber. Another of Koenraad II's sisters was the wife of Commander Adriaan de Wit. Their brother Dirk, the last of the generation, was a commander for the Zealand Chamber, like his brother and his cousin. He died in Batavia in 1741. Four years earlier he had married a woman from Delfshaven. Koenraad II was the only one to have a son who reached adulthood. He later became an apothecary in Goes in Zealand.[4]

The Van der Poel family and the Company were as tightly bound up with each other as were the Pomp family in Enkhuizen or the Ben and Bent families in Hoorn. Generally speaking, the West Frisians remained faithful to their own Chambers but the Van der Poels and their in-laws had no problem with changing from Chamber to Chamber. They sailed not only for the Delft Chamber but also for its counterpart in Rotterdam and sometimes for that of Zealand. In these families, sailing to the East represented a good income and a rising standard of living. However, premature deaths sometimes meant that social mobility was cut short. This could not be said of Jakob van der Poel. He owned two houses in Delfshaven. When his widow died in 1745, she also owned bonds worth ƒ. 20,000.

The widow of another commander chose a less passive investment for her money. Maria van Breen was one of the four daughters of Commander Jan Huigen van Breen. When she married First Mate Huig Goedhart in 1728, a licence fee of ƒ. 15 was paid for each of them but there was no marriage settlement drawn up for the union. The reason was that Maria owned too much and Huig too little. Maria brought ƒ. 7,000 to the marriage in annuities as well as houses and a quarter share in a merchant vessel and a similar share in a haddock fishing smack. Huig had barely ƒ. 1,000 in East Indian wares to call his own. After Huig's death while a commander off the Cape in 1733, Maria continued to pursue her business interests. One remarkable purchase, made with her sister, was that of a gin distillery on the Schie, for which she took out a loan for ƒ. 6,000. Her father-in-law, who was a tinsmith, had two other sons who signed on with the VOC. Her brother-in-law Teunis became a commander and died in 1738 in Batavia.[5]

When he was left a widower, Jan van Heemstee, who had been born and bred in Delfshaven, looked for his second wife in his own community. However, in 1742, when he left the sea behind him at the age of thirty-seven, he lost no time in moving to neighbouring Rotterdam. There he was able to enjoy what few of his colleagues did – a long second career on land. He took part in the local Rotterdam economy, putting his Company service to excellent use. His first step was to buy shares in two merchant vessels. Over time he increased the

[4] Rotterdam, GAR, Archief Delfshaven 2347, fols 584–648, 2496, fols 317, 3870, fol. 115 and 3880, fol. 265.
[5] Rotterdam, GAR, Archief Delfshaven, 3881, fols 232–54 and 3892, fols 573 and 608.

number. He became ship's husband of one of these vessels, the 180-ton hoeker the *Juffrouw Johanna Barbara*. The ship was primarily involved in carrying grain and wine. Van Heemstee's father-in-law, his brother and later his son were part owners. In 1768, he bought a 10/64 share in a *bootschip*, a type of vessel commonly used in the merchant marine. Besides these maritime ventures, he traded in 'brandy and distilled waters' and he even owned his own distillery. This was by no means the extent of his ventures. He owned several houses and even had a second distillery in Rotterdam, not to mention some land in Delfshaven. Two years before his death in 1776 the value of his possessions was estimated at *f.* 100,000. When he died there was a great deal to be divided among his five children. Van Heemstee was one of the few retired commanders who took a real plunge into the business world. Naturally, the highest fee was paid for his burial in the Great or St Lawrence Church in Rotterdam.[6]

After his return from his final voyage in 1753, Maarten van der Meer did not have to live off his investments entirely. He mixed in circles which opened the door for him to be appointed to a lucrative Company position on land. This good fortune was primarily thanks to his marriage in 1754 to the daughter of the Superintendent of the Shipyard in Delft, Leendert de Wit, who was himself a wealthy man. De Wit's wife's maternal grandfather had occupied the same post. However, it is possible that Van der Meer's father-in-law died at a rather inopportune moment – he died in 1751 when the younger man was far away in the East. It was only in 1758 that Van der Meer himself became Superintendent of the Shipyard, a very important position and one which was often occupied by retired commanders, both at home and overseas. Jakob Bruijn in Enkhuizen was an example. A shipyard superintendent was responsible for the purchase of all the materials required for the construction and fitting out of Company ships, and the eventual sale, and all the finances pertaining to those tasks.[7] He appointed the personnel in the yard and in the storehouses. He was required to be present at the loading and discharging of ships and, if necessary, he had to confiscate private goods. In the shipyard the *Zeemagazijn* offered him commodious accommodation, but even before he reached those heights, Van der Meer was a *commissaris van de wet*, a job for which he apparently qualified. His father-in-law, two uncles and a brother-in-law had all occupied this position before him. From his wife's side of the family, his wealth was augmented by an inheritance consisting of houses, shares in ships, bonds and annuities. Maarten's wife died in 1761 and was given an expensive funeral costing *f.* 30. Perhaps her loss was the reason Van der Meer chose to resign his position in 1762 and return to Schiedam, where he had been born in 1710. Not long after, he sold some of his

---

[6] Rotterdam, GAR, Verkopingsboek 703, fols 135–6; Oud-notarieel archief 2271, fol. 263, 2339, fol. 57, 2425, fols 577–8, 2428, fols 44, 111–12, 1032–4, 2555, fols 603–12, 2556, fols 107–8, 2618, fol. 315, 2871, fol. 88, 2990, fols 227–8, 3089, fol. 249, 3220, fols 490–7, 3276, fols 505–10, 3277, fols 727–9, 3292, fols 122–54.
[7] The Hague, NA, Archief Van Vredenburch 13, no. 35.

shares in ships, and in 1770 he died in his house located in one of the oldest streets in Schiedam. He was childless. His brother, Ary, had died as commander on his homeward voyage in 1749.[8]

Van der Meer's successor as Superintendent of the Shipyard, Stoffel Hoek, was not a retired commander. He allowed himself to be lured into the building of a new type of East Indiaman by the Rotterdam Master Shipwright, Pieter van Zwijndregt. The *Heren Zeventien* were not wildly enthusiastic about the venture and permitted only two experimental vessels to be built, the first in the shipyard in Rotterdam and the other in Delfshaven. The result was the *Vreeburg*. Hoek was so proud of this product of his own shipyard that he painted her in 1764, and this painting still hangs above the overmantel of the former boardroom of the directors of the Delft Chamber in the *Zeemagazijn*.[9]

In the second half of the eighteenth century, the shipping activities of the Delft Chamber also diminished, but the people of Delfshaven still continued to go to sea in the service of the Company. Nevertheless, for the retired commanders in the village there was very little employment on offer. Kornelis Leendertsz de Wit, a scion of the prominent family of that name, stopped sailing in 1788 and turned his back on life in Delfshaven and moved to Amsterdam. Probably his marriage to a woman from that city helped him make the decision. De Wit had begun his maritime career in 1764 at the age of fifteen, sailing on the *Vreeburg* (see above).

Commanders and Retired Commanders in the City of Delft

In the first half of the eighteenth century, in contrast to the situation in Delfshaven, in Delft there was probably only a handful of families fully dependent on Company shipping. These included families with various relatives and kinsfolk who had sailed to the East year after year and had achieved the rank of first mate and commander. As a consequence of a great deal of intermarriage, these families were often closely related. Such inter-relatedness was not as regular an occurrence in Delft as it was in Delfshaven, Enkhuizen or Hoorn. Unfortunately data for establishing this sort of connection are missing for Middelburg.

The Company did fulfil an important function as an employer in Delft. This was not because it required a large number of permanent workers on its premises in the town; the number was never large. However, much more numerous were the hundreds of people hired annually to be sailors and soldiers on the ships, people who came from different places. If these men survived the voyage

---

[8] Rotterdam, GAR, Archief Delfshaven, 3890, fol. 202, and Weeskamer (Orphanage Board) 516, fols 173 and 218; Schiedam, Gemeentearchief 919, fol. 65. Houtzager *et al.*, *Delft en de Oostindische Compagnie*, p. 35; G. van der Feijst, *Geschiedenis van Schiedam* (Schiedam, 1975), pp. 60–1 and 172; W.F.H. Oldewelt, 'De beroepsstructuur', p. 175.
[9] Van Gelder and Wagenaar, *Sporen van de VOC*, p. 101.

8. An anonymous mate. On his voyage out to Batavia on the *Holland* in 1778–1779, the Lutheran minister Jan Brandes had one of the ship's officers pose for him. The man is wearing a long brown coat, a white waistcoat, a knotted white stock as a neck cloth, a tricorn hat and a wig. Under his left hand on the table is a vaguely sketched octant.

they returned to the Dutch Republic after three to four years on average. Until around 1745, among them there were still a relatively large number of men from Delft. Sometimes that group even made up half of a ship's crew. Up to mid-century some 120 to 260 townspeople sailed away every year on Company ships. After 1745 the number of men from Delft dropped to only fifty to seventy, even though the total number of men required continued to rise, and so the extra sailors and soldiers had to be recruited from elsewhere. In the period after 1775, the number of men from Delft halved again. The supply of men from Delft dropped in all ranks, from the highest to the lowest. The Company was always a great devourer of men and boys from Delft. Fewer returned than sailed away because of deaths on board and overseas. The lengthy absences also contributed to the drop in the town population. This was especially marked in the period around 1770. As a consequence, there was a large surplus of women in the town: 30 per cent of them remained unmarried. Large groups of orphan boys were a common sight aboard the Company ships of Delft. In the course of the eighteenth century the Chamber registered a total of more than 10,000 Delft men in its pay books. Moreover, the other five Chambers mustered 2,000 to 3,000 men from the town. Any researcher interested in the development of the urban population of Delft would find it impossible to overlook the effect of VOC recruitment.

The ships of the Delft Chamber made a total of 206 outward-bound voyages in the eighteenth century.[10] Twenty of the commanders of those ships have been investigated in more depth.[11] These men were natives of Delft or had settled in the town. In total, they sailed forty-two times as commanders, accounting for one-fifth of all voyages. With two exceptions, they did well out of their service with the Company. Their social status improved, at least when this is measured by their place of residence and the fees they paid when they married or were buried. Almost half of them had to pay the highest fee. The remainder, as far as it is known, paid either $f.$ 15 or $f.$ 6. These were the fees paid for them personally and for their wives.

It was rare that later in his life a commander was still living in the same house he had lived in at the time he married. Nearly all the commanders owned their own houses. Only Jan Lokeman, a childless widower, lived in rooms, where he cherished his compass, sextant, map of the world and his logbooks, not to mention a few weapons and some medicines. From the $f.$ 2,361 in cash which he kept in his rooms before his death it was possible at least to pay his outstanding doctor's bill of $f.$ 123. Another childless widower, Ary van Veurden, lodged with

---

[10] K.L. van Schouwenburg, 'Het personeel op de schepen van de kamer Delft der VOC in de eerst helft der 18e eeuw', *Tijdschrift voor Zeegeschiedenis* 7 (1988), pp. 76–93, and 8 (1989), pp. 179–86. The total of Delft men was provided by T. van Velzen (The Hague, Nationaal Archief).

[11] Jakobus van den Berg (1727–1819), Emond Colier (1722–1783), Willem Dona (1740–1782), Georg Philip Gas (1760–1808), Gerrit Harmeyer (1718–1784), Jan Kristoffel van Heemskerk van Beest (1721–before 1778), Pieter Hogendorp (1718–1775), Adriaan van Katersveld (1723–1793), Aarnout van Kleef (1674–1727?) and son Joris van Kleef (c.1702–?), Kornelis van Kolster (c.1685–1735), Johannes de Kort (1748–1780), Jan Lokeman (?–1708), Kornelis Lorein (1749–1804), Bartholomeus Schut (?–1787), Johannes Snijders (?–1782), Pieter Verkerk (1738–1778), Ary van Veurden (c.1702–1774), Melchior de Vos (1652–before 1710) and Jakob Welgevaren (1725–1787). The commanders from Delfshaven investigated are Jan Huigen van Breen (?–?), Huig Goedhart (1698–1733), Teunis Goedhart (1701–c.1738), Jan van Heemstee (1705–1776), Kornelis de Klerk (1739–1786), Leendert de Koning (c.1680–after 1728), Maarten van der Meer (1710–1770), Dirk van der Poel (1709–1741), Jakob van der Poel (?–c.1730), Koenraad (I) van der Poel (1704–1743), Koenraad (II) van der Poel (1715–1744) and Kornelis Leendertsz de Wit (1749–1796 or 1804). Together these commanders were responsible for a quarter of all Delft voyages. If five commanders of the Rotterdam Chamber who sailed ten voyages for the Delft Chamber are included, the total rises to roughly 30 per cent.

his niece and nephew for twelve years. When he died in 1774 they inherited nearly ƒ. 15,000.[12]

Retired commanders and those who were still in service could afford to live in some of the smartest areas of the town.[13] The Brabantse Turfmarkt was especially popular as no less than fourteen of the twenty commanders investigated lived there, and two more lived in the Voorstraat. Both of these areas are very close to the Old Church which was the most important religious building in the city. The closer a residence was to the church and the centre, the more desirable it was considered. The size of the houses in these areas could vary considerably, from houses with two façades and two full storeys plus an attic, to tiny dwellings consisting of no more than two or three interconnecting rooms, sometimes without a passageway. A stepladder gave access to a loft and sometimes an extension at the back offered some storage space. It was in this latter sort of house that Adriaan van Kolster lived in the 1730s. However, the majority of the commanders had a two-storey house and an attic.[14]

Jakobus van den Berg had a special bond with the Oude Delft canal, the most prestigious canal in the town. As a four-year-old orphan in 1741 he had been placed in the Reformed Church orphanage on the canal, and in 1746 he had gone from there to the VOC as an apprentice cooper. Ten years later, having become a fully fledged cooper, he married a girl from his former orphanage. In less than twenty years, he was a commander and he made three voyages at that rank. At a certain point Van den Berg had reached a position which made it possible for him to move back to the Oude Delft, number 58 to be exact. Not long afterwards his daughter and son-in-law moved to number 50. His son-in-law was a German, Georg Philip Gas, who came from the area around Coblenz. He had sailed with the man who was to be his father-in-law in 1788, and later also reached the rank of commander. In 1816 Van den Berg and his wife celebrated their diamond wedding anniversary. They died shortly after one another, he in 1819 and she in 1817.[15]

Another Delft orphan who achieved the rank of commander was Johannes de Kort. However, he always sailed for the Amsterdam Chamber, not for that of Delft. Thanks to the fact that he possessed 'the necessary qualities' which would make him 'an apt pupil', at the age of fifteen he was transferred from the Reformed orphanage to the premises of the Foundation of the Baroness of Renswoude (*Fundatie van de vrijvrouwe van Renswoude*) which was located further along the Oude Delft. In her will, this Baroness had left a large sum of money to pay for accommodation and training so that 'some of the most sensible, intelligent and skilled boys, not younger than fifteen', housed in three orphanages

---

[12] Delft, Gemeentearchief (GAD), 2378, fols 100–8 (with thanks to Dr Th. Wijsenbeek-Olthuis who died in 2010), and for Van Veurden, *ibid.*, 2978, fol. 92.
[13] Wijsenbeek-Olthuis, *Achter de gevels*, pp. 158–61.
[14] See M. Zeilemaker, *Op zoek naar het historisch interieur* (Hilversum, 2005), pp. 28–35.
[15] See also Houtzager *et al.*, *Delft en de Oostindische Compagnie*, pp. 51–3.

in Delft, The Hague and Utrecht, could have a proper skilled training.[16] De Kort made no bones about his preference for going to sea. He started with a theoretical education in navigation and followed this with practical training. In his case, this meant gaining experience on board a specially selected merchant vessel and on a ship of the Admiralty of Amsterdam. In 1769 De Kort was appointed third mate by the Amsterdam Chamber. The governors of the Foundation had good connections with the directors of this Chamber. From his first voyage to Asia, De Kort, the grateful orphan, brought back a porcelain tea-service decorated with the Renswoude coat-of-arms for the governors of the Foundation. De Kort now began his steady progress in his profession. Until he was twenty-five the bulk of his earnings went to the Foundation, with De Kort being allowed to keep one-third. He sailed for the first time as a commander in 1777 but it was to be his final voyage. On his voyage home, during a severe gale, his ship hit a reef off Cape Agulhas and sank with all hands. De Kort had not had the time to marry.

From its three different centres, the Foundation supplied the VOC with a total of eighteen ship's officers. De Kort was the only one to achieve the rank of commander. The boys who pursued training with the Company were privileged in their education and in their treatment on board. For example the mathematician Johannes van der Wal was a very prominent scholar and from 1764 he was the examiner of Delft officers. At the Admiralty, De Kort was examined by the well-known mathematician and astronomer Pybo Steenstra.[17] The establishment of the Foundation offered De Kort opportunities not available to the orphan Van den Berg, who was a good twenty years older. The two never met on board because they worked for different Chambers. Eventually, Van den Berg was promoted to commander, just one year earlier than De Kort.

Jan Kristoffel van Heemskerk from Beesd in the province of Guelders was also among those fortunate enough to own a house on the Oude Delft. In 1758

---

[16] In Seville (Spain), the Royal School of San Telmo, in principle a charity institution, provided orphaned and abandoned boys, mostly from the 'respectable poor', with maritime training. The wards (about 150) were given a primary school education, followed by a further education devised to accustom them to shipboard life, which included navigation, handling artillery and piloting. Sailing under the auspices of the orphanage was considered part of the instruction. There was even a model ship with working parts in the courtyard of the Institute, which was one of the tools of instruction. Many boys reached high naval positions. See V.K. Tikoff, 'Saint Elmo's Orphans. Navigation, Education and Training at the Royal School of San Telmo in Seville during the Eighteenth Century', *International Journal of Maritime History* XX, no. 1 (2008), pp. 1–32.

[17] A. Verbout-Wamsteeker, 'Navigatieopleidingen aan de Fundaties van Renswoude 1756–1795', *Tijdschrift voor Zeegeschiedenis* 17 (1998), pp. 37–55; E.P. de Booy and J. Engels, *Van erfenis tot studiebeurs. De Fundatie van de vrijvrouwe van Renswoude te Delft. Opleiding van wezen tot de 'vrije kunsten' in de 18de en 19de eeuw. De fundatiehuizen. De bursalen in deze eeuw* (Delft, 1985), pp. 40, 123–4; C.A. Davids, *Zeewezen en wetenschap. De wetenschap en de ontwikkeling van de navigatietechniek in Nederland tussen 1585 en 1815* (Amsterdam, 1986), pp. 327, 354, 399 and 401.

he bought this residence for the sum of *f.* 5,760. The house had a summer-house, a coach-house, stables and a garden. Van Heemskerk was only in Company service for a very short time. He first served twelve years with the Admiralty of the Meuse (Rotterdam), where, at the age of twenty-five, he was promoted to captain in 1746. In 1752 he became a commander for the Delft Chamber. In the Navy he had commanded a ship-of-the-line during a voyage to the Mediterranean in 1749. In this period it was not usual for a naval officer to serve with the Company. Van Heemskerk made only one round-trip voyage to the Indies. In the middle of the trip he spent two years taking part in intra-Asian trade. At the end of 1755 he had returned home, where he lost no time in returning to the Admiralty. In 1758 he was appointed Superintendent of the naval shipyard in Rotterdam, four months after he had purchased his house on the Oude Delft. His new position offered him an official residence next to the naval supply depot, the *Zeemagazijn*. He had that house altered and painted at Admiralty expense. In 1774, Van Heemskerk requested and was granted an honourable discharge, and was also allowed to retain his annual salary of *f.* 1,280. He then returned to live on the Oude Delft with his wife. After both of them had died, the house was sold to a former burgomaster and director of the Delft Chamber. Jan van Heemskerk was a Roman Catholic and related to patrician families of the same name in Rotterdam and Delft. The reasons for his seeking temporary employment with the Company are not known.[18]

Fewer foreigners sailed for the Delft Chamber than for the Chambers of Hoorn or Enkhuizen. Van den Berg's son-in-law, the German Gas, is one example. In the pay books beginning from 1739, there are only twenty-one names of ship's officers of foreign origin, who originated from Schleswig-Holstein, Denmark, Sweden and Norway. In 1749 there was only one commander of foreign origin. Seven others eventually followed.[19]

Former Commanders Living off Their Investments

Generally speaking, commanders and retired commanders did not make any great direct contribution to the economic activity of their town. Indeed, it was much the same story as with the other Chambers. The majority of commanders retired from the sea around the time they turned forty.

Occasionally notarial deeds do offer some insight into the economic pursuits of eighteenth-century people, but there is not much for the historian to find for Delft. It seems that the retired commanders there seldom visited a notary to record investing their money in gin distilleries or potteries. Their colleagues in

---

[18] Delft, GAD, Koopbrief inv. D II, e 134; The Hague, NA, AA 1149 and coll. XXXI. See various resolutions of the Admiralty of the Meuse in the years 1758–1774 in nos. 132–5; The Hague, NA, Archief Van Vredenburch 1, 15.7.1752.

[19] S.W. Aarsbog, *Med Mars og Merkur*, appendix II.

Delfshaven were much more likely to take such steps. There certainly were plenty of notaries in Delft, some twelve or thirteen, officially appointed by the town council. The path to becoming a notary was not a very difficult one.[20] Sometimes the inventories of possessions drawn up for probate give some hint of economic activities of the deceased. For instance, there were two retired commanders who did invest their money in Delft industries. Other retired commanders did not venture beyond bonds and real estate. From the inquisition post mortem it appears that Jan Lokeman, who died in 1708, had sunk *f.* 10,500 into the mortgages of two potteries. He also owned a garden with two gazebos. The other commander who invested in local industry lived much later in the century. In 1772, Jakob Welgevaren put *f.* 2,000 belonging to his wife, who was the widow of a potter, into the purchase of the pottery the *Jonge Moriaanshoofd*.

The note alongside the name of a retired commander in the tax register of 1750, 'lives off his interest', could in fact have been said of many of his colleagues.[21] None of them had shares in the VOC. Later in the eighteenth century there was a growing tendency to put money into the usual Dutch bonds and private loans, usually at 3 per cent. Some commanders also ventured to invest in foreign bonds. In 1787 Bartholomeus Schut owned shares in the Bank of England worth around *f.* 12,000, as well as *f.* 3,500 in French bonds, over and above Dutch bonds worth nearly *f.* 11,000. This means that Schut had invested 60 per cent of his capital abroad, an exceptionally large amount for a Delft man in those days. Gerrit Harmeyer was one of the very few townsmen who invested money in loans to Suriname plantations.[22]

Furthermore, many a commander, retired commander or his widow earned money from selling porcelain and other goods which had been brought from Asia. Such wares were constantly sold to private buyers. Inventories made of estates of the deceased sometimes mention very large quantities of such goods which were stored in the hallway or the kitchen. In Enkhuizen this was the case with Ype Engelsman. In 1742, the widow of Jurriaan Wolberg kept a chintz shop in her home on the Kloverniersburgwal in Amsterdam. In 1705 the wife of the Amsterdam commander Jacob Regenboog, who was in the East at that time, owned a remarkable quantity of porcelain. Under the bedstead and in a cupboard between the bedstead and the chimney she had more than 900 pieces of porcelain.[23] In three of the six estates of deceased Delft commanders, commercial volumes of porcelain were quite clearly present in their possessions. In 1710, there was a great quantity of porcelain noted among the household goods and chattels in the estate inventory of the widow of Melchior de Vos. He

---

[20] Wijsenbeek-Olthuis, *Achter de gevels*, pp. 88–92; Verburg, 'De Vlaardingse notarissen'.
[21] Delft, GAD, Impost 1750, 1ste afd., no. 602, vol. 2, 1371 (2).
[22] Delft, GAD, 3205–89–1787; Wijsenbeek-Olthuis, *Achter de gevels*, p. 125.
[23] Dr Wijsenbeek-Olthuis pointed this out to me. See Delft, GAD, 2552–11–9–1710, 2857–11–9–1743 and 2983–13–1779. For Regenboog: Amsterdam, Gemeentearchief, Not. Arch. 5114, 606–18.

had completed his final voyage just two years earlier in 1708. At such an early date in the eighteenth century such goods were incredibly valuable. In 1743, as well as a great number of small houses, the Widow Van Kolster owned a quite considerable number of miniature Japanese kettles, rinsing bowls and other objects. At that time Japanese porcelain was especially expensive. Pieter Verkerk also brought porcelain back from the Indies in the form of various coloured dinner services. His personal cargo included Chinese curtains as well. The usual pattern among commanders when they remarried was to choose a woman who was better off than their first wife had been. The upward shift in economic and social status suggests that through their careers they were usually able to enhance their position. The import of porcelain and other Oriental goods helped in that process.

It would seem that, by preference, commanders and retired commanders put their money into real estate, principally in houses. Probably with money from his second wife, Welgevaren bought properties in two of the best streets, as well as the pottery mentioned earlier. He purchased the last around 1770. Van Veurden had invested his money in some more modest houses in 1738. The best example of a slum landlord is Van Kolster. When he was still a ship's officer, he bought some small houses in the Bagijnhof. After that he acquired yet more houses, though in less desirable areas. When Van Kolster was at sea, his wife ran the business. When she died as a widow in 1743 she owned eight rental properties and six mortgages on other houses at the then fairly extortionate interest rate of 4 per cent. The payments were weekly and varied from 4 to 15 *stuivers*.[24]

With the exception of the porcelain, the interiors of the houses of commanders and retired commanders sometimes revealed very little about the people who lived in them. Barometers tended to give the only clue. Why Adriaan van Katersveld left his octant behind when he sailed on his maiden voyage as commander in 1778 is unknown. He did not have to take it with him because the Company made arrangements to ensure that all required navigational instruments were present on board. In 1783 Harmeyer owned a globe, three rolled-up maps, two Chinese landscape paintings and a Chinese lantern with a compass. The widow of Melchior de Vos had no fewer than seventy-five paintings hanging in six different places in her house in 1710. Unfortunately what they depicted is not recorded.[25]

---

[24] Delft, GAD, Huizenprotocol 6z, fol. 188 and 7a, fol. 181 (Welgevaren), 6L, fol. 155 (Van Veurden); for Van Kolster see Oud-rechterlijk Archief 5x, fol. 95, Verpondingskohier (pawn book) 1733, 175, fols 89–91, and Not. Arch. 2857–11-9–1743.
[25] Delft, GAD, 2552–11-9–1710 and 2983–101–1779 (with thanks to Dr Wijsenbeek-Olthuis); K. van der Wiel, *Op zoek naar een biografisch portret van het verleden* (Hilversum, 2003), p. 75.

Two Unfortunate Men

Harmeyer's career with the VOC ended in a kind of bankruptcy. He was a native of Amsterdam and he had sailed for the Amsterdam Chamber until 1763. In the following year he obtained an appointment with the Delft Chamber. Two years after the death of his first wife he remarried in Delft, in 1765. Once again he chose a woman from Amsterdam, the widow of a colleague. A prenuptial agreement was made for this second marriage. Harmeyer sailed no fewer than six times as commander. During his travels he also did his best to trade in his own name and took out loans to cover the investments in goods. However, as time passed, the terms and conditions for such loans grew ever less advantageous, especially in 1779. Shortly after that, everything began to go wrong. On his homeward-bound voyage from China in August 1781 he had to forfeit his ship to the British in Saldanha Bay, north of the Cape of Good Hope. It was one of five ships which were lost in the British raid. The Cape Government was not very happy about the way the commanders had behaved at the surrender since four of them had not set their ships on fire in time. Harmeyer was suspended and was even incarcerated for a while in the fort at the Cape. Most of his private trade goods fell into British hands and so were effectively lost. Harmeyer's wife was obliged to leave their house to evade debt-collectors. The house was boarded up and she had to move in with her daughter in Maassluis; and she was forced to pawn items such as a gold watch and silver tobacco boxes. In January 1783 a notary compiled an inventory of the contents of the house. Then, in the spring, Harmeyer and his young son Koenraad suddenly came home. He and his colleagues had found a passage on a neutral ship. He managed to organize another appointment for himself. In September 1783 he set off on his seventh voyage as a commander. He died just before the ship arrived in Batavia, short of his sixty-sixth birthday. His widow refused to accept the inheritance because of the 'numerous debts which had turned up' as the consequence of the commander's 'borrowing considerable capital sums and taking on businesses' which had not succeeded. She moved back to Amsterdam where she died shortly after. The two sums, amounting to $f.$ 4,430 and no less than $f.$ 20,236, which were sent to her from the East as bills of exchange in 1784 and 1785, were probably collected by the creditors. Harmeyer had overplayed his hand and the evidence suggests he lacked business acumen. His investments in plantations in Suriname point in this direction, because it was generally known that these were risky. They paid less interest than promised and very few of them were redeemed on maturity.[26]

---

[26] The Hague, NA, VOC 14054; Delft, GAD, 3436, fol. 25; Cape Town Archives, resolutions C. of P., 3.8.1781, 7.5 and 17.12.1782 (www.tanap.net); Van der Wiel, *Op zoek*, pp. 75–91; J.P. van de Voort, *De Westindische plantages van 1720 tot 1795. Financiën en handel* (Eindhoven, 1973), pp. 187–96; *DAS* II, no. 4425, and III, nos. 8071–5. The ships' papers which were confiscated in 1781 are preserved in the National Archives in Kew, London

The second commander of the Delft Chamber to be cursed by bad luck was Adriaan van Katersveld. During a lengthy career with the Company, which began in 1744, he never managed to make his fortune. He only reached the rank of commander in 1778 when he was fifty-five. The path of his career was tortuous. For instance, in 1765 an application for the position of first mate was turned down. He had to wait another eight years to be promoted. The director Gerard van Vredenburch in Delft made a note of the long delay in promotion. Van Katersveld's second and final voyage as commander ended in 1786. He then requested a pension for life from the Company. It was granted and paid to him twice a year. The directors consented to this, 'having borne in mind the lengthy service of the applicant and the fatal situation as a result of which he found himself through a coincidence of circumstances'. Exactly what happened is not known. Possibly he had suffered a physical collapse or even something worse. His second mate on the final voyage, young Jan Kornelis Baane from Flushing, noted that his commander was 'sometimes dull-witted' and 'did absolutely nothing on board'. Van Katersveld died in 1793.[27]

In 1773, in view of his advanced age, the long-serving Van Vredenburch gave a farewell address to his fellow directors of the Delft Chamber. The tenor of his discourse was sombre: 'Will the Company collapse or can it not be rescued from its deplorable situation, laden with debts, as Your Excellencies here present must surely be aware of how far they have mounted up …?', he asked his audience. Van Vredenburch was very pessimistic about the chances of survival of the Company of which he had been a director for eighteen years.[28] The end was to come only two decades later. By that time Van Katersveld was already dead. The Company disappeared from Delft and Delfshaven, but the main buildings still survive. For by far the great majority of its commanders, the Delft Chamber had opened a road to greater prosperity and opportunities to live off their investments in later life. A few did engage in trade and industry and grew rich. Two others were appointed as Superintendent of the Shipyard, a pattern repeated in other Chambers. This was a very attractive post, one which offered boundless possibilities to earn extra income over and above the regular salary. It came with a free official residence as well. It was a job which required its occupant to travel frequently to buy materials and to deliberate with colleagues in other Chambers such as Amsterdam and Middelburg.

Though some Delft commanders did well there was no spectacular case of amassing a fortune like that of Roelof Blok in Enkhuizen. There were no

---

(High Court of Admiralty 30/712 (1 and 2)). Information kindly provided by Dr R. van Gelder.
[27] The Hague, NA, VOC 14060, and Archief Van Vredenburch 1, 15.5.1765; Delft, GAD, Not. Arch. 3202, fol. 86; E. Crone, *Cornelis Douwes 1712–1773. Zijn leven en zijn werk met inleidende hoofdstukken over navigatie en zeevaart-onderwijs in de 17de en 18de eeuw* (Haarlem, 1941), p. 4; *DAS* II, no. 4457, and III, no. 8163.
[28] Van Gelder and Wagenaar, *Sporen van de Compagnie*, p. 93.

intriguing personalities at Delft like Stavorinus and Reynders in Zeeland. There were, however, following the example of Van der Plas in Middelburg, two orphan boys worthy of attention who rose to the rank of commander.

5

Rotterdam

The achievements of Jan van Heemstee from Delfshaven in Rotterdam may perhaps raise expectations that more retired commanders developed a spirit of enterprise in the city. However, such expectations are doomed to disappointment, despite the fact that the situation in Rotterdam offered commanders promising opportunities to launch commercial and industrial initiatives. In contrast to the four preceding towns, all mired in difficulties, Rotterdam was a city which was growing. In the other four towns, the population was in steady decline, houses stood empty or were being demolished, and the local economy was contracting at an alarming rate. There was scarcely a trace of these problems to be seen in Rotterdam. After explosive growth in the seventeenth century, and population growth from 20,000 in 1622 to 51,000 in 1690, the number of inhabitants did drop slightly to between 44,000 and 47,000 around 1750, but half a century later it had risen again, reaching 58,000. The *Personele Quotisatie*, the personal income assessment for tax purposes, of 1742 offers insight into the financial circumstances of the upper echelons of the Rotterdam population. In that year the Province of Holland placed a tax on all its inhabitants who had an annual income exceeding *f.* 600. In Rotterdam, 2,600 people – 5 to 6 per cent of the total population – were liable to pay the tax. The large majority of this group, 90 per cent, had an income of between *f.* 600 and *f.* 4,000. The remaining 10 per cent enjoyed even higher incomes. A closer examination reveals that almost half of the households paying this tax (1,177) were connected with the harbour in one way or another.

This was a conspicuous characteristic of the Rotterdam economy, just as the relative stability of urban trade and industry was. The situation did not change markedly in the eighteenth century. The fishery had since lost its importance and by that time it was flourishing downstream in Vlaardingen and Maassluis. Shipbuilding, rope making and sawing remained strong, however. Tobacco and sugar were important products in the processing industries that thrived in the town. Indeed, the tobacco industry employed 3,500 people in fifty-six businesses. In the second half of the century, the importance of sugar waned, but distilleries and a few other industries still provided plenty of work.[1] One of the tried and

---

[1] A. van der Schoor, *Stad in aanwas. Geschiedenis van Rotterdam tot 1813* (Zwolle, 1999), pp. 315–32.

tested sources of business in the town was the Rotterdam Chamber of the VOC. It was responsible for one-sixteenth of the whole of the Company's activities.

The Chamber and the Population of the City

Newcomers from outside the city were always very important to Rotterdam. Citizenship (*poorterschap*) could be purchased for *f*. 12. For people who moved to the town the poor relief boards of the various religious denominations in the immigrants' places of origin were required to guarantee that the newcomer would place no call on the services of their counterparts in Rotterdam. Immigration never assumed significant levels, but after approximately 1730 it rose steadily. Every year around 200 Rotterdam men signed on as crew on Company ships – just as many as in Delft. In the course of the century, this number halved. A growing number of personnel never returned from the East. Originally this percentage was two-fifths, but after 1770 it was more than three-quarters. This sort of death rate was fairly normal in many urban populations. Indeed, it was true of Rotterdam itself. In the course of the century, immigration compensated for the losses. Taken as a whole, these developments meant that the urban population grew after 1750.[2] Although it is true to say that the economy and employment opportunities did not decline, they also did not grow. That meant that in Rotterdam as elsewhere unemployment and poverty were inescapable. In 1784, 5,500 people needed support, and by 1795 the number had doubled.

In Rotterdam the Company was not the 'economic giant' it was in Middelburg, but, just as in the other Chambers, it did have an effect on the composition of the population because of its constant demand for personnel. A large number of men who signed on Company ships never returned and that reinforced the already uneven balance between the number of men and women in the city. There are no exact figures for the ratio in Rotterdam but in Delft 30 per cent of women remained unmarried because of the shortage of men.

Another common occurrence among the poorer sections of the urban population was illegitimate births. Unquestionably, Company personnel contributed their share to this. Illegitimate births rose during the eighteenth century from 1 per cent to 5 to 6 per cent of the total number of births.[3] The name of the natural father was almost always known. Similar incidents have already been

---

[2] P. Grimm (ed.), *Heeren in zaken. De kamer Rotterdam van de Verenigde Oostindische Compagnie* (Zutphen, 1994), pp. 29–43. G.J. Mentink and A.M. van der Woude, *De demografische ontwikkeling te Rotterdam en Cool in de 17e en 18e eeuw* (Rotterdam, 1965), p. 67.

[3] M. van der Heijden, 'Achterblijvers. Rotterdamse vrouwen en de VOC (1602–1750)', in M. van der Heijden *et al.* (eds), *Rotterdammers en de VOC. Handelscompagnie, stad en burgers (1600–1800)* (Amsterdam, 2002), pp. 181–212, see pp. 182–3; Wijsenbeek-Olthuis, *Achter de gevels*, p. 414; Mentink and Van der Woude, *De demografische ontwikkeling*, p. 49.

mentioned in relation to the adulterous wife of Commander Russeplukker in Enkhuizen. Inevitably various Rotterdam commanders also ran into difficulties with or fell foul of eighteenth-century morals which forbade sexual intercourse outside the bonds of matrimony. It is probable that in 1711, when he was first mate, Jakob Brouwer begot a child under precisely these circumstances, but he was only tempted into matrimony when he was a retired commander. In 1736 he married a woman who was living in his house. Thirteen days before the marriage was solemnized he buried a newborn son. In 1729, Jan Hokkeling resolved a case of putative paternity in a different way. He denied it, but a few weeks before his maiden voyage as commander the mother was suddenly paid the sum of *f.* 180, and she renounced any further claims. A brother of Commander Kornelis Quack did exactly the same. Payment of *f.* 89 and no more 'claims or botheration' were conditions of the agreement.[4]

Hokkeling, like Russeplukker, was something of a womanizer. Shortly before he settled the paternity claim with cash in 1729, he developed a relationship with another woman of whom his mother did not approve. She felt so strongly she was even moved to alter her will in March 1731. Her son was only to receive the usufruct of his share of the inheritance. He would receive his full inheritance only when he married another woman who 'behaved honestly and who never courted notoriety by anything she did or said'. Hokkeling's mother achieved her goal. On 16 September, the commander was betrothed to someone else. However, two days later the banns were 'forbidden'. A woman with a minor daughter objected to the marriage on the grounds that he had made earlier promises of marriage to her. The affair was able to be settled amicably, and despite the challenge the marriage took place on 30 September 1731. It did not last long because Hokkeling's wife died in childbirth a little more than a year later, at the end of 1732.[5] As a commander and in his personal life Hokkeling was the cause of a number of problems.[6]

Nearly half of the people who sailed for the Rotterdam Chamber were natives of the city itself and sometimes the share was even as high as two-thirds. A random sample of the ships' pay books revealed the proportions. However, in contrast to their confreres in Enkhuizen, when they appointed a commander the directors did not always give preference to a native of the city. Not even half of the 120 eighteenth-century commanders were sons of the city on the

---

[4] For Brouwer, see P. Moree, 'Gezagvoerders op VOC-schepen van de Kamer Rotterdam in de achttiende eeuw', in Van der Heijden *et al.*, *Rotterdammers*, pp. 136–60, see p. 151. For Hokkeling, see Rotterdam, GAR, Not. Arch. 2501, fols 540–641; for Quack, see *ibid.*, 2576, fol. 270.

[5] Rotterdam, GAR, DTB 2170, fol. 239, and 2843, fol. 226, and Not. Arch. 2362, fol. 728 (15.3.1731), and 2628, fol. 543 (21.9.1731).

[6] See Chapter 15.

Meuse (57). Nine of them came from nearby Delfshaven.[7] In contrast to the men serving the other Chambers, among Rotterdam commanders there were no remarkable personalities or careers which stand out. There were not even any orphans. One-fifth of the commanders have been examined in more detail, including a few Rotterdam men who sailed for the Delft Chamber. None of the commanders came from the ruling classes or the gentry. Willem Koelbier was perhaps the commander who died the richest. He began at the bottom of the Company hierarchy and reached the rank of commander by 1768. He made three voyages at that rank and retired ashore in 1778. In 1781 he was examiner of ship's officers and commanders, and he also became Superintendent of the Shipyard and its 'overseer' in 1791. He also acted as an agent on behalf of many former colleagues.

From 1694 the Company shipyard was located outside the city, beyond the Oostpoort on the Boerengat and so opposite the naval dockyard. In 1790, 209 men were employed there. The Superintendent of the Shipyard was not personally involved in shipbuilding, but was in charge of the whole complex, and it was his duty to ensure that all departing ships sailed fully equipped. His supervision of private goods which those on board brought with them on their return was a very important part of his job. He held the keys to the stores for the ship's supplies. At the end of the seventeenth century a completely new *Oost-Indisch Huis*, the administrative centre of the Chamber, was built. It was completed in 1698 and remained standing until the German bombing of 1940.[8]

Humble Beginnings

Nearly all of the commanders had begun their careers with the VOC as deckhands or sailors. Only a few had previously sailed with the merchant navy. Many were lower middle-class and from the circles of labourers and ordinary seafarers. Their fathers were employed as ship's carpenters, tailors, bakers, or tobacconists.

---

[7] Grimm (ed.), *Heeren in zaken*, pp. 29–30; Moree, 'Gezagvoerders', pp. 152–6 for a complete list of names. The commanders examined in more detail are: Willem Jakob Andriessen (1755–after 1795), Jean Belleveau (?–1759), Jakobus Bogaard (1672–1743), Gijsbert Bonekamp (c.1708–1751), Kornelis van Brattem (1732–1781), Arie Brouwer (1685–after 1746), Jakob Brouwer (1680–1765), Jan Hokkeling (c.1692–1734), Andries Laurens Kanters (1762–1794), Willem Koelbier (1736–1799), Jan Krielaard (?–1738), Dirk Krijne de Munnik (1659–1727), Kornelis Lans (c.1690–1733), Kornelis Leempoel (1704–after 1761), Hendrik Lont (?–after 1727), Kornelis Overraad (?–1709), Kornelis Quack (1707–1757), Arnoldus Rogge (1758–1802), Dirk van der Schilde (1710–1781), Willem Smalt (1760–1819), Arie van Stolk (1699–after 1737), Dirk Dirksz Varkevisser (1758–1805), Pieter Verkerk (1738–1778) and Willem de Wijs (c.1690–1756).

[8] Grimm, *Heeren in zaken*, pp. 18–23; Van Gelder and Wagenaar, *Sporen van de Compagnie*, pp. 104–21; see also Bulletin no. 2 (1988) of the Historisch Museum Rotterdam devoted to Rotterdam and the VOC.

Kornelis Lans' father died in the poor house in 1722. The Roman Catholic Parish Poor Relief in Leiden had to stand surety for the parents of four-year-old Pieter Verkerk if it were to come to light after they moved to Rotterdam in 1742 that they were destitute.[9] Many retired commanders also moved throughout the rest of their lives in the circles of craftsmen and shopkeepers. This is revealed by the occupations stated by their relatives and other witnesses at marriages and christenings.

During the first decades of the eighteenth century, there were a few families whose lives were closely bound up with sailing for the Company. In the 1710s three Brouwer brothers, Jakob, Barend and Arie, regularly sailed to the East, often together. Jakob and Arie reached the rank of commander, in 1716 and 1722 respectively. Barend sailed as a ship's carpenter and later became a shoemaker. Their sister married Jan Krielaard from Woudrichem, who became a commander in 1724. Jakobus Bogaard's father worked for the VOC and he himself started working for the Company at a young age. In 1706 he made it to the rank of commander. Between then and 1722 he made four voyages with that rank; he died in 1743. His son, Barend, died at sea as third mate in 1727. His brother-in-law gave up the sea in 1725 after he had returned home from his fourth voyage as commander.

In 1714 Bogaard moved house from outside to inside the walls of the city and he continued to live there in his retirement. Jakob Brouwer never left his parental home. He lived there on his investments and from what he earned as a money-lender to his family and third parties. In 1734 he invested in a share of a herring bus.[10] Commanders and retired commanders lived dispersed throughout the city, some of them in the better parts in the vicinity of the town hall and the church of St Lawrence, very desirable addresses. There were a number of good addresses in Rotterdam, of which the Haringvliet and the Boompjes were the best.[11] Brouwer lived in the vicinity of those streets but other commanders tended to live further away from the centre of the town. In such districts it was sometimes possible to buy expensive houses. For instance, in 1736 Hokkeling's house in such a neighbourhood was sold for ƒ. 5,700 after his death, and Gijsbert Bonekamp's house on its sale raised ƒ. 3,850 in 1751. His timber business which was close by was also sold at the same time.[12] The Poor Relief Board of the Reformed Church received a legacy of ƒ. 5,872 from the sale of Dirk van der Schilde's house, which was also located a little way outside the city.

Kornelis Lans' father, who had died in the poor house, could never have imagined that, shortly before his final voyage in 1731, his son could have afforded to buy a house on the Wijnhaven. It was a two-storey house with an attic storey, a

---

[9] Rotterdam, GAR, Oud-Archief 810, fol. 135.
[10] For Bogaard, see Rotterdam, GAR, Not. Arch. 1800, fol. 861, and 2635, fol. 183; for Brouwer, see Moree, 'Gezagvoerders', pp. 147–51.
[11] Van der Schoor, *Stad in aanwas*, p. 331.
[12] Rotterdam, GAR, Not. Arch. 2747, fol. 504, and 2876, fol. 638.

loft and a cellar. It had built-in cupboards which were 'lined with gilded leather'. After the deaths of Lans and his wife, who died within a short time of each other, this house and its contents were sold at public auction. A great deal of furniture and many articles of clothing as well as vast quantities of Chinese and Japanese chinaware, textiles and jewellery went on the block. In the attic there were charts, navigational instruments and books about sailing and navigation. There was also a copy of the *Groote Christelijcke Zeevaert*, the traditional book of homilies, prayers and hymns for seaman by Adam Westerman, of which the first edition was printed in 1625 and the last in 1743.[13] Lans also had a Bible, a book of psalms and a catechism. Lans' only son turned his back on the sea and later became a prominent apothecary in the city.[14]

Sailing to Riches

The VOC commander who had managed to reach the highest rank on board but whose origins lay in the lower middle class or even lower in the social hierarchy could usually expect to enjoy a degree of material prosperity which his parents had never known. Often his social status also improved. Nevertheless, it is still difficult to delve more deeply into what such a commander did after his sailing career ended.

This is true of Jean Belleveau, who came from Rochefort and had married a fellow Frenchwoman. This mariner earned considerable amounts of money on his voyages. Initially he had sailed as boatswain on a coastal trader before he signed on with the VOC. In 1733 he was a third mate for the Delft Chamber. During a voyage in 1733–1737, he rose to the rank of first mate, this time sailing for the Rotterdam Chamber. Initially his family had to make do with what they had. For *f.* 72 per annum, they lived in what was not much more than one room, in a house in which four other families lived. In 1740, the Belleveaus' living space was doubled, as indeed was the rent. The Frenchman also displayed an enterprising spirit and in 1739, for instance, sold various chests of tea to a Rotterdam merchant. His career was flourishing. In 1740 he became a commander for the Delft Chamber and in 1742 he obtained the prestigious command of the *Herstelder*, a new ship which the Amsterdam Chamber had bought from the local Admiralty. On board was no less a personage than the newly appointed Governor-General, Gustaaf Willem, Baron van Imhoff, on his way to the East where his orders were to carry out reforms in Company policy. Van Imhoff had personally recommended Belleveau for the command. The officer returned home via China in 1748, accompanied by his son Jean Daniël who had sailed with his

---

[13] S.J. de Groot, 'De "Groote Christelycke Zee-vaert" and "de God-vreezende Zeeman", hun meer dan driehonderdjarige rol als toeverlaat voor de zeevarenden', *Mededelingen Nederlandse Vereniging Zeegeschiedenis* 34 (1977), pp. 5–18.
[14] Rotterdam, GAR, Weeskamer 2568, fols 805–904.

9. Gold commodore's medallion. One of the commanders in the returning fleet was always appointed commodore, unless there happened to be a former member of the *Hoge Regering* in Batavia on board, who would assume the role of admiral. After a safe voyage home, the commodore would report in person and in writing to a meeting of the *Heren Zeventien*. In October 1745, Jan de With from Denmark was appointed commodore by Batavia. He made his report on 2 September 1746 and was presented with the usual gift of a fine gold medal (with inscription) on a gold chain. De With's medal had a diameter of 8.5 cm and, with the chain included, weighed 315 grams. Often this gift was melted down and sold, but De With forbore to do this. After making his report to the *Heren Zeventien*, the commodore, accompanied by a few of the directors, also made his report to a commission of the States-General in The Hague. The Scheepvaartmuseum in Amsterdam also possesses a medal and chain presented to Maarten Haringman dating from 1753.

father as a midshipman. Still in Asian waters, Belleveau sailed several times to Mocha (al-Mukha) on the Red Sea, where he operated successfully in the dual role of commander and supercargo. He traded spices for coffee on behalf of the Company. Since the VOC had closed its factory in Mocha in 1739, all trade had to be transacted in the roads.[15] Based on the evidence of a stream of bills of exchange which began to arrive from the East from 1744, it is clear that Belleveau, who had chosen to settle in Rotterdam, was very effective in looking after his own interests. An amount of nearly *f.* 68,000 was remitted, a sum which was over and above the *f.* 10,000 earned from his salary and various perks. At Van Imhoff's suggestion, his salary had been set at *f.* 100 per month, payments at that level prevailing during the years he spent in the Indies. This sum was far higher than was usually earned by a man in his position. In 1747 his wife moved to a house in a much better neighbourhood.

After 1748 Belleveau left the sea behind. By this time he was able to buy the manor *Bergzicht* near the leafy village of Hillegersberg, north of Rotterdam. For the 'spacious, solid, strong and well-constructed gentleman's residence', he paid *f.* 4,300. The estate included an 'orangery', a gardener's cottage, stable accommodation for four horses, a 'very pleasant tea-house on the road', a garden and a Turkish tent; a kitchen garden with 'two fine hot houses' as well as a few statues scattered here and there in the garden came with the house. A gardener whose annual salary was *f.* 200 was part of the deal. Belleveau died in his town house in 1759. The fee at his burial was *f.* 15, which indicates a fortune of between *f.* 6,000 and 12,000. There can be no doubt that Belleveau was an immigrant who made his mark as well as being a successful Company commander.[16] His son Jean probably died as third mate on board a Zealand ship shortly before its arrival in Batavia in 1754.

Some born and bred Rotterdam commanders were well-to-do. The Brouwer brothers were wealthy. Jakob had enough money to be able to lose *f.* 20,000 when one of his brothers went bankrupt. Bonekamp was able to leave his widow comfortably off. Six years after his death, her property was assessed at *f.* 20,000 for a capital levy, showing that she was certainly not destitute. Quack, who had been assessed at less than *f.* 4,000 in 1736, was given a second-class burial with a licence fee of *f.* 15 in 1757, which means that his assets, like Belleveau's, must have been between *f.* 6,000 and 12,000. In 1781, the childless widower Dirk van

---

[15] Jacobs, *Merchant in Asia*, 260–6; J.E. Schooneveld-Oosterling, *Generale Missiven* XI, pp. 13, 221 and 569. For Van Banken see: Rotterdam, GAR, Not. Arch. 3007, fols 1137–40 (23.6.1777); The Hague, NA, VOC 123, res. Heren XVII, 16.3.1742; Rotterdam, GAR, Not. Arch. 2405, fol. 240 (17.8.1728), 2641, fol. 444 (11.11.1731), 2461, fol. 480 (6.10.1739), 2785, 10.11.1740, 2693, 21.9.1746 and 17.11.1747; and Oud Stads Archief, Verkoopboek 678, fols 231 and 689, fol. 110.

[16] The Hague, NA, VOC 123, 16.3.1742; Rotterdam, GAR, Not. Arch. 2405, fol. 240 (17.8.1728), 2641, fol. 444 (11.11.1731), 2461, fol. 480 (6.10.1739), 2785, 10.11.1740, 2693, 21.9.1746 and 17.11.1747; and Oud Stads Archief, Verkoopboek 678, fols 231 and 689, fol. 110.

der Schilde bequeathed more than just his house to the Reformed Church Poor Relief Board. The minister with the help of an elder drew up a list of all his porcelain. The gems, jewellery, furniture and cash he left on his death amounted to a value of ƒ. 8,500. The Board invested the bulk of the legacy in various sorts of bonds valued at ƒ. 22,500. In addition he held 3 per cent annuities worth £2,500 from the Bank of England. As in the case of his Delft colleague Schut, more than half of his money had been invested in foreign currency. The legacy was assessed at approximately ƒ. 100,000, ƒ. 7,000 relating to outstanding bills from, among others, his bookseller for newspapers, his barber for services, his laundry, a plumber, a carpenter and a wigmaker for the refurbishing of his wigs, as well as payments for medicines, a pair of slippers and two pairs of black leather breeches. Possibly seventy-one-year-old Van der Schilde had not been able to make the payments personally for some time. His housemaid, who had been with him for five years, received ƒ. 50 for each year she had been with him plus an extra ƒ. 150. The costs incurred for his funeral, ƒ. 603, were noted in scrupulous detail. These included the making and lining of the coffin, the delivery of the coffin by the coachman, the cambric shroud which cost ƒ. 211, mourning bands, gloves, hats for the coachmen, stocks, money for those holding the vigil, servants at the funeral which cost ƒ. 252, cards announcing the death, varnish and, last but not least, wine.[17] In contrast to other commanders and retired commanders, Van der Schilde did not have a country residence with acreage, let alone anything like the manor house owned by Belleveau.

During his sailing career and in his later life on land – he retired in 1756 – Commander Van der Schilde was absorbed with his financial affairs. A whole host of notarial deeds bear witness to this. For instance, he made arrangements so that his mother would have an income. She often received a monthly payment. He was still sailing under the aegis of the Delft Chamber and he often lent colleagues money, among them Welgevaren and Schut. Merchants gave him permission to act as their agent buying goods in the East and collecting what was owed them. In Batavia he personally traded in wine, supplied by A. and J. Crasser. This firm also supplied the wine for his funeral. Once he had finally established himself on shore, he acted as agent for other commanders and ship's officers, including Koelbier. Van der Schilde also handled the sale of the contents of their sea chests on their return, lent them money and on many occasions was named their executor. One of his jobs, to which he was appointed in 1758, was examiner for the Rotterdam Chamber.

---

[17] For Brouwer, see Rotterdam, GAR, Not. Arch. 2628, fols 757–60 (18.7.1732); Oud Stads Archief, Verkoopboek 664, 1.5.1736; *ibid.*, Minuut Kohier P.Q. 4169, fol. 1054; for Bonekamp, see *ibid.*, 2201, fol. 506 (24.3.1758); for Quack, see *ibid.*, 3004, fol. 853, and 3608, fol. 160; and for Van der Schilde, see GAR, Giftebock 583, fol. 201, and Not. Arch. 3463, fols 553 and 960.

The Trade of the Van Brattem Brothers

Notarial acts often reveal to the researcher what sort of business affairs a first mate, commander or retired commander was involved in with colleagues, merchants and money-lenders in the places where they lived. The arrangements of the Van Brattem brothers for carrying out their private trade and the sorts of sums involved are a good example. Kornelis became a commander and later Superintendent of the Shipyard in Colombo in Ceylon. Teunis died young while he was still a first mate. Their father had been a master in the merchant navy but they sailed alternately for the Chambers of Rotterdam and Delft. In the purely personal sphere, as the situation warranted, they made their wills and organized monthly payments to be made to their mother or their wives. Before sailing, they exchanged powers of attorney with a few of their fellow crew members, with an eye to taking care of or settling their kit in case they should die on board or overseas. Sums of money were mentioned in the documents in connection with loans and trade in commodities. Their brother Jakob often looked after their interests during their absence. After they started their careers at sea, Kornelis and Teunis did not see much of each other, unless perhaps they happened to run into each other overseas. They did meet at the beginning of 1759 and for the last time in 1767.

In pursuing trade in European goods in the East and at the Cape, commanders and their ship's officers were able to use their own networks of contacts which they had built up during previous voyages. Besides these, at home in Rotterdam their suppliers also had their own contacts, especially in Batavia and Cape Town. The commanders and ship's officers were obliged to pay their business contacts fixed sums of money under agreements which had been registered with a notary. The going rate of interest was half a per cent per month on money borrowed for buying trading goods. Letters of recommendation could be especially useful overseas in developing or exploiting contacts. Of course, the sum that goods fetched over and above the amount agreed with the merchant was profit for the commander or ship's officer. Experience and relations were what counted in earning money in any particular branch of private trade. In order to lay his hands on more space for trading commodities, a commander could purchase sea chests from those of his shipmates who had no particular use for them. Each person on board, according to rank, was permitted to take along a certain quantity of commodities. The greatest risk run by using another man's sea chest was that he might die during the voyage. Making an open claim on the deceased's chest would reveal the transgression of the rules governing private trade of those on board.

The Van Brattem brothers made the fullest possible use of the opportunities available. They purchased their trade goods in Rotterdam, Delft and Amsterdam, as well as further afield in Germany. They frequently patronized the same firms. Andries Crasser in Rotterdam supplied a large quantity of wine to Kornelis, for instance, in 1767, to the tune of ƒ. 2,698. On his return home, Teunis sold all his sea chests directly to dealers. In 1761, when he was third mate, he was entitled to a sea chest measuring four and a half by two feet, and in 1764, as second mate, he had a somewhat bigger one measuring five by two feet, branded with his own name; by 1766 he was entitled to three sea chests. After his departure in 1769, Kornelis remained in Asia, where he died in 1781. Until his death in 1777, retired commander Jakobus van Banken was his most important supplier in Rotterdam. When he died, Teunis switched to three Amsterdam suppliers. It required no less than nine Rotterdam notaries to record all his transactions. In the East, Kornelis initially participated in the intra-Asian trade, and he was then appointed Superintendent of the Shipyard in the important port of Colombo. This position placed him in a situation in which he could earn large amounts of money. Evidence of this is three bills of exchange which were transferred to suppliers in 1781, 1782 and 1785. They amounted to the sums of ƒ. 12,342, ƒ. 66,461 and ƒ. 3,615 respectively. All Kornelis' earlier investments paled in significance beside them.

Table 5.1 Wages and financial transactions of Kornelis and Teunis van Brattem

	Voyages	Rank	Wages (ƒ)		Loans/purchases (ƒ)		Bills of exchange/sales (ƒ)	
			Kornelis	Teunis	Kornelis	Teunis	Kornelis	Teunis
Kornelis	1756/58	3rd mate	821					
Kornelis	1759/60	2nd mate	831		744			
Teunis	1759/61	3rd mate		855				750
Kornelis	1761/62	2nd mate	862		426			
Teunis	1762/64	3rd/2nd mate		791				825
Kornelis	1763/66	1st mate	1,845		5,220			
Teunis	1765/66	1st mate		2,702		3,687		7,250
Kornelis	1767/69	comm.	514		6,710 8,000		6,646	
Teunis	1768/69	1st mate		982		1,010		?
Kornelis	1769/81	comm./superint.	12,650		390		9,600 2,342 4,615	
			17,523	5,330	21,490	4,697	23,203	8,825

Table 5.1 records the financial data pertaining to both Van Brattem brothers. It contains only those figures which are mentioned in notarial deeds, bills of exchange and ship's pay books, and not what was paid to Kornelis posthumously. In other words, these are minimal amounts. Undoubtedly, both gentlemen would have had trade commodities stored at home as well. Only the sums raised by Teunis on his sales are known; these are given in the final column. It is quite obvious that ship's officers also invested many thousands of guilders in their

10. East Indiaman, the *Blijdorp*. Model of the *Blijdorp* of the Rotterdam Chamber, sister ship of the *Padmos*, both constructed in 1723. On her fourth voyage, the *Blijdorp* ran aground on the West African coast north of Cape Verde, in August 1733. Commander Jan Hokkeling was involved in this affair. The model, which was presented to the museum at the end of the nineteenth century, is built to a scale of 1:36, and is 168 cm long, 73 cm at the beam and 152 cm high. The stern frame is carved and painted.

private businesses. According to the figures in the table, the two brothers were involved in monetary transactions worth approximately 88,000 guilders, including their wages. During the seafaring years 1759–1769 alone, exclusive of their wages and bills of exchange, they had a turnover of at least *f.* 58,215 from loans, purchase of trade goods and the sale of those goods. These figures are for only two ship's officers, one of whom became a commander in 1767. On average, the turnover of the Van Brattem brothers was well over *f.* 5,000 per annum from their trade in European and Asian commodities. When these figures are placed in the context of the 200 sailings of the Rotterdam Chamber between 1700 and 1794, in which around 800 commanders and ship's officers were employed – that is some four per voyage – it is possible to get an impression of the amounts which were generated by the private trading activities of these people. Moreover, in the second half of the century, the opportunities to undertake such enterprises were greater than they had been in the first half.[18]

These calculations make no claim to completeness. They are put somewhat in perspective when they are placed alongside the annual expenditure of the Rotterdam Chamber on the building and fitting out of ships, which reached somewhere in the region of ƒ. 125,000.[19] What was happening in other Chambers will not in fact have deviated greatly from this pattern. Moreover, the Van Brattem brothers were not outstanding figures who were particularly conspicuous among officers engaged in trade for personal gain.

Rogge and Smalt: Portents of Different Times Ahead

From the beginning of the 1740s, almost without exception the Rotterdam Chamber signed on a Scandinavian, usually a Dane or a Swede, as third mate or higher. At the same time the stream of men from Rotterdam and Delfshaven gradually shrank. Counts made by a Norwegian researcher reveal the arrival of the Scandinavians. A number of them were promoted to commander and some made a number of voyages. Erasmus de Vries from Helsingør had lived in Rotterdam for a long time as a married sailor. He died on his second voyage to Asia as a commander in 1768. This fate had already befallen Laurens Kok from Moss in Norway in 1756. Six Scandinavians in total reached the highest rank.[20] By the 1780s, the geographical origins of the Rotterdam upper ranks had become even more dispersed. There were both more foreigners and more men from other parts of the Dutch Republic than from Rotterdam.

Around 1790 a great deal changed in the pattern of private trade. A few commanders and retired commanders of the Rotterdam Chamber were prominently involved in this. Up to that time it had been the custom that a commander could fill his sea chest with trading commodities he had purchased himself – whether or not he had had to borrow money to do this – and that after his arrival in the East he was free to sell the goods. However, merchants also rented the sea chests of commanders and their shipmates for specified sums of money and then filled the chests with their own wares. The sea chests were shipped on board under the brand of one particular sailor. Sometimes in lieu of rent the officer concerned got a proportion of the profit in the East. The initiative in this transaction lay with the merchant.[21] During the outward voyage at the Cape or in Asia, these goods were essentially European commodities, of

---

[18] See Chapter 12.
[19] P. van de Laar, 'Rotterdam. De koopstad en de VOC', in Van der Heijden *et al.*, *Rotterdammers*, pp. 30–55, see pp. 48–52.
[20] Aarsbog, *Med Mars og Merkur*, Appendiks II.
[21] Examples of this are in Bruijn, *Ship's Surgeons*, pp. 235–42.

which the Company itself only took a portion on its own account. When it was plunged into financial difficulties after the Fourth Anglo-Dutch War (1780–1784), the Company considered leaving the field of European goods entirely to private traders. It would transport the commodities of these private individuals 'as cargo'. In 1791 certain conditions governing this practice were adopted. Long before this decision was taken, various merchants had already tested and transgressed the rules of what was officially allowed. One of these was Anthony van Hoboken, who had taken over an already existing network of business contacts in Batavia and Cape Town from a senior colleague. Van Hoboken was a dynamic man. In that very same year, he sent goods to Asia with Arnoldus Rogge, and over the years that followed with a number of other commanders, including Willem Smalt.[22]

Rogge and Smalt were fairly junior officers. The former was a native of Bremen and the latter was from Rotterdam. They seized with both hands the opportunity to increase their earnings with this bit of business on the side offered them by Van Hoboken. They took his goods with them and they made thorough use of his contacts at the Cape and in Batavia. Among these contacts in Batavia, there was their somewhat older colleague, Willem Jakob Andriessen. Shortly after his divorce from his wife on the grounds of adultery in April 1787, he had sailed for the second time as a commander and had remained in the East. In 1789, he was Deputy-Superintendent of the Shipyard in Batavia, and in 1792 he was Superintendent. In association with his predecessor, retired commander P.H. de Hoedt, Andriessen became deeply involved in business. He took Van Hoboken's goods on consignment and sent Asian commodities to the Republic as freight, officially allowed since 1791, that is, after paying the cost per ton for shipping. His salary of $f.$ 80 per month must certainly have paled in comparison with his commercial earnings.[23]

After their first voyage carrying Van Hoboken's cargo, Rogge and Smalt remained in close contact with him. There was no need to hide the relationship since the Company had legitimized private trade. Even orders for exotic animals, 'small birds, monkeys and other rarities' were perfectly acceptable. After his maiden voyage, in 1791, Rogge had it recorded that he already had a personal fortune which fell under $f.$ 20,000. On his second voyage, he took another cargo for 'the king of trade'. However, caught up in the war then raging, Rogge's voyage ended in Ireland in 1795. Van Hoboken took good care of Rogge, who had become penniless, and in March 1796 gave his consent for him to marry his sister, who lived with him. The marriage spelled the end of Rogge's sailing career. However, he did invest a quarter share in two small merchant vessels belonging

---

[22] Dillo, *De nadagen*, pp. 186–96; A. Hoynck van Papendrecht, *Gedenkboek A. van Hoboken & Co. 1774 –1924* (Rotterdam, 1924), pp. 22–36; B. Oosterwijk, *Koning van de koopvaart. Anthony van Hoboken (1756–1850)* (Rotterdam, 1983), pp. 27–37.

[23] Rotterdam, GAR, Schepen archief 452, fol. 179 (28.4.1787); Dillo, *De nadagen*, pp. 1524 and 194.

to his new brother-in-law, which were destined to be employed in the grain trade to the Baltic. The same year, the two men also bought a large gin distillery in Delft, for which each paid the sum of ƒ. 7,300. This was followed later by the purchase of a malt house. Rogge moved to the prestigious address of the Oude Delft, where he lived until his death in 1802.[24]

Smalt's father was a tobacconist. After a few voyages in minor ranks, just before he set sail for his maiden voyage in command, Smalt registered that he possessed less than ƒ. 2,000. His father was poor enough to be buried free of a fee by the parish. After his return in 1792 and the settling of his accounts with Van Hoboken, Smalt married the daughter of a shopkeeper. At that point he was registered as being worth less than ƒ. 8,000. On his subsequent voyage in 1793, he again did business for Van Hoboken but this voyage ended in Batavia in the summer of 1795 after a great deal of time spent sailing around in Asia. At that point the war was at its height. Smalt reached his homeland, the newly founded Batavian Republic, as a passenger on a neutral ship. He was to set sail one more time, in 1802, as captain of Van Hoboken's own ship the *Rendier* on a voyage to Batavia. However, the peace between France and Britain was short-lived and, on the return voyage in 1804, the British stopped the ship as one from an enemy state and took her to Ireland. The ship and her cargo were confiscated. What happened to Smalt after this is a mystery. He died in Rotterdam in 1819.[25]

In the twilight years of the Company, Rogge and Smalt were able to profit from the opportunities offered by the opening up of trade to private individuals. The Batavian Revolution after the French invasion of 1795 and the liquidation of the VOC brought almost two centuries of the old pattern of sailing to and trading in Asia to an end. From that time, commanders, who were now permanently named captains, no longer sailed in the service of the enormous enterprise of the VOC, which had enjoyed a wide monopoly, but instead sailed for private ship owners. Van Hoboken was one of those ship owners/merchants who made optimal use of the opportunities which were then offered.

Once again, it is remarkable that some of the commanders finished their seafaring careers as superintendents of shipyards, either at home or abroad in Batavia or Colombo. From a financial point of view, this was an extremely attractive proposition. A number of retired Rotterdam commanders also benefited from being appointed to the position of examiner.

---

[24] Rotterdam, GAR, Not. Arch. 3310, fol. 990; Hoynck van Papendrecht, *Gedenkboek*, p. 40; Oosterwijk, *Koning van de koopvaart*, pp. 29–33 and 40–2.
[25] P. Moree, 'Met vriend die God geleide', pp. 133 and 224–5; Hoynck van Papendrecht, *Gedenkboek*, pp. 52–4; Oosterwijk, *Koning van de koopvaart*, pp. 56–8.

6

Amsterdam

The Amsterdam Chamber was the largest of all of the six Chambers. It was responsible for half of all the commercial and shipping activities of the Company. Each year it fitted out half of all the ships and appointed half the commanders. Certainly, compared to the four small Chambers, the numbers involved were large. Examining the appointments of commanders as a whole, certain aspects of their professions and lives in Amsterdam tend to stand out conspicuously in comparison with the commanders of the other Chambers. For instance, to a far greater extent than elsewhere, the Amsterdam commanders lived outside the city. For this reason, in the next chapter special attention is devoted to commanders who continued to live in their native places after they had been appointed commander or first mate by the Amsterdam Chamber. Using a random sample, fifty commanders from the city itself or from outside are examined in greater depth.

Almost No Commanders Resident in Exclusive Neighbourhoods

The Jordaan was a part of Amsterdam that was home to a few commanders and retired commanders of the Company. This section of the city was part of the third expansion of Amsterdam which took place in the years 1610–1615. The Jordaan was on the western side of the semicircle of canals which in its turn had expanded out from the medieval centre of the city. It had been designed as a residential and small business quarter. In the eighteenth century it housed a great many tradesmen and labourers. It hummed with small-scale industry. A maze of small alleys and passageways lined with extremely cramped apartments, often in cellars, wound between the streets and the canals. Many of the Amsterdam commanders had spent their youth in the Jordaan. Their fathers and other family members had been coopers, coppersmiths, gold-thread makers, carpenters, grocers, inn-keepers or mariners. Later, after attaining the rank of commander, they continued to live in the Jordaan, albeit at better addresses. Eleven of the twenty-one commanders registered in the *Personele Quotisatie* of 1742 gave their addresses in Quarters 49–53 which were situated in the western part of the city. The *Personele Quotisatie* listed each person's share of a new tax

11. Jakobus van Dam. This man was a native of Amsterdam and as first mate assumed temporary command of the Zealand ship the *Pasgeld* on the voyage out in 1753 after the death of the commander. At the end of 1755, he was sent back to the Republic from Batavia, 'as a useless subject', stripped of his rank and stipend. This small seated statuette from Canton is said to represent Van Dam. Many officials of the European companies had such images made in the era of the tea trade. At least sixteen such statuettes are still preserved in public and private collections.

imposed on residents of the province of Holland with an annual income of more than ƒ. 600. It was a list of the well-to-do.[1]

The Jordaan was densely populated and buzzing with life. A disturbance of the peace, such as that in August 1702 involving Commander Jakob Regenboog, could erupt spontaneously. Regenboog had only been back from his maiden voyage as commander a few weeks. A group of his crew members felt that they had a score to settle with him. Seven of them set off in search of Regenboog, but failed to find him either at home or at his half-sister's. Led by the rigger Pieter Koetsier, they finally tracked Regenboog down in an inn called the *Brakke Grond* on the Overtoom outside the city walls, not far from the Jordaan. His former crew members dashed a glass of beer in his face and attacked him 'physically, smiting, cursing and fulminating terribly'. Other customers at the inn managed to rescue the hard-pressed commander, who had in the meantime 'been injured on the crown of his head, so that as a consequence the blood streamed down over his face'. Flushed with victory, Koetsier and his mates moved on to another inn. They proudly displayed their trophies – Regenboog's wig and rattan walking stick – and they boasted that they had landed 'handsome punches' on the 'blackguard'. Koetsier placed the wig on his own head. The crewmen threatened to dish out the same treatment to the first mate. Recovered from his shock, Regenboog had witnesses make depositions in front of a notary. Koetsier was jailed by the magistrate. The attack had no unfortunate consequences for the victim. Three months later he married a carpenter's daughter from the Jordaan, and in January 1703, he set sail again. In 1721, in the course of his fifth voyage to Asia, he was dismissed for muddle-headedness, but it is unlikely this was related to the blow to the head he had received during the incident at the *Brakke Grond* almost two decades earlier.[2]

Seldom did a commander or a retired commander live within the semicircle of exclusive canals just to the west and south of the centre of the city. Around 1720, Adriaan Timmerman, who had sailed until 1713, lived on the Prinsengracht, but only in the first most northerly section opposite the Jordaan. A relatively large number of commanders and retired commanders lived in the heart of the old centre and the areas just to the east of it. This picture changed little over a century.

Only a very few retired commanders lived at the most expensive addresses. One such was Jacobus Verleng who retired from the sea in 1750 and, just over four months after he arrived home, bought a house in a prestigious part of the Keizersgracht for ƒ. 27,000. His house had once been the property of the patrician Boreel family. Verleng had made the money to pay for the purchase in

---

[1] W.F.H. Oldewelt (ed.), *Kohier van de personeele Quotisatie te Amsterdam over het jaar 1742*, 2 vols (Amsterdam, 1945); this source contains 12,655 names and addresses. See also W. Frijhoff and M. Prak (eds), *Geschiedenis van Amsterdam. Centrum van de wereld 1578–1650* (Amsterdam, 2004), II 1, pp. 36–7, II 2, pp. 268–9 and 285.
[2] Amsterdam, Gemeentearchief (GAA), Not. Arch. 6355, fols 1131 and 1141.

Batavia. During his fifth voyage as commander in 1746, he had been appointed Commander of the Roads and Superintendent of the Shipyard (*commandeur van de rede en opperequipagemeester*) in Batavia, succeeding his deceased fellow-townsman and colleague Hendrik Opmeer. Verleng occupied this lucrative post until the end of 1749. When he left Batavia he took with him personal bills of exchange worth ƒ. 48,738. Shortly after the purchase of his new residence, Verleng, a widower, remarried. He made a testamentary provision that he had reserved the sum of ƒ. 25,000 for the daughter of his first marriage. Verleng did not live long to enjoy his prestigious address, at which the previous occupants had kept a gig and two horses. He died just three years after taking possession, in 1753. Even by that time, not all his money had been transferred from Batavia. Another ƒ. 93,600 arrived after his death.[3]

Generally speaking, in the large city of Amsterdam Company commanders were able to live in greater anonymity than their colleagues in small towns and cities like Enkhuizen and Delft. Perhaps in their own immediate surroundings they enjoyed a certain degree of social prestige. They often lived amongst shops and small businesses. In 1742, Frederik Schouten was taxed just as much as his neighbour who was a pastry cook. His other neighbours lived off their investments and had more money than he did. Retired Commander Simon de Groot also obtained an income from his investments and lived at a good address on the Brouwersgracht, close to a tea seller, two itinerant beer sellers, purveyors of butter and wine, a grocer, an inn-keeper, and a few others who also lived off their investments. Their annual incomes of at least ƒ 1,500 were about as high as, if not higher than, that of De Groot. People with incomes of less than ƒ. 600, of course, formed the majority of the local population in the area. In fact, De Groot returned to his old profession in 1747 and set sail again to the East. Originally he had said farewell to his sailing career in 1731. At intervals, he had still received money from Batavia, the last transfer being in 1743. Initially the sums involved were substantial, for instance ƒ. 9,600 and ƒ. 19,200, but later the amounts dwindled. It is possible he engaged in a little trade during the period he lived off his investments. His colleague Jurriaan Wolberg lived on the Kloveniersburgwal, where he kept a shop selling Indian chintzes among a number of other shops specializing in textiles.[4]

Directors showed a preference for appointing fellow townspeople as ship's officers and commanders and the Amsterdam directors were no different from their confreres in other Chambers. There was always a call for sizeable numbers of ship's officers in Amsterdam. This is perhaps the reason that foreigners stood a good chance of appointment there, as many of them climbed through the ranks

---

[3] Amsterdam, Gemeentearchief (GAA), Not. Arch. 12807, fol. 719 (11.12.1751), and Kwijtscheldingen serie (Exemption Series) VI 1732–55, fols 124, 255–64; Oldewelt, *Kohier*, II, p. 322, no. 4474; Schooneveld-Oosterling, *Generale Missiven* XI, pp. 538, 763 and 845, and XII, p. 275.

[4] Oldewelt, *Kohier* II, p. 24, no. 985, p. 63, no. 2814 and p. 199, no. 5739.

and settled in the city. Sailors from other parts of the province of Holland also had a good chance of an appointment as a commander in the city. This pattern changed slightly during the second half of the eighteenth century. Many of these Holland commanders did not move to Amsterdam after their appointment but remained resident in the town in which they had been born. Here they enjoyed a respected social position through their appointment as commander with the Company, which would not have been so easy in Amsterdam.

In the *Personele Quotisatie* of 1742, commanders and retired commanders were assessed at an average annual income of ƒ. 1,000. In total, twenty-four of them were registered. Three were retired, and ten were assessed at the lowest level. This means that a good 5,000 of their fellow townsmen had much higher incomes than they did, often having a number of servants and owning coaches or boats and horses. There were certainly commanders without even one servant. House rents in Amsterdam were after all conspicuously higher than they were in any other town in the Republic.[5]

The City

Amsterdam was the biggest city in the Dutch Republic. From the late sixteenth century until well into the seventeenth century the population grew explosively and the inhabited area expanded enormously. By 1680 there were between 210,000 and 220,000 people living in the city. After that growth flattened out a little. Fifty years later, in 1730, the city had between 230,000 and 240,000 inhabitants. This number did not rise further, but actually fell slightly to 210,000 by the end of the century in 1795.[6] The contrast with what was happening with the population figures in four of the other five Chamber towns was dramatic. In the other towns there were enormous decreases in numbers of inhabitants. Rotterdam, which experienced spectacular population growth of more than 25 per cent during the second half of the century, reaching a total of 58,000, was the sole exception.

Generally speaking, economic conditions in the towns and cities of Holland in the eighteenth century were not good. Decline and deterioration were often the norm. Enkhuizen was the saddest example of all. C. Lesger argues that the slow growth and later only slight decline in the numbers in Amsterdam are an indication that employment opportunities and the economic climate in the city were initially good, but, with the passage of time, signs of stagnation and some decline began to intrude. There was a sort of pendulum effect between the situation in the trade and shipping sector and the industrial sector. In the first half of the eighteenth century, merchants and ship owners concentrated more heavily than ever before on products from the East and West Indies and on expanding

---

[5] Oldewelt, *Kohier* I, pp. 7–21; Frijhoff and Prak, *Geschiedenis van Amsterdam* II 2, 257–8.
[6] Oldewelt, *Kohier* I, pp. 21 and 219.

12. Flower boat. This so-called 'flower boat' was brought as a souvenir from Canton in 1746 by Commander Jan de With and displayed in his country house in Oenkerk (Friesland). The ship's model (75 cm long, 27 cm in the beam and 55 cm high) is made entirely of ivory and is beautifully carved to the smallest details. Various male figures stand about on the model, some with a steering oar in their hands. There are various open and closed rooms, some richly furnished. Lanterns are suspended at various points. Flower boats on the Pearl River were places where Chinese prostitutes entertained their clients.

their contacts with the German hinterland. The port was still as busy as ever, with approximately 3,000 ships putting into the harbour around 1730. However, a century earlier the number had been higher, by nearly 50 per cent. In the same period, industry in Amsterdam was flourishing. This prosperity was attributable to the import of enormous quantities of tobacco, sugar, silk, cotton and diamonds. The processing of these products provided work for thousands of people in the various branches of industry. After 1750, the situation changed. Selling the various manufactured products was made difficult as a result of protectionist measures in, and competition from, other places. Commerce in general was severely hindered by protectionist measures taken by various European countries. The traditionally high wages in Amsterdam took their toll. The rising price of food made it virtually impossible to introduce any wage cuts. The pendulum effect in Amsterdam then hit the commercial and shipping worlds, which experienced a strong revival. More incoming ships were registered in the harbour than ever before: 3,546 in 1778 in comparison with 2,760 in 1742. Especially intensified were commercial links with the coastal areas of North Germany, known as the Little East. The bustle in shipping activity meant more work in the construction of new vessels and in repairing the old, which spilled over into suppliers' businesses and the transport sector. Nevertheless, it was inevitable that, with food growing increasingly more expensive and a fall in employment after 1770, there was more poverty and destitution. In 1765, 10 per cent of the population received financial assistance, and in 1799, 18 per cent were 'on poor relief'.[7]

Only sporadically did retired commanders take an active interest in the economic life of the city.[8] One example of such a man who did better himself economically is Wessel van Neercassel, the son of a shoemaker, who first sailed as a commander in 1704. Like Jacob Verleng later in 1746, during his third voyage in 1712 Van Neercassel was appointed Commander of the Roads and Superintendent of the Shipyard in Batavia. He also exploited all the opportunities this lucrative position offered him. Among other commodities, Van Neercassel traded in sugar and slaves. In this trade he collaborated with his colleague and fellow townsman Tobias Uilenberg. However, on his return home, crew members reported Uilenberg to the *Heren Zeventeen* of the VOC for illicit trading, and they dismissed him. Van Neercassel's name was also mentioned in the matter and eventually in November 1715 the Superintendent was sent back home accused of 'fraud'. This dismissal spelled the end of his sailing career. Van Neercassel became a merchant and later an underwriter. In 1722 he bought a

---

[7] *Ibid.*, pp. 21–87, 219–65 and 291.

[8] Besides the fifty commanders for whom only their place of birth was checked, the following commanders were investigated in more depth: Pieter Angelvorst (1735–1777), Rijkmanus ten Bem (1678–1732), Jan de Boer (?–1778), Swerus Magnus Cederborg, Johan Carl Clemens, David van Elteren (1707–1753), Simon de Groot (1688–1750), Willem 't Hoen (1717–1765), Frederik Kelger (1722–1775), Dirk Klinkert (c.1724–1766), Jan de Koning (1676–1727), Diedelof Kroes (c.1670–1714), Gideon Kuiper (1685–1729), Gerrit van Lanschot (?–1715), Willem de Leus (1674–1728), Jan Lindeboom (?–1721), Jan de Marre (1696–1763), Bastiaan Mol (1697–1747), Jurriaan Molensteen, Douwe Jansz Mout (c.1705–?), Dirk Muller (1758–1834), Pier Muntz, Wessel van Neercassel (1671–1759), Jakob Onkruid (1661–1729), Hendrik Opmeer (1702–1745), Jochem Outjes (c.1707–1767), Johannes Pleen (c.1750–1791), Jurriaan Popta (1687/8–1742), Wopke Popta (1734–1800), Jakob Regenboog (1669–1727), Pieter Scharf (1684–1743), Jan Schellinger (1724–1769), Hendrik Schoon (1688–1736), Frederik Schouten (1705–1773), Herman Schutte (1703–1751), Benjamin van der Spek (1737–1787), Damiaan Hugo Staring (1736–1783), Anthonius Franciscus Steffers, Karsten Suniksen (c.1731–1763), Abraham Swart (1709–1756), Adriaan Kornelis Timmerman (1674–1726), Jan Tobias Toon (1691–1751), Reindert den Uil (1738–1779), Tobias Uilenberg (1673–?), Jurriaan Verburg (1735–after 1795), Jakob Verleng (1704–1753), Pieter Verley (1687/8–1736), Jakob Wiebe (c.1704–1766), Jan de With (1715–1781), Jurriaan Wolberg and Matthijs Zwaan (1690–1738).

property on the Prinsengracht near the Westerkerk for *f.* 8,500. He had this demolished and a large warehouse built on the site. Thirteen years later, in 1735, he and his family moved to the Herengracht. The house was a large one, 8.5 metres wide, three storeys high, with a stepped gable and a stone staircase to the front door. In the *Personele Quotisatie* of 1742, Van Neercassel was assessed at an income of *f.* 6,000 per annum. He had two servants and a covered carriage drawn by two horses at his beck and call. The retired commander died in 1759 at the age of eighty-eight. One of his granddaughters later married into the Amsterdam gentry. Van Neercassel's son, who bore the same name and lived close by, was the owner of the brewery the *Zwaan*. He also lived in great state. Their father and grandfather, Floris, did not live to enjoy this newly acquired wealth. He died much earlier, in 1727, and was buried at the cost of the parish in the Noorderkerk.[9]

Retired commanders were not employed in any of the many municipal positions, such as pensionary – a man who acted for the town in legal matters – town clerk, bookkeeper in the town hall, or real-estate agent, bargeman or professor, jobs held outside the town hall. In 1749, the corps of civil servants numbered 3,200 men and women.[10] This figure meant that the municipality of Amsterdam, not the Company, was the largest employer, and no former commander was counted among those city employees.

The Company in the City

The VOC did not play a dominant role in the midst of all the many activities in Amsterdam. Various industrial sectors offered people more work than the Company did. Nevertheless, the VOC was engaged in a variety of activities, all directed and co-ordinated by the board of twenty directors. These activities could range from buying cattle for slaughter, to launching a new East Indiaman, to purchasing more hemp for the ropewalk. In the 1740s, the Company employed more than 1,300 people in various jobs. Roughly 180 people had permanent employment in the *Oost-Indisch Huis* and on the artificial island of Oostenburg where the ships were built. Over 1,100 skilled and unskilled workers toiled there for a daily wage. By 1790 this group had risen to 1,319, of whom at that date '254 did no actual work every 14 days'.[11]

---

[9] The Hague, NA, VOC 116, 4.10.1714; Coolhaas, *Generale Missiven* VI, p. 894, VII, p. 197; J.E. Elias, *De vroedschap van Amsterdam* (Amsterdam, 1903–1905), pp. 395 and 831; Oldewelt, *Kohier* II, p. 153, no. 3057, and p. 240, no. 2538. It can be expected that the Amsterdam notarial archives, which are still very difficult to access, will contain more data.
[10] Frijhoff and Prak, *Geschiedenis van Amsterdam* II 2, p. 345.
[11] J. Gawronski, *De Equipagie van de Hollandia en de Amsterdam. VOC-bedrijvigheid in 18de-eeuws Amsterdam* (Amsterdam, 1996), pp. 43–5.

The *Oost-Indisch Huis* was the heart of the Company. It stood at the corner of the Kloveniersburgwal and the Hoogstraat, very close to the Dam. It is now part of the University of Amsterdam. It was a complex of buildings which had been constructed at the city's expense between 1603 and 1661. Until it purchased it all from the municipality in 1722, the Amsterdam Chamber rented the entire complex which consisted not just of boardrooms and offices but also abattoirs and stores for victualling the ships and warehouses for trade goods. The shipyard was situated on the island of Oostenburg, in the north-easternmost corner of the city alongside the island of Kattenburg where the Admiralty workplaces were located. It was at least a half hour's walk from the centre. The shipyard and the main stores were protected by two bastions on the city wall. Oostenburg was built around the same time as Kattenburg and Wittenburg, that is between 1655 and 1660. More or less the whole area was set up for the building and repairing of ships. The Company had bought the terrain in 1661. It was dominated by an enormous, four-storey-high store-house which measured 177 by 20 metres. A second store was built in 1720 and in 1752 a separate sailmaker's shop and a meat warehouse were added. The ropewalk was 500 metres long. The shipyard for the building of new ships and for carrying out repairs was the biggest in the Republic. There were three slipways. Many of the workers lived in the immediate neighbourhood. In the eyes of the directors who had to supervise it, Oostenburg was an out-of-the-way place in the back of beyond. They had themselves transported there in coaches in tow. That was necessary because there was a prohibition on keeping ordinary coaches in the city.[12]

The commanders did not have to walk to Oostenburg to board their ships. Usually they only went on board when the ships lay off the island of Texel some distance north of Amsterdam. The crew members did not have to go to Oostenburg either because they were ferried to their ships on flat-bottomed lighters which they boarded near the *Montaalbaanstoren*, the tower on the waterfront of the city's centre. The numbers of both sailors and soldiers were enormous. For instance, in 1730 there were nearly 4,000 men for nineteen ships, and in 1751 there were 5,400 men for eighteen ships. Fewer than half of these men would ever return to Amsterdam.

Of all those mustered, two-thirds to three-fifths were sailors. The remainder were soldiers plus a few tradesmen. Table 6.1 shows where the sailors came from. The total number of seamen amounted to about 2,400 in 1730, and some 3,500 in 1775.

---

[12] Van Gelder and Wagenaar, *Sporen van de Compagnie*, pp. 63–80 (illustration of a coach in tow on p. 68).

Table 6.1 Geographical origins of sailors of the Amsterdam Chamber[13]

Origin	1730		1775	
Amsterdam	800	(33%)	830	(24%)
Rest of the Republic	500	(21%)	830	(24%)
Foreign	1,100	(46%)	1,840	(52%)
Total	c.2,400		c.3,500	

These figures reveal that, until well into the eighteenth century, Amsterdam men remained loyal to the Company. In fact, their numbers increased slightly, even if their proportion of the total fell. Shortage of other employment will have played a role, just as did dire necessity and gentle prodding from the institutions which doled out charity. Nevertheless, over time more men and boys came from other parts of the country and from abroad. Work was scarce. Newcomers enthusiastically seized the employment opportunities the Company offered. The figures for the Company are consistent with the slow growth in the number of first marriages of men from outside the city, a rise which began in 1720.[14] However, totals of first marriages do not tell us everything about immigration. In fact, many of the newcomers never married, because they did not survive their Asian adventure.

Foreigners also appointed Commander

Abroad the Company had a reputation for always paying its wages on time, if need be to wives or parents. This proved a powerful attraction because in most countries such punctiliousness did not exist. When they arrived in one of the port cities of the Republic, either Amsterdam or elsewhere, people knew the names of inns which were run by their compatriots. Foreign mariners never lacked opportunities to rise to the higher ranks on board a Company ship. They could also become commanders, although sometimes the literature paints another picture.[15] It is certainly striking that, after 1740, various North Germans, Scandinavians

---

[13] Based on *DAS* I, pp. 146 and 155, and II, sailing departures in 1730 and 1775; random samples taken by W.M. Jansen and P. de Wilde for their MA thesis in history, 'Het probleem van de schaarste aan zeevarenden in de 18e eeuw' (Leiden University, 1970).

[14] S. Hart, *Geschrift en getal. Een keuze uit de demografisch-, economisch- en sociaal-historische studiën op grond van Amsterdamse en Zaanse archivalia, 1600–1800* (Dordrecht, 1976), pp. 142–3 and 146–7.

[15] R. van Gelder, *Het Oost-Indisch avontuur. Duitsers in dienst van de VOC* (Nijmegen, 1997), pp. 56–7 and 186–8; E. Kuijpers, *Migrantenstad. Immigratie en sociale verhoudingen in 17ᵉ-eeuws Amsterdam* (Hilversum, 2005), pp. 250–1. For the reputation of the VOC, see E. Göbel, 'Danes in the Service of the Dutch East India Company in the Seventeenth Century', *International Journal of Maritime History* XVI (June 2004), pp. 77–93, see pp. 82–3 and 90.

and other Northern and Eastern Europeans were appointed commander. Up to that time such appointments had indeed been sporadic. Men from Amsterdam were the first preference or, if none was available, ship's officers from the province of Holland. Of the forty-five commanders in the random sample of those who received their first appointment from the Amsterdam Chamber between 1700 and 1740,[16] twenty-eight were natives of Amsterdam and fourteen were from outside the city in Holland. The same pattern could be found in the other Chambers. Admittedly mariners from the Danish Wadden Sea Islands and the adjacent continent had always regularly risen to the rank of commander. They always adopted the Dutch version of their names. When Johan de Klerk was appointed commander in 1775, he was given permission to resume his own name: Johann Alexander von Schkopp.[17] The random sample also reveals that, later in the century, only ten Amsterdam men were appointed against seventeen foreigners. The only possible answer to this mystery of what caused the shift must be a great reduction in the quality of the Amsterdam men who applied. There were also, for instance, more new commanders' places for men from Katwijk and Texel in the province of Holland.

It is not necessary to search far for good examples of immigrants who enjoyed success both professionally and socially, and it was the Company which had given them the opportunity. Frederik Schouten, who had once been registered with an income of $f.$ 800, is a good example of such a man. When he was very young he had left Stettin in Pomerania for Amsterdam, where he married in 1731. In 1740, at the age of thirty-five, he became a commander. Schouten was a Lutheran and had three children, one of whom died in Company service as a first mate. Schouten retired from the sea in 1757. He had often spent long periods in the East and had earned a good deal of money. In the year he retired, he received a last bill of exchange for $f.$ 12,657 and he had earlier received nearly $f.$ 10,000 in bills of exchange. Later another sum of nearly $f.$ 12,000 followed. Besides the money, he also brought two new housemates back with him on his final voyage: a foster son, the son of a junior merchant in Batavia, and a female slave, Johanna van Bengalen. When Schouten made his will in 1762, it appears that the foster son, Johanna and a serving maid, Antje, were living with him in his house. In his will Schouten stated that he had paid for Johanna's return voyage to Asia, but that after his death she could also make her home with his daughter-in-law. His property was assessed at nearly $f.$ 50,000. The retired commander seems to have been a rather restless man, because after his return home he moved house three times. Schouten also provided very well for his wife, because she was to receive an annuity from the Funds for Sea Officers Sailing to the East Indies (*Fonds der*

---

[16] See note 8.

[17] P. Dekker, 'Drei Hooger Befehlshaber auf niederlandändischer Ostindienfahrt im 18. Jahrhundert', *Nordfriesisches Jahrbuch* 7 (1971), pp. 56–61; The Hague, NA, VOC 308, 26.6.1775; *DAS* II, no. 4244.

zeeofficieren op Oost-Indië),[18] enough for her to continue to live in 'appropriate and respectable' circumstances. The annuity from the Fund as it turned out was never paid because Mrs Schouten predeceased her husband. Her funeral in 1767 was carried out in the grandest style. When Schouten died in 1773, his foster son paid the second highest death duty of *f.* 15 for his funeral.[19]

Jakob Wiebe, from Elbing in Poland, is another example. He had a splendid career at sea, but was unable to enjoy his considerable earnings as a retired commander. He died in 1766 during his seventh return voyage as commander. Wiebe had become a specialist in Chinese and Ceylonese trade. He sailed home four times from Ceylon and three times from China. His private business affairs in the East flourished. Between 1746 and 1764, bills of exchange worth more than *f.* 44,000 were made out in his name and, over and above his stipend, on five occasions after his arrival home he was paid the usual bonus of *f.* 2,000. At the age of forty-two, Wiebe was fairly old when he was given his first command, but he had not delayed marriage until this milestone. In 1731, he had already married a woman from North Friesland in Amsterdam. They had four children, one of whom, Jakob, like his father, died in the service of the VOC.[20]

Eschel Juel from Hadersleben in South Jutland was unfortunate. His maiden command in 1764 was a voyage to the Cape, while his second ended in Ceylon in 1766. There he was dismissed from his command for misconduct. He spent years trying to restore his good name, claiming that he had been maltreated by his officers. He was never reinstated but in 1775 he was finally given a weekly allowance of *f.* 7.[21] Another Dane from Jutland had come earlier and he had had a very successful career. As a fourteen-year-old boy, he had left Aarhus to go to Amsterdam with two brothers. There he changed his name from Jens True to Jan de With. Having begun as a boy, by 1736 he had climbed to the rank of third mate, and four years later he was made a commander on the return voyage of a ship of the Rotterdam Chamber. He made another return voyage for that Chamber, and concluded his sailing career with a return voyage for the Amsterdam Chamber. At the very last minute, he was appointed commander of the whole return fleet after the sudden death of the intended commander, Christoffel Blom. This voyage with a fleet of seven ships passed propitiously and, in September 1746, De With was presented with the usual tokens of approval by the *Heren Zeventeen*. These consisted in his case of a gold chain 120 cm long and an inscribed gold medallion with a diameter of 8.5 cm. De With did not lose much time before departing for Dokkum in the province of Friesland, where he married a wealthy widow. The Admiralty of Friesland appointed him captain, a sinecure which he held for several years. More importantly to him personally,

---

[18] See Chapter 11.
[19] Amsterdam, GAA, Not. Arch. 13012, 12.9.1762, and means for burials 5005, vol. 149, 10.11.1773; The Hague, NA, VOC 6259.
[20] The Hague, NA, VOC 222, 12.10.1756 and 6465.
[21] The Hague, NA, VOC 134, 15.10.1771, 308, 19.10 and 19.11.1767 and 23.10.1775.

in 1758 he bought the estate Staniastate in Oenkerk, which he named after his first command, the *Hofwegen*. He died in 1781. In the house on his estate, De With kept something special, a finely carved model of a ship in ivory from Canton. It was not a junk but what was known as a flower boat which sailed back and forth on the Pearl River. It was the sort of vessel on which Chinese prostitutes received their clients. They were absolutely forbidden territory for Europeans. Whether De With's staff and visitors understood the true nature of this model is not known. The model is now in the *Fries Scheepvaartmuseum* (Maritime Museum) in Sneek.[22]

Generally speaking, the behaviour of the foreign commanders did not differ from that of their Dutch colleagues. Usually by the time they were appointed, they had been settled in the Netherlands for years and had married. Pieter Angelvorst from Molde in the far north of Norway was able to organize his private trading activities in the East during his three voyages just as well as his Dutch counterparts did. Nine bills of exchange worth a total of nearly ƒ. 45,000, which were the fruits of his labours, were transferred to Amsterdam between 1771 and 1779. These monetary transactions were carried out in the same way when commanders left orphaned children behind. The wife of Frederik Kelger from Koningsbergen (Kaliningrad) had died in 1764 and their two surviving children lost their father in 1775, when he died in the East. The governors of the orphanage in Batavia assumed control of Kelger's possessions there. These were sold at public auction, the bulk of them to Chinese merchants. The sum raised was ƒ. 6,955. Kelger's salary and other credit were paid out to the Amsterdam Orphanage. Among Kelger's possessions in Batavia was a ring set with seventeen diamonds and also two young Bengali slaves. The man from Koningsbergen had made five voyages as commander between 1762 and 1775. In this period, private trade had earned him nearly ƒ. 35,000 in cash. In 1751 he had married as someone who had no possessions. Kelger, Angelvorst and others were and remained Lutherans. Their children were often baptized in the Lutheran church, though this of course also depended on the religious denominations of their wives.[23]

Characteristics of the Commanders

The commanders of the Amsterdam Chamber typically remained loyal to their Chamber. The directors regularly gave them new commands. The breaks between

---

[22] M.J. Seffinga, 'Het ivoren "Bloemenschip" van Jan de With – 1746', *Jaarboek Fries Scheepvaart Museum en Oudheidkamer* (2004), pp. 65–8; F.S. Gaastra, 'Friesland en de VOC', in P.H. Breuker and A. Janse (eds), *Negen eeuwen Friesland-Holland. Geschiedenis van een haat-liefdeverhouding* (Zutphen, 1997), pp. 184–96; Schooneveld-Oosterling, *Generale Missiven* XI, p. 222.

[23] Amsterdam, GAA, Weeskamer 5073, akte 165 (22) and 166 (9 and 41); The Hague, NA, VOC 6861, akte 4079.

voyages were often only very brief. For instance, Jakob Onkruid returned from his third voyage in July 1717, and six months later he sailed again. In 1719, the turnaround was even quicker: back in August, he sailed again in November. His sixth and seventh voyages also started barely six months after his arrival home, and by that time Onkruid was no longer a young man – he was born in 1666. In that period, it was not exceptional for a commander to sail home in a ship belonging to another Chamber. This was how Onkruid arrived in the roads of Rammekens in 1722. He did not survive his seventh voyage as a commander. He died in the East in 1729.

A more regular system developed in the shipping patterns of the Company in the eighteenth century. After their arrival in Batavia most of the ships quickly set sail for home. The commanders participated in this sort of regularity, which more closely resembled that of a regular line service. At least that is what they did if they were not overtaken by exceptional circumstances.

Among the group of the Amsterdam commanders in the sample, Jochem Outjes from Stockholm is the only one who left the service of the Company to sail with another employer. He did not do this of his own free will. In 1755 he was given a dishonourable discharge with confiscation of his salary, bonuses and private goods. He had summoned out the boat, which brought the pilot on board, from neighbouring Den Helder twice. He had used this opportunity to tranship 'various contraband goods' and was caught red-handed. Outjes later resumed his former career of ship's master sailing to Surinam and St Eustatius. Before he had been appointed commander by the Company in 1747, he had already sailed to the West Indies. However, when he was appointed he had not fulfilled the usual requirements for being a commander.

Pieter Verley also did not choose the time of his retirement. In 1773, after the completion of his fifth voyage as commander, he had brought twenty-nine chests of tea and a quantity of porcelain with him as private freight. He had these goods stored in the warehouse of a merchant in Cape Town who sold them. This smuggling was discovered. Verley lost not only the salary he had earned, but also the money he had invested in his own trade, and his job as commander. This sort of trading in contraband 'with connivance' was a common occurrence. However, Verley was caught conspiring with his supercargo, the senior merchant on board, who had 'a large quantity' of chests loaded and unloaded at the Cape and then had these chests taken away at Texel on two lighters. This last case in particular was taken very seriously and was heard, along with the charges against Verley, before the chief magistrate of Amsterdam.[24]

In other Chambers, in the first half of the eighteenth century the various interlinking family relationships among the commanders were striking, as was the presence of families which produced a great many ship's officers and commanders.

---

[24] For Outjes, see The Hague, NA, VOC 172, 21.10.1755; Fr. Beijerinck and M.G. de Boer, *Het dagboek van Jacob Bicker Raije 1732–1772* (Amsterdam, n.d.), pp. 237, 244 and 246. For Verley: GAA, 5061, series number 170 (schoutenrol 1734), and *DAS* III, no. 6869.

In Amsterdam this pattern did not extend much further than father and son, as we saw in the examples of Schouten and Wiebe. Perhaps because it was a large immigrant city, family connections among officers in Amsterdam were less prevalent than they were, for instance, in Delfshaven or Enkhuizen, or perhaps there was just little tradition of real seafaring families.

Almost all of the Amsterdam commanders were married and had more than one child. Twins were born to Jacob Onkruid in 1700. If a wife died there was the possibility of marrying for a second time. The improved financial status of a commander meant that he had to pay at a higher rate for a marriage licence the second time. Gerrit van Lanschot was divorced, but it seems that the terms of the divorce were unclear. When he died in Persian waters in 1715, the proceeds from the sale of his goods and chattels and his salary, to the value of $f.$ 12,000, went to the orphanage since the authorities in Batavia were unsure about what rights his 'separated housewife' still had. Two commanders had their wives with them in the East. In 1750, David van Elteren left for Batavia with his wife and adopted daughter of eighteen. The daughter went instead of a servant. When Jurriaan Molensteen realized that his appointment as Superintendent of the Shipyard in Colombo meant that he would be spending a long period in Asia, he had his wife join him there. They returned to Amsterdam together in 1775.[25]

The commanders in Amsterdam never became excessively wealthy, nor were they accepted into the highest social classes. Van Neercassel's granddaughter is the only example of such a rise in status. The commanders did not own country estates, with the exception of Jan de With in far-off Friesland. In a class-conscious era, only one-fifth of the couples marrying in Amsterdam were able to pay for a marriage licence at the highest rate. Half of them paid for the fourth- or lowest-class licence. No commander purchased a first-class marriage licence. Often commanders bought third- or fourth-class licences. Simon Hart, the Amsterdam archivist who has done so much to unlock the quantitative data about baptismal, marriage and burial registers, has shown that nearly a quarter of those being buried paid for a burial licence at the highest rate. Among them were only a very few (retired) commanders. They were far more likely to have paid at the second-class rate.[26]

Sometimes commanders were able to earn a great deal of money in the East, as did Van Neercassel. An Amsterdam commander was often appointed to the lucrative position of Commander of the Roads and Superintendent of the Shipyard in Batavia. Besides Van Neercassel and Verleng, this position was held by Hendrik Opmeer from 1742 to 1745. As time passed, it also became more usual for commanders and ship's officers to participate in private trade. The money

---

[25] For Van Lanschot: Amsterdam, GAA, Weeskamer 5037, fol. 207 (15.3.1718); Coolhaas, *Generale Missiven* VII, p. 313. For Van Elteren Den Haag: NA, VOC 126, 25.8.1750; for Molensteen: The Hague, NA, VOC 6494, 1.

[26] S. Hart, *Geschrift en getal*, pp. 188–9.

they earned was transferred by bills of exchange.[27] Although most of the bills of exchange in the first half of the century were made out to the commander or to family members, in the second half the number of bills addressed to merchants at home in the Republic increased considerably. It reached a peak in the period around 1770. The average amount a commander transferred doubled from approximately ƒ. 10,000 in 1710/1720 to an average of ƒ. 20,000 after 1770.[28] There can be no doubt that commanders in the latter period were able to earn more in the East than their predecessors had earned. However, in Amsterdam this rise in fortune was not marked by any conspicuous social advancement. Perhaps this was explicable in a city in which only the existing upper class continually grew richer.

Jan de Marre: Theatre Director and Playwright

There are some concrete data about at least two commanders and about what they did after their retirement: Jan de Marre and Jan de Boer. The former launched into an entirely different life after he came back from his only return voyage as commander of the ship the *Heesburg*. He had entered Company service as a thirteen-year-old boy in 1709. Four years later he had already risen to the rank of quartermaster and finally, in 1728 at the age of thirty-two, he was appointed commander. However, De Marre's whole life was not concentrated on the sea. He had other interests. On his maiden voyage out in 1728, he had already begun on a poetic epic, *Batavia, begrepen in zes boeken* (Batavia, understood in six books), which was eventually published in 1740. After he left the Company, he made friends with playwrights and poets in Amsterdam and with people in Amsterdam theatrical circles. It was not long before he was appointed manager of a theatre, a position which was described in the tax register of 1742 as bookkeeper of the theatre. When he took over its management, the reputation of the theatre was fairly mediocre. In collaboration with his fellow managers, De Marre breathed new life into it. For far too long its repertory had consisted of translated French pieces and no new original plays had been performed. Under his management, the Amsterdam elite once more put a visit to the theatre on its agenda. The quality of the actors was high. De Marre retained his connection with the theatre until his death in 1763.[29]

Jan de Marre also wrote plays. Sometimes repeat performances drew full houses, and the plays were reprinted in various subsequent editions. In 1736, his drama *Jacoba van Beieren: gravin van Holland en Zeeland. Treurspel* (Jacoba

---

[27] This will be discussed in more detail in Chapter 13.
[28] Taken from Wolvers, 'Het wisselverkeer', pp. 28, 30 and 40.
[29] J.A. Worp, *Geschiedenis van den Amsterdamschen Schouwburg 1496–1772 (met aanvulling tot 1872)* (Amsterdam, 1920), ch. XXIX; Frijhoff and Prak, *Geschiedenis van Amsterdam* II 2, pp. 388–91.

13. Jan de Marre (1696–1763). Jan de Marre was a very versatile man. He began to sail with the Company at a very young age and finished his career at sea as a commander in 1732. Later he became director of the Amsterdam theatre and wrote various poetical and theatrical works. From 1745 he led a double life because he was also examiner in seamanship for the Amsterdam Chamber. In this capacity, he launched a number of innovations. Anonymous engraving from a portrait by J.M. Quinkhard, to which a eulogy by Lucas Pater has been appended.

of Bavaria: Countess of Holland and Zealand. Tragedy) was performed. In an innovative manner which was imitated for a long time afterwards, this piece dealt with the fourth and forbidden marriage between Jacoba and Frank van Borselen in the fifteenth century. The retired sailor depicted the countess as a passionate, loving woman. One high point in the theatre was the celebration of its centenary on 7 January 1738. The play was preceded by an allegorical masque, written by De Marre. This masque lauded the stage as Apollo's true training school. Music by Antonio Vivaldi, especially composed for the occasion, was played in the interval. *Batavia*, written in 1740, was a rhymed history of the VOC, which sounded a few critical notes. The Company had ensured that the Javanese, 'the industrious farmer', enjoyed 'a sweet peace' thanks to the cultivation of coffee, De Marre claimed in his lines. This work was followed by various verses and farces. His somewhat bigger work composed in 1746 was a description of the Cape Colony.[30]

Jan de Marre in His Role as Examiner

Another position possibly kept De Marre from more poetic and theatrical works. It was a job which brought him back to the world of shipping and navigation. In 1745, the Amsterdam Chamber appointed him to be the examiner in seamanship for the examinations set for ship's officers. De Marre would not have accepted the job just for the money. According to the tax register of 1742, he enjoyed an annual income of *f.* 1,200 and the rent of his house on the Keizersgracht was set at *f.* 425. The Chamber paid not much more than *f.* 300. This multi-talented retired commander now threw himself enthusiastically into sea charts and navigational instruments. He apparently still had time for this alongside his work at the theatre. He immediately made a number of suggestions for all manner of changes and improvements, often with and at the initiative of his colleague examiner, the mathematician Martinus Martens. They were convinced that the 1731 list of the charts and navigational instruments on board VOC ships needed to be revised. It resulted in improvements in the Jacob's staff, the bearing and the steering compasses, the list of charts and books, and the introduction of the octant and the azimuth compass. In previous years, De Marre had brushed up his own mathematical knowledge by attending Martens' lectures at the *Athenaeum Illustre*, the forerunner of the University of Amsterdam. The revised list was published in 1748.

De Marre's workplace in the *Oost-Indisch Huis* was in what was known as the navigation officer's room. It was crammed with sea charts. He also studied this material thoroughly, which led to the first published atlas of charts and sailing

---

[30] O. van Marion, 'Vechtlust of verliefdheid? Dichterlijke verbeeldingen van Jacoba van Beieren', *Tydkrifvir Nederlands en Afrikaans* 5, no. 2 (1998); see also www.antenna.nl/wvi/nl/nest/marre.html. C.A. Davids drew my attention to this.

instructions for the waters within the chartered territory of the Company in the East. In 1753 it became the sixth publication in the originally five-volume atlas series the *Zeefakkel* (The Sea Torch), initially compiled by Johannes van Keulen in 1681. De Marre personally supervised the compilation of the charts. Up to this point commanders and ship's officers had only had manuscript charts of the area.[31] De Marre, who was an intensely practical man, had persuaded the directors of the value of printing the charts by pointing out that the many inaccuracies through compass points in the old charts, which might also have crept in when they were being copied, hindered rather than helped navigation.[32] This multi-faceted man – retired commander, theatre director and examiner – died in 1763. His fellow-examiner Martens had predeceased him by only a few months.

Once again the Amsterdam directors succeeded in finding a couple of examiners of a high standard. They were the mathematician Pybo Steenstra and retired commander Jan Gerritsz de Boer from Buiksloot, then a village outside Amsterdam. The 1743 division of the examinations into one practical, on seamanship, and one theoretical, on navigation, had proved a success. The goal of innovation in navigation had been well and truly met. In the examinations and the sailing orders, both aspects, theory and practice, were assigned equal importance.

De Boer certainly fulfilled expectations. He was a man of wide experience. He had sailed twice to China as a commander. On his second and last voyage in 1746–1747, after departing from Canton there were so many dead and ailing on both his own ship and one of the Hoorn Chamber that the two commanders and their officers decided to cast one ship adrift and leave her fate to the waves. The survivors were to be assembled on one ship. Suddenly, five British men-of-war hove into view and they rendered 'substantial and essential service with the transfer of people and others' so that, 'in part owing the Divine Providence' people were saved. After this, De Boer never went to sea again.[33]

Nevertheless, the Company and De Boer did not lose sight of one another. In 1751, the directors had already taken him into service again as loading supervisor or wharfinger. This position meant that De Boer could fill in for the Superintendent of the Shipyard when necessary. If a director or the Superintendent was absent when ships sailed from or returned to the Texel Roads, the loading supervisor was in charge. In the shipyard in Amsterdam, in collaboration with the Superintendent, he drew up stowage plans for the goods on the ships. De

---

[31] The significance of this publication will be discussed in more detail in Chapter 16.
[32] Oldewelt, *Kohier* II, p. 342, no. 5676; Davids, *Zeewezen en wetenschap*, pp. 173–5, 197–9, 207, 225 and 350–2; Gawronski, *De Equipagie*, pp. 67–70, with a reproduction of De Marre's portrait by Quinkhart; W.F.J. Mörzer Bruyns, *Schip recht door zee. De octant in de Republiek in de achttiende eeuw* (Amsterdam, 2003), pp. 53 and 92; G. Schilder and W.F.J. Mörzer Bruyns, 'Navigatie', in *Maritieme Geschiedenis der Nederlanden* III (Bussum, 1977), pp. 191–225, see pp. 200, 202 and 218.
[33] The Hague, NA, VOC 222, 5.12.1747, and 225, 1.4.1748.

Boer held this position until he was appointed examiner in 1764. This appointment took place a year and a half after De Marre's death. De Boer also launched a number of initiatives. Working in co-operation with Steenstra he renewed the sailing directions for the route to Asia. The use of the variation of the compass in order to determine longitude was once again raised. In putting this forward he gathered evidence from reading through thirty-four ship's logs dating from 1764–1765 and all manner of reports. The improved sailing instructions were introduced in 1768.

De Boer also advised the directors about potential economies that could be made in the fitting out of ships, and about better observation and reception of the returning fleet by warships. In 1769 he published a ninety-five-page book about practical seamanship entitled *Zeemans oefening over de groote zeevaart, alsmede een nauwkeurige beschrijving van het drijfanker and deszelfs gebruik* (Exercise for sailors about sailing on the high seas, as well as a description of the driving anchor and its use). In this book De Boer revealed his enormous knowledge and experience. Among the matters he discussed was how it was best to sail before the wind in a storm with few or no sails, which was known as scudding, and advice for commanders on anchoring.[34] De Boer died in 1778. One of his successors as examiner in 1794 was Arie Kikkert from Texel, an individual whose career is discussed in the next chapter.

The Last Commanders of the Amsterdam Chamber

The appointment of a man from Texel, even one who had moved to Buiksloot, as examiner for the Amsterdam ship's officers was an indication that there had been some changes in the group of commanders. Such an appointment would have been impossible in earlier times. As has been pointed out, in the first half of the eighteenth century, men who were Amsterdam born and bred were given the majority of the appointments as commanders. There had already been a slight drop by the middle of the century. This situation meant that men from other places in the Republic were given more chances, and these opportunities quickly spread to foreigners. As a large shipping business, the Company constantly needed trained men, for whom it set minimum qualifications tested by examination. For people from outside – ship's officers and commanders from the merchant navy and the whaling fleet – it was always difficult to obtain similar positions with the VOC. Jochem Outjes was an exception, but he failed to measure up to Company standards. In the 1740s, the VOC accepted naval officers to overcome a temporary shortage, but there were not very many of them. Forty years later, there was such a shortage of people of its own mould that the *Heren Zeventien* were forced

---

[34] The Hague, NA, VOC 134, 27.3.1771 and 31.3.1773, 267, 3.2.1755, and 308, 8.5.1764; Davids, *Zeewezen en wetenschap*, pp. 192–3 and 350–2; Bonke, 'De Verenigde Oost-Indische Compagnie', pp. 19–20; Gawronski, *De Equipagie*, p. 104.

14. Dirk Muller (1758–1834). Dirk Muller was born in Amsterdam, where his father was employed in the Company shipyard. He passed through the ranks of the ship's officers and was appointed commander in 1788 (captain). After his return in 1791, he settled on a modest country estate in the Achterhoek and devoted himself to agricultural pursuits. This 1793 portrait, in which Muller is shown in uniform with two globes and a partially unrolled chart, is the work of an unknown artist.

to accept officers from the merchant navy, especially from the moribund whaling fleet, and naval officers were also appointed again. In order to make a position with the Company more attractive, the old titles of commander and mates were discarded in favour of captain and lieutenants. Foreigners now also had more opportunities than they had ever had before. The Company could no longer cling to its old criterion that candidates had to climb up through its ranks to its financially extremely attractive commands.

A random sample of seventeen of the fifty-seven commanders who sailed for the Amsterdam Chamber between 1790 and 1794 reveals these enormous changes.[35] Not even one-quarter of them were from Amsterdam. The rest came from outside the city. More than 40 per cent were foreigners, natives of such familiar places as Karlskrona, Stralsund or Bergen in Scandinavia. Of this group, some had made their careers with the Company while the rest had begun either

---

[35] Counts in *DAS* II, nos. 4657–787 (departures from Amsterdam); Moree, 'Met vriend die God geleide', pp. 155–235; Van Eyck van Heslinga, *Van Compagnie naar koopvaardij*, see under J. Sem and D. Smith.

with the merchant navy or the whaling fleet. Three were from the Navy and they had already visited the East with a squadron from the fleet. It was usual practice for Lutherans to be appointed, but by the end of the eighteenth century no one seemed to be bothered by the promotion to commander of a practising Roman Catholic like Anthonius Franciscus Steffers from Zwolle. In 1792, while he was still in the East, he was also appointed a captain in the Admiralty of Friesland. The names of foreigners were no longer changed into Dutch equivalents. For instance, in the administration, Clemens and Cederborg kept their original Christian names Johann Carl and Swerus Magnus.

Fortunately, even in this final phase of the life of the VOC there were still Amsterdam men who commanded ships for their own Chamber. One of them was Dirk Muller whose father worked in the shipyard. Beginning as a young lad, Muller worked his way up through the usual ranks and was appointed commander in 1788. After his return at the end of 1791, he stopped sailing when he was barely thirty-three years old. In total he had earned more than *f.* 26,000 and the income altered his life completely. First he had his portrait painted, dressed in uniform with two globes and a half-unrolled sea chart next to him on a table. Then he married his second cousin from the Achterhoek in the province of Guelders and farmed his own estate there. He had six children and all of his three sons joined the Navy. At the end of his life, he still took an interest in the tactics of sea battles. He died on his estate in 1834.[36]

Another Amsterdam man was Gerrit Scheler. He was the last but one commander to set sail for Asia from Amsterdam on board a ship of the Hoorn Chamber, on 22 December 1794. His fatal voyage is described in Chapter 2 on Hoorn.[37] In the city of Amsterdam today, the *Oost-Indisch Huis* and a few buildings on Oostenburg are reminders of the Company. In 1822, the *Zeemagazijn*, the large storehouse on the water, collapsed when it was used to store grain instead of lighter Asian wares. Recently, archaeological research has revealed how solid the slipways were.[38]

---

[36] R.B. Prud'homme van Reine, 'Dirk Muller: portret van een VOC-kapitein', *Zeemagazijn* 28, no. 4 (2002), p. 4.
[37] See Chapter 2.
[38] Overvoorde and De Roo de la Faille, *De gebouwen*, pp. 44–5; J. Gawronski, 'Vals plat en de VOC. Opgravingen op Oostenburg, Amsterdam', in Akveld *et al.*, *In het kielzog*, pp. 163–73.

7

Commanders from Outside the Six Chamber Towns

Invariably there were some commanders without any close links with the town or city in which their Chamber had its headquarters. They had not been born there and they continued to live in their place of birth. This situation was by no means a coincidence in towns such as Flushing, Dordrecht, Leiden or Gouda, for fellow townsmen held appointments as directors on the boards of Chambers and such men were not indifferent to the interests of fellow citizens. Nevertheless, apart from such instances there were also commanders from other parts of the Dutch Republic, from Brielle in Holland to Harlingen in Friesland and the city of Groningen. One commander might choose to move to the town in which his employer was located while another preferred not to uproot himself. In the case of Jakob Rijzik of the Zealand Chamber, he opted to return to Brielle with his wife after the end of his maritime career in 1773. In the random sample of geographical origins, a few regions stand out as sources of commanders, but mostly only during a specific period. Examples were the Meuse towns of Vlaardingen and Maassluis, the coastal village of Katwijk-aan-Zee (Katwijk on Sea) and the island of Texel. At no time was there ever a set pattern of movement from any of these regions to any one particular Chamber.

Vlaardingen and Maassluis

During the eighteenth century, Vlaardingen and Maassluis were the most important fishing communities in the Republic. For quite a long period of time they were relatively prosperous, and had approximately 5,000 and 4,000 inhabitants respectively. The ship owners in both places managed to keep their boats at sea for the majority of the year by practising other forms of fishery alongside their principal one. The herring catch prevailed in Vlaardingen; in Maassluis the cod catch was more important; but in each town the other sort of fishery was pursued as an alternative. The first half of the century was marked by strong growth in both towns. In 1741 Maassluis had 1,000 fishermen. In the years around 1750, there were local complaints about a shortage of men for the herring busses and the hookers used for the cod fishery.[1]

During this same period of economic growth various men from Vlaardingen and Maassluis are to be found in the Company records as first mates and commanders. Then their participation ebbed away again. In Maassluis, the reason for the lack of enthusiasm for serving with the Company was probably that there was plenty of work in the then still flourishing and less risky fishing industry. For the inhabitants of both these Meuse towns, voyages to the East were certainly not without risk. The eight men from Maassluis in the random sample who served as first mates and commanders all died overseas, one after the other between 1718 and 1751.[2] Two years after his death, the widow of Kornelis van der Velde was extremely pleased to receive a bill of exchange for *f.* 11,498 for her family. This was a huge amount since at the time a widow of an Amsterdam guild member received *f.* 3 per week. The heirs of Abraham van het Hart, who had sailed for the Zealand Chamber, also received his business profits which were transferred from Batavia. The bill of exchange went to the Rotterdam Chamber where the ferryman (*marktschipper*) from Maassluis – a man who ferried people and goods over the river or between places on the river, usually on market day – picked up the money for the family.[3]

Around the same time, five men from Vlaardingen were also employed as commanders, all of them in the service of the Amsterdam Chamber. The brothers Kornelis and Maarten de Breems did not survive their service at sea and died abroad, in 1738 and 1747 respectively. Their father had been skipper of a herring bus. The other three commanders were able to serve out their time and retire from the sea. Later, still sound of mind and body, they assumed prominent positions in Vlaardingen, something which they probably would never have achieved in Amsterdam.

The parents of Frank Verzijde were poor and illiterate. Possibly through the intervention of an uncle in Maassluis who was a commander with the Company, Verzijde found himself on board an East Indiaman. He became a commander in 1715, when he was thirty-two. He retired in 1722 after his second voyage. He had earned enough to purchase real estate in Vlaardingen as well as shares in ships. Verzijde built up good contacts in the herring world. In 1723 he became the ship's husband of three busses and had a share in the old tannery, where

---

[1] L.M. Akveld, 'Noordzeevisserij', *Maritieme Geschiedenis der Nederlanden* III (Bussum, 1977), pp. 318–44, see pp. 320–1 and 329–30; H.A.H. Kranenburg, *De zeevisscherij van Holland in den tijd der Republiek* (Amsterdam, 1946), p. 46.

[2] These were: Jan de Graaf (?–1730), Abraham van der Hart (1700–1737), Hendrik van Oudheusden (?–1751), Gilles Oudemans (1692–1742), Kornelis van der Velde (1706–1742), Jakob Verzijde (?–1718) and First Mates Hendrik Sneeuwbal (1712–1747) and Kornelis Sneeuwbal (1714–1745).

[3] Bos, '*Uyt liefde tot malcander*', p. 75; The Hague, NA, Not. Arch. Maassluis 5546, aktes 20.1.1739.

the nets were tanned to make them more durable. Two years later Verzijde was chosen to be a member of the town council which was composed of twenty of the most prominent citizens of Vlaardingen. This position, which was for life, meant that he would be eligible to become a burgomaster, alderman, treasurer and administrator responsible for the orphans of the town. Verzijde held all these positions with the exception of burgomaster. He married a woman from the nearby village of Schipluiden in 1726. It would seem from his application for what was known as a 'Turkish passport', which he requested in 1731 to protect his ship against capture by Barbary privateers from North Africa, that he also employed his fishing boats for trade. Verzijde died in 1736 and the highest rate for a burial licence was paid for his funeral in the Great Church.

Jakob Goosen Hoogstad began his Company career in the same way. As a sixteen-year-old youth in 1718 he sailed with his fellow-townsman Frank Verzijde. Both his father and grandfather had been skippers on herring busses. Hoogstad's rise up the social ladder was therefore not as spectacular as Verzijde's. Nevertheless, his appointment as first mate in 1729 was quite an achievement. He married the daughter of one of the most prominent men in Vlaardingen, Barend de Wit, who had been on the town council since 1703 and had been burgomaster several times. Naturally he was also an owner of herring boats. A year after the marriage Hoogstad was appointed commander. It was in this capacity that he set sail on his third voyage in February 1736, but this ended when his ship and another of the Company ships ran aground on the Goodwin Sands off Dover. The ship's officers were blamed for the stranding of the ships. Hoogstad and the others were suspended and then dismissed. In some ways this was not as great a disaster as it might have been for Hoogstad. His father-in-law had died shortly before the mishap and the dismissed commander was free to take over the ship-owning and business ventures of his family by marriage. He was to remain active as a ship's husband for forty years. Moreover, in 1738, the commanders and ship's officers who had been involved in the disaster of 1736 were completely exonerated. Nevertheless, Hoogstad did not return to the Company. Instead, he considerably expanded his economic activities in Vlaardingen. In 1756 he became a member of the town council and eventually he was to be burgomaster five times. He died in 1766. One of his two sons was already the owner of herring boats. The other became a Protestant minister.

Verzijde and Hoogstad are examples of men who achieved social status in their own community through their careers with the Company and gathered the financial means to be able to invest in the local economy. They benefited enormously from the time they spent at sea. The fifth man from Vlaardingen who was appointed commander was just as successful. Huibert van der Linde resigned from the Company in 1750 after just one voyage as commander. At the end of 1748 he had been the first to bring the news to Batavia of the birth of a new Prince of Orange on 8 March, the later Stadtholder Willem V. This was accompanied by news of the armistice in the War of the Austrian Succession. As a reward, the government in Batavia promoted him. However, on his return home the *Heren Zeventien* refused to release goods he had not been authorized to sell. Later Van der Linde became a merchant and finally in 1777 Bailiff of the town of Breukelen (Brooklyn) in the province of Utrecht.[4]

Katwijk-aan-Zee

The men and boys who left the relatively closed communities of Vlaardingen and Maassluis were rather unusual. They had not done what by far and away the majority of their fellow townsmen had done which was to go into fishing. They plunged into what was relatively unknown, voyages to Asia. For men from Katwijk this took exceptional courage and ambition. Their village was a small settlement of approximately 3,000 people in the dunes, and it was only possible to reach the closest town, Leiden, on foot or by cart. The main industry was coastal fishing using flat-bottomed boats which could be hauled up onto the beach. Incomes were meagre and there was not even a harbour. During the eighteenth century, a few men from Katwijk regularly went to Rotterdam or Amsterdam to look for work in the merchant navy. Dirk Dirksz Varkevisser was just such a man. He exchanged Katwijk for Rotterdam, where he married in 1749, and worked his way up to be a master on the European routes, and finally became a ship owner.[5] Another six Katwijk men are known to have reached the rank of commander with the Company. On their voyages, they usually had one or more young men from their village on board with them. After a safe end to their sailing careers, they went back to Katwijk to their families, where they mostly became prominent members of the community, taking their place alongside a few local ship owners and merchants. Their preferred place of residence was on the much sought-after Voorstraat near the sea.

Dirk Reinsz Varkevisser rose through all the ranks in the Rotterdam Chamber. In 1767, when he was fourteen, he became a ship's boy and by 1770 he was a sailor, two years later a gunner and in 1775 a third mate. He was re-appointed to the rank in 1777 and finally he was made a commander in 1783. He died in this highest rank, however, just shortly after his departure on his maiden voyage. His cousin Dirk, the son of the previously mentioned Dirk Dirksz Varkevisser, was also employed by the Company and he disembarked in Cape Town and settled there. A few decades earlier, Bastiaan Verdoes had enjoyed a longer career as a commander. He died in the East in 1757 during his fifth voyage in charge of a Company ship. His seventeen-year-old son was then on board with him

---

[4] P. Moree, 'Jacob Hoogstad (1702–1776). Een Vlaardinger in dienst van de Verenigde Oostindische Compagnie', *Historisch Jaarboek Vlaardingen* (1988), pp. 77–87; P. Moree, 'Reders en vroedschapsleden in Vlaardingen in het jaar 1750', *Netwerk, Jaarboek Visserijmuseum* (2000), pp. 21–29. See also Chapter 14. For Van der Linde, see The Hague, NA, VOC 222, 27.3.1751.

[5] Hoynck van Papendrecht, *Gedenkboek*, see index under Varkevisser and Dorrepaal.

as a cadet, but his son behaved in such a brutish way that he fomented serious tension among the ship's officers. Verdoes was a professional but also a very difficult man who drank too much.[6]

Maarten Hakker was one of the happy few who were able to end their life at home on dry land. His brother-in-law and fellow commander, Matthijs Fierman, was not so lucky. His ship went down with all hands in the Indian Ocean when she was bound for the Cape in the hurricane season of 1770. This Katwijk man had been in peril of his life once before in the same area, in 1754. His ship was bound for the Cape when she ran into a severe gale and was badly damaged. The drinking water had been exhausted and, as the man in charge of the ship's boat, Fierman's task had been to look for fresh water in a bay along the African coast. Once ashore high seas prevented him and the boat's crew from returning to the ship. With two other men he made the journey to False Bay east of the Cape on foot, where he was finally able to board his ship again. The journey on foot lasted from 13 May to 30 July. Hottentots and the widely dispersed Boer population had supplied them with food. They had made the very last stage of the journey by ox cart. After Fierman's drowning in 1770, his widow and two of his five surviving children received a large sum of money from Batavia.

Hakker gave up the sea in 1774. He had made four voyages as commander and had probably visited the Tropics nine or ten times, always in the employ of the Rotterdam Chamber. He could call himself a rich man and was well set up. In 1762, when he was second mate, he had married, paying at the lowest rate for a marriage licence, but when he died his heirs paid the highest required fee for his burial licence, *f.* 30. Hakker had managed his overseas trade very well. Between 1771 and 1774 sums which reached a total of almost *f.* 30,000 were transferred to Amsterdam, either to him personally or to his business associates. After his death, his widow received another *f.* 4,500.

Hakker was forty-eight when he died in July 1777. Tragically his last child was born posthumously four months later. His wife was then forty-one. She remarried a year later, her new husband being a surgeon from The Hague. Both paid the highest fee for the marriage licence.[7] Hakker had ensured that his wife was a wealthy woman. His good fortune was not the fate of his fellow villagers who died young or in low ranks in the service of the Company. The great uncertainty about whether or not they would ever return meant that, at the outset of a

---

[6] He will be referred to again in Chapters 13 and 15. Van Gelder, *Naporra's omweg*, pp. 294–7, 360–1 and 447.

[7] Some of the data about the commanders has been taken from J.P. van Brakel, 'Katwijkse koopvaardijkapiteins', *Rijnland. Tijdschrift voor sociale geografie en streekgeschiedenis van Leiden en omstreken* VI (1969), vol. 23–4, 84 1–859, nos. 23, 35, 42, 87 and 107, not no. 53. These cover Matthijs Fierman (1726–1770), Maarten Hakker (1729–1777), Kornelis Philipsz Hoek (1748–1784), Dirk Kornelisz Plokker (1742–? abroad), Dirk Reinsz Varkevisser (1753–1783) and Bastiaan Verdoes (1702–1757). For Hakker, see also: The Hague, NA, Archief Katwijk, Not. Arch. 5037, akte 74, 5039, akte 2 and 10, and 5041, akte 15 and 24.

voyage, men from the same place gave each other notarial deeds authorizing one of their counterparts to take charge of their affairs should they die. This power-of-attorney made it much easier for heirs to demand personal property from the VOC administration. In running this administration, it was a great help if their patronymic was consistently used alongside their own first name. In such small communities as Katwijk and Texel, this was essential to be able to distinguish among members of the various extended families, of which Varkevisser is just one example. It helped to prevent confusion.

Texel

On the island of Texel, the sea provided work for almost half of the male working population. In 1742, 545 out of a total of 1,202 worked as pilots, skippers of flat-bottomed coastal boats, fishermen, or in the merchant navy, the whaling fleet, the Navy or the VOC.[8] In the second half of the century, the number of families who were involved in shipping to the East is striking. Earlier in the century, there were examples of such family involvement in Delfshaven, Rotterdam, Hoorn and Enkhuizen, but the trend seems to have developed later on in Texel. In 1778, De Ruyter from Den Burg sailed on a ship of the Hoorn Chamber as second mate with two of his sons, aged sixteen and eleven, on the same vessel. However, the family most closely linked to the Company was the Kikkerts. There were many branches of this family and various Kikkerts became commanders. They were also inhabitants of Den Burg, the biggest village on the island. Some of them were well-to-do. Albert Albertsz was certainly not the first in the family to sail for the Company but he was the first Kikkert to be appointed commander, in 1766. He died in Batavia in 1771 during his second voyage. Later his widow sorrowfully had it recorded that, because he had died so far away, she could not follow the custom of 'placing the key of the doors of the house on the coffin of her husband and walking in front of the bier'. Lambert Kikkert, himself a seaman and not without substance, was able to boast that not only his great-nephew but also his own three sons, Albert, Arie and Harmanus, had risen to the rank of commander. When he died in November 1783, his eldest son had been buried a year earlier in Huisduinen near Den Helder, and Arie and Harmanus were at sea. Harmanus was still a first mate and was to become a commander in 1785. Research carried out by P. Moree has allowed an extraordinary glimpse of Harmanus' domestic life. In the National Archive in Kew (London), Moree discovered nineteen letters from Harmanus' wife, Aagje Luytsen, to her husband, written in the years 1776–1780. During the Fourth Anglo-Dutch War, in 1781 British warships captured five Company ships in

---

[8] Bonke, 'De VOC', in Roeper and Vonk-Uitgeest, *Texel en de VOC*, p. 39.

15. The *Wezenputten* on Texel. The inexhaustible Wezen wells (until c.1781 there was only one), in the vicinity of Oudeschild, provided the inhabitants of Texel and many outward-bound ships with drinking water. The water which had been pumped up was conveyed via a wooden conduit into open barrels on a flat (*praam*), moored in the Schilsloot. This flat carried the barrels to the sea dike, over which they were hauled using a windlass. Ship's boats then carried them to the ships in the Koopvaarders (Merchantmen) Roads. In the eighteenth century these activities attracted the interest of such visitors as the artist P. van Cuyck in 1759 when he made a drawing of the scene. F. de Roode made an engraving from this drawing.

Saldanha Bay north of Cape Town and confiscated all of Harmanus' personal possessions, including the letters.

Aagje married very young in 1776. She was twenty. Scarcely had she been married before she became pregnant. By the time the baby was born, Second Mate Harmanus was far away on the high seas. The letters cover a period of five years, in which the wife of the second mate had to scrimp and save to make ends meet. Aagje could never be certain if her husband was dead or alive and still earning a wage. His employer, the Amsterdam Chamber, was dilatory and negligent about transmitting the quarterly advances. She refused to ask for help from either her parents or her parents-in-law, even though they were all regular visitors to her small house. Should her husband die, she wrote, 'I have absolutely no idea what I shall do for money', certainly not with small children at home. Aagje had been determined to marry a sailor but once she had married she realized 'what a sad and lonely life' she had. Friction with her sisters-in-law was sometimes inevitable. When the shed behind the house was broken into, she felt very frightened. Friends from her former life told her: 'We go to all the fairs [kermesses] and parties … we don't plan to marry for a long while yet.' In those days a married woman was not supposed to seek entertainment outside her own home without her husband. The one time she did this, she explained to Harmanus in great detail why she had done it. In fact, Aagje was more or less cloistered at home. She clung to her unconditional love for Harmanus and longed passionately for his physical presence. For a man such as Russeplukker in Enkhuizen she would never have been a type like Bregje Schaap. Kikkert's portrait, painted when they married, had pride of place in the parlour. Her small son Lammert gave her a great deal of pleasure. Unlike his little brother Klaas, whom Harmanus never knew, he survived the smallpox epidemic in Den Burg. Since her own youth Aagje's own skin had been slightly pock-marked. In her house, Eastern objects, especially 'beautiful porcelain', made an immediate impression. Aagje regularly prompted Harmanus to bring her a 'lovely chintz skirt', while Lammert was hoping for 'a monkey in a skirt'. A little later, full-time household help lightened her load. In the small community of Den Burg, everything and everyone was at no more than a stone's throw away. Little escaped neighbours and fellow villagers. When Harmanus had to tarry longer than expected in Amsterdam where he was making preparations for a voyage, Aagje went to visit him, travelling with the skipper of a flat-bottomed boat. They lodged in an inn near the harbour.

In later years, life improved for Aagje. Fortune finally smiled on her, and her loneliness and straitened circumstances came to an end. It was not long before Harmanus could spend more time at home, and in 1785 he was appointed a commander. He made only one voyage in that rank because he retired from the sea in 1787. This was a step not many Texel men had the opportunity to take. A survey of the 175 men from Texel who had worked for the Company during the eighteenth century reveals that 100 of them perished overseas and three deserted there. In short, 60 per cent of the total never made it home to live out their lives. Moreover, on his final voyage Harmanus had been involved in some profitable business dealings. Between 1786 and 1789, five bills of exchange worth ƒ. 23,000 were transmitted to him. Earlier he had invested money in the debt obligations of VOC personnel. Now that he was in a position to buy land on Texel and in Den Burg he was counted as a prominent citizen. In 1788, he became a member of the magistrates' bench which had seven members, of whom Den Burg contributed two. This appointment was speedily followed by that of burgomaster and administrator of the orphanage. However, Harmanus was a supporter of the House of Orange and the Batavian Revolution of 1795 cost him his positions. He was only reappointed to the magistrates' bench in 1804. He died in 1806 at the age of fifty-seven. Aagje had predeceased him in 1797.[9]

---

[9] Based on P. Moree, *Kikkertje lief. Brieven van Aagje Luijtsen geschreven aan haar man Harmanus Kikkert, stuurman in dienst van de VOC* (Texel, 2003), *passim*. Of the 175 deceased men from Texel, 119 are mentioned in I. Vonk-Uitgeest, 'Texelse opvarenden in dienst van

The career of Harmanus' elder brother, Arie, both as seaman and later on land, was even more impressive. He crossed the Equator just as many times as his brother, probably eight crossings in all, but he progressed more swiftly through the ranks. Harmanus sailed two times as third and two times as first mate. Arie made three voyages as commander, including a visit to China. He retired from sailing one year after Harmanus, in 1788 when he was forty-two. Between 1781 and 1790 he cashed bills of exchange worth ƒ. 47,500. The income was over and above the usual stipend and perquisites he received in his position as an officer. Unquestionably Arie was a rich and very prominent man, partly as a consequence of his marriage. After the local Patriots' anti-Orange disturbances on Texel in 1789 were under control, another Kikkert loyal to the House of Orange was given a place on the magistrates' bench, and on 3 August of that year, Stadtholder Willem V breakfasted at Arie's house during a visit to Texel.

Arie Kikkert also retained his ties to the Company. Perhaps he had more of the sea in his blood than his brother. In November 1790, the outward-bound VOC ship the *Negotie* was wrecked on the North Sea coast of Texel and scavengers lost no time in finding their way to her. The directors in Amsterdam put Arie in charge of guarding and salvaging the wreck. In this process, 'a machine which could plunge even to great depths under water', an invention of two islanders, was put to use. Arie Kikkert continued to be involved in the salvage operation until 1800.

In 1794 he was appointed examiner in practical seamanship by the Amsterdam Chamber, making him a successor to De Marre and De Boer. So that he could do this work properly, Arie and his family moved to Buiksloot, north of Amsterdam. It was not the changes in the VOC, which began in 1795, but his election as *dijkgraaf*, the official in charge of the board which oversaw drainage and control of local waters, in September 1796, which prompted him to resign from his position as examiner and return to Texel. He won the election by an overwhelming majority, but failed to obtain the approval of the provincial government. The latter was displeased with his earlier emphatic support of the House of Orange. After this, he devoted his time to managing his not inconsiderable property and to new attempts to salvage the *Negotie*.

In 1788 Arie Kikkert had bought a house in Den Burg and pieces of land on various parts of the island. He had also leased the *Eyerlandse Huis* with its postal link to the island of Vlieland. Eyerland was a dune area on the north side of Texel, which in May every year produced several tens of thousands of birds' eggs which the lessee then sold to biscuit manufacturers in Amsterdam. It also had thousands of head of small game and game birds. To manage all this, the

---

de VOC', in Roeper and Vonk-Uitgeest, *Texel en de VOC*, pp. 149–204. The other glimpses from more recent information in 2005.

lessee had to employ staff, whose number could rise to as many as six or seven in the busy month of May.[10]

Arie Kikkert died in 1807 a wealthy man. In a will dated 1804 he declared that he possessed property worth almost *f.* 100,000. When his legacy had to be divided up it became clear how much he really owned. The notary needed 107 pages to describe it all. His real estate consisted of four houses, three of which were rented out. He lived in the fourth with his youngest daughter, his wife having died in 1800. He owned 14 hectares of land which was divided into fifteen plots. On one piece of land there was a sheep stall. Arie had not invested much in maritime businesses. All he possessed was a one-eighth and a one-ninth part of two pilot ships. Two fishing nets in the loft of his house bear silent witness to his lack of active interest. Arie invested almost all his money in domestic debt, namely annuities and obligations, worth a total of *f.* 30,000. It is interesting that the interest rate between 1800 and 1804 fluctuated from 2.5 to 4 per cent. He had only *f.* 3,000 in foreign funds, but considerably more in mortgages and private bonds, a total of *f.* 37,000 and almost all of it debts of dozens of people from Texel. Among these was a loan of *f.* 7,792 to his eldest daughter and son-in-law. In the last years of his life, Arie enjoyed an annual income of *f.* 3,000 a year from interest, leases and rented property. When he died, *f.* 2,050 in cash was found in the house.

In many corners of its interior and in its contents, his large residence betrayed evidence of Arie Kikkert's life at sea with the VOC. A variety of textiles and items of clothing were noted as being East Indian. Costly porcelain was placed in two glass-fronted display cabinets. Fifteen scenes of China hung on the wall of the drawing room. In the front room, the retired commander kept his ship's papers, spyglass, telescope, 'an octant in its case', and a dagger with a copper sheath. He still had an old compass and a barometer hanging on the wall. In the office there was a painting 'depicting the whole family'. Behind the house there were a shed and a stable. There was a man to care for a sheep, a ram and two lambs destined for the pot.[11]

Arie and Harmanus are examples of men who prospered in their sailing careers in the service of the Company and they earned plenty of money. They were also given the chance to lead an active life on land. They invested their money safely and did not take many risks. Although these two brothers were certainly not the only Kikkerts to reach the highest maritime ranks in the VOC or indeed the Navy, in the eighteenth century they were the only ones of the nine

---

[10] C. Reij, 'De geslaagde Texelse VOC-schipper: Arie Lambertsz Kikkert, 1746–1807', in Roeper and Vonk-Uitgeest, *Texel en de VOC*, pp. 65–85; V. Roeper, 'De schipbreuk van de Negotie. Een scheepsramp bij Texel in 1790', in *ibid.*, pp. 123–35. See also Davids, *Zeewezen en wetenschap*, pp. 399 and 453.

[11] Rijksarchief in Noord-Holland (National Archive of North Holland), Oud Not. Arch. 185/4914, akte of 13.11.1804, and 4916, akte of 29.5.1807.

men born and bred on Texel to be able to round off their shipboard life with a long and prosperous life back on land.[12]

Two Whaling Fleet Commanders to the East

By the 1770s it was painfully obvious that whaling catches were no longer flourishing and the fishery was in decline. The number of whales caught was dropping steadily. Many whaling ships returned empty-handed. By degrees other forms of employment, especially the burgeoning shipping trade to the West Indies, attracted various whalers to tropical waters. Around 1780 this was still just as a form of winter employment, but later it became their main occupation. Klaas Keuken Junior and Simon Vaartjes were men who had made this transition but, after some years, they applied for posts as commanders with the VOC.

Keuken's father, who bore the same name, had been a successful whaling skipper in his own day. In all, he caught 208 whales, while his son could claim no more than thirty-three and at that number the younger Keuken gave up whaling. Both lived in the small, largely Mennonite community of Oude Sluis in the Zijpe polder near Den Helder. The Keukens were rich. For his marriage in 1773 to a woman of his own age, also a Mennonite, Klaas Junior paid a licence fee of *f.* 30. In 1779, he made his final voyage to the northern regions. He then changed his course westwards. As master of a 206-ton merchantman he picked up sugar and other produce from the Caribbean. This earned him a lot of money. In 1783, he was worth nearly *f.* 20,000. Even though he was a Mennonite, he could not avoid carrying some armament on his ship and, in fact, he transferred to a fully armed East Indiaman in 1789. Without any experience of navigation south of the Equator, he was appointed a commander by the directors of the Amsterdam Chamber, which had had to forgo some of its former more stringent requirements for its commanders. He began by sailing to the Cape on a Company *hoeker*. Then he took command of a merchantman which had been purchased and he sailed her to Batavia and finally on to Ceylon. In 1790 he travelled back home on board a Company East Indiaman. His first full command was in 1791–1793. In June 1795, on his following command, his ship was captured by the British off St Helena and was taken to Plymouth via Ireland to be sold as a prize. Two bills of exchange worth together *f.* 10,500 were waiting for him when he finally arrived home.

There had been great changes on the home front because, a few months before his return in June 1793, his wife had borne another man's child. During his

---

[12] The nine commanders were: Pieter Klaasz Daalder (?–1716), Pieter Jansz Foute (1652–?), Albert Albertsz Kikkert (1738–1771), Albert Lambertsz Kikkert (1737–1782), Arie Lambertsz Kikkert (1746–1807), Daniël Paulusz Kikkert (1749–1793), Harmanus Lambertsz Kikkert (1749–1806), Simon Vaartjes (1753–1795) and Willem Theunisz de Wijn (1746–1787). I thank Mrs I. Vonk-Uitgeest for her data and her advice.

16. Uilke Barends (1757–1810). Uilke Barends from Heerenveen had his portrait painted by Thomas Gaal in Middelburg in 1802, shortly before he sailed to Asia. In 1790 and 1792 he made two voyages for the Zeland Chamber. His wife wrote that the portrait: 'was a speaking likeness'.

subsequent voyage, Keuken transmitted none of his salary to her. His adulterous spouse died in 1801 in Oostzaan, where her son organized her funeral. Shortly afterwards, Keuken remarried in Oude Sluis and in 1802 set sail for Batavia once again. He died on his voyage home in 1808.[13]

Simon Vaartjes from Den Hoorn on Texel was another whaler who was entrusted with the command of his own VOC ship. He came from a hamlet in which many men earned their living from whaling. His father-in-law had been skipper of a whaling vessel. Vaartjes sailed for three seasons as a skipper-captain (1777–1779), but on the third and last voyage he did not catch a single whale. The following spring he signed on a merchantman bound for the West Indies as the first mate. Three years later he was master of the 400-ton *Broeders Lust*, and this ship was chartered by the Enkhuizen Chamber of the Company at the end of 1786. Vaartjes retained his position as master but the Company did not pay his stipend, even though his first mate was taken under the Company wing. The Company's own officers were unhappy with this situation and this created tension. Vaartjes told one of those men who had refused to obey the first mate that he was no longer needed, and added: 'you are free to go and to put your pipe into your mouth and to smoke it'. This voyage was followed by another two on Company ships, of the Delft and Rotterdam Chambers. As in the case of Keuken, the size of the ships increased.

Vaartjes died in Batavia in March 1795. He left his second wife – he had remarried as a widower in 1786 – behind in Den Hoorn with seven children, all of whom were still minors. Initially his widow demanded back the money which Vaartjes had lent various inhabitants of the island, and in 1796 she was granted a licence to work as 'a small retailer in salt and soap, as a seller of flour, butter, coffee and small beer by the jug and a dealer in oil and candles'. A year later she was also permitted to sell strong drink by the glass in her small shop and to sell 'weak brandy'. Life continued to be a battle for her, certainly when Vaartjes' first three children demanded and were granted their portion of the inheritance. Vaartjes' widow also spent some time as a pensioner in an almshouse of the Reformed parish. She died in the house of a son in Harlingen in 1831.[14]

---

[13] The Hague, NA, VOC 297, 20.7.1789; Archief Den Helder, Not. Arch. 1789, aktes 1270 and 1271, and 1814, aktes 113 and 114; P. Dekker, 'De walvisvaarders uit noordelijk Noord-Holland van 1770–1783', *West-Frieslands Oud en Nieuw* 40 (1973), pp. 51–2; P. Dekker, 'De financiële toestand van de bewoners langs het Marsdiep gedurende de tweede helft van de 18e eeuw', *West-Frieslands Oud en Nieuw* 48 (1981), pp. 154–5.

[14] I. Vonk-Uitgeest, 'Schipper in poolijs en tropenzon. Simon Jansz Vaartjes, 1753–1795', in Roeper and Vonk-Uitgeest, *Texel en de VOC*, pp. 95–121; Dekker, 'De walvisvaarders', pp. 51–2.

8

Naval Officers Employed by the Company

Generally speaking, naval officers and the commanders and ship's officers employed by the VOC came from two different social worlds. Some naval officers were middle-class, but in the eighteenth century they were usually scions of the upper class, even the aristocracy. In contrast, the ship's officers in the Company were a group of professionally and socially upwardly mobile men. Among the commanders of the Zeeland Chamber, an appointment as naval captain in the Admiralty of Zeeland betokened greatly sought-after social advancement.[1] Consequently, there was little interest in a move in the opposite direction downward. When the Admiralties were plunged into financial difficulties at the end of the War of the Spanish Succession (1702–1713) many of the warships of the Republic were either mothballed or destroyed. Opportunities for active service shrank and many high-ranking naval officers went abroad to seek appointments in the Russian or Portuguese navies. They scarcely cast a second glance at the VOC as a potential new employer. In 1713 and 1714, only three lieutenants – the lowest rank for officers – of the Admiralty of Amsterdam joined the VOC. The Board of the Admiralty granted them permission to take this step. Another three followed in 1717. They retained their naval rank. After that, only sporadically did any other lieutenant venture to take the same step. No captain ever did.[2] The Company offered these lieutenants posts as second or third mates.

Changes in 1742

In 1742, there was a sudden change in the pattern. The initiative was taken by the VOC. The Navy still had a numerous, rather over-crowded officer corps, which it only rarely employed at sea. Around 1720, the Admiralty of Amsterdam, by far the largest of the five Admiralties, had twenty-two commanders – the naval rank between lieutenant and captain – and thirty-five lieutenants in service. There was little work for them and their opportunities to earn any money were

---

[1] See Chapter 3.
[2] The Hague, NA, AA 1452 (14.12.1713), 1453 (12.1 and 21.8.1714) and 1456 (14.9, 28.10 and 16.11.1717). See also Bruijn, *De admiraliteit van Amsterdam*, ch. IV.

severely restricted. Suddenly, in 1742, the VOC offered them a new opportunity. For some time the Company had been suffering problems with its shipping. Many ships had been lost in recent years, eight ships in the returning fleet on one occasion. As a consequence, doubts were openly cast on the quality of the ships and the professionalism of the ship's officers. The situation was exacerbated because unusually large numbers of commanders and ship's officers had succumbed to malaria in Batavia. The Company was facing a shortage in its officer corps and measures to rectify the situation were inevitable. Nor were these the only problems. Various affairs overseas were not faring well. When they realized how serious the situation was, the *Heren Zeventien* took drastic action. The newly appointed Governor-General, Van Imhoff, played a leading role in the transformation. On the basis of his personal experience in the East, in November 1741, he handed the *Heren Zeventien* a plan for the recovery of the whole of the Company's overseas business including the shipping. In meetings held between 14 March and 3 April 1742, the *Heren Zeventien* took a series of radical decisions.[3]

The sizes of the three classes or rates of the East Indiamen were altered. The Company now decided to adopt other ideas developed by English shipbuilders in the construction of large ships. The Admiralty of Amsterdam had already adopted English practices almost a decade earlier. The Amsterdam Chamber bought the new warship *Edam*, constructed along English lines.[4] Rechristened, significantly, *Herstelder* (*Recovery*), she set sail for Batavia on 27 October 1742. As well as carrying Van Imhoff on board, her commander was Jean Belleveau from Rotterdam.[5] The flagship was accompanied by three other new ships and the ceremony when they left from Texel was more elaborate than usual.

The ships were not the only improvement introduced in 1742. The treatment of ship's officers was also subjected to radical changes. The ranks were made equivalent to those in the Navy, giving them more cachet. Stipends were raised as well. Belleveau was now a captain, no longer a commander, as was Verleng of Amsterdam on the *Eendracht*. Serving under each of them were two lieutenants, not mates. The highest ranks on the East Indiamen were now captain, captain-lieutenant and lieutenant. Not only were the stipends raised but the usual perks and bonuses were also adjusted upward. In the East, the Company ships were not only to be carriers of cargo with an emphasis on speed, as Van Imhoff had advocated, but they were also to radiate military power. A Commander of the Indian Seas held the highest naval authority in the East.

These new measures were specifically introduced by the *Heren Zeventien* and Van Imhoff to arouse interest among naval officers in entering Company service.

---

[3] N.J. Krom, *Gouverneur Generaal Gustaaf Willem van Imhof* (Amsterdam, 1941), pp. 83–97. See also J.E. Heeres, 'De "Consideratiën" van Van Imhoff', *Bijdragen Taal-, Land- en Volkenkunde van Nederlandsch-Indi* 66 (1912), pp. 441–621, see p. 458.
[4] DAS I, 46–7.
[5] See Chapter 5.

'Decent people' were to be there to take the lead in the whole process of the improvement of shipping. 'Men of good family' were better and more skilled at sea than 'the type of person who has usually been employed', Van Imhoff argued. This was because such men regarded it as an honour to do their work well and 'the shame of incompetence' affected them more deeply 'than those types of people who shrug off all admonitions and reproaches as if these did not concern them and did not give a damn about suspension or dismissal'. The differences in social background could not have been expressed more explicitly. Any lack of experience in working in the tropics was naturally compensated for by social status.

Unfortunately for Van Imhoff, no steady stream of naval officers beat their way to the doors of the six Chambers. In one month in 1742, one midshipman, three lieutenants and two Navy commanders asked the Board of the Admiralty in Amsterdam if it would be possible to get permission to take temporary service with the VOC. A few months later they were followed by a fourth lieutenant. Perhaps there were a few more but data from the other Admiralties do not survive.[6] Although the number of naval officers remained remarkably small, something can be said about a few of those who did serve with the VOC.

Van Imhoff's Favourites

Through Van Imhoff's intervention, suddenly a new breed of officer was able to take command of East Indiamen, men who did not have any knowledge or experience of sailing in Asian waters. Dirk Wolter van Nimwegen had always been restless and ambitious. Born into a good family, he became a lieutenant in 1729 at the age of seventeen. He was eager to find action and a few months later asked to be discharged so as to fight in the army of the States-General. His father, who had died young, had been a high-ranking army officer. In answer to his request, the Admiralty speedily appointed him to a ship. By 1736 Van Nimwegen was a commander, a rank for which he had been passed over two years earlier. He regularly put to sea but in 1739 he had to forgo a voyage because the 'banns had been called' for his marriage. He married an older, but prominent widow from Hoorn who was the daughter of an eminent *regent*, Nanning Kaiser. They married with a prenuptial agreement. In 1740, Van Nimwegen set sail to escort a convoy to Curaçao. His wife had asked him to look after some business interests for her there which her first husband had had on the island. When he returned to Hoorn, he came into contact with Van Imhoff. The introduction was made by the Judge Advocate of the Admiralty, Jakob Boreel, who recommended Van Nimwegen and several other officers to the newly appointed Governor-General.

---

6   The Hague, NA, AA 1477 (15.3, 21.3, 27.3, 17.4, 18.4 and 15.5.1742), 1480 (29.9.1746, only the resolutions of four months have been preserved), 1481 (23.3.1747) and 1482 (12.9.1748).

From that moment everything ran smoothly and prosperously for Van Nimwegen. The Admiralty granted him leave to enter the service of the Company. The VOC appointed him 'Commander of the Indian Seas', the newly created position and one which placed him above all other captains and commanders.

Van Imhoff was impressed by Van Nimwegen's qualities. He wrote to Boreel that he found him a good seaman and one he thought must have been 'an excellent subaltern officer'. He gave a comic description of the way in which Van Nimwegen and Belleveau, who was born in France, got on well on board. There were occasional misunderstandings between the two because 'the one spoke bad Dutch and every so often in his expressions the other is rather more impolite than he is aware of himself, a habit which could be forgiven a seaman'.[7] Van Nimwegen did not linger in the East, staying no more than five months. While he was still in Java, he sailed to Bantam in the *Herstelder*, where the Sultan gave him two sealed packets of diamonds for Van Imhoff. He prudently forwarded them back to the Netherlands. In October 1743, Van Nimwegen sailed for home in the *Herstelder*. He was allowed to take as much luggage as a member of the *Hoge Regering*. He also received a bonus of ƒ. 4,000. While he was still in Batavia, in consultation with Verleng and Superintendent of the Shipyard Opmeer, he put forward suggestions for a more practical method of stowing cargo. On his arrival home, he found that his Admiralty had promoted him to captain. For one year, in 1745, he commanded a naval frigate which cruised the North Sea and escorted merchant ships in convoy to the Bay of Biscay. He had scarcely returned home when he asked for and was granted permission to 'sail' for the VOC again. He left at the end of 1746. In the East Van Nimwegen made various intra-Asian voyages and died in Batavia in August 1750. His wife had not made use of the opportunity to travel to the East, a perk which Van Nimwegen had been granted in 1747. Later, she received ƒ. 25,000 as the profit from his private trade. Van Imhoff had been careful to see that Van Nimwegen was given voyages which were profitable to him. The voyage to Bantam in 1743 had been 'a good beginning'. Two more very profitable voyages to China followed after that.

The character of Dirk Wolter van Nimwegen is still somewhat shrouded in mystery, especially because of his contacts with men in the highest circles of power. For instance, in 1746 he corresponded with the future Stadtholder Willem IV, for whom he took a small parcel to Van Imhoff when he left again that year for the 'Nederlands Indiën'. It probably did nothing to damage his position when his nephew Pieter Hendrik, who had worked as supercargo in Mokha and China, suddenly had to return home in 1749 because of complaints and an

---

[7] The Hague, NA, AA 1470 (5.8.1734) and 1474 (2.9.1739); Kooymans, *Onder regenten*, p. 34; Bruijn, *De admiraliteit*, p. 124; H. van Malsen, 'Briefwisseling van den gouverneur-generaal Gustaaf Willem baron Van Imhoff met den advocaat fiscaal der Amsterdamsche admiraliteit mr. Jacob Boreel Janszoon (1738–1750)', *Bijdragen en Mededelingen Historisch Genootschap* 50 (1929), pp. 321–426, see p. 336; Schooneveld-Oosterling, *Generale Missiven* XI, pp. 14, 18 and 20.

increasing tendency to squander. In 1751, the *Heren Zeventien* refused to give Pieter Hendrik a new appointment, which did not prevent the Admiralty of Amsterdam from appointing him a commander in 1750 and a captain five years later.[8]

Among Van Imhoff's front-rank favourite naval officers right from the time of his appointment was Lieutenant Ficco van Rheede, who, like the Governor-General himself, hailed from the harbour town of Leer on the Ems in East Friesland, not far from the Dutch border. In April 1742, Van Rheede was given permission to take service with the Company. He found he was well suited to it and in December 1746, as there was no experienced officer to take charge of the homeward-bound fleet, Captain-Lieutenant Van Rheede was put in command. In fact, Van Rheede was not really ready to go home and he insisted that, as soon as he had returned to the Netherlands, he should immediately be granted the command of an outward-bound ship. All went well for him and in May 1749 he was in Batavia again. It has to be said that Van Imhoff was never completely convinced of Van Rheede's qualities. He was 'of good character' and was very familiar with money matters, but in Van Imhoff's opinion he was 'never really dashing nor did he greatly excel'.[9]

As a consequence of the large-scale fitting out of the fleet during the War of the Austrian Succession in 1744 and 1745, some time elapsed before other naval officers followed the 1742 example of Van Nimwegen, Van Rheede and their like. During these years, at the request of the British, an auxiliary Dutch squadron supported the British Navy against the French fleet. During this period, most of the officer corps was mobilized.[10] In 1746 and thereafter, the naval authorities in Amsterdam gave permission to two commanders and two lieutenants, but no captains, to enter Company service. One of these men was Nikolaas de Beer, a native of Holstein, who had been made a lieutenant in 1734 and a commander in 1741. He was another who was encouraged by Judge Advocate Boreel in 1746. There was nothing to bind the unmarried man from Holstein to the Dutch Republic. He sailed as the captain of an East Indiaman. He was given special commissions by the *Hoge Regering* in Batavia. Four times – in 1748, 1749, 1750 and 1752 – he made the unusual voyage to Manila, the Asian headquarters of the Spanish. In 1754, De Beer came back to the Republic in command of the returning fleet. At a sitting of the *Heren Zeventien* in October 1754, he gave a report on the return voyage, after which he was presented with the customary gift of a gold chain, worth *f.* 500. During his absence, De Beer,

---

[8] The Hague, Koninklijk Huis Archief, archief Willem IV, 173, letters Van Nimwegen of 8.9 and 31.10.1746; The Hague, NA, AA 1330, fols 9, 38–9 and 95, 1480 (20.9 and 28.9.1746) and 2378 (journal/diary) and VOC 308, 7.10.1751; Schooneveld-Oosterling, *Generale Missiven* XI, p. 820 ; Van Malsen, 'Briefwisseling', pp. 404 and 420.

[9] Van Malsen, 'Briefwisseling', pp. 391 and 398; Schooneveld-Oosterling, *Generale Missiven* XI, pp. 204 and 474; Bruijn, *De admiraliteit van Amsterdam*, p. 124.

[10] Bruijn, *De admiraliteit van Amsterdam*, pp. 32–8.

who was a Lutheran, had been promoted to captain by the Admiralty in 1750 and in that rank he was to command warships on four occasions. He did so for the last time in 1766. He died in 1772 in The Hague at the age of sixty-six, 'a man beloved by all'.[11]

There was still a continued interest among officers in serving temporarily away from the Navy, but it was always on a modest scale. Besides the VOC, occasionally the West Indies Company and the merchant navy would also appoint a naval officer to command ships. Van Imhoff hoped that, at the end of the war in 1748, more naval officers would join 'our Company so as to be able to earn a little money to tide them over when they are on half-pay'. He did not live to see that his wish was fulfilled, even if it was to a very limited degree, as he died in 1750. Interest among naval officers might indeed have been greater at that time, because once again the Admiralties drastically reduced the number of ships fitted out. There was insufficient employment in Amsterdam for the seventy-seven commanders and lieutenants in 1750. Nevertheless the conditions and the prestige of sailing with the VOC were apparently not great enough to tempt these men. Despite a great lack of enthusiasm there were some naval officers who did seek employment with the Company, indeed with some regularity, but always on a temporary basis.[12]

Back and Forth between the Navy and the Company

It was always expected that a naval officer would return to the fold of the Admiralty. Permission was indeed always granted with the retention of 'rank and quality'. Promotions were continued. Unless the person concerned happened to die overseas, when he returned he always went back to the Navy. When the system of ranks of 1742, with the naval titles of captain, captain-lieutenant (lieutenant-commander) and lieutenant, was cancelled by the *Heren Zeventien* in 1755, this had no marked impact on the existing interest of naval officers in making the transition to the Company. Stipends were also reduced to the same level as earlier. The 1742 system had caused a great deal of discontent among the Company's own officers. Outsiders had taken their places and those outsiders did not always behave with as much tact as they might have. Many Company commanders and ship's officers felt that they had been relegated. It was the

---

[11] A few other officers were Commander Boudewijn Molen (1721–post 1751), Lieutenant Kornelis Eike (?–1763) and Lieutenant Frederik Jan Karel van Honsdorf (?–1765) of the Admiralty of Amsterdam and the Admiralty in Friesland Annaeus Lodewijk Betting. Schooneveld-Oosterling, *Generale Missiven* XI, p. 474; P. Dekker, 'Der "Admiral" Nis de Bombell (1706–1772). Ein Nordfriese in niederländischen Seediensten', *Nordfriesisches Jahrbuch*, Neue Folge 13 (1977), pp. 107–33.

[12] The Hague, NA, AA 1485 (June/July 1753); Maritiem Museum Rotterdam, Aantekeningen (Notes) by J.C. de Jonge V (Aug. 1749, Aug./Sept. 1750 and 1764); Van Malsen, 'Briefwisseling', p. 392.

17. Jan Zacharias Nauwman. Pastel drawing by A. Boon (probably dating from 1791) of Jan Zacharias Nauwman in naval uniform. In his right hand he holds half a rolled chart, with a pair of protractors lying next to it. In the 1750s and 1760s Nauwman sailed for the Company. Before and after this period, he was a naval officer in the service of the Admiralty of Amsterdam.

18. Mrs Nauwman, born Rebecca Schuller. Pastel drawing of Rebecca Schuller, wife of Jan Zacharias Nauwman, commander and naval officer. Signed: 'A. Boon fecit 1791'.

Amsterdam Chamber which took the initiative of restoring the pre-1742 situation. Whoever wanted to continue to sail with his newly acquired rank was free to do so, but this was only nominal. Van Mensburg and Rijzik had proudly retained theirs, as we have seen. However, it was not long before the title of commander had once more come back into general use. The naval officers who entered Company service after 1755 became either ordinary commanders or mates.[13]

A closer look at a few of them indicates how the system worked. Jan Lodewijk Philippi from Leeuwarden was appointed captain by the Admiralty of Amsterdam in 1750 but he left to go to the VOC in 1752. He was immediately appointed captain, even though he had never sailed for the Company before, as the Amsterdam Chamber noted in his letter of appointment. His military background stood him in good stead in 1754 when he and other ships joined battle with the fearsome Angrian pirates off the west coast of India. He managed to inflict considerable damage on them, but was unable to prevent his own and one other ship with everyone on board blowing up. The explosion was caused because his ship was rammed by a burning pirate vessel and the fire caught hold in his ship and reached the powder magazine. The former naval officer could do nothing to prevent the loss. The authorities in Batavia were full of praise for Philippi's conduct. He had behaved like a true naval hero and had shown that 'neither courage nor leadership had deserted our young men nor had they been degenerated'. The *Nederlandsche Jaerboeken* of 1754 said that the Frisian had performed a deed 'braver' than 'Roman courage', because he had personally set off the gunpowder in the magazine to prevent his ship being captured.[14]

Jan Zacharias Nauwman from Darmstad in Germany had begun his seafaring life in the Navy. One time when he was filling the water barrels as his ship lay in the Texel Roads, he met a young widow in Oudeschild. This probably happened in 1747 or 1748 – it is difficult to pinpoint the date accurately. Nauwman married in 1748 and settled in Oudeschild. In 1750, his reputation was such that a declaration had to be made in the presence of a solicitor in which a woman denied 'a rumour' which was doing the rounds 'in the village' that she had had 'carnal conversation' with Nauwman. It had been, she said, not with him but with his colleague Hendrik Andries Franke. Two years later, as a sub-lieutenant, Nauwman entered VOC service. By 1757 he was a commander. Meanwhile his naval career continued. He was made a commander in 1753 and a captain in 1758. On his maiden voyage as commander, Nauwman took along his young son who was barely nine years old. During the course of that voyage in 1758 his wife died. When Nauwman returned in 1759, he remained ashore for two years. For some of that time he took over Jan de Boer's work in the Texel Roads for the Company. In 1761 his Admiralty again gave him permission to leave

---

[13] The Hague, NA, VOC 128, 15.10.1755.
[14] The Hague, NA, VOC 308, 17.7.1752, and 2841, fol. 697; Schooneveld-Oosterling, *Generale Missiven* XII, p. 475; Van Gelder, *Naporra's omweg*, pp. 352–4.

for the East for six years. His son once again accompanied him, but the boy died in 1765. Nauwman himself returned home in 1768. He remarried, settled down in IJsselstein in the province of Utrecht and resumed his career with the Admiralty.[15]

These examples reveal the strange intermingling of careers in the Navy and the Company. As was demonstrated in Chapter 3, in Zealand it was a well-established custom for Company commanders to be appointed captains by the Admiralty of Zealand. From 1742, especially in the Amsterdam Chamber, the same pattern of switching between the two services took hold. Paulus van Rauwenhoff, the son of an Amsterdam merchant, became a naval commander in 1759 and three years later was promoted to captain. Before this he had been a commander for the Company but had been dismissed by the *Heren Zeventien* because on his return to Texel he had been caught transferring contraband goods. He had been one of Van Imhoff's 'golden boys', having sailed as a twelve-year-old midshipman on the *Herstelder* in 1742. At that time he was a model of good behaviour or, as Van Imhoff wrote: 'The boy Rauwhoff is a real little rogue, but is simultaneously the brightest [chap], can climb like a cat, knows the workings of the compass and was acquainted with all the rigging over the whole ship and everything indicates that he promises to be a fine officer.'

After one voyage to the East in 1761 Commander Jan Werner Falck again reported to the Navy. Indeed his voyage had turned out to be a protracted one, because up to 1760 he had served as Superintendent in Surat for some years. Like Philippi, he did battle with the local pirates, in 1757. Naval officer Hendrik Otto de Haard, the son of a solicitor from Nijmegen, became successively lieutenant, commander and captain in 1756, 1759 and 1766, and it was with the rank of captain that he sailed to the tropics in 1765. He died in 1771 just before he reached home on his return from his second voyage. In 1766 when he was in Canton, the Company staff had found him a stiff and formal man.

Isaak Louis de Bellon kept working for the Company, even though the Admiralty of Amsterdam continued to promote him. In 1761, when he was a lieutenant, he was given permission to transfer to the VOC for four years. Meanwhile in 1763 he became a naval commander. In 1777, after he had been a commander for nearly three years and was far away in Batavia, he was promoted to captain. He was granted leave to join the VOC again in 1780 and in 1794 he was still registered as a naval captain. During his service with the Company, De Bellon was squarely confronted with the strictness with which its authorities applied the rules. In 1776 the commander of a ship which was berthed in

---

[15] The Hague, NA, AA 1330, fols 29 and 57; Rijksarchief in Noord-Holland, Oud Not. Arch. 185/4870, deed of 24.1.1750, and 4874, deed of 16.3.1759; De Jonge, *Geschiedenis* IV, pp. 407 and 412–14; Bonke, 'De Verenigde Oost-Indische Compagnie', in Roeper and Vonk-Uitgeest, *Texel en de VOC*, pp. 22–4 and 28–30; Vonk-Uitgeest, 'Texelse opvarenden', in *ibid.*, pp. 188–9; Van Gelder, *Naporra's omweg*, pp. 447–9. I would like to thank Mevrouw I. Vonk-Uitgeest in Oudeschild for this information.

Plymouth for a thorough overhaul died. De Bellon was transported to Plymouth in a specially chartered vessel to take his place. On his arrival on board, he discovered that a large number of the kitchen utensils from the galley and other goods were missing, but he did not trouble to make a list of the missing items. At the end of the voyage, the sum of ƒ. 954 was deducted from his stipend to cover those goods. He lodged a protest and finally managed to have the amount reduced by one-third, but he did not completely escape the penalty. He was not able to demonstrate convincingly that the missing items had not vanished after his arrival and it proved a lesson to him that he should have been more attentive to his record-keeping.

Two naval officers must certainly not be overlooked in this survey: the half-brothers Willem and Jakob Pieter van Braam. Both were officers in the Admiralty of Amsterdam and their father was a successful merchant in East Indian linen and Chinese wares in the city. Willem van Braam became a captain in 1762, his brother in 1766. These promotions were made when both men were sailing as commanders for the Company with the permission of their Admiralty. Between 1761 and 1770 Willem made three voyages. Jakob Pieter sailed in 1764 and remained overseas for a very long time. In 1767, he married in Batavia, and the same year he was appointed Superintendent at Hougli in Bengal. He remained in the post until 1773. Jakob Pieter van Braam returned to the Republic in 1776 after spending some time with his family-in-law at the Cape. He returned to the East Indies one more time in 1783 as commander of the first squadron of warships sent to support the Company. Both these ex-commanders then enjoyed long careers in the Navy, reaching the flag rank of vice-admiral. However, as supporters of the exiled Stadtholder Willem V, they found themselves unemployed in 1795.

Both the Van Braams had made their fortunes as the result of their Asian voyages. A bill of exchange transmitted by Jakob Pieter offers a good illustration of just how profitable one such voyage could be. In 1765 he had a bill of exchange worth ƒ. 19,200 transmitted from Batavia to his father in Amsterdam. In 1776 he had the financial wherewithal to purchase the 'Engelenburg' estate in Brummen in Guelders. Its value was somewhere in the region of ƒ. 70,000 to 80,000. The income from the estate did not live up to expectations and, after Jakob Pieter's wife's death in 1781, the family decided to sell it.[16]

---

[16] For Rauwenhoff, see The Hague, NA, VOC 128, 12.10.1758; Van Malsen, 'Briefwisseling', p. 336; Schooneveld-Oosterling, *Generale Missiven* XI, p. 592. For Falck, see The Hague, NA, AA 1330, fols 29 and 78–9, and 1487 (18.8.1761); Schooneveld-Oosterling, *Generale Missiven* XII, pp. 480 and 588; and s'Jacob, *Generale Missiven* XIII, pp. 190, 593 and 600; Van Gelder, *Naporra's omweg*, p. 331; for De Haard, see Bonke, *De Jonge Lieve*, pp. 207–8; for De Bellon, see AA 1330, fols 70, 92 and 147 and 1487 (27.10.1761), and VOC 135, 29.3.1776 and 222, 9.10.1778 and 12.4.1779; for the Van Braams, see Staring, *Damiaan Hugo Staring*, pp. 33–4 and 37–9; De Jonge, *Geschiedenis zeewezen* IV and V, *passim*; S. van der Leest, 'Jacob Pieter van Braam (1737–1803). De jaren 1787–1803, de nadagen in de carrière van een achttiende-eeuwse marineofficier' (MA thesis, Leiden University, 2005).

At the Cape, fellow commander/captain Damiaan Hugo Staring had shown an interest in 'Engelenburg' when he heard rumours about its possible sale. He had become acquainted with the Van Braams at the Cape. He was looking for an estate in the province of Guelders, preferably in the Achterhoek, one of the ancient quarters of the duchy of Guelders near the German border, but he was not averse to the south-east corner of the Veluwe, a forest-rich ridge of hills. He was worried that the 'Engelenburg' would be an estate 'which did not yield revenues in proportion to the capital'. The estate had been sold three times in quick succession, which Staring did not think was a good sign, so he looked elsewhere. He finally bought 'Wildenborch' near Vorden in the Achterhoek, which remained in his family for many generations. Accusations were made by citizens of Cape Town about the way he laid his hands on the necessary sum for the purchase price of ƒ. 95,000. During his appointment as Superintendent of the Shipyard, Staring had seized every opportunity to make money. His behaviour had been so bad he was known as the 'blood-sucker'. When the top administrators in Cape Town were accused of various outrages by a group of inhabitants in 1779, Staring's name was one of those mentioned. The matter was investigated and Staring readily admitted he pursued business like any other man, especially in timber. He used crew members on ships in the roads for his own private purposes and he was also not averse to making use of Company vessels. Wisely, in the wake of all this uproar, he handed in his resignation in 1781, and because of the Fourth Anglo-Dutch War he returned to the Republic on a neutral Danish ship. He had transferred his money expeditiously. He did not live long to enjoy the 'Wildenborch', though. He died in 1783.[17]

Naval Ranks After All

For a long time there had been agreement in Admiralty circles that many of the naval officers serving at sea did not receive 'a suitable stipend' and that a growing number 'had nothing or very little income of their own'. A man in search of a fortune sailed for Asia.[18] Such men never came in droves but there was a steady stream of them. One example is Frederik Alexander Meurer. In 1773–1775, this sub-lieutenant worked for the Company as second and then first mate. He was able to put his knowledge of the seas south of the Equator to good use in the 1780s when he participated in naval squadrons dispatched to the East,

---

[17] T. Landheer, *Oranje of Napoleon? De wisselvallige levensloop van Christiaan Antonij Ver Huell 1760–1832* (Utrecht, 2006), p. 48; Staring, *Damiaan Hugo Staring*, chs 2–3 and appendices II–III; G.J. Schutte, *De Nederlandse Patriotten en de koloniën. Een onderzoek naar hun denkbeelden en optreden, 1770–1800* (Groningen, 1974), ch. IV; C. Beyers, *Die Kaapse Patriotte gedurende die laaste kwart van die agtiende eeuw en die voortlewing van hul denkbeelden* (Pretoria, 1967), p. 64. Mr T. Landheer drew my attention to this.
[18] The Hague, NA, AA XXXVII, 82 and 83.

19. Damiaan Hugo Staring (1736–1783). Staring had his portrait painted by an unknown artist after his return from the Cape of Good Hope in 1782, when he had settled at 'Wildenborch' near Vorden (Achterhoek) and had re-entered the service of the Admiralty of Amsterdam. In 1771, he had left his post as a naval captain to take service with the Company as a commander and Superintendent of the Shipyard in Cape Town. In the foreground of the portrait is a map of Africa showing Cape Town. In the middle left are two ships: an unrigged three-master and an imagined four-master under sail.

with the rank of captain. Later he would reach the rank of vice-admiral. The dispatch of three squadrons of warships to Asia in the final years of the VOC obviously reduced the attraction among naval officers of serving temporarily with the VOC. Now they could also wear their naval uniforms in the tropics and they were on full pay for a far longer period than had been usual.

At the end of the eighteenth century, the difference between the jack-tars and the 'people of good birth' was steadily decreasing. Broadly speaking, the traditional division of labour at sea began to blur. Men who had been involved in whaling sailed to the West Indies and even signed on with the VOC. Masters in the merchant navy transferred to the Company or the Navy. Finally, besides opting for the VOC, naval officers also joined the merchant navy. During and after the Fourth Anglo-Dutch War (1780–1784), the corps of naval officers expanded considerably, which made it impossible to retain the fairly elitist character of the group. In 1793 the two largest Admiralties, those of Amsterdam and Rotterdam, had 194 lieutenants in service. The rank of commander no longer existed but twenty years earlier there had been no more than 144 commanders and lieutenants combined. This indicates that the number of junior officers had increased by one-third.[19]

The VOC also contributed to these changes in the seafaring pattern of the Republic. During the Fourth Anglo-Dutch War, the commanders of a number of ships which were more heavily armed were given the rank of captain. This was a one-off decision. After the war, the Company was confronted with a shortage of ships and was forced to charter or buy a number of ships from the merchant navy. In order to 'raise the spirits' of its own personnel, in 1784 the *Heren Zeventien* decided that all the existing officer ranks would be renamed. Thereafter, the commander would be called captain, the first mate captain-lieutenant, the second mate lieutenant and the third mate sub-lieutenant. Their ranks might have changed but their stipends did not. Likewise, from that time, two cadets would be assigned to each ship, replicating the two midshipmen who were to be found on naval ships. Each rank had an appropriate uniform with the ranks clearly indicated by insignia. The VOC commander had definitely become a captain. Retired commanders were also permitted to call themselves captain. Christiaan van Veerden, who had remained at the Cape in 1782, indicated in his enquiries concern about the changes. Presumably he was not alone.[20]

The now completely forgotten Jan Kornelis Baane, who was a hero to his contemporaries, had many of the typical characteristics of a commander in the closing years of the Company. Baane was from Flushing, born there in 1762. In 1780 he served, as a sailor, for the Zealand Chamber, returning in 1786. Over-

---

[19] Count based on the printed Registers of Names of the Boards of the Admiralties of 1773 and 1793.

[20] To prevent any sort of confusion, in this book every man who was in charge of a Company ship will be consistently referred to as commander. The Hague, NA, VOC 138, 3.5.1784, and 308, 7.6.1787, and Archief Van der Heim 92, 21.6.1784.

seas he sat the examination for ship's officer. He built up extensive experience of the violence of war, because he took part in such engagements as the battles of naval and Company ships against the ruler of Riouw (Riau) and Buginese pirates from South Sulawesi. In 1787 he was appointed lieutenant on a ship of the Delft Chamber and in 1790 he was back in Flushing. His arrival was followed not long after by a bill of exchange worth ƒ. 8,615. A year later he was captain with his original Chamber, that of Zealand. Climbing the ranks from sailor to the highest post on board was still possible in 1791, as it had been at the beginning of the century. Baane ended his seafaring career in a fight. In 1794, when he was on his way from Batavia to Japan with another ship, he came across a French frigate which had taken a Company ship as a prize. A skirmish developed in which Baane managed to retake the Company ship and to beat off the French attack. His 'outstanding courage' was only rewarded in 1816. Baane, whose body was seamed with the scars of many wounds received in the course of duty, was then appointed naval captain-lieutenant, a position which brought with it an annual salary of ƒ. 1,000. By that time there was no longer any question of social discrepancies.[21]

---

[21] Engelberts Gerrits, *Gedenkstuk* II, pp. 440–2; S. Kalff, 'Een zee-officier van de O.-I. Compagnie', *Onze Vloot*, no. 1 (1925), pp. 4–8; Crone, *Cornelis Douwes*, pp. 4–19.

PART TWO

COMMANDERS AT SEA

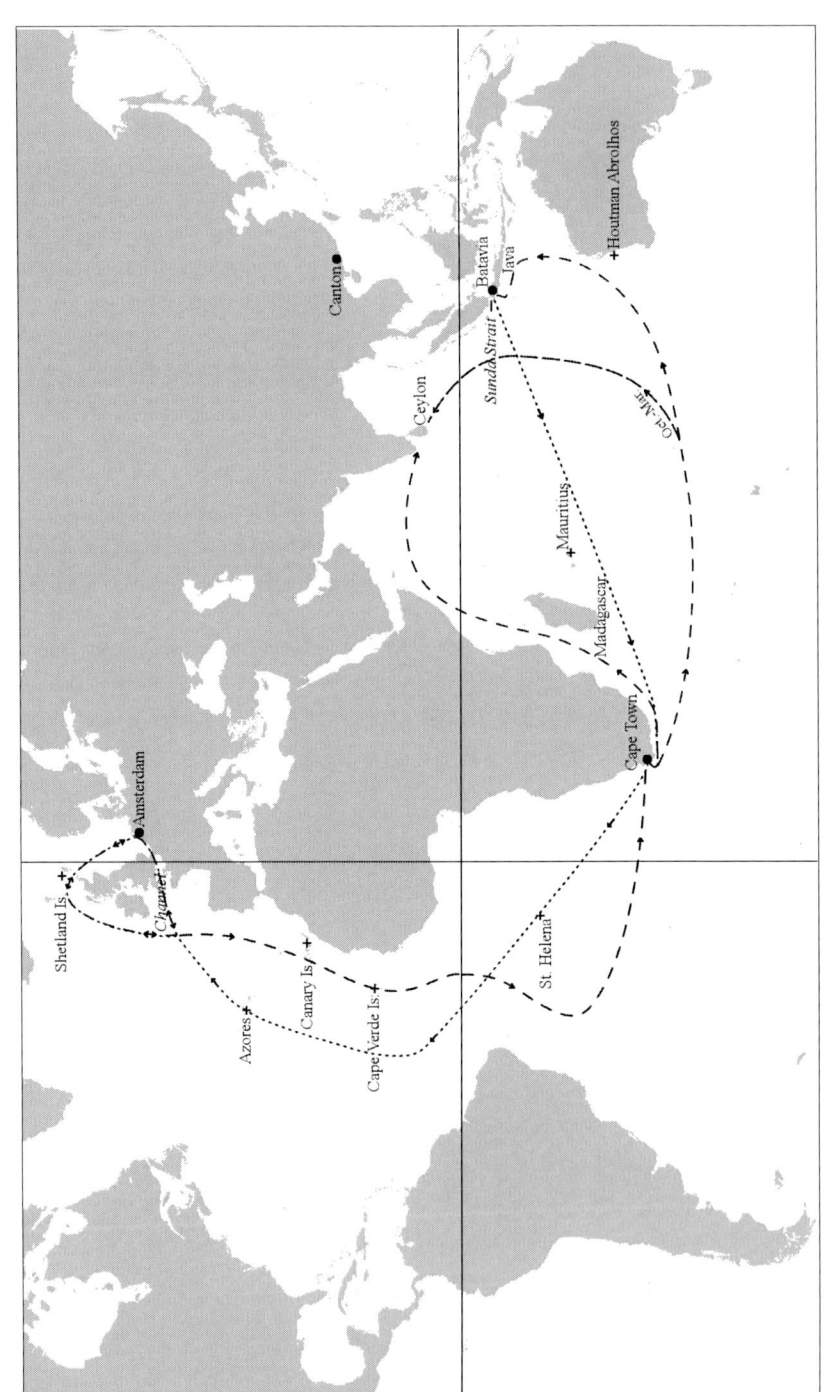

Map 2. Shipping routes to and from Asia

Introduction to Part Two

Part One of this book gave a picture of the sort of men who were in command of the ships of the six Chambers. This picture contained information about their geographical origins, their family backgrounds, their financial circumstances and their rise in social status in the towns in which they lived. It was also possible to catch a glimpse of their administrative and commercial activities after they had retired from the sea, if they happened to become involved in such matters once they settled on land. This information has helped to produce a multi-faceted picture of how eighteenth-century Company commanders lived ashore. However, many never returned home but died overseas or during their voyages to the East. Nearly one in six of the commanders have been mentioned, either in the text or in the notes, more from some Chambers than others.

The focus of Part Two is the Company commander in the performance of his duties. The procedures which were followed for the appointment of a commander are discussed in Chapter 9. Each director of a Chamber took his turn to make a nomination of a man he wanted to sponsor. Ship's officers had to sit a whole series of examinations before they were able to present themselves as candidates for an appointment as commander. These examinations are the theme of Chapter 10, which also includes some discussion about the new names proposed for the existing ranks and the ways in which a commander acquired his professional expertise. In Chapters 11 and 12, the financial side of the profession of commander is investigated. It begins with a discussion of normal earnings and then various aspects of private trade carried on by these men are sifted through. This is followed by an assessment of the commander's role on board, in which particular attention is paid to his accommodation in the stern, his social life and the host of vicissitudes which were inseparable from departures, arrivals and returns.

Of course, the Company ships were not always safe or soundly constructed. Every so often, these points were discussed extensively in the meetings of the *Heren Zeventien*, in the Chambers, by the master shipwrights and by the commanders themselves. In the period around 1740, these discussions reached a height and a real attempt was made to find explanations for and solutions to a series of shipping disasters, not all of which could be blamed on human error. Serious talks were held about other improvements which could be made and

Governor-General Van Imhoff was an important participant in these discussions. Despite all the measures taken, ships continued to disappear without trace and frequently the blame for the loss of a ship was laid fairly and squarely on the shoulders of a commander.

Naturally the commanders represented all sorts and conditions of men, from very human individuals to absolute brutes and some very nasty specimens. Others were troublemakers. At this point, it is worth remembering that for the historian the deviant behaviour of people is usually the only moment at which it is possible to obtain any information at all about the running of a ship and life on board. The standard of navigation, the lagging behind of the introduction of improvements in the sea charts of Asia, and the discussion and implementation of plans in relation to the traditional East Indiaman come under the spotlight in Chapters 14 and 15, in which the ever-increasing stream of regulations issued by the *Heren Zeventien* is also touched upon. The professional expertise and skills of the commanders are reserved for the second to last chapter. Finally, Chapter 17 offers a glimpse of the commanders of four other East India companies, with the emphasis falling on the captains of the English East India Company. This comparison throws the most conspicuous facets of the lives and careers of VOC commanders into sharper relief.

Once more a whole list of names passes in review, often names of men already introduced, but there are new ones as well. The names are no longer drawn from a random sample but are those of commanders who were involved in various aspects of the actual performance of their duties as VOC commanders, and are singled out in this connection in the sources. In contrast with Part One, no further investigations are made into the course of their lives, because this is not relevant in this context. Completely different sources from those referred to in Part One, in which the main focus was the random sample of individual commanders, were used for the research for Part Two. This section required research in serial sources in the archive of the VOC. Long series of the resolutions of the *Heren Zeventien* and of the Amsterdam Chamber, Instructions, the General Reports (*Generale Missiven*) from the *Hoge Regering* in Batavia to the *Heren Zeventien* (published up to 1761) and the Netherlands-Indies Book of Decrees (*Nederlandsch-Indisch Plakaatboek*) were combed. Some research was also carried out in the private archives of a number of the directors.

9

Appointment as Commander

The directors handled the appointment of personnel to the higher ranks on board East Indiamen in accordance with a set procedure. Commanders, ship's officers and petty officers were usually appointed during a meeting set for a specific date. Announcements were posted on placards stating that candidates for specific positions on certain ships could apply. The privilege of applying was not restricted to commanders and senior ship's officers. Even third mates were given the opportunity to 'give a presentation' of their qualifications in person during the meeting. The same procedure applied to a number of other functions, such as those of senior and junior surgeon. To give one example, on 21 June 1784 the Rotterdam Chamber decided to post (*affigeren*) an announcement stating that 'on the 5th July next, Monday afternoon at 4 o'clock' candidates could give personal presentations. Sometimes this sort of announcement was made at even shorter notice. When they were on shore, potential applicants were apparently supposed to make sure they did not stray too far from the neighbourhood of their Chamber.

By Rotation and Drawing Lots

In the eighteenth century, in any administrative system it was usual for directors to take turns in nominating their own chosen candidates for vacant positions. This was a system known as gifting places (*ambtenvergeving*), the rules of which were often set down in secret contracts. The system used by the VOC was no different from that which operated at the Admiralty Boards or in town councils. Each of the four smaller VOC Chambers had seven directors, the Zealand Chamber had twelve and the Amsterdam Chamber twenty. All of the Chambers used what was more or less the same form of presentation of qualifications (*dienstpresentatiën*) at the interviews of applicants. At first glance, the whole system seems to have been open and above board, and, indeed, a number of candidates were allowed the opportunity to offer their services. Applicants attended the meeting of the directors at the agreed time. They gave accounts of their previous appointments and their voyages. For each of the ships in question, various points were noted for the benefit of the directors. Several of the directors preserved their papers related to these presentations plus lists of names and positions so that they could use the information in making a decision at a later meeting. In Rotterdam Jakob van der Heim kept these sorts of documents, supplemented by his own notes and observations, for the years 1771–1787. In Zealand, Samuel Radermacher collected complete reviews for the period 1737–1760.[1] His son, Daniël, also made notes concerning various matters. There were other Zealand directors who kept Company documents among their family papers. During their directorships, grandfather Johan Constantijn Mathias and his grandson, Bonifacious Mathias-Pous, kept lists of the appointments of commanders and ship's officers, thereby preserving data for the periods 1738–1764 and 1771–1780. In the Zealand papers there is often a note of which director made the particular choice for a position. In the Delft Chamber, if there had been a discussion about appointments Adriaan van Vredenburch and his son, Gerard, made notes on their copies of the minutes, which cover the period 1730–1761. Finally, for the Enkhuizen Chamber, material has been handed down thanks to two directors who were close friends, Jan Minne and Dirk Haak. They preserved lists of applications and appointments for the period 1725–1765.[2] On the basis of this sort of information, handed down by men who were personally involved with making appointments, it is possible to paint a picture of how a commander and his officers obtained their appointments on board East Indiamen.

Nevertheless, one aspect is unfortunately still shrouded in obscurity. It is unclear if a commander paid for his appointment and, if he did, what sort of sum he paid. Perhaps he simply promised to perform certain services for a director while overseas. In the Republic, and hence also in the VOC, it was customary to pay for obtaining a particular position, including a relatively humble one. It was also common practice for a patron to propose his own acquaintances, relations and clients. There was no publicly acknowledged scale of payments for the positions. The VOC had a draconian regulation forbidding every form of payment. Each time a candidate was appointed to a position, he had to swear an oath that he had neither paid nor promised anything to get the job. Contravening this rule meant being cashiered from the Company and prohibited from working for the VOC ever again. The same applied to the individual who sponsored the offender for the position. In 1712, directors were obliged to sign a statement in which they declared that, 'for the selecting or assisting in the selection,

---

[1] There is a possibility that these are actual copies of the minutes of the Chamber.
[2] These papers are kept in The Hague, NA, Archief Van der Heim 92 and 93, Archief Van Vredenburch 1 and 13, and Archief Radermacher 235; Middelburg, Zeeuws Archief (ZA), Archief Mathias-Pous-Tak van Poortvliet 16 and 227; Hoorn, WA, Oud Archief Enkhuizen 1561 and 1568–86. See also The Hague, NA, VOC 253, 1.11.1728; and also J.R. Bruijn, 'Commandanten van Oost-Indiëvaarders in de achttiende eeuw', *Tijdschrift voor Zeegeschiedenis* 20, no. 1 (2000), pp. 4–13, see pp. 6–8. Mr H. de Vos from Schoorl shared his knowledge of the system of the allocation of positions by the Enkhuizen Chamber with me.

20. Voting in a meeting of directors in 1741. In this year three fellow townsmen applied for the post of commander on the *Ida* of the Enkhuizen Chamber. Roelof Blok was elected on the nomination of one of the directors, by grace of the votes of all five gentlemen present; two were absent. Neither of the other two candidates obtained a single vote, but were given commands in 1742. Blok sailed on 1 June 1741. Of the five applicants for the post of assistant-merchant the last obtained all the votes. Directors Haak and Minne were both present at the meeting.

appointing or assisting to appoint' personnel, either in the Republic or overseas, they 'had enjoyed or will enjoy nothing at all whether money or anything of monetary value'. In 1713, the *Heren Zeventien* put the same restraint into words as a 'silent interdiction and prohibition of veniality or the sale of offices, services and appointments'. A number of directors objected to signing the document, which was introduced at a time when there was a general campaign in the Republic to try to curb bribery and the sale of offices. Later in the eighteenth century, a newly appointed director was still obliged to sign the document and to declare under oath that he would not sell any appointment.[3] The Sautijn case, discussed below, demonstrates that the content of the 1712 document was nothing more than a dead letter.

On the day which had been assigned for the presentations, the commanders, ship's officers, surgeons and others who wanted to apply presented themselves at the *Oost-Indisch Huis*. Interviews were invariably held on a Monday. Candidates were seeking places on a ship which would set sail some four or five months later. The directors asked them about their experience in the service of the Company and with other employers. In the case of surgeons, 'How long they had practised their art' was important. For others the important factor was the number and sorts of voyages they had made. Answers to questions such as 'How long have you been at sea?' and 'When did you arrive here?' were recorded. Afterwards the date of the examinations was fixed and it was agreed which of the directors would be present at these as invigilators. Usually the examinations were held directly afterwards either on a Wednesday or a Saturday, at ten-thirty or noon or later. A week after the presentations, the directors made their choices.

In most cases there was more than one candidate and a choice had to be made. For eighty-eight commands on the ships of the Enkhuizen Chamber in the period 1725–1765, there were 324 applications, which means that 236 candidates were turned down. The same commander could show interest in more than one ship. There were 292 applications for the position of first mate on the eighty-eight ships and 363 for that of second mate. Willem van Mensburg is a good example of the way the course of events ran in Enkhuizen. In 1728 he applied four times for the position of second mate and was finally appointed third mate. Three years later, his second application for second mate was successful. The same pattern occurred again in 1734 for the position of first mate. Between 1737 and 1740 he made nine unsuccessful bids to become a commander but he did become a first mate once more in 1740. In 1744 he again missed out on an appointment as commander. He finally won that highest post the following year and again in 1748 and 1752, in those cases with no difficulty. Roelof Blok became a commander on his third attempt in 1740–1741, and in the period 1725–1732 it took Jakob Sombeek nine attempts to be appointed to the three ranks of second

---

[3] The Hague, NA, VOC 115, 29.7, 26.9.1712, 12.8.1713, 116, 13.3.1716, 118, 23, 28.8.1727, 9.3.1728 and 11.397, art. 55; The Hague, NA, Archief Van Vredenburch 10, fol. 28. See also Van Gelder, *Naporra's omweg*, p. 352.

21. List of appointments on the recommendation of directors in 1773–1774. List of the nominations for the posts of commander, first and second mates for the 1773–1774 fitting out of the Zealand Chamber. The names of the directors who made the nominations are on the left in order of their own appointment. Radermacher is number 6 in order of seniority; Pous is number 12 in the sponsorship list for commanders. For the post of mate, as number 4 Van Citters put forward the first nomination; as number 12 again Pous did not have a turn. Stavorinus was Radermacher's nomination for the post of commander of the *Ouwerkerk*; Justinus van Gennep was director Buteux's candidate for the same post on the *Bartha Petronella*.

and first mate and commander. In 1730, First Mate Kornelis van der Hoeven apparently enjoyed the right connections to be appointed commander the first time he applied.

A commander who asked for a new command when he got back and did not get it was said to stand 'still'.[4] Later in the century, in general there were fewer applicants and among them there were more who had never sailed before with the VOC or who had come directly from abroad. This situation is clearly revealed in Van der Heim's lists. In their time, Haak and Minne in Enkhuizen were able to appoint no fewer than seventy-four Dutchmen as commanders. The directors in Enkhuizen also took turns in making their choices for various lower-ranking functions. In total there were twenty-seven positions to be filled on each ship, including the petty officers such as the boatswain, the sailmaker and the steward and their assistants. The directors of the Zealand Chamber handed out only nine positions for each vessel. As well as the commander and the ship's officers there were those of assistant, junior merchant, senior surgeon, commander of the soldiers and an almoner. Each Chamber had its own unique customs.

'Unanimity' was not necessary to make the final choice. A majority of the votes sufficed. The candidates were written on a list according to the position for which they were applying, and the votes were marked after their names. Almost without exception there was unanimity. In Enkhuizen sometimes all seven directors were present while at other times there were only three to five. The choice was made by the director whose turn it was. His candidate was appointed if the examination results were 'competent', 'well answered' or 'answered all questions perfectly'. On a few occasions, either 'lamentable' or 'incompetent' had to be recorded. If a candidate arrived too late for the examination, the record showed 'said person too late and disqualified'. Of the twenty directors of the Amsterdam Chamber, only those in charge of the fitting out of the ships were eligible to submit a nomination for a commander's place. Those in charge of the warehouses could make recommendations for the ship's officers.[5] In Zealand all twelve directors participated in the nominations, which was probably the situation in the other Chambers as well.

In 1719 in Amsterdam, the candidate of director Willem Sautijn, Jan Pietersz Keizer, was rejected because 'his hand shook'. Thereupon, Sautijn made a deal with an Enkhuizen colleague by which Siewert Pool went to Amsterdam and Keizer, to the town of the Dromedaris – that large tower of the southern gate near the harbour which is still a prominent feature of Enkhuizen. Two years later Keizer was indeed appointed in Amsterdam. In Delft, Gerard van Vredenburch regularly held heated discussions with certain colleagues about the suitability of candidates. Sometimes his anger got the better of him: 'All for nothing!', he

---

[4] Taken from the counts made by Mr H. de Vos in Schoorl. See also Hoorn, WA, Oud-Archief Enkhuizen 1578.
[5] The Hague, NA, VOC 307, 16.9.1716.

noted, 'the man who had to be [appointed] was from Rotterdam!' He was also perturbed about the appointment of ship's officers who did not comply with the prescribed sailing experience for a commander.[6]

In Rotterdam, besides the allocation of appointments, lots were drawn. In this case, approximately twenty-five of the lower-ranking positions on a ship, what were known as 'the small places', were decided in this way. Among these positions were the third mate, provost marshall, almoner and boatswain. Most of these were petty officers' places. These positions were divided up into groups of three among the directors and lots were drawn. One of Van der Heim's lots is still to be found in his archives. It is a piece of paper 10 by 7.5 cm on which are written the three places to be allotted. These nominations and appointments took place outside the meetings. For instance, Van der Heim personally organized the appointment of the chief sailmaker, a quartermaster and the provost marshall on the ship the *Huis te Krooswijk* which was due to sail in February 1772. On the same occasion, his colleague Hugo Cornets de Groot, who had been a director since 1738, looked after the appointment of the third mate, the senior cooper and the second corporal. When the positions were being apportioned, the directors took their turns by order of seniority. At the next fitting out of ships, each director was again given another set of three positions, sometimes even a list of four positions which were in his gift.[7] Seniority among directors was set according to their dates of appointment. A new member had to take his place at the bottom of the pile. New members were infrequent since appointments to Chamber boards had no time limit. Many directors had other business interests quite apart from those of the Company to absorb their time. They were members of town councils, even burgomasters, and they could be merchants.

In the Zealand Chamber, the turns allotted to directors and the results of their sponsorship of candidates can be closely followed for more than twenty consecutive years. Samuel Radermacher kept annual lists of 'appointments or recommendations' from 1737 to 1760. These lists contain the nine positions per ship fitted out mentioned earlier. The directors were numbered in order of seniority, from one to twelve. There were eight ships fitted out in 1740–1741 while in the following year there were only seven. In 1740 the directors who held numbers three to nine consecutively chose their candidates for the eight commanders' positions. The following year numbers ten to twelve and then one to four took their turns. The year after that, 1742, number five and those holding higher numbers got their choices. For the other eight positions exactly the same procedure was followed. Depending on the circumstances, a director might have a year in which he was unable to nominate either a commander or a first mate for any of the ships. It appears that in 1741 Johan Mathias was responsible for the nomination of Kornelis Vis as first mate, and in 1749 as commander.

---

[6] The Hague, NA, Archief Van Vredenburch 1, 22.12.1755, 30.6.1756 and 17.9.1758. For Sautijn, see Elias, *De vroedschap*, p. cxliv; and *DAS* II, nos. 2405, 2420 and 2481.
[7] The Hague, NA, Archief Van der Heim 92.

In 1773 Stavorinus had Daniël Rademacher to thank for his nomination, and Justinus van Gennep had Pieter Buteux to thank for his, and in fact again on two consecutive occasions in 1773 and 1776.[8]

In the various departments or commissions into which the directors of every Chamber were divided up, the same system of rotation was observed for the granting of other vacant positions. The Amsterdam Chamber had four departments, those of fitting out, warehousing, reception of goods and the counting house; while the Zealand Chamber had three commissions: fitting out, mercantile matters (*koopmanschappen*) and bookkeeping (*thesaurie*). The smaller Chambers worked along lines similar to those of Zealand. In 1786 patronage for positions in the fitting out department of the Amsterdam Chamber gave rise to some 'dubiousness' which led to the making of a new agreement that 'turns will be taken, albeit with the understanding that a newly appointed director will not be given an opportunity before all the sitting members ... have already made their nominations.'[9]

Did a Commander Pay for his Position?

One of the thorny problems encountered in the history of the *ancien régime* and of the eighteenth century in particular is finding concrete evidence that occupants of certain positions paid money to obtain the positions and, if they did pay, then what was the cost. Generally, it is accepted that payment was normal. It is likewise assumed that those people who were appointed – relatives, minions and any personnel – were dependent on the grantor of a particular position. However, tangible evidence which might confirm these assumptions is often lacking.[10] Naturally, the problem of documentation extends to the VOC. Theoretically there was no sale of offices and anyone who trespassed the prohibition could expect to be severely punished. Nevertheless, the grumbles of the directors when they were asked to sign the 1712 document is an indication that such sales did occur, and also perhaps that they had qualms of conscience about signing the document. The solution was the use of a go-between, an intermediary or agent. The agent sold the particular vacant position which was in the gift of the director who commissioned him. Under this system, a director of the Company did not violate the obligations of his own position. The money paid for his services reached him under another designation. The converse was equally true. The agent would present a candidate and such an introduction was perfectly normal. A very good example of this is a notarial deed from Amsterdam dated

---

[8] The Hague, NA, Archief Radermacher 235; Middelburg, ZA, Archief Mathias-Pous-Tak van Poortvliet 227.
[9] The Hague, NA, VOC 4927, res. 8.1.1787; see also Gaastra, *De geschiedenis van de VOC*, pp. 160–1.
[10] Examples in Bruijn, *De admiraliteit van Amsterdam*, pp. 59–62.

2 November 1702. In it, the mother of Commander Haye Jansz declared that her son had paid *f.* 1,500 for his appointment. A former Company surgeon, the agent, had secretly handed the money over to somebody else. Before Jansz had set sail on 15 May 1702, the former surgeon had been a regular visitor to his home and so was able to tell him about favourable progress toward 'the desired goal'.[11]

The state of affairs with illegal payments could give rise to problems, if it suited a certain person to put another in a bad light. The result was sometimes a legal case and a hearing with witnesses, which generated useful material for later historians. This sort of situation occurred in Amsterdam in 1724. In 1707, Willem Sautijn (1678–1731) was appointed a director and he plunged himself enthusiastically into the sale of Company positions. He had two agents, the widow Evertje Vlaming and a German immigrant, Pieter Bakker, who both regularly visited the director privately. That went on until, on one occasion, Bakker insulted a prominent guest of Sautijn, which led to a breach in their relations. As a consequence, Vlaming and Bakker spread stories to Sautijn's political enemies in the city about sales of offices. The reports set in train a protracted legal battle, one which only came to an end with Sautijn's death in 1731. In the period 1717–1724, Sautijn is alleged to have earned *f.* 22,820 from selling positions. In the course of the investigation, several directors from the fitting out department who appointed commanders told the chief magistrate 'expressly' and without being asked that they had never perjured themselves, they had abided by their oaths and they would never award positions for money. Sautijn's colleagues were obviously afraid that the investigation would also involve them. All sorts of witnesses were summoned and because of the investigation we have the story of the shaky hand of Commander Keizer (see above). In 1720–1721, on Sautijn's behalf Evertje Vlaming had sold three commanders' positions to Isaac de Vries, Jan Geerse and Gerrit Loot for *f.* 2,000 each in cash. An unnamed applicant paid *f.* 2,500 for a commander's position in March 1724, but he never got appointed because in April the first accustations against Sautijn were made, so the 'victim' had his money returned. The post of third mate cost *f.* 300. However, this was not enough for Sautijn. He forced newly appointed men to borrow money from him at a usurious interest rate of 8 to 10 per cent. The price of *f.* 2,500 for a commander's position was not unusual in Zealand, nor were the sums of *f.* 1,200 for the job of first mate and *f.* 600 for that of second mate.[12]

The sums which a commander needed to purchase his command were high. Prices could vary but were the equivalent of two to three years' stipend. This is a clue that the position of commander opened the door to other opportunities

---

[11] Amsterdam, GA, Not. Arch. 5651, fols 458-462 (2.11.1702); *DAS*, no. 1895.
[12] Amsterdam, GA, Rechterlijk Archief 382, fol. 33ff (18.4.1724), 535, fols 15–16 (26.8.1724), 641A (dossier Backer/Sautijn) and 860, fol. 132; Elias, *De vroedschap*, pp. cxli–cxlv; Lequin, *Het personeel*, p. 47; *DAS*, nos. 2445, 2447 and 2469; Roos, *Zeeuwen en de VOC*, p. 173.

to earn money and considerably more than the wages paid by the Company. A third mate on the other hand would have earned enough to cover the price of his position in less than a year. Being a third mate was not as lucrative as being a commander. In a business which had so much continuity in its rules and customs over nearly two centuries and whose directors held office for scores of years without any break, the use of patronage to acquire the posts of commander or first mate probably never changed much. The records kept by the Radermachers and other directors also point in a similar direction. The two Radermachers, father and son, between them held the position of director for sixty years. Jakob van der Heim occupied his directorship for twenty-three years. In 1784 an attempt in Rotterdam to withdraw the position of third mate from the system and to have the candidates for this post present themselves personally sank without trace. The idea behind the proposal was that this step would lead to the appointment of more competent people, but any such change would have thrown the whole system into chaos, hence the veto of the reform.[13]

The court case against Sautijn and the notarial deed of 1702 reveal the presence of various sorts of intermediaries. A brief letter from Rotterdam, written on 28 January 1775, and kept by Van der Heim, offers a glimpse into the way a sailmaker was appointed. It reads: 'Most Honourable Gentleman ... you can be assured that this person, Jan den Otter, is competent to sail to the Indies as a sailmaker. I remain Honourable Sir, your most obedient servant Jan van der Pijpen.' It did not need to be any shorter than this. Jan den Otter did indeed sail as chief sailmaker on board the *Jonge Hellingman* on 6 April. He had been junior sailmaker on his previous voyage. A man called Morgans wrote a similar letter for a chief gunner. This is certainly the way the system worked but the amounts of money involved remain shrouded in mystery. For instance, what the words 'for the general account' – found in the Radermacher papers in a reference to the appointment of Adriaan van den Boer in 1750 – mean precisely will never be known.[14] Unqualified applicants were given short shrift by those directors with a conscience. Good applicants probably stood a much better chance. Keizer's appointments show the other side of the coin.

Asking Around

After a commander had been appointed, there was still one more hurdle to be cleared. The other Chambers had to be consulted about whether they agreed with the appointment or not and whether they knew anything to the detriment of the person concerned. There were various cases of commanders and ship's officers who had previously sailed home on the ships of other Chambers. If there were some objection, the appointment was provisionally withheld. On

---

[13] The Hague, NA, Archief Van der Heim 92, extract 21.6.1784.
[14] The Hague, NA, Archief Radermacher 234.

one occasion Van der Heim noted that an appointment was agreed, 'if there is no objection from Zealand'. In 1758, Amsterdam reported to Delft that it was withholding its consent for the appointment of First Mate Jakob Welgevaren as a commander, unless the directors in Delft could offer some cogent arguments why it should be approved. At that point, there were a great many other suitable officers available ashore. Welgevaren did get his ship, because the commander who had been the first choice fell ill. A few days after his departure, he stranded the ship off Calais. Director Gerard van Vredenburch blamed his fellow directors for Welgevaren's appointment.[15] Van Vredenburch recalled a similar blunder in 1747 noted in his father's papers. In that same year, a fellow townsman, Paulus Verschuur, was appointed commander of the *Rust en Werk*. The ship sailed off course far away along the coast of Surinam, which was a rare occurrence. The Governor of Surinam said of the officers that he had never seen 'more stupid and incompetent people ... who barely knew how to drop anchor'. The first mate 'was the least incompetent to navigate, nevertheless the others were all embittered against him'. The *Rust en Werk* returned home and set sail again in 1749, this time with a different commander. Hopefully this time it was not with another 'sprig of the faceless masses' on board.[16]

The system of consulting the other Chambers was often used to obtain more information about would-be commanders, rather than to thwart their being appointed to a post. At the very most an appointment might be postponed. The rules were followed faithfully and people were on the alert to see that they were not violated. In July 1754 the appointments of Paulus Rauwenhof and another colleague were already announced in the newspaper even though the round of consultation had only just been set in motion. The Zealand Chamber immediately asked Amsterdam for elucidation. In 1778 the Amsterdam Chamber informed the directors in Rotterdam that, although 'nothing direct could be found against' Pieter van Prooien which might have stopped his appointment from being approved, it was perhaps worth letting them know that Van Prooien had a reputation for treating his crews brutally. He had been guilty of such conduct on three earlier voyages. The Rotterdam directors were not pleased with this piece of information because three earlier candidates had failed to appear for the examination after presenting themselves for interview. So Van Prooien got his ship in part by default, and it was also not to be his last command.

There were two situations in which this consultation with other Chambers was important: if it was a first appointment or if the candidate had been suspended for some time.[17] When a first mate was promoted to commander, due attention had to be paid to his earlier appointments and to his examination

---

[15] The Hague, NA, Archief Van Vredenburch 1, 17.9.1758, and 13, no. 43 (18.9.1758); The Hague, NA, VOC 308, 18.9.1758.

[16] The Hague, NA, Archief Van Vredenburch 13, 14.8.1748.

[17] The Hague, NA, VOC 308, 18.7, 25.7, 5.8.1754 and 12.2.1778; The Hague, NA, Archief Van der Heim 92, 19.1.1778.

results. At the end of the 1720s, the *Heren Zeventien* warned against the employment of new officers since, they said, now 'there are senior men who apply for posts and no fault can be found with them'.[18] Pressure to make promotions too quickly had to be curbed. Much later in the century, this surplus of officers was very much a thing of the past. There was a shortage of good candidates. The door was opened wide to ship's officers from outside the Company. Though their backgrounds differed a great deal, that did not lead to their being rejected. In 1789 the Delft Chamber asked permission to appoint Simon Vaartjes who had been a whaler and had also sailed to the West. He had even made one voyage to the East in a chartered ship.[19] Another example is the identical request made by the Amsterdam Chamber on behalf of twenty-seven-year-old Lodewijk Willem van Rossum from Franeker, in Friesland. He was an officer with the Admiralty of Friesland and had no experience at all with the Company to offer. However, in 1789, at the insistence of the Amsterdam Chamber, it was also decreed that Dutchmen who had served with foreign Asian companies could only be appointed with the express permission of the *Heren Zeventien*. Amsterdam had thought it 'extremely dubious' that the Rotterdam Chamber had appointed one of its townsmen, Jan Mulder, commander since he had served with the German Emden Company as a second mate.[20]

The second really useful purpose of consultation concerned candidates who had been suspended by a Chamber and who had then tried their luck with another Chamber. If the candidate's ship had sunk or had run aground, the suspension invariably lasted until blame for the mishap had been apportioned. Suspension was also the punishment applied if rules and instructions were infringed for such offences as less than the registered cargo being found on board or smuggling. A suspension meant that a commander or ship's officer was 'unfit' for a new position. If the matter was cleared up or if the term of suspension had elapsed, the commander had to request rehabilitation from the Chamber that had punished him before he could submit a fresh application for a position with the Company. After he had done so, he was declared 're-admissible'. Nearly every year a commander was suspended either for a serious breach or for a somewhat lighter misdemeanour. This did not spell the end of his career. In almost every instance, the suspension had no effect whatsoever on his further career. In 1701, Jakob Onkruid was found guilty of prohibited private trade and made several vain requests to be rehabilitated, but afterwards he suceeded and was able to enjoy a long career as a commander. He was just one of many.

Hendrik Hilverduin was an example of a commander whose suspension had more serious consequences. After the end of a voyage on the *Admiraal De Ruyter* he was declared 'unfit' by the Amsterdam Chamber, for which he had already

---

[18] The Hague, NA, VOC 221, 10.8.1728.
[19] See Chapter 7.
[20] The Hague, NA, VOC 223, 30.10.1789, 297, 9.3, 24.4, 17.9, 23.10.1789, and 298, 10.5.1790.

served nineteen years. He was not given any new post and was threatened with poverty. He had, he wrote to the Chamber in 1766, done nothing wrong and he wanted to clear his name of the 'erroneous' report which had reduced him to such circumstances. Calumny spread about his behaviour during his latest voyage had cast him in a bad light. His letter had no effect so he tried to offer his services to the Enkhuizen Chamber. The directors there conferred with those in Amsterdam. Afterwards Hilverduin was given a command by Enkhuizen and sailed in January 1769. On the domestic front, the need for money was apparently extremely pressing. Hilverduin signed both a monthly and a transport letter. His finances recovered and such measures were no longer necessary when he was given another ship by the Enkhuizen Chamber in 1774.[21]

Agreements among the directors, written down in formal documents, determined many facets of the business of the Company. The appointment of a commander was only one of these. To the outside world, the boards of the Chambers presented a picture of harmony and 'unanimity'. After all, they were part of a collegiate administration. Unanimity radiates from every page of their resolutions. Only a few individual directors betrayed the fact that decisions were taken by a majority of votes. Certainly emotions could run high, ranging from dissension to outright anger. Commanders applying for posts who appeared before the directors at meetings unquestionably had to field very critical questions. Despite all this, it was the choice of the director whose turn it was which decided the fate of the applicant, and that choice was not necessarily the best one. Those applying for the positions as ship's officers faced the same procedure. Probably some money always changed hands in obtaining a post as commander or ship's officer. It was not any different with other positions in the Republic. Nevertheless, having the right contacts and money did not always guarantee the success of an application with the Company. There were still the official examinations and regulations for promotion, which had some effect in the selection process, so that talent did count.

---

[21] The Hague, NA, VOC 308, 23.6.1766 and 29.8.1768.

10

Examinations, Ranks and Training

The average Company commander was a professional seaman and a person bent on improving himself in life. He had gone to sea at a young age and had passed through the ranks in the Company from ship's boy, deckhand, sailor or petty officer before, somewhere around the age of twenty, he was appointed third mate. Gunner's mates in particular took this step. Overseas or during a voyage, this promotion to third mate could be an emergency measure passed by the ship's council. Because of the death of a commander or first mate and the subsequent promotions to fill vacancies, the lowest rank of the ship's officers fell open. Anyone with some knowledge of navigation, and there were such men always at hand among the crew, had a good chance of suddenly finding himself third mate. Once he had returned home, before his next voyage this man could present himself at one of the Chambers or he could pass his name on to a director through an agent in order to be able to receive a properly acknowledged appointment as a third mate from one of the Chambers. However, it was not quite as easy as it sounds. First the candidate had to pass an examination.

Examinations

In 1619, the VOC, specifically the Amsterdam Chamber, had taken the revolutionary step of introducing examinations for its ship's officers. The Amsterdam directors were convinced that sailing to Asia put higher demands than normal on the officers' knowledge of navigation. Before they were accepted for service, each first and second mate had to sit an examination, in which he was questioned on his knowledge of the instruments and techniques available for navigating the high seas to the East and back again. Simultaneously with the introduction of this requirement, the Chamber had also appointed an examiner. It was nearly half a century before the Zealand Chamber decided to follow the example set by Amsterdam. The four smaller Chambers took even longer to follow suit. It may be that they required their candidates to take some sort of test of competence, but the appointment of their own permanent examiners came only in the eighteenth century. The Rotterdam Chamber was the last to put such a system in place, and that was not until 1737.

On the international scene, examinations to test competence to make voyages to Asia were a rarity. It was not until 1720, a century after the VOC, that the French *Compagnie des Indes* required both practical and theoretical training of those who wanted to become officers, even though earlier the VOC system of examinations had already attracted some attention in France.[1] The English East India Company introduced tests only much later. The VOC also far outstripped the Dutch Navy in establishing criteria to test the knowledge of its officers. In 1677, the English Navy had introduced a sort of examination for its lieutenants. Mates in the Admiralities of Zealand and Amsterdam, petty officers in the Navy, were examined in the years 1670 to 1700. From 1702 naval officers in Rotterdam were required to sit an examination in which their knowledge was tested by flag officers and captains. However, it was only in the middle of the eighteenth century that every naval officer in the Dutch Republic was required to have his knowledge tested. Simultaneously, the same requirement was re-introduced for the petty officers and this time it was stipulated for all five Admiralties.

In the meantime, the Company had already made far greater progress in terms of checking the competence of its officers. In 1658, the Amsterdam Chamber decided that future third mates, those young men typically rising up through the ranks, had to prove their knowledge in an examination. This was followed by a refinement in the regulations in 1681. Anybody who had sailed to the East once as a ship's officer was no longer required to sit the examination for the same post, but he would have to sit an examination if he applied for a higher rank. Even though the other Chambers did not employ their own examiners directly, their freedom in terms of appointment policy was restricted. In 1657, the *Heren Zeventien* had stipulated that only commanders 'who had knowledge of navigating on the high seas' should be appointed and particular attention should be paid to 'experienced commanders, as this is the most serious concern of the Company'. In 1661, it was decreed that no commander could be appointed without having had experience as a first mate. At the beginning of the eighteenth century, coinciding with the appointment of their own examiners by the smaller Chambers, the regulations were tightened even more. The 1661 regulation was re-issued in 1700. Three years earlier, it had been decreed in Batavia that no second mate could be promoted to first mate in the East unless he had first been examined by a committee composed of two commanders and the Superintendent of the Shipyard. Moreover, any appointments made overseas always had to be confirmed by the *Heren Zeventien*. In 1718, these gentlemen decided that each first mate had to sail first as a second mate and each second mate had to sail first as a third mate before promotion. A decade later, a ship's officer had to hand a written report of his examination results over to his direc-

---

[1] Mörzer Bruyns, *Schip recht door zee*, pp. 66–7.

tors. In principle, after 1718 every first mate who became a commander would have had to have been examined three times.[2]

The instructions issued in 1720 by the Zealand Chamber to Abraham Anias upon his appointment as examiner show how the regulations worked in practice for certifying the competence of ship's officers. The candidate had to present himself at the shipyard, where he was obliged to give written answers to the questions on a printed examination paper. He was forbidden to take instruction in 'navigation or the skills of ship's officers' from Anias beforehand. The candidate was expected to have garnered his knowledge from his study of one of the many editions of Claes Hendricksz Gietermaker's *'t Vergulde licht der zeevaert ofte konst der stuurlieden* (The Gilded Light of Navigation or the Art of Navigation) or Klaas de Vries' *Schat-kamer ofte konst der stuurlieden* (Treasury or the Art of Navigation), with the help of a private tutor. At the back of these books were lists of questions and answers on the subject matter. Later, the examination questions were made available in a printed version, such as *Examen der Stierlieden* (Examinations for Ship's Officers) by the Hoorn examiner Pieter Warius, published in 1751. The written examination was followed by an oral, held after the examiner had read the 'examination paper' and had pointed out any errors to the examinee. If all was well in 'figures and in calculations', the oral examination took place in the office of the Superintendent of the Shipyard, in the presence of two directors (*heren van de equipage*, directors of fitting out). If the candidate showed that he understood the work he had done thoroughly, he was awarded a certificate. This piece of paper was his passport to an appointment. Anias was given a fixed sum for every examination successfully sat. For a first mate this was ƒ. 15.30, for a second mate ƒ. 12.00 and for a third mate ƒ. 7.65.[3] If a candidate failed, Anias received nothing. It seems likely that the examination questions, set on the basis of the known texts, would have been highly predictable.

Later, once again it was the Amsterdam Chamber that intervened in certifying navigational skills. In 1743 it split the function of examiner into two, one for theory and one for practice. Jan de Marre was the man appointed for seamanship in 1745.[4] From that time, both examiners had to check the ship's logs of vessels coming back from Asia, which had to be handed in at the completion of a voyage. The examiners were to be vigilant and check that the commander and his officers had adhered faithfully to the sailing instructions. After a while,

---

[2] Davids, *Zeewezen en wetenschap*, pp. 294–5; *Nederlandsch-Indisch Plakaatboek* III, 22.2.1697; J.R. Bruijn, 'Seafarers in Early Modern and Modern Times: Change and Continuity', *International Journal of Maritime History* XVII, no. 1 (2005), pp. 1–16, see pp. 3 and 6.

[3] The Hague, NA, Archief Radermacher 234; C.A. Davids, 'Het navigatie-onderwijs aan personeel van de VOC', in P. van Mil and M. Scharloo (eds), *De VOC in de kaart gekeken. Cartografie en navigatie van de Verenigde Oostindische Compagnie 1602–1799* (The Hague, 1988), pp. 65–74. Gietermaker's book was published in Amsterdam in 1660, 1677, 1697, 1725, 1731, 1748 and 1774, and De Vries' book in 1702, 1713, 1736, 1749, 1777 and 1818.

[4] See Chapter 6.

the other Chambers also adopted this procedure. The crowning moment of the examination structure came in 1751 when even a commander could not escape having to sit an examination personally before he could be appointed to his maiden command. In Zealand this requirement was only introduced in 1766.

The last radical change in the examination system took place in 1793. The reason was differences in the examination of knowledge of calculating longitude at sea. Great improvements had been made in these calculations in the two preceding decades. The Chambers of Amsterdam and Zealand designed a joint new instruction for the examiners. For each of the four examinations, from third mate to commander, a description was given of what the subject matter should be. Before the examination was held, each candiate had to give his name, place of residence and religion, as well as a detailed account of his earlier appointments. The examination continued to be both written and oral. Article 5 of the 1793 Instructions expressly forbade any secret consultation of the candidate's own notes or books. In other words he could not crib. The report of the examination had to note whether any of the candidate's errors had been caused by sheer ignorance or could be attributed to inattention and simple mistakes of calculation. All this made the task of the examiners more demanding. Therefore their stipends were raised in 1794, in Amsterdam to *f.* 1,200, in Zealand to *f.* 600 and in the other Chambers to *f.* 150. To what extent examinations before that time had taken place without cheating is impossible to say. In 1796, someone who knew his Company inside out at the time of its collapse said that the permanent examiners 'generally ran a sort of business ... with their examinations and testimonials'.[5]

Just as in the case of applications, much of the information about examinations remains obscure. To what extent the Chambers actually resorted to reciprocal agreements in the selection and appointment of their ship's officers and commanders is not known. When Jan Pietersz Keizer was appointed in 1719, Enkhuizen disregarded the regulations which Amsterdam insisted on upholding. In 1778, Director Van der Heim in Rotterdam was clearly annoyed when Frederik Godert Wever and two others failed to turn up for the examinations after having appeared for interviews. His mood would not have been improved when he heard that, shortly afterwards, Wever had sailed as a commander for the Amsterdam Chamber.[6]

'1742'

In the cold, extraordinarily cold months of March and April 1742, during their spring meeting in Amsterdam, the *Heren Zeventien* decided on a drastic reorganization of the tried and tested system of ranks, stipends and promotions.

---

[5] The Hague, NA, VOC 144, 3.12.1792, 301, 2.5.1793, 302, 11.6.1794 and 11528, no. 67; Davids, *Zeewezen en wetenschap*, pp. 295–6 and 454.
[6] The Hague, NA, Archief Van der Heim 92, 19.1.1778; *DAS* II, no. 4331.

22. Octant. Parts of an octant were found by divers in the 1743 wreck of the *Hollandia*. They are tangible evidence of the early use of this new navigational instrument on board Company ships. The octant shown here is a reconstruction made from the salvaged parts. The frame is new.

In their efforts they left no stone unturned but in the end they failed to make a really lasting impression. The main instigator was Van Imhoff, who had just been appointed Governor-General. He had spotted deficiencies on the ships and had expressed grave doubts about the quality of the officer corps.[7] The practical effectuation of Van Imhoff's *Consideratiën* (Considerations) meant a militarization of the highest ranking ship's officers, and the *Heren Zeventien* gave their consent. It was not long before there was even talk of setting up a supreme war council and the appointment of flag officers.[8]

Nobody could remember a time when the Company had not employed commanders and ship's officers. The latter were divided up into three ranks:

---

[7] See Chapter 8.
[8] The Hague, VOC 222, 27.3.1745. For the weather see J. Buisman, *Duizend jaar weer, wind en water in de Lage landen* 5 (1675–1750) (Franeker, 2006), pp. 731–2.

the lowest, the third mate, always earned a monthly wage of *f.* 26, the second mate received *f.* 32 and the first mate *f.* 48–50. The amount of the commander's stipend depended on his experience. On his maiden voyage, he earned *f.* 66 a month and after that his stipend rose to *f.* 72 on his second voyage and on his third and subsequent voyages it reached *f.* 80. The 1740 rates were the same as they were in 1650. In 1742 a new top stipend of *f.* 100 was added for the new rank of captain. A far more important change was that from that date commanders and mates were no longer sailing on the big East Indiamen, but captains, captain-lieutenants and lieutenants, and even cadets. These were all ranks which were used in the Navy and the underlying idea was to attract naval officers to seek service with the VOC. In the first instance, the highest stipend of 100 guilders was intended for such men.[9]

The regulations introduced in 1742 and in subsequent years actually failed to generate any great interest among naval officers. Fewer than had been hoped for reported to the Company. Nevertheless, there were a few commanders who profited enormously from the new regulations. Jean Belleveau had only made one voyage as commander and Christoffel Blom had yet to make his maiden voyage. Instantly both were promoted to captain and were paid a stipend of *f.* 100 per month. There can be no doubt that they were Van Imhoff's protégés. Jacobus Verleng in Amsterdam and Willem De Wijs in Rotterdam were also promoted to captain, but they each had three voyages as commander behind them. For many of their colleagues, the resolutions made in March and April 1742 were not any better than the then prevailing bitter north winds. Commanders and lieutenants from the Navy who were junior in years and experience were given command of the big ships and as captains enjoyed higher bonuses and more profitable perks. A few relative outsiders reached the rank of captain apparently with little or no effort, while existing commanders were made masters of only the smallest charter ships.

In 1746, the new appointments policy was given greater clarity. The *Heren Zeventien* decided that in future all Chambers had to follow a uniform policy. No longer would any first mate be able to be promoted to any rank other than that of commander, the lowest of the commanding ranks. Having completed two round-trip voyages to Asia with a stipend of *f.* 66 and subsequently *f.* 72 per month, a commander was able to call himself a captain-lieutenant on his third voyage, with a corresponding stipend of *f.* 80. With the exception of their ranking, nothing had changed from the situation before 1742. The opportunities to generate extra income were also unchanged, with the exception that a commander was now allowed to bring a small military chest filled with tea and porcelain home with him from the East. Only on his fourth voyage could he call himself captain and earn *f.* 100 a month, with suitably increased bonuses and perks. Consequently, from the moment of any new appointment all the available

---

[9] The Hague, NA, VOC 116, 11.7.1718, and 222, 14.3.1742 with the first resolutions.

commanders were placed on the revised scale. Many could call themselves either captain-lieutenant or captain and they eagerly availed themselves of the opportunity to do so. What is more, as captains they earned more.[10]

In 1746 the *Heren Zeventien* also passed a regulation that although appointments would continue to be made by individual Chambers, one of the two Company advocates who acted as permanent secretaries to the *Heren Zeventien* had to sign the letters of appointment of the captains and captain-lieutenants. They were not required to perform this duty for a commander. Moreover, there were regulations about which officers were to staff East Indiamen. A captain had to have a first mate with the rank of first lieutenant, a second lieutenant, a second mate, a third mate and two naval cadets under him. A captain-lieutenant had a first mate with the rank of lieutenant, a second mate, two third mates and a cadet. There was no clarification, however, of how the staff officers were to refer to their commander. The requirements for staffing opened opportunities. For example, as captain-lieutenant, Commander Van Mensburg took his son with him as a cadet in 1748.[11]

The Return to the Old System

The regulations of 1742 and 1746 were soon rescinded. They irritated the old guard and did not produce the desired influx of naval officers. To make matters worse, they were more expensive because of the top stipends and the higher bonuses and perks. It surely could not have been the intention of the *Heren Zeventien* that a Dirk van der Schilde or a Kornelis Quack now earned more than he would have done under the old system as an ordinary commander. In October 1755, all the innovations were revoked. Once again the highest position was that of commander. The salaries were cut back to the levels they had been at prior to 1742, so the highest monthly wage was *f.* 80. All the opportunities to earn extra money reverted to the former level, including opportunities overseas. There was a proviso that in wartime, any naval officers serving with the Company would be paid the same wage as they would have been paid by their Admiralties, at least if they had commanded a warship two or three times. In peacetime, naval officers would earn the same as the Company's own personnel.[12] It was under these conditions that naval officers such as Stavorinus later sailed with the VOC.

The commanders who were hardest hit financially by the 1755 regulations were those who had reached the rank of captain. Their only consolation, and also

---

[10] The Hague, NA, VOC 123, 18.8.1742, and 222, 24.7.1742 and 17.11.1744, and Archief Van Vredenburch 11, 23.8.1746; see also Chapter 8.
[11] The Hague, NA, VOC 14757.
[12] The Hague, NA, VOC 128, 15.10.1755, and 308, 18.9.1755; *Nederlandsch-Indisch Plakaatboek* VII, 7.9.1756.

that of their colleague captain-lieutenants, was that they could continue to use their rank, which pleased them. In 1768 Commander Christiaan Blom tried to obtain that right and submitted a petition asking that he also be appointed with the rank of captain. The Amsterdam Chamber had no hesitation in turning the request down flat. After all, the title had been abolished in 1755.[13]

In Batavia, Van Imhoff's ideas about the militarization of the officer corps held sway as long as he remained Governor-General. In 1743, he asked Batavia to pay more attention to 'sea power' in the East. There were too few ships available which, when armed with extra cannon, could patrol against pirates and smugglers or maintain order in wartime. Furthermore, a 'reasonable gradation of rank among the officers and attention paid to and love of the profession of sea service' would be strengthened, he thought, by the appointment of several high-ranking officers. He had in mind a vice-admiral, a rear-admiral and two commodores as 'heads of squadrons' – the Governor-General had become familiar with naval jargon. One of the two commodores was appointed. He was Dirk Wolter van Nimwegen, who was to earn not $f.$ 100 but $f.$ 120 a month. The other flag ranks did not materialize, but in 1753 the nucleus of Van Imhoff's plan was laid down in a set of regulations.[14]

Suddenly, around 1760 the appointment of a vice-admiral surfaced once again. Probably the presence in Asian waters of large British and French naval squadrons during the Seven Years War (1756–1763) had stirred up some anxiety in Batavia. Nikolaas Houting was appointed vice-admiral. He was a scion of the Monnickendam gentry and held the position of rear-admiral in the Admiralty of the Northern Quarter. He had commanded warships as captain on various occasions. In 1761 he and his family left for Batavia as passengers on an Amsterdam ship. He took up his duties in 1762 but these can hardly be said to have been impressive. They certainly diverged from what Van Imhoff had once envisaged. Commander Stavorinus, himself a naval officer, met Houting on several occasions in 1769 and 1770, when he was anchored in the Batavia Roads. Stavorinus said Houting supervised repairs to ships, inspected the ship's logs, signed sailing orders and permits for the victualling of ships and took care of other maritime matters. His was a shore posting. There was no question of generating 'sea power' on his part. In fact, as a vice-admiral earning $f.$ 200 a month, Houting was doing the work of a Superintendent of the Shipyard. In 1772 the latter official was reinstated after Houting had died at the age of sixty-six. Earlier, this job had often been done by commanders and that practice was revived after 1772. Hence another of Van Imhoff's innovations disappeared without a whisper. Houting had been able to rejoice in the fact that his Admiralty had appointed him a

---

[13] The Hague, NA, VOC 128, 15.10.1755, and 308, 18.9.1755; *Nederlandsch-Indisch Plakaatboek* VII, 7.9.1756. The Hague, NA, VOC 308, 5.9.1768.
[14] Schooneveld-Oosterling, *Generale Missiven* XI, pp. 5–6, 485 and 725; *Nederlandsch-Indisch Plakaatboek* VI, pp. 475–7.

full vice-admiral in 1766, with the same stipend as he was already receiving in Batavia from the Company.[15]

The Commander Becomes a Captain After All

Despite all these changes of plan, eventually the men who commanded the Company ships were all made captains and captain-lieutentants. The reason for this change of heart was the war which had broken out with Great Britain in December 1780, the Fourth Anglo-Dutch War. In July 1781, the Amsterdam Chamber appointed the tried and tested commander Jan Paardekoper and another four of his colleagues captain. Their ship's officers were also given corresponding naval ranks and their ships were fitted out with heavier armaments. Nevertheless, it was only in May 1784 that naval ranks were generally introduced.[16] None of the changes incurred higher costs for the Company. The alteration applied purely to the ranks used, just as it had in 1755. Even a commander/captain who sailed on his fourth voyage did not receive a stipend any higher than for his first.

The Company commanders would never become the equal of naval officers. Indeed, some naval officers such as Baron Van Kinckel continued to speak of them with disdain. For their part, the directors of the Company sometimes found it difficult to find the right touch in dealing with naval officers. After all, it was an era in which such concepts as respect, precedence and ceremonial played an important role. The *Heren Zeventien* even promoted naval rear-admiral Houting to vice-admiral and so the commander of their own naval forces. He was given the same rank as a member of the *Hoge Regering* and his title of address was 'Noble Sir'. However, in order of precedence he came only after the most junior member of the Government in Batavia. He was expected to attend its sessions, but could only speak when maritime matters were discussed.

In 1783, the naval squadron, referred to above, sailed for Asia – an event which had never happened before. Its purpose was to assist the Company by boosting its waning military power. The captain in command of the squadron, the commodore, was Jakob Pieter van Braam, and Stavorinus was one of the other captains. As former commanders, both knew how affairs were managed in Batavia and had had experience with Houting. One of the points which concerned the *Heren Zeventien* when they were compiling the Instructions for the naval squadron was that, if he were to remain ashore in Batavia, the commodore might detract from the 'splendour' of the VOC Government. After some humming and hawing, it was agreed that Van Braam would be given the same

---

[15] The Hague, NA, VOC 222, 6.10.1760 and 14.4.1761; *Realia* III (Batavia, 1886), p. 180; *DAS* II, no. 3821; Bossaers, '"Van kintsbeen"', p. 57; Wilcocke, *Voyages ... Stavorinus* I, pp. 297–9.
[16] The Hague, NA, VOC 222, 3.5 and 27.11.1784, and 308, 19.7.1781; *DAS* II, no. 4392.

military honours – salutes and the like – as an ordinary member of the *Hoge Regering*. The other captains would be given the honours due to an extraordinary member. In the order of precedence, Van Braam and his captains would be placed below the most junior extraordinary member of the Council. As matters transpired, it seemed that, as long as the Government in Batavia and Van Braam co-operated in military matters, there were no problems. Difficulties arose only towards the end of the squadron's stay. Then animosity began to materialize. Van Braam insisted on his prerogatives and got his own way. However, the members of the *Hoge Regering* got their revenge. In Batavia the naval officers were socially isolated. They were not invited to dinner parties or other social occasions. Furthermore, the commanders who were in Batavia behaved in the same fashion towards the naval officers, among whom were sometimes men who had formerly been their colleagues, albeit briefly.[17] After 1742, naval officers and ranks in the Company never really managed to come to terms with each other on matters of status and precedence.

The *Académie de Marine* in Batavia

Van Imhoff had an overall vision for improving the officer corps and militarizing it. He was convinced that it was essential that the Company should run its own training programme. A school with boarding facilities was a revolutionary idea and such an institution was not to be found anywhere else abroad. On his way to Batavia on the *Herstelder* in 1742–1743, he worked out a plan for an *Académie de Marine* (Naval Academy). Shortly after his arrival, a definite decision was made to establish such an institution. This step, it was said, signalled the establishment of 'a corps of cadets to be trained to be naval officers', and this would 'cost the Company very little in comparison with the promised benefits which could be anticipated in due course'.

Training lasted four years. The third of these was a year of practical work on board a ship. There was room for twenty-four boys between the ages of twelve and fourteen from 'decent' Protestant families. The *Académie* was housed in spacious premises situated in one of the best parts of the city. Subjects studied included arithmetic, mathematics, navigation and artillery. This was combined with training in the use of arms, and language classes, including Latin, Malay, the Malabar language (probably Malayalam) and Persian, so that graduates could command the Moorish (Muslim) sailors in their own languages. Writing,

---

[17] The Hague, NA, Staten-Generaal 9223, fols 735 and 738; AA VIII, 59 (14.7.1784) and 61; Archief Meerman van der Goes 10 (26.12.1781) and 18 (10.1.1783); these references have been borrowed from J.R. Verbeek, 'Kapitein Jacob Pieter van Braam. Commandant van het eerste landseskader in Indië 1783–1786' (MA thesis, Leiden University, 1981). See also S. Dörr, *De kundige kapitein. Brieven en bescheiden betrekking hebbende op Jan Olphert Vaillant kapitein-ter-zee (1751–1800)* (Zutphen, 1988), pp. 146–8 and 153.

drawing, shipbuilding and divinity were also part of the course. Lessons ran from 7 a.m. to 5 p.m. On Wednesday and Saturday mornings, there was instruction in dancing, fencing and horse-riding. The head of the *Académie* was a governor. From 1745 to 1750 this was Paulus Paulusz, the chief cartographer in Batavia. The school was supervised by a board of governors which included a member of the *Hoge Regering* and the Superintendent of the Shipyard. The domestic side was looked after by a European steward, a cook and six ship's boys. The cadets received pocket money of *f.* 10 per month.[18]

From the 1690s, the Company had run a training course for ministers and catechists in Ceylon. When he was governor of the island in 1737, Van Imhoff had introduced improvements in this seminary in Colombo. Hence, an academy for maritime personnel was not a new departure for him. He also established a second seminary in Batavia in 1743. Everything had been carefully thought through, including the finances. The money from fines imposed on Company personnel went to the *Académie*, although sometimes half of it was destined for the seminary. This was how Commander Verdoes forfeited four months' stipend to the *Académie*, when he and a colleague were punished for not co-operating adequately against the pirates on the west coast of India. Many of the newly appointed officials in the East paid a tax which went to naval education. The receipts from all sorts of other new taxes ended up there as well. In order to ensure that the standard of the education was kept high, in 1747 the reader in navigation at the *Athenaeum Illustre* and examiner of the Amsterdam Chamber, Martinus Martens, was appointed correspondent. Martens informed the *Académie* about new developments and was paid *f.* 240 a year for this work. A similar sum was spent each year on the purchase of books and instruments. There were masters for teaching navigation and mathematics, French and fencing.[19]

There were sufficient graduates from the academy (*académisten*), some of whom were the sons of high-ranking European army men. Examinations were held every year on 23 December. If he passed these, the cadet was given the rank of lieutenant and went to sea. In 1747 three of them passed, including Paulus Rauwenhof, Van Imhoff's 'golden boy'. A year later there were four and in 1749 as many as five who could be promoted to lieutenant. The expectation was that the *Académie* could train enough students each year that 'shortly as a result all the shipping of the Company will assume a completely new guise'. Indeed, some progress was made in this direction because at the beginning of the 1750s there

---

[18] Schooneveld-Oosterling, *Generale Missiven* XI, pp. 24, 338, 362, 446, 453 and 477. See also J.P. Nieborg, *Indië en de zee. De opleiding tot zeeman in Nederlandsch-Indië 1743–1962* (Amsterdam, 1989), pp. 20–6.

[19] J. van Goor, *Jan Kompenie as Schoolmaster. Dutch Education in Ceylon 1690–1795* (Groningen, 1978), ch. IV; C.W.Th. van Boetzelaer van Asperen en Dubbeldam, *De Protestantsche kerk in Nederlandsch-Indië. Haar ontwikkeling van 1602–1939* (The Hague, 1947), pp. 245–6.

were so many officers available for the returning fleet that the *Hoge Regering* in Batavia appointed two men to the same post, a move which incidentally failed to please the *Heren Zeventien*.

Van Imhoff was the driving force behind the institution. After his death in 1750, the *Académie* fell into decline, the training being considered too expensive. At the end of 1755, the *Académie* was closed, much to the relief of many of the inhabitants of Batavia who had had to pay a whole array of taxes to support it. The seminary also closed its doors in the same year.[20]

The *Académie* had certainly had its uses. Of the twelve young lieutenants produced at the examinations between 1747 and 1749, four achieved the rank of commander. Apart from Rauwenhof, they were Willem van der Nieuwpoort, George Christiaan Honsdorp and Johan Willem Munts. They had all enjoyed a well-rounded education in maritime matters and were well acquainted with the etiquette which reigned in naval circles. In earlier days, a mate could never have counted on such an education. As far as Batavia was concerned, it would have been better if mates had been trained at home in the Republic. Perhaps the unspoken thought behind this idea was that in the Navy such ship's officers were no more than petty officers. Moreover, during the last few years before the *Académie* closed, a sort of small school had been established in the shipyard in Batavia. There a host of ship's boys were given shelter after their arrival. Without the facility the fear was that they would have just roamed around. Future ship's officers would certainly be found among the boys in the shelter.[21] The annoyance among the older Company commanders and ship's officers about the 1742 reforms and the *Académie* was understandable. The same could be said for the 'old sea dogs' who had to overcome a great aversion to 'being made subordinate to the command of a freshly hatched naval lieutenant from among the cadets'. By 1755, everthing had disappeared.

The Usual Course of Instruction and the Changes Introduced

A ship's officer had to have a good understanding of certain aspects of mathematics and astronomy. In order to fix the course, he had to be able to calculate, and this skill was also essential in determining the distance covered in a twenty-four-hour period. He also had to have mastered plane trigonometry in order to discover the estimated position of the ship, or at the least he had to know how to use tables of the compass points. Concepts derived from astronomy such as the latitude, altitude and declination of a heavenly body were necessary to check

---

[20] The Hague, NA, VOC 222, 15.10.1755; Schooneveld-Oosterling, *Generale Missiven* XI, pp. 592, 725 and 838; F. de Haan, 'De "Académie de Marine" te Batavia, 1743–1755', *Tijdschrift Indische Taal-, Land- en Volkenkunde* XXXVIII (1895), pp. 551–621.
[21] D.B. van Heuven, 'Nautisch onderwijs op Java in vervlogen dagen', *Marineblad* 63 (1953), pp. 544–52 and 1256–65.

the estimated latitude by reading the height of a star or of the sun at midday. Determining latitude at a time other than noon could be done, as could every calculation, without the use of logarithms, but these facilitated the calculations and decreased the chance of mistakes. The calculation of compass variations had to be done by taking a bearing from the sun. The determination of longitude using distance to the moon was done by spherical triangulation.[22]

These subjects were taught at the *Académie* in Batavia, but ordinary ship's officers had to learn such things on their own. They could use the textbooks mentioned earlier, by Gietermaker and De Vries, which were frequently reprinted and supplemented. In these books, matters such as determining courses and recognition of shallows were also explained in a conversation between a commander and a ship's officer, cast in the form of questions and answers. Instructions from the Company about the characteristics of winds in various oceans were also printed in the book and detailed explanations were given. A third book appeared in 1766, written by Pybo Steenstra, examiner to the Amsterdam Chamber. Entitled *Grondbeginzelen der stuurmanskunst* (Principles of Navigation), it was based on the latest insights and innovations. There were also all kinds of tracts dealing with specific aspects of navigation, such as calculation of latitude and using octants and sextants. Tables and almanacs were also readily available.

Instruction in these subjects took place partly at sea and partly ashore. During a voyage, a third mate was expected 'to be making calculations and studying navigation', and indeed this is what happened. He had to be present at noon when all the officers measured the height of the sun.[23] Ashore, in the home ports and in many towns and villages there were a number of private tutors in navigation. Many versatile schoolmasters in country villages also set themselves up as such. The lessons, for which the pupils paid at least *f.* 36, lasted six weeks or more. This was the tariff of schoolmaster Pieter Holm (1696–1776) for the course at his small school *Schip recht door zee* (Ship Dead on Course) in his home in the old centre of Amsterdam. The 'lecture room' was furnished with two desks at which to write, three tables at which to determine a position, and six benches. Between 1737 and 1774, Holm taught more than 500 pupils, a proportion of whom were from the Company. Some attended for cramming for examinations. Holm also sold all sorts of navigational instruments and aids. The various other small schools will not have been very different.

The bookkeeping of Holm's school shows what has always been suspected. Naturally, on Company ships there were always sailors and petty officers who wanted to climb up higher through the ranks. Ship's officer was always a sought-

---

[22] Davids, *Zeewezen en wetenschap*, p. 335.
[23] *Ibid.*, pp. 319–26; E. Crone, 'Pieter Holm en zijn zeevaartschool', reprinted from *De Zee* (1930), pp. 5–20. In the ship's papers of East Indiamen captured by the British (kept in the National Archives, Kew, London, Prize Papers) there are copies of various calculations made by lower-ranking ship's officers on board, as I was informed by Dr R. van Gelder.

after post. Boys from seafaring families, like those from Enkhuizen and other towns, were aware from their earliest childhood that they had to study if they were to make progress on board. In his cash book, Holm noted who took lessons with him and what instruments they happened to purchase from him. Alongside many names, but not all of them, he wrote down what their rank was and for what route their studies were intended. Among his pupils, forty-four sailed for the Amsterdam Chamber and three for that of Hoorn. By far the great majority of them took lessons in navigation, while five came to cram for their examinations. Of the nineteen pupils whose rank Holm noted, twelve were ship's officers of all ranks and the rest were sailors, gunner's or boatswain's mates. Presumably, among the remaining twenty-eight pupils there were many sailors. Holm showed some prophetic vision in 1765 when he wrote alongside the name of David Westvaal of the Hoorn Chamber, 'not much given to learning'. Six years later Westvaal was still a sailor.

When he sailed on board the *Kronenburg* of the Amsterdam Chamber in December 1758, Commander Willem Hoogland had with him a gunner's mate, a quartermaster and a third mate, all of whom had taken navigation lessons with Holm. The three ship's officers of Commander Jan Spek had all attended Holm's school together in August 1759, studying navigation, and cramming for their examinations. From sailor, to gunner's mate to first mate, all had paid *f.* 36 out of their own pockets for the lessons in navigation, or *f.* 6 for cramming. They did not buy many instruments as these were supplied by the Company. Each ship's officer bought the new octant which had come into general use around 1748.[24]

Besides practical education on board, private study, and lessons at a small seaman's school, some new forms of education in navigation were added in the eighteenth century. At certain periods during the seventeenth century lectures were given in mathematics, astronomy and navigation at the *Athenaeum Illustre* in Amsterdam, but from approximately 1710 there was always a permanent member of staff who taught these subjects, usually a reader. Commander, dramatist and theatre director Jan de Marre attended some of these lectures. From 1743 to 1763, Martens was reader there. Ordinary ship's officers and commanders did not avail themselves of such educational facilities.

The *Zeemanscollege* (Seaman's College), established by Cornelis Douwes (1712–1773), was a completely new departure. Douwes, a colleague of Holm, had put forward a plan to establish this school – the aim being to train seamen in the theory of navigation – to the Admiralty, the Amsterdam Chamber and the Amsterdam Town Council. These three institutions financed the school on the Oudezijds Achterburgwal. The actual education was free. Among the seventy-four pupils enrolled there in February 1750 were twenty-two boys from orphanages or who had indigent parents. Enrolling such pupils was a condition made

---

[24] Crone, *Cornelis Douwes*, pp. 4–19 (the navigational log of J.C. Baane); Crone, 'Pieter Holm', pp. 40–60; Mörzer Bruyns, *Schip recht door zee*, pp. 71–87 and 155–204 (text from Holm's cash book); DAS II, nos. 3749 and 3796.

by the town council for its co-operation and support. Practical instruction on the water was part of the programme. The vast majority of the pupils came from the Admiralty and its officers were given separate lessons in the mornings. The others had their lessons in the evenings. The initial enthusiasm of the Amsterdam Chamber rapidly waned. In 1750, only ten of its ship's officers were enrolled, even though the Chamber paid one-third of the costs. When a similar school was established in Rotterdam in 1751, the Company abstained from sponsoring it. It was said that the Seaman's College in Amsterdam 'is of such little use, how much less use it would be for the Rotterdam Chamber which fitted out only one-eighth the ships the Amsterdam Chamber did'. After Douwes' death in 1773, the Company withdrew its sponsorship from the Seaman's College.[25] The lectures which they attended at the *Zeemanscollege* were the first compulsory education naval officers had ever had to follow.

With a very few exceptions any aspiring ship's officer with the Company in search of an education in navigation was in fact dependent on his own perseverance and on private schoolmasters. He was given precious little assistance by his employer, which set requirements about his knowledge and examinations to test it before an appointment. There was more chance of finding this sort of education in Amsterdam than anywhere else, with opportunities slim to non-existent in the other Company towns. The Renswoude Foundation in Delft was one possibility.[26] A few selected orphans such as Johannes de Kort were given the opportunity to train there. The same sort of education was also offered in the branches of the Foundation in Utrecht and The Hague. In all, the Foundation produced eighteen ship's officers for the Company, but only De Kort ever became a commander. From 1785, the *Kweekschool voor de Zeevaart* (Navigational College) in Amsterdam offered boys aged from twelve to sixteen professional training to become a ship's officer. It was a boarding school. In 1787–1789, ten trainees sailed to the East as cadets. Between 1790 and 1794 this number rose to no less than ninety-five, but by then they included not just cadets but also boys training to be petty officers. Initially the trainees sailed only on ships of the Amsterdam Chamber but gradually they could also be found on the vessels of the other Chambers as well.[27]

This *Kweekschool* was the result of a private initiative in which Guillelmus Titsingh (1733–1805), one of the bookkeepers of the Amsterdam Chamber, played a leading role. A similar foundation had been established three years

---

[25] Crone, *Cornelis Douwes*, pp. 122–43; Davids, *Zeewezen en wetenschap*, pp. 326–8.

[26] See Chapter 4.

[27] N.D.B. Habermehl, 'De Kweekschool voor de Zeevaart vanaf de oprichting in 1785 tot de vernietiging in 1811. Een Amsterdams antwoord op het kwantitatieve en kwalitatieve tekort aan zeevarenden', *Mededelingen Nederlandse Vereniging voor Zeegeschiedenis* 42 (1981), pp. 5–40, see pp. 28–9; J.C.M. Warnsinck, *De Kweekschool voor de Zeevaart en de Stuurmanskunst 1785-1935* (Amsterdam, 1935), pp. 74–6. For the Foundation, see Verbout-Wamsteeker, 'Navigatieopleidingen'.

earlier, in 1782, in Semarang on the north coast of Java. Johannes Siberg (1740–1817), who had once sailed for the Rotterdam Chamber as a gunner's mate and had risen high in the East, becoming rich and powerful, financed the navigation school there out of his own pocket. It offered a three-year course and in many ways it resembled the defunct *Académie*. Boys aged between twelve and fourteen could enrol to study a broad range of subjects. The Company even gave the pupils places on board its ships as cadets, with the prospect of becoming sub-lieutenants. This school, which was also called the *Marineschool* (Naval School), produced many cadets for the Company and did not cost it a penny.[28]

The 1619 Resolution of the Amsterdam Chamber which led to the introduction of examinations for ship's officers and the appointment of examiners was gradually expanded and refined. The other Chambers followed the example of Amsterdam, albeit rather tardily. When it came to the actual training of their ship's officers, the Chambers were not greatly bothered. With a few exceptions, ship's officers had to make their own way. The result was that right up to the liquidation of the Company, for ship's boys who wanted to get ahead the possibility of becoming a ship's officer was always open. Christiaan Lond is a late example of this rise through the ranks. He arrived in Batavia in 1784 as a deckhand on an Enkhuizen ship. He was promoted to sailor and, during a voyage from Ceylon to Batavia, his commander died and it turned out that Lond was the only person on the ship who had an understanding of navigation. Sailor Lond guided the ship safely to the harbour of Padang on the west coast of Sumatra. Afterwards, the *Marineschool* in Semarang proudly announced in 1788 that Lond had once taken several lessons there.[29]

---

[28] Nieborg, *Indië en de zee*, pp. 28–32.
[29] *Ibid.*, p. 31.

11

Normal Income

For the vast majority of employees, the financial remuneration for their employment in the Company consisted of a wage or stipend, calculated by day, week or month. Everybody who sailed on board one of the Company ships was paid by the month, and the commander was no exception. He also received a monthly stipend, the bulk of which was paid out only after the completion of a voyage. Any extra days over and above a full month were paid proportionally, calculated on the basis of a thirty-day month. The chapter about Enkhuizen showed that a part of the commander's stipend was paid out to his family members during his absence and this could be picked up at the *Oost-Indisch Huis* of the Chamber concerned in the form of an advance, as a monthly letter or as a monetary transfer.

It was not the remuneration which made sailing with the Company an attractive proposition. The greatest incentive was the extra opportunities to make money which a voyage to the East offered. There were various bonuses which could be earned, depending on the length of the voyage and the route taken. Besides these bonuses, there were gratuities linked to specific achievements. These bonuses and gratuities were usually shared only by the commander and his ship's officers, but everybody on board looked forward to taking private freight along on both the outward-bound voyage and the voyage home. The carrying of trade goods was hedged in with a plethora of rules and regulations. The higher the rank a man reached, the more goods he was allowed to take. There was strict control over these private cargoes, particularly when they were unloaded, and there was always a chance that they could be confiscated. After the completion of a voyage, a commander often had to wait a long time for his payment because, if there was the slightest doubt about deviation from the rules, his payment was postponed.

Monthly Wages

The Company prized experience. On his maiden voyage, a commander never earned the highest stipend and this had been the rule since the foundation of the Company. In the seventeenth century payment also depended on the type of ship. The stipend for commanding a yacht or a fluyt was lower than that earned for being in charge of an East Indiaman. At various times, for instance in 1662 and 1685, the Company fixed the upper limit of wages, including those of the ship's officers, in regulations. The remuneration was the same in each Chamber. In 1718, the *Heren Zeventien* decreed that a commander would earn ƒ. 66 on his maiden voyage, ƒ. 72 on his second command and for his third and all subsequent voyages ƒ. 80. These sums remained unchanged for years although before each appointment a note was made of which voyage this was. A first mate was paid between ƒ. 48 and ƒ. 50, a second mate ƒ. 32, and a third mate ƒ. 26. With the exception of the period 1742–1755,[1] these sums were never altered. At the end of 1793 the stipends were raised, but a commander, then a captain, still earned ƒ. 80 per month, which was in fact the same as his predecessors had earned nearly two hundred years earlier for third and subsequent voyages. From the end of 1793 a second voyage earned him ƒ. 100 and a third ƒ. 125. The monthly wages of the ship's officers were raised at the same time to ƒ. 60, ƒ. 46 and ƒ. 34 respectively.[2] The recipients did not have much time to profit from these rises in salary as these changes were introduced just a few years before the liquidation of the Company.

Quite often a lengthy period of time could elapse between appointment to a post and the actual departure of the ship. Every sailor on board was given an advance which was the equivalent of two months' wages, known as earnest money (*handgeld*). Initially no exception was made for the commander but in 1794 his earnest money was extended from two to three months, to give him some leeway in purchasing his goods for private trade. The stipend proper was paid only from the moment the ship sailed out of the roads. When the final account was made, the earnest money was invariably meticulously subtracted from the last payment. The Company regulated every aspect of salaries paid. For instance, in 1742 in order to be rid of the usual quarrels which a promotion during the voyage encouraged, it was decreed that during the voyage one half of the money earned would be calculated according to the old scale and the other half according to the new.[3]

At the end of the voyage, a commander had to wait to pick up the stipend he had earned. Before he could claim his stipend, he had to make a report to the directors of his Chamber about the voyage and the vicissitudes which had been faced. This rule was established as early as 1613. On very rare occasions a commander was paid an extra month's stipend. This happened to Lambert Bot after he had weathered a severe storm in the Indian Ocean on 10, 11 and 12 January 1717, in his ship the *Boekenrode*. From the day on which the storm broke his monthly stipend was raised from ƒ. 72 to ƒ. 100 and this rate was maintained until he arrived home at the end of July. On one single night on 21 May 1737, during which the Cape was ravaged by a horrendous storm, seven homeward-

---

[1] See Chapter 10.
[2] The Hague, NA, VOC 144, 9.12.1793, 221, 30.3.1662 and 11.7.1718, 301, 6.5.1793 and 4683, 6.9.1685.
[3] The Hague, NA, VOC 221, 21.9.1678, 301, 27.1.1794 and 11.397, art. 56.

bound ships were wrecked. But once again, in 1738, the directors were disposed to be fairly flexible. More than a year after their ships had been wrecked, without too much fuss having to be made, four of the seven commanders and their crews received their wages up to the day on which their ships went down. In fact, this sort of payment was a general maritime custom.[4]

Bonuses and Gratuities

The monthly stipends were the basis for employment and, as a consequence of their power to deduct fines from these earnings, the directors were able to ensure that their commanders carried out their duties properly. One of the sanctions which they could use was to withhold a proportion of the money at the end of the voyage or to delay payment. The matter of fines will be dealt with in more detail later. There were also ways and means to encourage good work. A voyage which was completed in less than average time was rewarded. This was an established custom. Ever since 1620 there had been such bonuses and 'recognitions' for a commander, first mate, second mate, and merchant, if on board. To ensure that the funds were divided equitably, one-sixth of the bonus went to the third mate and five-sixths to the others. If a voyage to Batavia took less than six and a half months, the bonus was *f.* 600, and within seven months the sum was *f.* 300, and within eight months *f.* 150. Time spent at the Cape or at S. Tiago in the Cape Verde Islands was not counted in calculating the sum. The ship's officers were fined *f.* 600 if they had not stopped at the Cape to take on supplies and had done so at some other place, unless the reasons for making the decision were unquestionably compelling.[5]

This system of seventeenth-century bonuses lasted a long time. It was only when Van Imhoff was Governor-General that the Government in Batavia decided to expand it. The reason for this decision was to try to speed up the voyages. If a ship arrived in the East within five and a half months, her officers could expect a bonus of *f.* 1,200. Within six months the sum was *f.* 900. In 1746, Jan de Boer, later appointed examiner, and his mates were the first to claim the *f.* 1,200. Their new ship, the *Lekkerland*, of the Amsterdam Chamber, sailed from Texel on 14 November 1745, and anchored in the Batavia Roads on 15 May; the ship had been anchored in Table Bay at the Cape from 4 to 26 February. The *Hoge Regering* congratulated itself on the success of its system of bonuses. By the end of 1747, twenty-two ships had claimed one of these bonuses,[6] but this system did not become a permanent fixture of rewards for officers.

---

[4] The Hague, NA, VOC 114, 23.10.1705, 221, 4.11.1713, 222, 2.9.1738, 307, 1.11.1717; *DAS* III, nos. 6992–3, 6998–9, 7000 and 7002–3.
[5] *DAS* I, 61.
[6] *Nederlandsch-Indisch Plakaatboek* V, 12.7.1746; Schooneveld-Oosterling, *Generale Missiven* XI, pp. 465 and 591.

Bearing in mind the possibility of the outbreak of war and safety in the Channel, not to mention keeping a weather eye on the potential for smuggling in southern English ports, the Company regularly issued its commanders with instructions to steer clear of this sea lane. They were instructed to set course to the north or around the back way (*achterom*); in other words to sail around Scotland. Because of the tempestuous autumn and winter weather in this region, this route was not popular and was thought to be longer. As compensation, every member of the crew was given two months' extra wages, over and above the total he could otherwise have expected if he followed the northern route. Homeward bound, shortly after leaving the Cape in a meeting of the ship's council the commander of the returning fleet opened a sealed envelope containing instructions which dictated whether he should sail via the Channel or around the north of Scotland and where he would meet the warships dispatched to escort his ships in convoy.[7] The bonus of two months' wages for the northern route is recorded in numerous settlements in ship's wage books.

The *Heren Zeventien* were not as liberal with other forms of extra payments or gratuities. These were dispensed only sporadically during the eighteenth century. During the Nine Years War (1689–1697) the Company had to dip into capital to make extraordinary payments to officers. In 1690, Commander Gilles Brouwer had fought three Algerian privateers for seven hours off the Canary Islands before he had been able to sail on. His reward was a gold chain valued at 100 silver ducatoons (*f*. 300). In 1696 his colleague Dirk Lovelt did not survive a similar attack by two Algerian ships. His widow received the sum of *f*. 1,000 as a token of esteem. The widow of Willem Kemp had received a similar sum earlier, after her husband, the commander of the returning fleet, had been attacked by French warships in the North Atlantic in September 1693. The convoy managed to escape but Kemp's ship went down with all hands.[8]

Aside from these monetary acknowledgements, examples of extra rewards were few and far between. Lambert Bots' payment in 1717 has already been mentioned above. In 1744 the Hoorn directors decided that Commander Gerrit Reindertsz Vos had earned a gratuity. In December 1743, he had picked up the ship the *Rijnhuizen* in Zealand, where it had landed on its homeward voyage, and brought her to Hoorn. The *Heren Zeventien* thought that a moderate reward had been earned, but they said it should be paid 'as thriftily as was feasible'. A gratuity of *f*. 600 was paid out to Jan Frederik Zegert for his role in a battle against the Bugis in the Straits of Malacca in 1784. The very last reward was paid to Captain-Lieutenant Kornelis van Dijk, who captured two French fishing boats off the Cape of Good Hope, taking them as prizes. Van Dijk was captain of one of the hookers which were normally stationed at the Cape. He was allotted

---

[7] DAS I, 87.
[8] The Hague, NA, VOC 221, 5.4.1692, 28.2.193 and 19.9.1698; *DAS* III, nos. 1594, 1599 and 1750.

one-third of the prize money. This was paid on 11 May 1795 at a time when the Dutch state had already become the Batavian Republic.⁹

In short, the Company regularly paid out bonuses for fast voyages as well as extra stipends for the route around the north of Scotland, the *achterom*. However, gratuities and extra rewards for exceptional achievements were rare. Therefore, for a commander the really financially attractive side of his post with the Company was the possibility it offered to trade on his own behalf (*negotie*), and his employer gave him ample opportunities to do so.

Personal Cargo

When he sailed to the East, every man on board carried with him his own baggage which consisted of his personal kit plus goods which he could use for his private commercial transactions, however limited these might have been. The same custom was followed in the merchant navy in which from time immemorial crew members, from the lowest to the highest rank, had had their own cargo space allotted to them in the hold of the ship where they could stow a small quantity of personal trade goods. This was called free freightage (*voering*) and seamen were not required to pay for it. When loading cargo and mustering were completed, understandings were reached on this matter. The seamen's goods were also exempt from import and export duty. In this matter, as early as 1603, the Company had established the regulation that the value of the free freightage could not exceed the sum of two months' wages of the person concerned. In order to limit the amount of cargo space taken up by private goods, the Company provided each crew member with chests at cost. Only commanders and a few other privileged people were allowed to have these chests made at their own expense, but such chests had to comply with the regulated measurements. Before the chests were loaded, they were branded with the monogram of the VOC and the first letter of the Chamber concerned, the year and occasionally the initials of the owner. Chests were checked to make sure that they complied with this requirement. In 1728, shortly before the *Castricum* was due to sail, some unbranded chests were discovered. The Amsterdam Chamber ordered an investigation and insisted that the belongings of Commander Thomas Fletcher, his first mate and his boatswain be unloaded. However, the *Castricum* had already sailed when the order reached Texel. Two wharf labourers who were also involved in the deception were dismissed.¹⁰

The commander was permitted two chests measuring five by two Rhineland feet (one Rhineland foot = 31 cm), ship's officers one. The system of checking

---

⁹ The Hague, NA, VOC 222, 10.11.1744, 298, 1.3.1790; *DAS* III, no. 7171; De Jonge, *Geschiedenis zeewezen IV*, p. 713. For Van Dijk, see The Hague, NA, VOC 209, 11.5 and 28.9.1795, and Cape Town Archives, resolutions C. of P., 30.5.1794 (www.tanap.net).

¹⁰ The Hague, NA, VOC 253, 28.10, 1, 4, 15 and 29.11.1728.

the contents of the chests was not uniform; 'the one Chamber dealt with a liberal, the other with a more stringent hand'. In 1671, it was decided that besides his two chests a commander could also take along food and drink. The quantities permitted were meticulously recorded.[11] These examples demonstrate that a commander and his crew were formally permitted to trade on their own account. Private trade is the subject of the next chapter. It is important to note that the possibilities for private trade on the outward-bound voyage were considerably expanded in 1742. If a tax (*recognitierecht*) were paid per chest, barrel or cellaret, a commander could transport a large quantity of what were referred to as *recognitiegoederen* (taxed items). This change meant that the ancient privilege of exemption from taxation was restricted but the principle of free freightage was still honoured. Around 1790, almost all types of goods were opened up to free trade, so no taxes were due on them in any case.

The procedures to be followed for the voyage home were more or less the same. Everybody on board, irrespective of rank, was eager to take Eastern goods, whether these were curiosities or commercial items, back to the Republic. As well as their kitbags and some provisions, many sailors had one or more chests on board. The *Heren Zeventien* fought an uphill battle to try to curb the quantities of private trade goods transported. The terms search (*visitatie*), examination and confiscation occur with great regularity in the resolutions passed in the seventeenth century. Nobody was permitted to take goods worth more than three months' wages. It was not fairly applied, though, because a 1682 resolution laid down that 'in searching the chests of commanders ... discretion' was the order of the day.[12] The rules regarding the strictness of the checks imposed on high-ranking officers were more flexible. Regulation followed regulation. In practical terms, the transportation of non-permitted Asian goods by crews was extremely difficult to control.

In 1742 there was also a drastic alteration to this policy. The tried and tested rules applying to what was called permitted baggage (*gepermitteerde voering*) pertaining to all members of the crew were abrogated and replaced by payment of a gratuity on arrival home. The amount of this bonus depended on rank on board, and the commander was included. His bonus was a very large sum, *f.* 2,000, which was even raised to *f.* 3,000 if he held the rank of captain. Furthermore, the commander was also still permitted to bring home some chests. As early as the 1750s, the rules had already been liberalized and weakened. Once again, crews were allowed to bring home private trade goods, albeit in officially fixed quantities, and the bonuses were not abolished.

---

[11] The Hague, NA, VOC 221, 7.8.1603 and 11.4.1756; F.W. Stapel (ed.), *De Beschryvinge van de Oostindische Compagnie* I, Rijks Geschiedkundige Publicatiën 63 (The Hague, 1927), pp. 653–7. See also S. Hart, 'De rederij', *Maritieme Geschiedenis der Nederlanden* II (Bussum, 1977), pp. 106–25, see pp. 116–21.

[12] The Hague, NA, VOC 221, 1.10.1682, and 307, 29.9.1659 and 26.4.1677.

Rising Incomes

For a very long period of time, the fixed earnings of a Company commander hardly varied. A change came in the 1740s and the innovations introduced in 1742 had significant financial consequences. The commanders still earned a monthly stipend, the amount never really being altered, and sometimes their wives, parents or children had taken an advance. Bonuses for a fast voyage or for sailing around the north of Scotland could occasionally alter the amount of the final accounting. Between the years 1705 and 1709, Kornelis van Overraad of the Rotterdam Chamber spent four years away. During his absence his wife took an advance of ƒ. 930. Upon his return his final payment, including his bonuses, was ƒ. 2,625, bearing in mind his monthly stipend had been ƒ. 70 for over forty months. Arie Turfkloot of the Delft Chamber earned a similar sum at the end of a fifteen-month voyage. Only the two months' earnest money was deducted and so in 1710 he had a sum of ƒ. 954 cash in his hands. In 1714, after a period of absence of forty-five months his final payment came to ƒ. 3,212.[13]

The amounts earned by regular commanders like Van Overraad and his colleague Turfkloot were not especially high. It was only in the 1740s that these amounts suddenly rose drastically. In comparison with former times, a golden age now dawned for commanders. The principal reasons were the gratuity of ƒ. 2,000 for the return voyage and the rise in the monthly stipend. At this time, Kornelis Quack was sailing for the Rotterdam Chamber. After the completion of three voyages between 1744 and 1755, his successive final settlements were ƒ. 3,662, ƒ. 6,422 and ƒ. 4,477. These sums included one ƒ. 2,000 bonus and two worth ƒ. 3000. However, in 1755 both the higher stipends and the super-gratuity worth ƒ. 3,000 were abolished. Simultaneously, the large contributions demanded to support the *Académie de Marine* in Batavia came to an end. To support this institution, on a maiden voyage and on promotion commanders and their officers had had to pay sums which fluctuated between ƒ. 300 and ƒ. 30.[14]

Despite the cancellation of the very generous payments in 1755, the money earned by commanders in the second half of the eighteenth century made the regular sums received by their predecessors pale into insignificance. The main reason for this was that the princely gratuity of ƒ. 2,000 still continued to be paid at the same time as greater regularity and so greater speed were introduced into Company shipping. In the second half of the eighteenth century, many more ships than had previously been the case were allocated for the voyage home directly after their arrival in the East, generally with the same commander and the majority of his crew. Consequently, on average ships and crews returned home much more quickly. A round-trip within eighteen to twenty months was now usual. The voyages and the final accounting of Frederik Kelger of the

---

[13] The Hague, NA, VOC 13.894, 13.898 and 14.110.
[14] *Nederlandsch Indisch Plakaatboek* VII, pp. 159 and 191.

23 and 24. Sea chests. The Hannemahuis in Harlingen in Friesland has two deal ship's chests found by the Hannema family when they moved into this house in the Voorstraat in 1744. Because of their size it would seem the chests belonged to a VOC commander: they measure 169 x 69 x 68 cm and 168 x 68 x 68 cm, a little larger than the measurements laid down by the Company for the carriage of private goods. On the lid of the chest illustrated here have been branded VOC 1730 and VOC 1732; on the other chest are the brands VOC A, VOC A 1720, VOC 1724 and VOC 1728.

Amsterdam Chamber testify to this. In the period between 1762 and 1771, the pages in his ship's pay books closed with the successive sums of *f.* 3,403, *f.* 3,276, *f.* 3,206 and *f.* 3,614. These were all voyages which lasted only a short time.[15] However, it was the gratuities which caused the big difference compared with earlier earnings. The large sums Kelger picked up at his pay office are regularly to be found in the final settlements of commanders from all the Chambers after 1742. At last it was possible to earn a princely stipend with the Company.

Some commanders received even higher amounts. The Amsterdam Chamber – and the same will have happened in the other Chambers – paid out extra bonuses if a ship returned with more cargo than had been planned. Every so often there was even talk of overloading so that crews could get these bonuses. In 1761, over and above his gratuity of *f.* 2,000, Jakob Wiebe received another *f.* 1,708 for extra cargo. In fact, Wopke Popta even made a habit of overloading his ships. He had learned this strategy from Wiebe when he had sailed with him as first mate. In 1767 his commander died during the return voyage and he had taken over the command. He then got *f.* 1,118 which was one-third of the total bonuses. On his next four return voyages as commander, Popta received bonuses for extra cargo of *f.* 4,925 in 1769, *f.* 2,221 in 1772, *f.* 2,124 in 1775 and *f.* 1,735 in 1778. Therefore Popta's final settlements after voyages which usually lasted twenty months involved sums ranging from *f.* 5,500 to well over *f.* 9,000.[16] Turfkloot and Van Overraad would never have dared dream of such amounts.

The Actual Payment

A commander could feel content if he and his men were paid their wages and bonuses fairly soon after the completion of a voyage. Payment was not automatic nor was it a matter of course. The Directors of Fitting Out of each Chamber always first had to inspect the ship, cargo and crew. These gentlemen were usually present when the ship arrived in the roads – at Texel, Goeree and Rammekens. Each Chamber possessed its own well-appointed yacht with a permanent crew which would transport the directors and high-ranking officials to places outside the town. They took care of the discharge of the majority of the ship's crew as quickly as possible. These men could then pick up their money at the Pay Office. The commander and his officers had to wait longer for their money. The directors of their Chamber made an official decision about each payment. Sometimes this happened within a month, but sometimes more than a year could pass before a decision was made. The checking and weighing of both the Company and private goods consumed a great deal of time and the weather also had to be good. The ship's logs had to be inspected as well, and that was the task of the

---

[15] The Hague, NA, VOC 14.200, 14.210 and 14.221 (Quack), and 6422, 6463, 6502 and 6530 (Kelger).
[16] The Hague, NA, VOC 6387 (Wiebe), and 6465, 6493, 6542, 6584 and 6637 (Popta).

examiners. Sometimes their report was ready within a fortnight, but it could be two to three months before the directors could discuss the findings around their boardroom table.[17]

The two most important causes of delayed payment to a commander and his officers were questions raised about the proper weight and the composition of the cargo, as well as suspicions about the smuggling of private goods. Elder Evertsz had his private doubts about the weighing of various products in 1789 when he was the commander of the chartered merchantman the *Handellust*. He noted inconsistencies in the procedures which caused him to think that the weighing during loading and unloading was done on trust, which meant that differences could creep in. What is certain about this procedure is that during unloading Company officials frequently detected what was called 'underweight' (*minwicht*). Smuggling however was always a much more serious matter. In 1778, before the arrival of two ships from China there were suspicions of unlawful doings on board. The commanders and officers were ordered not to disembark until the ships had been completely unloaded.[18] Furthermore, fines levied for violations of regulations at overseas trading posts were also deducted from the final payment to the person concerned.

When the accounting was protracted or the stipends earned were declared forfeit, the commanders involved sought refuge in petitions in which they insisted on a speedy decision or asked for a mitigation of the measures taken against them. Widows of commanders who had died on their return voyage sometimes lodged objections to posthumous fines. Such petitions or appeals were generally dealt with by the *Heren Zeventien* at one of their three annual meetings in Amsterdam or Middelburg.

Despite all these precautions, the number of irregularities discovered by the directors was not conspicuously high. Perhaps the check carried out on arrival home was not overly strict or the supervision during loading was lax. In reviewing the relatively few cases of fraud and other irregularities which were discovered and prosecuted, it is important to remember that some twenty to thirty ships annually returned to the Company ports. Below are a few examples which give some idea of what sorts of cases were dealt with in practice. The first examples pertain to Company cargoes and the later ones to fines and the withholding of bonuses or gratuities. Smuggling will be discussed in the next chapter.

An Incomplete Cargo

Throughout the history of the VOC, problems to do with missing goods appeared with a certain regularity on the agendas of meetings of the *Heren*

---

[17] Examples in The Hague, NA, VOC 297, 28.9.1789, and 302, 28.5 and 25.9.1794.
[18] The Hague, NA, VOC 297, 7.9.1789, and 308, 3.8.1778; *DAS* III, nos. 8010, 8012 and 8238.

Zeventien or of the *Hoge Regering* in Batavia. Generally speaking, the checks carried out when cargo was unloaded revealed very few suspicious cases which warranted reporting. Around 1740, it is clear that a number of commanders were having problems in Batavia about the correct contents of the chests of silver destined for the intra-Asian trade. In the Republic, the relevant reports of 'short weight' were examined in greater detail. After the investigation was completed, the commanders concerned were exempted from having to make up the missing quantities. They were able to show that the chests involved had been closed and sealed upon arrival in the Netherlands. One possible explanation is that too little had been put in when they were being filled. Officially the packing of the silver chests – made from thick deal planks and reinforced with iron bands – was surrounded by the greatest precautions. This work took place in the *Oost-Indisch Huis* under the supervision of the directors. The coins were packed in bags and peat was placed between the bags to ensure that they would not be split by having been shifted around. A chest had two heavy locks to keep it shut and it was also sealed and then wrapped in sailcloth, which was nailed on, and the chest was then bound up with rope. Before the ship sailed, the commander and the junior merchant signed a bill of lading (*cognossement*) on which the chests and their contents were recorded.[19]

Tin caused the commanders even more problems. The tin pigs were used as ballast. In 1769, Commander Arie Fransz had to pay compensation worth *f.* 1,169 for a deficit of a good 4,000 pounds of tin. His defence was that the loading of the tin had been done 'outside his authority' and that when the ballast was unloaded he had long since disembarked. His disclaimer was rejected. In 1776, the Hoorn Chamber fined Commander Marten Schoning and his first mate by withholding *f.* 883 on account of a deficiency of twenty-eight pigs.[20]

Sometimes the submission of a petition did help. Eventually, in 1775 Maarten Hakker was paid his full stipend when it was revealed that the goods which were missing when the ship returned to the Republic had been unloaded in Bengal. Upon his arrival in Batavia in 1776, Hans Hansen had to be informed that vats of white lead were not on board. Therefore, the sum of *f.* 1,006 was deducted from his final settlement. However, in 1778 the Amsterdam Chamber had to acknowledge that the white lead had never been loaded.[21] Short weight could also be discovered and a fine imposed in Batavia when a ship arrived from the Republic, as the example of the silver demonstrates.

The majority of the cases recorded in the resolutions of the *Heren Zeventien* concern larger or smaller quantities of one specific product in the cargo. In 1737,

---

[19] The Hague, NA, VOC 222, 23.8, 24.11.1740 and 10.10.1741. See also R. Paesie, *Het VOC-schip Ravesteyn. De laatste reis van een Zeeuwse Oostindiëvaarder* (Amsterdam, 1999), pp. 558–61.
[20] The Hague, NA, VOC 222, 19.4.1769 and 23.3.1776; *DAS* III, nos. 7740 and 7928.
[21] The Hague, NA, VOC 308, 13.7.1775 and 29.1.1778; *DAS* II and III, nos. 4521, 7910 and 7972.

Lukas Krootjes was eight bales of coffee short for the Enkhuizen Chamber, and Jakob Pols of the Delft Chamber was missing five sacks of saltpetre in 1743. Two years later, sailing for Enkhuizen, Maarten den Breems had one 161-pound basket of mace too few, and Pieter Jellesz was eight bales of pepper short for the Amsterdam Chamber. Later examples are Pieter ten Droge who had a deficit of saltpetre for the Zeeland Chamber in 1774, and Benjamin van der Spek who was short on fine sugar and camphor for the Amsterdam Chamber in 1780.[22]

One outstanding fine was imposed on Stavorinus, who has appeared elsewhere in this book. When he returned in 1771, he was no less than 536 pounds of sugar, 736 pounds of tamarind and 841 cans of Cape wine short, which had a total value of $f.$ 205. In his defence, Stavorinus said that he had divided these products out among the crew as the result of heavy weather and many cases of illness on board, but he had omitted to note this in the ship's victualling book. The response was not unsympathetic. The fine was halved, but Stavorinus still had to forgo a month's stipend on account of his 'careless housekeeping'.[23]

Dirk de Veth, Pieter Alkmaar and a colleague were caught out in 1738 because of short weights in cargoes of tea. De Veth was missing eleven chests and twenty-five canisters and Alkmaar six chests and fifty-six canisters. The commanders defended themselves and put the blame on the warehouse master in Batavia. The case dragged on and De Veth and Alkmaar both died before it was settled. Eventually, their heirs paid the fines imposed, in 1743. The sum of $f.$ 2,366 was deducted from De Veth's final payment.[24] The Amsterdam Chamber deducted more or less the same amount from a bill of exchange worth $f.$ 6,645, which had arrived from Batavia for Commander Alkmaar.[25]

Amounts Withheld from Stipends

When the ship's papers were checked by the examiner, care was taken to see that all the rules and instructions issued for the voyage had been scrupulously observed. Adherence had to be both literal and in the true spirit of the instructions. The chief source of information was the ship's log, but there were also papers to do with items of the ship's tackle on board, and the victualling book which recorded consumption. Once again, in these matters the directors were sparing in the number of fines they imposed. Years passed without any record of violations of this sort being mentioned in the books of resolutions.

---

[22] The Hague, NA, VOC 222, 12.11.1737, 16.3.1744, 22, 24.3.1746 and 29.3.1775, 308, 27.11.1780; *DAS* III, nos. 6988, 7163, 7219, 7249, 7903 and 8043.
[23] The Hague, NA, VOC 222, 15.4.1772, 308, 19.9.1771 and 23.1.1772; *DAS* III, no. 7821.
[24] See Chapter 2.
[25] The Hague, NA, VOC 222, 3.9.1739, 16.11.1742, 14 and 18.11.1743; *DAS* III, nos. 7042, 7043 and 7046.

Nevertheless, there is one period which stands out – the years 1764–1778, when retired commander Jan de Boer was examiner. He paid attention to every little detail of every sort and this led to various rebukes. De Boer was examiner in seamanship and therefore he checked the correct use of drift anchors or drogues, a subject on which he had published a booklet in 1769. Stoffel Kok and Joost Koen each forfeited three months' wages in 1775 because they had not dropped this anchor during stormy weather. Failure to install, or the non-use of, a new type of ventilation system or air pump which could reduce the high temperatures below decks cost commanders two months' wages. Arguments such as that their ship was too fully laden or that there was no room for the ventilation system or that the system did not work cut no ice. In the 1771 returning fleet, the ventilation system was not used on six ships. Only the widow of one of the six commanders was excused from paying the fine after she made an appeal. In the following year, a widow was once again excused, although two of her husband's colleagues, Jan Balthus Meyer and Pieter Andriessen, had to pay up. Neglect of the fire hoses could bring down wrath on a commander's head. In 1767, such carelessness cost Jakob de Vries two months' stipend. Jurriaan Verburg was an even worse offender. The use of neither the ventilation system nor the fire hose were noted in his logbook. This meant a double punishment: four months' stipend.[26]

In De Boer's era, yet another case, occurring in 1762, was settled in 1766. As they approached the Grounds (*De Gronden*), the stretch of sea between Ushant in France and the Scilly Isles in England, Commander Pieter van Dalen and his first mate had actually constantly adjusted their position, but had not recorded these corrected positions in the ship's log. Eventually, this oversight cost Van Dalen a fine of one month's stipend and his mate a reprimand. They were paid what they were owed only after their joint negligence had been documented and punished.[27]

The directors took matters very seriously if the commanders failed to make the rendezvous with the warships sent to escort them on the last leg home. The meeting or crossing point was located either in the western part of the Channel or east of Scotland. The escort of warships was vitally important for the safety of the returning ships and to prevent smuggling using other ships or in British ports. Examiner De Boer, with or without his Zealand colleague, interrogated commanders on this point, both orally and in writing. In this connection, De Boer was sometimes asked to attend the meeting of the *Heren Zeventien* to answer questions. In 1769, Thomas Brunel did not keep to the prescribed course and had not spotted the cruising warships. This oversight cost him two months' stipend. In 1771, two commanders missed the crossing point in the Channel,

---

[26] The Hague, NA, VOC 222, 2.10.1767, 27.9.1770, 27.3, 10.10.1771 and 2.10.1775, 308, 29.8.1771, 26.11.1772 and 2.10.1775; *DAS* III, nos. 7716, 7809, 7815, 7818, 7820, 7828, 7829, 7831, 7924 and 7925.

[27] The Hague, NA, VOC 222, 1.10.1760; *DAS* III, no. 7618.

and in 1772 there were no less than six who committed this apparent breach of discipline. These six had sailed in a convoy from the Cape and that year made up the second of the three smaller convoys. In their defence, the commanders could show that they had been at the crossing point, but had drifted off course. The wind and the weather had prevented them from returning to it. The fines imposed, ranging from three to six months' stipend, were eventually dropped.[28] Naturally, De Boer was not the last to hand out punishments. Fines were levied by others but their imposition was much less frequent.

In 1756 a ship of the returning fleet sailed off course. In their investigation into this error, the *Heren Zeventien* heard that crews often tried to dissuade commanders from looking for the cruising warships. Their objections were that looking for the rendezvous caused delays. Not meeting the warships also reduced the chances of contraband goods being detected. The Gentlemen's reaction was to make all the members of the ship's council culpable for failing to make the rendezvous, but the proposed fine of the loss of six months' wages was never imposed on a commander, not even in De Boer's day. Another cause of punishment was that in the previous years apparently more than one East Indiaman had arrived minus her ship's boat or boats. In 1744, the *Heren Zeventien* took the sudden decision that a commander and his first mate would have to cover the costs. This is the reason that Kornelis Stevens and his first mate saw their stipends drastically reduced in 1746.[29]

Occasionally the directors were disposed to be milder. In 1721 Pieter Visser sailed past Cape Town, which was strictly forbidden. He only dropped anchor off St Helena and he was unable to produce a convincing reason for his action. In fact, Visser caused the Company 'a fair amount of embarrassment'. His ship would have been the only one at the Cape at that moment and should have collected the Cape papers for the *Heren Zeventien*. As punishment, Visser had to wait slightly longer for a new command, but by 1724 he had once more set sail.

During the Fourth Anglo-Dutch War, the directors were extremely worried about the safety of their fleet. After the commander of the returning fleet, Kornelis Kornelisz, had brought six ships safely into Cadiz, he was presented with a gold medal worth *f.* 500. Sometimes commanders of chartered ships shared in the bonuses. In 1790, at his own request, Harmen Ruurdsz was awarded the fixed bonus for a 'successful voyage'.[30]

---

[28] The Hague, NA, VOC 133, 16.10.1769, 134, 10.10.1771, 222, 6.4.1770, 31.3.1773 and 26.10.1780; *DAS* III, nos. 7789, 7826, 7827, 7843, 7846, 7849, 7852, 7854, 7855 and 8047.
[29] The Hague, NA, VOC 128, 12 and 13.10.1756, 222, 12.3.1744, 24.3.1746, 25.10.1757, 13.10.1759 and 24.11.1783, 298, 12.5 and 29.9.1790, 307, 30.3.1722 and 14329 (zeilorders/ sailing orders); *DAS* III, no. 7460.
[30] The Hague, NA, VOC 222, 24.11.1783, 298, 12.5 and 29.9.1790, 307, 30.3.1722; *DAS* II and III, nos. 2598, 6507, 8063 and 8255.

Benevolent Fund

The normal sources of income ensured a commander and his family a comfortable existence, but one which was constantly threatened because of the risk of death during a voyage or overseas. In the middle of the eighteenth century, an unexpected surge of solidarity, and perhaps insecurity, must have gripped the commanders of the Amsterdam Chamber. In October 1750, thirteen commanders, twelve first mates and a retired commander set up a fund to help their colleagues and their next of kin, not overlooking themselves in the process. Five commanders and two first mates at that moment waiting at Texel to sail also gave their support and joined as well. It was an entirely Amsterdam initiative. Jochem Tarncke was the only outsider. Not long before, he had sailed for the Enkhuizen Chamber and had only just moved to Amsterdam. The reasons which prompted these men to take the initiative remain obscure. There had been very few shipping disasters in the previous three years, only the stranding and the loss of the *Amsterdam* on the south coast of England near Hastings in January 1749.[31] The commander of the *Amsterdam*, Willem Klump, was among those who took the initiative. He was due to sail out again on another ship in December. At this particular period, the founding of voluntary self-help funds was very popular. These were mutual, professionally-based funds. Membership was voluntary. The greatest concern of the participants in such a fund was to ensure that in the event of age and illness, above all their wives, but also they personally, would not have to become a burden on public charitable institutions. It was usual to pay an entry fee and after that annual contributions. Those who participated in such a fund were financially able to do so.

The fund was a benevolent society open to 'all highly qualified officers', commanders and ship's officers employed by the six Chambers. Colleagues who participated in the fund were eligible for an allowance if they were to become poverty-stricken as the result of an accident or some similar disaster. Their next of kin – widows or dependent parents and children – also received financial support. The criterion by which this was measured was that without help from the fund people could end up in 'obvious degradation'.

Commanders and first mates still active at sea paid an annual premium of one month's stipend, to be deposited every 1 May. When participants retired ashore, the premium was linked to age: the younger the contributor, the lower the fee. For a commander or first mate aged around forty the fee was ƒ. 35 and ƒ. 21 respectively; if they were fifty-five it rose to ƒ. 60 and ƒ. 36. The compulsory entry fee was also graded according to rank and age: for a thirty- or fifty-five-year-old commander ƒ. 110 and ƒ. 160, and for first mates of the same age ƒ. 66 and ƒ. 96 respectively. Allowances from the fund were paid for as long as this was necessary. The sums paid were devised so that the recipient could live 'prop-

---

[31] See Marsden, *De laatste reis van de 'Amsterdam'*.

erly'. Widows received an allowance until they died or until they remarried. The amount depended on the initial fee and the annual premiums which their spouse paid. The sums were between ƒ. 60 and ƒ. 100 per year.[32]

Very little can be said about how the fund operated. Apparently it managed to get off the ground, it covered all the Chambers and it existed for quite a long time. In his will in 1762, retired Commander Schouten mentioned that his wife had the right to an allowance from the fund. While her husband was overseas in 1765, as well as her monthly letter, the wife of Gerrit Harmeyer also received an allowance from the fund. After his return home the commander deposited money in it. Upon his death, Commander Bartholomeus Schut of the Delft Chamber possessed bonds worth three times the amount of ƒ. 2,000 which he had deposited in the High-Ranking VOC Officers' Fund in exchange for an annuity. This was in 1787. Generally speaking, this sort of fund, especially one for widows, was fairly short-lived. Often the premiums were too low to cover all the allowances which had to be paid.[33]

After the first four decades of the eighteenth century, the regular earnings of a Company commander underwent an enormous change. In practice, the ƒ. 2,000 gratuity dating from 1742 meant more than a doubling of normal earnings. Because the shipping to the East was transformed into a sort of regular service, for many commanders the length of a command shrank considerably. Consequently, they were more quickly allocated a new ship for the next voyage with the chance of a new bonus. The upshot was that a commander earned more money in less time. If he also managed to have more cargo on board than had been agreed upon, he could also expect extra money. These earnings were completely separate from any of his personal commercial transactions, the subject of the next chapter.

Naturally breaches of the rules and regulations occurred. However, the number that were spotted and punished was not very high. If the Company did take steps in the case of short weights in cargo or errors or negligence in the ship's inventory, the punishment was harsh, but this happened only infrequently.

---

[32] The Hague, Koninklijke Bibliotheek (Royal Library), 595/A97 (Reglement); F. Lequin, 'Het personeel van de Verenigde Oost-Indische Compagnie in Azië in de achttiende eeuw, meer in het bijzonder in de vestiging Bengalen' (PhD thesis, Leiden University, 1982), pp. 61 and 257.

[33] J. Van Genabeek, *Met vereende kracht risico's verzacht. De plaats van onderlinge hulp binnen de negentiende-eeuwse particuliere regelingen van sociale zekerheid* (Amsterdam, 1999), pp. 71–7; M.H.D. Leeuwen, *De rijke Republiek: gilden, assuradeurs en armenzorg 1500–1800* (The Hague/Amsterdam, 2000), pp. 100–1 and 111–17; Schmidt, *Overleven na de dood*, pp. 206–10; Van der Wiel, *Op zoek naar een biografisch portret*, p. 83.

12

Private Income

In the first part of the book, many references were made to the private trade pursued by the commanders and their officers. This sort of commerce was a perfectly normal practice. The official rules and regulations pertaining to this trade, the transfers of money to the Republic, punishment of violations and the earning of considerable amounts of money overseas are the themes of this chapter.

It was very common indeed for Company commanders and others to have large amounts of porcelain in cabinets in their houses. Commanders of the Enkhuizen and Delft Chambers have been cited as examples of men who had large quantities of tableware and other pieces at home. They or their wives sold some of the pieces on to fellow townspeople or merchants. Many other pieces of porcelain were auctioned by the Company and consequently disappeared from sight.

Generally speaking, it is difficult to obtain a satisfactory picture of the way in which such private commercial activities were conducted. If a commander had sufficient amounts of ready money at his disposal, he was not required to register his purchase of goods. However, it was a different story if he bought such goods on credit, since his suppliers then set down in a contract how much and when he would pay the money he had borrowed from them – for instance, after arrival in Batavia and at an interest rate of half a per cent per month. Drawing up a contract required the services of a notary. Before Willem Klump sailed on his fatal voyage on the *Amsterdam*, he borrowed a total of *f.* 12,020 from four different creditors in the autumn of 1748. He undertook to repay this sum in Cape Town and in Batavia. In this case, the amount concerned was the equivalent of at least twelve years' stipend.[1] The notarial deeds drawn up on behalf of the Van Brattem brothers of the Rotterdam Chamber have already allowed a glimpse of their transactions. By using proxies taken out in the names of shipmates, the crew were able to ensure, as far as it was possible to do so, that one or other of these proxies would take care of their estate should they happen to die. An example of this practice is provided by Commander Koenraad van der Poel. On 11 October 1737 he and three of his officers visited a notary where

---

[1] Marsden, *De laatste reis van de 'Amsterdam'*, pp. 23–4.

they drew up a document which stated that, in the event of the death of one of them, one of the others was empowered to take charge of administering his estate. Six days later, their ship the *Hofvliet* sailed from Goeree. The proxy was carried with them in duplicate and authorized at the factory in Bengal, after the death of the second mate.[2]

Usually, the commanders had built up a network of traders in the East, similar to those that merchants in the Republic maintained overseas at the Cape, in Batavia and other ports. However, it was not always easy. Harmeyer of the Delft Chamber had to learn this the hard way around 1780. Piling loan upon loan without having the income to back up these borrowings could only lead to disaster. A successful commander earned a great deal from his private trade, frequently very large sums indeed. The Van Brattem brothers were only one case. Other, even more striking examples were Wiebe, Kelger and Angelvorst of the Amsterdam Chamber, and again they were only three among many.

Regulations for the Outward Voyage

In 1693 the Company made some slight adjustments to the existing rules and regulations governing private trade. A further revision in 1713 did not usher in any real change. In the first decades of the eighteenth century, on his departure from the Republic a commander had permission to take with him two pipes of *mom*, three *amen* (*aam* = c.155 litres) of wine, four cellarets with Dutch gin, twelve hams and eight pieces of smoked meat, fifteen cheeses and two quarters of butter (in total 160 pounds). *Mom* was a beer probably made without hops which was brewed especially for the route to Asia and transported in elongated tubes which contained 400 to 500 litres. Cellarets were small chests with rectangular sections for fifteen bottles approximately 27 cm high. In total the allotted meat was not to weigh more than 500 pounds. Besides these comestibles, the commander could also have with him a box for hats, a chest of glasses and one containing pipes, each chest measuring 3 × 3 × 2 Rhineland feet (one foot = 31 cm), a small chest of supplies and a portable writing desk, that is a slope measuring 3 × ½ × ½ feet with the writings materials to be used with it. An extra basket measuring 3 × 2 × 1 feet for smoking pipes might also be taken along. The quantities and sorts of goods permitted a first mate were proportionally about two-thirds of those of the commander. The measurements given for the sea chests were all for the inside. The chests had to be square. All the goods had to be the commander's own property.[3]

---

[2] The Hague, NA, VOC 2427 (OPB 1739), fols 355–7; *DAS* II, no. 3084.
[3] The Hague, NA, VOC 5013, 30.10.1713. A handy manual for all sorts of Company terms is the *VOC-Glossarium*, published in 2000 by the Instituut voor Nederlandse Geschiedenis te Den Haag (Institute of Dutch History, The Hague). Gawronski, *De equipagie*, 123ff. offers plentiful information about the supply of everything that was needed on board.

It was not easy to cheat with the measurements of the chests. They were always the same and had been fixed for a very long time. Apparently, the exceptions were the hat box and the cellaret. In 1726 a regulation was made which said that the hat box could not be higher than 1½ feet, or 46½ cm. From time to time, chests without a brand were spotted. Informers who drew attention to a load of forbidden cargo were promised one-third of the profits obtained from these goods. Sometimes informing could backfire, as the soldier Philip Frederik Weiland found out to his cost in 1771 when he had to forgo a reward. He discovered contraband trade being pursued by the Amsterdam Chamber and reported this at the Cape, but was then banished to Robben Island without a trial as a consequence of a false accusation by the Chamber. He survived his incarceration and asked for compensation in 1788, probably in vain.[4]

No rule or regulation could ever be passed which would guarantee that all ranks from the highest to the lowest actually took with them no more goods than the permitted maximum quantity. Van Imhoff was deeply perturbed by this aspect of the Company business. He complained that, 'recently the Company trade [has been becoming] a sideline and private trade the main work'. He was referring to the personnel in the trading posts in Asia, where it had become such an ingrained habit 'that people almost assume it to be a right to trade alongside the Company in the Indies'.[5]

On the voyage out, the main commodity preferred was alcoholic drink, a contraband product, for which there was always a high demand. Van Imhoff proposed that overseas personnel be allocated an amount of money, 'each to his own predilection', which could be spent on drink, and this change was indeed introduced in 1742. Control on import from the Republic was lifted. After this, crew members with the rank of chief carpenter, chief sailmaker and higher, namely those who earned *f.* 20 a month or more, could take a quantity of liquor with them for sale in Asia, though within reason. To avail themselves of this privilege, before departure they had to pay *recognitierecht*, which was a sort of tax. For each chest, pipe or cellaret containing beer, wine or strong drink, of which the quantities were minutely circumscribed, they were required to pay *f.* 5 on departure and *f.* 5 rix-dollars on arrival overseas. A first mate was allowed twenty-five chests, a commander a maximum of fifty, whereas a captain might be permitted up to eighty. These were certainly large numbers but they did not damage the Company because on the outward-bound voyage the whole cargo capacity of the ship was seldom needed for its own goods. In order to purchase their own merchandise, the commanders and the crew members often went into debt. When the new rules were introduced in 1742, the quantity of drink a commander could take with him was halved.

---

[4] The Hague, NA, VOC 198, 9.12.1788.
[5] The Hague, NA, VOC 118, 5.3.1726, and 221, 5.3.1726; Heeres, 'De "Consideratiën"', pp. 472–3.

The chests with the contents that had been taxed (*recognitiekisten*) were smaller in size than standard chests. They measured 114 by 72.6 by 77 cm, and were transported in a sealed section of the hold which was opened only after arrival. In 1771, new, even smaller chests were introduced. In 1791, in the Texel Roads, before the chests were put into the sealed compartment, unbranded *recognitiekisten* were discovered. Crew members had reported the illegal goods because they were disgruntled about their treatment by their commander and officers. The chests had been taken on board some days after the last muster roll had been called. Actually this was probably what often happened in practice, as a German crew member recorded how in the middle of the night in May 1727, while the ship still rode at anchor in the Texel Roads, he had been awakened to help carry the chests full of contraband. 'The commander, mates and other petty-officers brought many private commodities to the ship, something which could not happen during the day without it being seen. At night while we are asleep one or two fully laden lighters arrived and so we had to get up and load the goods into the big ship.'[6]

The Company often could only stand by helplessly with its hands tied unable to keep private trade within the self-imposed limits. This is illustrated by the private transport of silver ducatoons. Large silver coins had a higher value in Batavia and elsewhere in the East than in the Republic because they disappeared from circulation overseas. In an attempt to prevent this drain abroad the Company had raised the rate of exchange of *reals* and rix-dollars. This re-valuation also applied to the ducatoons, called silver riders. Instead of a value of 63 *stuivers* ducatoons fetched 72 or 78 *stuivers* in the East. This re-valuation led to the introduction of a 'light' *stuiver* because the 'heavy' silver *stuiver* which circulated in the Republic fetched about 1½ *stuivers* on the overseas market. There was a great demand for the ducatoon among the Chinese who regarded it as having the highest value. Consequently, in commercial transactions in Asia ducatoons traded at 90 to 97½ light *stuivers*. Under these circumstances, it was worth the while of every crew member to take ducatoons to the East. At the end of the seventeenth century the ducatoon was withdrawn from circulation, but around 1710 an impressive supply of old ducatoons was put into circulation by the Amsterdam Exchange Bank (*Amsterdamse Wisselbank*) and more ducatoons were struck. The Company profited from the difference between what

---

[6] The Hague, NA, VOC 123, 28.3.1742, 223, 11.5.1792 and 9.12.1793, 299, 5.12.1791, 4707, 11528, no. 26 and 14329 (regl. 1742); Moree, 'Met vriend, die God geleide', pp. 188–9, 198–9 and 212–13. The chests measuring 4 feet ¼ thumb (inch) in length were 2 feet 6¼ inches wide and 2 feet and 8 inches high. This time the outside of the frame was taken, measured in Amsterdam feet of 28.3 cm. The measurements prescribed in 1771 were approximately 100 x 74 x 73 cm. I would like to thank Dr R. van Gelder for the German quotation; the manuscript is kept in the National Library in Berlin (Ms germ oct 437, fol. 62 v). See also R. van Gelder, 'Van Saksen naar Batavia. Gottfried Preller 1726–1735', in P. van Zonneveld (ed.), *Naar de Oost! Verhalen over vier eeuwen reizen naar Indië* (Amsterdam, 1996), pp. 17–43.

was known as the 'heavy' and 'light' money and 'private, profit-oriented people' were quick to recognize a prime opportunity to smuggle an excessive quantity of ducatoons to the Indies.

The Company forbade the private transportation of ducatoons but its prohibition fell on deaf ears. It meant profit to any man on board who had a few ducatoons with him. The demand for large supplies of these coins was constant. Officially there was a total embargo on exporting them but finds on wrecked Company ships provide ample evidence that those who sailed in them ignored the ban completely and had plenty of ducatoons with them. On their arrival in Batavia, almost all the survivors of the ship the *Zeewijk*, which sank off the coast of Western Australia in 1727, had ducatoons with them, packed in small bags or hidden in 'handkerchiefs ... shoes, coats, shirts and belts ... all sewn with ducatoons in them'. In 1736, the *Hillegom* sank just after she had set sail from Texel. Officially she carried no money, yet shortly after she went down, more than 4,000 ducatoons, packed in tin boxes with the initials or the names of consignees in Batavia on their lids, were taken from the wreck. Earlier, in 1725, a 'large quantity of money belonging to private persons' was brought up from the wrecked *Slot ter Hoge* by a diver. In 1990, it was revealed that *'t Vliegend Hart*, which had also sunk, contained many chests of ducatoons. The re-valuation of the ducatoon in 1743 meant that the profit which could be obtained from appreciation gradually shrank.[7]

At the end of the 1780s, all the regulations governing private trade were slowly abandoned. Outsiders were now allowed to send goods on Company ships. Merchant Van Hoboken, who collaborated with Commanders Rogge and Smalt of the Rotterdam Chamber, is an example of this new development. In 1791, merchants and traders were officially given the right to ship their commercial commodities to the East as 'freight'. There was no longer any room for the *recognitiegoederen* of a commander or others and the system was abolished. Stipends were raised, and even more importantly an indemnification of *f*. 180 was given for a certain amount of cargo (one 'last') which the *recognitiekisten* would otherwise have taken up in the hold.[8] This change meant that there was now room for the cargo shipped by outsiders. There was no longer any obstacle preventing a Company commander from taking his own goods to the East openly and independently 'as freight' and later trading them there. Once he would have only been able to do this by first overcoming a great many hurdles. Now, he was free to do as he pleased.

---

[7] F.S. Gaastra, *Particuliere geldstromen binnen het VOC-bedrijf 1640–1795*, Van Gelder lecture (Leiden, 2002), pp. 11–20; A. Pol, "'Tot gerieff van India". Geldexport door de VOC en de muntproduktie in Nederland 1720–1740', *Jaarboek voor Munt- en Penningkunde* 72 (1985), pp. 65–195, in particular pp. 88–96; Paesie, *Het VOC-retourschip Ravesteyn*, pp. 38–40; Jacobs, *Merchant in Asia*, pp. 300–2; DAS II, nos. 2600, 2680, 2978 and 3016.

[8] See Chapter 5 on the Rotterdam Chamber, p. 104; The Hague, NA, VOC 299, 31.10.1791.

In short, prior to 1742 the opportunities open to a commander to transport private goods to the East to earn some extra income, if he abided by the official regulations, were fairly restricted. If he wanted to earn extra money he had to resort to illegal practices and, if the stories are true, these were rampant. In 1727, when the *Luchtenburg* went down in the Wielingen, a channel off Cadzand at the entrance to the West Schelde in the province of Zealand, it appeared that, without official permission having been granted for this, she had been carrying a coach on board.[9] The door for earning some extra money was opened a little wider in 1742, when trade in strong drink was allowed. In 1771, the door was closed again slightly, but from 1791 there were virtually no restrictions at all. Merchants had also prepared themselves for the change in policy.

A Glimpse of Private Trade on the Voyage Out

Divers both in the past and recently have found tangible evidence from shipwrecks that those who sailed in the ships carried prohibited silver ducatoons with them. However scattered these wrecks are, a wreck represents a ship in active service that had its life abruptly cut off. The inventory of the estate of a commander who died on board is to some extent comparable. In both instances, the life of a ship and that of a commander, clues are left by an unexpected end. The inventories of the possessions of crew members who died on board were always put away in the back of the ship's pay book, which is where a researcher can sometimes still find them. More than fifteen inventories of the possessions of commanders who died, compiled during the voyage to Asia, the vast majority of them dating from the first half of the eighteenth century, have been investigated in more detail in search of references to commodities of private trade.[10]

These inventories reveal that commanders only sporadically indulged in the transportation of ducatoons. Daniël van Staden in 1738 and Dirk Pomp in 1740 had these coins with them, the former 231 and the latter 195, neither a considerable number. Simon de Groot had forty-nine ducatoons and a considerable quantity of Spanish *matten* with him, as well as various other bags of money,

---

[9] The Hague, NA, VOC 221, 6.8.1728; *DAS* II, no. 2709.
[10] Mrs A. Meddens-Van Borselen collected and described the estate inventories in the framework of a research seminar. Her work concerns the estates in VOC 12704 (Le Fain 1704, *DAS* II, no. 942), 12766 (Maljaard 1716, *DAS* II, no. 2250), 6928 (De Leus 1728, *DAS* II, no. 2713), 14735 (Blom 1738, *DAS* II, no. 3097), 14422 (Van Staden 1738, *DAS* II, no. 3119), Davidson 1739, *DAS* II, no. 3155), 12966 (Van de Woestijne 1739, *DAS* II, no. 3144), 14741 (Pomp 1740, *DAS* II, no. 3185), 12996 (Marijnissen 1743, *DAS* II, no. 3262), 6169 (Broeder 1745, *DAS* II, no. 3309), 6231 (Waag 1749, *DAS* II, no. 3434), 13067 (Ruts 1754, *DAS* II, no. 3597), 13104 (Ruis 1759, *DAS* II, no. 3756), 6374 (Elsevier 1759, *DAS* II, no. 3750) and 14072 (Forster 1792, *DAS* II, no. 4685). To these can be added 14.449 (Jan Tuinman 1751, *DAS* II, no. 3498). P. Grimm transcribed the inventory of Simon de Groot dating from 1750 (*DAS* II, no. 3513, and VOC, 6261).

25. A silver ducatoon. Silver ducatoons were often smuggled to Batavia from the Republic. They have been able to be recognized on various occasions in shipwrecks because of their anomalous packaging. This ducatoon was struck in the Overijssel mint in Kampen in 1734. The text on the coin is the well-known aphorism: *Concordia res parvae crescent*, 'unity makes small things grow'; also 'unity makes small things powerful'.

'in all likelihood because of private orders', it was noted alongside the entry. Commercial items are usually easily recognizable. In two inventories which date from 1759 not a single restriction was noted and the goods were simply listed in separate columns. It was noted that Commander Reinier Jan Elsevier had trade goods (*negotiegoederen*) with him and Pieter Ruis had merchandise (*koopmanschappen*), according to the description given. Elsevier had no fewer than nineteen different sorts of wine, as well as three different types of beer (*roskammer*, *truwelle* and *hane*), textiles including black knitted breeches and embroidered camisoles, 300 spectacle cases, 56 pairs of flintlocks and 30 pistols. Besides these he had 24 men's hats, 12 crystal fruit dishes, 400 lamp chimneys, 66 wine glasses and 320 panes of glass. In the comestibles department, he had considerable quantities of cheese, butter, herring, ham, smoked meat, ox-tongue and salmon. Ruis apparently had other ideas about commercial items as he had less drink and foodstuffs. His main interest seems to have been ironmongery (*Neurenburger cramerij*), which included spectacles, scissors, knives, looking-glasses, nails, razors and buttons. Moreover, he had reams of paper, woollen breeches and stockings, as well as 153 rolls of tobacco and a large number of pipes. He had hardly any wine, but he did have some Dutch gin as well as the usual foodstuffs. He had three sorts of cheese: 'Edam, cumin (Leiden) and green cheese'. More remarkable were seven telescopes, two violins and their bows, eighteen perpetual almanacs, two small chests containing paintings and French glassware.

Ruis and other commanders also had sealed, brand-marked chests in their charge destined for people overseas. In the estate of Jan Maljaard listed in 1716 were seven chests in the names of the people to whom they were addressed. They included the director in Bengal, a merchant and a cashier in Batavia Castle, the wife of a minister of religion, a free merchant, one person who is not described in any further detail and a widow who was to receive some money in the name of her brother in Middelburg. These small chests were described as goods on order (*bestelgoederen*). In 1753, Jozias Ruts had thirteen chests of wine, with explicit instructions to deliver these in Batavia. Some of the wine which was being transported by Anthonie Marijnissen in 1743 was partly for a half-share in the profit, partly for his personal profit.

Generally speaking, the goods registered to Commanders Elsevier and Ruis are similar to those listed in the other inventories. Among Willem Leus' commercial items were wooden knives, jack knives, black knives, curry combs, fifty dozen each of all these items, and twenty dozen barber's razors. Even Stolwijk cheese from South Holland went to the East, as did white leather gentlemen's gloves. Ruts had with him boxes of violin strings, three violins and their bows, two 'sweet flutes', two small ordinary flutes and two French horns. If a commander died after leaving the Cape, Cape wines were also to be found among his possessions.

Many goods were the same as those mentioned in the 1693 regulations. Apparently these were commodities for which there was a ready market in the East. The general merchandise contained articles for everyday use for which it seems there was a constant demand. Perhaps they were even imported to order. It is difficult to discover whether the amounts recorded of such bulk articles as drink were kept within the set boundaries, or just what share of the capacity of the ship they took up. Any possessions which happened to have been stowed in the hold or between decks were not mentioned specifically.

When he arrived in Batavia, or indeed even earlier at the Cape, the commander was careful to see that his own private goods were unloaded safely and as discreetly as possible. Connivance must have been very common in the ports everywhere. A personal contact or a business contact of the supplier in the Republic organized the transfer and sale of the goods. Money which had been borrowed was repaid to this agent.

Commander Pieter Scharf ran into difficulties when he tried to deliver his fifty-four flintlocks in Cape Town in 1726. Shortly after his arrival at the Cape, these firearms were sold at auction to the inhabitants of the Cape, but they were so shoddy that they could not even fire half a shot with loose gunpowder without falling apart. One person had already lost a hand. Scharf was aware that the flintlocks were not of that quality 'which Europeans traded to each other, but had instead been expressly manufactured [to be sold to] people in the West Indies or others about whom people were not greatly bothered', or so it was recorded in the resolutions of the government of the Cape on 19 November. This provides a disconcerting insight into eighteenth-century ideas about trade. Scharf was obliged to take his firearms, even 'the bits and pieces of those which had exploded', back on board and had to pay back the money which he had collected. The same day Scharf sailed for Batavia on the *Meerlust*. Apparently, this affair did nothing to damage his career as a commander as he made two subsequent voyages.[11]

The complaint lodged against Staring mentioned earlier makes it plain to the researcher that the highest-ranking official in a port, the Superintendent of the Shipyard, could also be immersed in private trade. Around 1778, Staring exercised what amounted to a reign of terror at the Cape. When a ship arrived, he would board her with two of his cronies in order 'to discover what trade goods' the commander and the ship's officers had brought with them. For the first three days, only Staring and his men and the doctor – to check the health of the crew – were allowed on board. The Superintendent bought everything which caught his eye and on which he thought he 'could make the most excessive profit', in other words what the inhabitants at the Cape could buy from him 'at the highest price'. Neither the transportation of the goods nor their storage cost Staring a penny. He simply used the Company lighters and the shipyard.[12]

Regulations for the Voyage Home

There were other regulations governing the voyage home. In 1717, in a meticulous set of rules and regulations the Company formulated what each member of a crew could bring with him on his return trip. A commander could have three chests measuring 5 × 2 × 2 Rhineland feet (155 x 62 x 62 cm), one of which could be filled with linen or textiles, though not white and painted, and silk cloth. Besides this, he could bring along some goods in a sailor's chest measuring 4 × 1½ × 1½ feet (124 x 46.5 x 46.5 cm), plus six pots of pickles (*atjar*). Goods which had not been claimed three months after arrival in the Republic were confiscated.

The rules were strict but nonetheless the crew members continued to display their ingenuity in finding extra space for their own goods. Their berths and kitbags were increasingly stuffed full of trade goods, often wrapped in sailcloth and bound up with rope. Naturally a commander was supposed to restrain himself from such practices. In 1732, he was given the right to bring twelve canisters of tea weighing 80 pounds each. Canisters were made of plaited reeds. His crew were also allocated proportional amounts.

The Company fought a losing battle and was ultimately completely unsuccessful. On their voyage back to the Republic the returning ships were supposed to be loaded to the gunwales with the Company's own trade goods. Indeed this is what the whole of the Company business was based on. On the voyage out, maximizing use of space was not particularly important. With all the years of experience he had built up overseas, Van Imhoff discovered that, remarkably enough, the returning ships were 'not just bursting at the seams, they were overloaded'

---

[11] Cape Town Archives, Resolutions C. of P. 19.11.1726 (www.tanap.net); *DAS* II, no. 2664.
[12] Staring, *Hugo Damiaan Staring*, p. 174.

with private goods. He calculated that on average each ship carried between 100 and 150 chests belonging to the crew stowed between decks alongside 2,000 to 3,000 canisters of tea, authorized and unauthorized. He thought this space would be better used for storing sails, water and victuals, which would mean that there would be more space available for the goods of the Company itself.

Van Imhoff was displeased with this situation. He made the fairly revolutionary suggestion that all 'authorized baggage' should be bought off for 'its monetary equivalent', so 'that everybody on board would make as much profit proportionally as at present' with his private trade. The Company would earn more money because of the larger cargoes of Asian wares. The *Heren Zeventien* adopted this plan and implemented it in 1742. For example, from that time instead of bringing back his chest and a canister, when he returned home a sailor would be paid the sum of *f.* 150. He was allowed to share only one chest for his clothes with his messmates. Besides their bonuses, petty officers whose monthly wages were higher than *f.* 20 were absolutely forbidden to bring more than one brand-marked chest with them, as had been laid down in the 1717 regulation. This same regulation also applied to the ship's officers, but without the 'other augmentations', which had become the custom. Over and above this, a third mate was given compensation of *f.* 300, a second mate *f.* 400, and the first mate the sum of *f.* 500. The commander, upon whose shoulders 'the burden of everything' was laid, received the highest payment, or sweetener (*douceur*) as it was called, the sum of no less than *f.* 2,000. Besides this, he also retained his right to the chests as laid down in the 1717 regulations. The only privilege he lost was his canisters. A man with the rank of captain was actually given *f.* 3,000, as well as four chests and two small sailor's chests.[13]

Van Imhoff's idea of paying by far the majority of the crew money instead of allowing them to bring goods with them made the whole process of embarkation much simpler. A small group of messmates could bring only one chest on board with them. Only the commander and the ship's officers had more. However, the *Heren Zeventien* undermined their own rule, because in 1750 and 1756 the crew were given more generous permission to ship merchandise and other wares. Only silk textiles and goods which were shipped by weight such as spices (*pondgoederen*) were forbidden. Tea and tamarind, a sweetmeat and also a medicine prepared from the pods of the tree of the same name, could once more be brought on board. Even more goods could be taken on board at the Cape and brought home to the Netherlands. Popular choices were Cape wines, furs, household utensils, clothes for personal use and for family, jewellery, gold and silver work and curiosities. These goods could be imported duty free on arrival home. All the rest of the wares were sold at the first auction to be held after landing in the Republic. Eight to 20 per cent of the profits went to the

---

[13] Heeres, 'De "Consideratiën"', pp. 472–9; *Nederlandsch-Indisch Plakaatboek* V, 18.6.1743.

Company. All this was over and above the *douceur* for lost cargo space which remained untouched.

The possibilities for earning large sums of money on the voyage home were therefore considerably expanded. The commanders and ship's officers were also allowed to trade their private goods in the intra-Asian trade. Because of rising discontent among the commanders, in 1752 they were permitted to double the amount of the private goods they transported. This was essential to them, they said, because of the 'impossibility of saving enough for themselves for their old age in the present unhealthy economic climate'. These opportunities were expanded again in 1760. The bigger the ship, the larger the number of *pikols* (= 100 *kati* = 62 kilos) that could be transported. The quantities for a commander increased to a maximum of 10,000 *pikols*, or 8,750 in a smaller vessel. Ship's officers could transport half or somewhat less than the commander.[14]

In 1790 a great discussion arose about authorized goods. Just as on the voyage out, in the framework of the new, more liberal policy on trade and freight, space had to be made for the goods shipped by private merchants. The Chambers disagreed about this, but the list was cut back. As compensation, the crew were paid a higher stipend. Once again it was a question of money instead of goods. Commanders were privileged in the amount of authorized goods they were allowed because, it was argued, they had to be able to make a decent profit to ensure their ambition was kept at fever pitch. Otherwise, the Company would lose good and honest men.[15]

Generally speaking, making rules and regulations to govern private trade contributed to greater opportunities for a commander and his men to earn more. After 1750, the *douceur* of 1742 became a real bonus. In observing the rules, everything depended on the vigilance of the checks during loading and unloading after arrival. If people were caught infringing the rules, they usually lost everything.

Transfers of Money from Asia to the Republic

Goods authorized or otherwise were loaded on board in the East on their way to their destination in the Republic where they would be transformed into money. A commander was not allowed to take the ready money he had earned overseas with him in his pocket. The Company did not allow its personnel to bring gold and silver, whether coin or specie, to the Republic. Money could only be transferred using bills of exchange (*wissels*), which were also called *assignaties*. The person concerned brought his ready money to the paymaster in Batavia, Ceylon or Cape Town, and later to offices in India. In exchange for this cash, he

---

[14] The Hague, NA, VOC 14329 (regulations from 1717, 1750, 1754 and 1756); *Nederlandsch-Indisch Plakaatboek* VI, 17.7.1752, and VII, 25.1.1760.
[15] The Hague, NA, VOC 223, 11.5 and 1.12.1792, 1.6 and 9.12.1793 and 4797 (1792).

was given a bill or promissory note for the amount concerned, which he could exchange for money at the office of the Company back home. By instituting this rule, the Company kept precious metals overseas. It was also advantageous for its personnel as well. Until 1738 the Company paid interest of 4 per cent on the balance of the bill of exchange, and even more importantly the monetary transactions overseas and in the Republic were carried out in the same currency. The ducatoon was an attractive monetary unit for this purpose. After 1700, bills of exchange were made out for 78 *stuivers* per ducatoon and these were later paid out at the same rate. Between 1719 and 1728, the Company tightened this policy and calculated 66 *stuivers* per ducatoon. Later, until 1738 it was again 78 *stuivers* and, after that date, 72 *stuivers*. From 1779, a ducatoon was calculated at 70 *stuivers*. It is not necessary to probe the reasons for these changes.[16] Unquestionably, the transactions which generated those bills of exchange sent to the Republic were profitable for those concerned. For instance, if a commander in the years 1738–1779 handed in 1,000 ducatoons in Batavia, he would later exchange this bill in the Republic for *f*. 3,600.[17] Hence, it made no sense to smuggle ready money into the Republic.

It was of increasing importance to the Company to see that the money earned in the private commercial transactions of its personnel in Asia, including those on the ships, remained there. Its need of capital grew inexorably because of the increasingly stronger competition in Asian markets for new products, especially after c.1760, as a consequence of the dominant role assumed by the English East India Company. Private activities satisfied this need to a growing extent, because in 1742 Van Imhoff had introduced a virtually irreversible policy of allowing Company personnel the freedom to pursue their own trade in an expanding number of products. Their steadily growing incomes from Asian activities ended up in the hands of the *Hoge Regering* in Batavia through the intermediation of the paymaster and, as already stated, the bills of exchange could only be converted into money in the Republic. After 1771, the opportunities for private individuals were expanded even more. Commanders participated in this system to the hilt.[18]

From their perusal of the Letters and Papers Dispatched (*Overgekomen Brieven en Papieren*) sent at set times from Asia and Cape Town, the *Heren Zeventien* were kept accurately informed about how many bills of exchange had been issued, to whom and for what amounts. As the eighteenth century progressed, the amounts steadily increased from being initially around 1 million per year to 4 million in the 1780s The profits made from private trade by Company

---

[16] See Gaastra's study of private flows of money mentioned in note 7.
[17] The amount of *f*. 3,600 is the sum of 72,000 *stuivers* divided by 20 *stuivers* per guilder. With a value of 63 *stuivers* for a ducatoon in the Republic, the return would have been *f*. 3,150.
[18] C. Nierstrasz, 'In the Shadow of the Company. The VOC (Dutch East India Company) and its Servants in the Period of its Decline (1740–1796)' (PhD thesis, Leiden University, 2008), chs 3 and 4.

personnel were only paid out in cash after their return to the Dutch Republic, or they could be made available to family members or business partners. Albeit on a modest scale, commanders took part in this traffic in money – not all of them by any means, but a growing number, which reached two-thirds in the 1770s. The value of their transfers in that decade was no less than $f.$ 2.7 million. In the first decade of the century it had been no more than 400,000 guilders. In total, the paymasters noted well over 2,000 times, 'paid in by the commander of the Honourable Company to be reimbursed by Their Honours upon [his] arrival in the Fatherland'.[19]

The growing use of bills of exchange by commanders can be traced to the 1740s, when the new policy governing private trade and return transportation of goods was introduced. Especially after 1760, on various occasions during their stay in the tropics commanders drew bills of exchange, and the amounts grew continually larger. From that period, the sums per commander ranged on average between $f.$ 7,000 and $f.$ 7,400. By this time, the majority of these bills of exchange were no longer addressed to their wives or business partners at home but to merchants. All the evidence indicates that commanders were playing a more active personal role in private trade abroad.

Besides the commander, other men on the ships were occupied with their own trade initiatives. Often on the voyage out, a chest would contain some European goods, which were probably going to be used for trade. The higher the rank, the greater the opportunities open to a man to pursue commerce. Nevertheless, the men in the lower ranks of the ship's company made relatively little use of bills of exchange. The profit to be made on the goods which they had brought with them was probably calculated to be able to buy a few authorized wares. In the East, it was the first mates who had the most ready money which they could transform into bills of exchange. In the period up to 1770, it would have been 5 to 10 per cent of them. Later the percentage rose to around 20 per cent. Below the ranks of second and third mate, the percentage was negligible. Occasionally in the bills of exchange it is possible to come across the name of a boatswain, chief sailmaker, surgeon or sailor, who had deposited some money with the paymaster in exchange for a bill.

The average amount of a bill of exchange sent by first mates fluctuated between $f.$ 2,000 and $f.$ 3,000, rising to around $f.$ 4,000 after 1770. The death of a first mate was frequently the reason that a bill was drawn up. In 1711/1712, for instance, two bills worth $f.$ 8,230 were sent to the guardian of the son of

---

[19] The passages about the traffic in bills of exchange are based on the MA thesis by Wolvers, 'Het wisselverkeer'. I am very grateful for this information, as well as for the opportunity to consult the file of microfiches concerned. I also thank A. van den Belt for large amounts of information about this material. The source of the bills of exchange mentioned in the text is the tables in the back of the *Overgekomen Brieven en Papieren* in the VOC Archive in the National Archive at The Hague and, up to and including 1760, bills mentioned also in the published *Generale Missiven*.

First Mate Isaak de Keizer in Middelburg. The widow of Jan Ongewassen in Amsterdam received no less than *f.* 15,452 in 1719. In Middelburg, between 1774 and 1778 the widow of Jan Frederik Lang, who had died in the hospital outside the city walls of Batavia, received four bills of exchange worth a total of *f.* 10,610. Usually the amounts sent home were much lower. As already mentioned, to an increasing extent, merchants were the beneficiaries. Frans Verschuur twice sailed home from Ceylon, in 1787 and 1790. There he deposited money with the paymaster for four bills of exchange worth in total *f.* 14,600. This money was destined for merchants in Amsterdam, one of whom was a dealer in wines. Among the first mates only a few names of later commanders are to be found. Angelvorst, Arie Kikkert and Rijzik, discussed in earlier chapters, are a few of the rare examples.

Caught and Punished

The traffic with the Republic in bills of exchange was an essential link in the private trade in money and goods. It was a highly profitable means of being able to rake in the money earned in Asia and send it back home at an attractive rate of exchange. The source of the money was never checked in the Republic. However, although far from all the commanders chose to use this means of payment, they all brought authorized goods with them and these were always the tangible extra earnings from a voyage. Naturally, all the visible goods in the ship's cargo to the Republic were hedged in by rules and regulations, and being caught infringing these rules inevitably meant punishment.

When the returning ships were being loaded, it was possible to check which private goods the crew took on board. When the cargo was unloaded after a ship's arrival back in the Republic it was the last opportunity for the authorities to inspect goods and discover whether a commander and his shipmates had observed the rules governing their property. However, there is very little that can be said about either the strictness or the keenness with which this inspection was carried out in the roads of Texel, Goeree and Rammekens, or during the transhipment of the goods to lighters. Why one commander was caught and others escaped scot-free has to remain guesswork but it is unthinkable that commanders always obeyed the regulations scrupulously.

Perhaps it would be better to look at the matter the other way around. Why is it that there are only occasional examples of infringements of the rules on contraband and smuggling recorded? Directors and their officials would only take action if the crew informed on their commander for smuggling or if there were unequivocal reports that goods were put aboard private vessels at sea off the Dutch coast, from officers on ships in the naval convoy. In such instances, the retribution of the Company was swift. The goods and the stipend of the commander concerned were confiscated and he was denied the bonus which, since 1742, should have been his by right. The commander was declared 'incompetent' (*inhabiel*), in other words he was either unfit to serve the Company further or he was suspended. Jan Koster of the Delft Chamber was punished in 1718 on the evidence of his second mate, who also informed on the first mate.

The transhipment of goods on the high seas was a regular occurrence in the eighteenth century, no matter what the Company did to try to prevent it. In 1703 a new rule was issued stating that no unauthorized vessel should be found in the vicinity of the returning ships. Nor should any ship's boats sail away during the discharge of cargo.[20] In 1755, Jochem Outjes and Pieter Eikels were caught because without there being any real need for it they had summoned the pilot boat and had handed various unauthorized goods over to men on board. They paid for this illegal activity with immediate dismissal. A year later, in 1756, the Company careers of Arie van der Aart and Paulus Rauwenhof were abruptly ended for similar reasons. After a round-trip voyage in 1778, Kornelis Bosch of the Amsterdam Chamber was discharged with no mercy shown. His attempts to smuggle had also been a failure. Quite apart from the loss of the confiscated goods, a commander who was caught also forfeited any stipend still owed him. Outjes had gambled away no less than ƒ. 5,287, which included a bonus of ƒ. 2,000.[21]

It was in fact normal for the pilot boat to be found in the vicinity of the Company ships. It was obligatory to have a pilot for sailing in and out of the passages to the sea on the Holland and Zealand coasts. The piloting of the returning ships was charged at the highest rate, which meant that it was a highly sought-after post. Pilots lived in the villages around the entrances to the sea along the Dutch coast and on the Wadden Islands. They were either professional pilots or also worked as fishermen or whalers. One examination was sufficient to qualify a man for being a pilot. Their vessels had a number on the mainsail or flew a white flag from the mast which made them easily recognizable. Each ship in the returning fleet was obliged to take two pilots on board. The first pilot usually came out on one of the warships in the convoy, on which until that moment he had been a sailor, or he came with the Company galliot, a small fast coaster which brought out welcome extra fresh victuals for the crew after the long voyage from the Cape. However, there was a rule that the second pilot always had to return to shore in his own boat, but it was a rule often more honoured in the breach than the observance. Constant problems arose about the division and payment of the pilotage and rivalries cropped up between villages.

---

[20] The Hague, NA, VOC 246, 27.8.1703. For smuggling on English East Indiamen, see H.V. Bowen, "'So Alarming an Evil": Smuggling, Pilfering and the English East India Company, 1750–1810', *International Journal of Maritime History* XIV, no. 1 (2002), pp. 1–31.

[21] For the cases mentioned, see consecutively The Hague, NA, VOC 116 and 221, 30.9.1718, *DAS* III, no. 6416; 222, 21.10.1755, *DAS* III, nos. 7431 and 7434; 128, 12.10.1756, *DAS* III, nos. 7461 and 7467; 222, 7.10.1778, *DAS* III, no. 8005. For Outjes and Eikels, see also the next note.

It was not difficult for Company commanders to come to an agreement with the pilots about supplying some extra services as this meant more earnings for all those concerned. The repeated accusations of the directors railing against the transhipment of goods in pilots' boats are certainly based on fact, just as are the reports of warships which had chased off such boats. In 1755 Eikels, one of Outjes' colleagues, and eight of his shipmates had had contraband on board the *Stralen* and before sailing into the entrance to the Texel Roads, these goods had to be offloaded. The *Stralen* flew a signal to summon two pilot boats. Eikels reached an understanding with both these pilots that they would put the goods ashore near Petten, a small coastal village in North Holland, for an agreed price. There the goods were to be loaded into wagons and conveyed to a particular place, where they would be unloaded. While the pilots were busy loading the wagons, they were caught by the bailiff.[22] The upshot was that the commanders involved had to bid the VOC an irrevocable farewell, and this was the fate of various others, including Jan Koenraad Lubken. In 1791 he did not even have the chance to start his maiden voyage as commander of the packet-boat the *Faam*, on which he had made several voyages as second-in-command in 1789 and 1790. He had made himself hated among the crew which is why they informed on him, reporting his illegal chests. Lubken was arrested straightaway and never returned to the Company.[23]

Nevertheless, the same fate did not befall everyone who was declared 'incompetent'. Many commanders managed to stage a comeback. There was even a fixed procedure to be followed for reinstatement. The dismissed commander petitioned his own Chamber for rehabilitation. However, it was not his own Chamber which made the decision about his petition but rather the *Heren Zeventien* after consultation with the other Chambers. In 1699, Anthonie Chef from Enkhuizen was caught transhipping several bales of tea and some other goods onto a small boat off the Dutch coast. In 1704 he was rehabilitated, and in May 1705 he sailed once more as a commander. The same fate befell Jakob Onkruid in Amsterdam. After a suspension in 1701, he was reinstated in 1708 and after that made another six voyages. Being temporarily 'incompetent' certainly did not mean that any further hope of a career with the Company was irrevocably damaged, but a few years had to pass before rehabilitation could occur. All in all, being caught smuggling was a financial setback. Perhaps this is why Kornelis Fret in Zealand regretted having permitted two small boats loaded with goods to come alongside in 1728. He was only allowed to go to sea again in 1734.[24] And there were more like him.

---

[22] P. Dekker, 'De pilotage te Petten in de 18ᵉ eeuw', *West-Frieslands Oud en Nieuw* 42 (1975), pp. 36–71, in particular pp. 48–51 and 61–2.
[23] See note 6.
[24] The Hague, NA, VOC 112, 21.10.1699, and 113, 21.10.1704 (*DAS* III, no. 6014 and *DAS* II, no. 1974; 113, 19.3.1701, *DAS* III, no. 6037 and *DAS* II, no. 2047; 221, 17.3.1729, *DAS* III, no. 6722 and *DAS* II, no. 2938.

Kornelis van Dijk was let off leniently at the Cape. When he returned from Batavia on his Cape hooker, private goods which were neither branded nor authorized were found in the hold. These goods, as well as two slave boys and two girls, had been ordered by various private citizens at the Cape. These so-called ordered goods were soon released because it was judged that by doing so precious space would be saved in the warehouses. However, Van Dijk and his officers had also brought along their own sacks of sugar, rice, floor tiles and woodwork. Some of these goods had been supplied and sold by such people as Willem Jakob Andriessen, formerly a commander with the Rotterdam Chamber and now Superintendent in Batavia. The remainder had been bought from 'various merchants among them Christians, Javanese, Moors, Chinese and yet others'. Van Dijk said that the authorities had supervised the loading and the Cape government demanded a written testimony of this claim. Van Dijk kept his ship.[25]

Sometimes during inspections goods which appeared to be prohibited were discovered. When the Enkhuizen directors checked his ship in 1750, it transpired that Maarten Haringman had six pots of conserved fruit on board. The pots were confiscated, but a year later they were to be returned to Haringman, unless they had been auctioned in the meantime. In the event of this happening, he was entitled to half the sum raised. In 1789, the directors in Amsterdam thought that a trunk of 'some considerable' weight in the possession of Paulus Kroon was suspicious and stored it in the warehouse, where its contents were investigated. It did indeed contain money; nevertheless, Kroon was allowed to pick it up. Around the time of the return of the summer fleet of 1737, rumours flew thick and fast that there had been eight stowaways on board the *Haamstede* commanded by Jakob Bernards, who had fled before the Company yacht of the Delft Chamber arrived. More stowaways were found on other ships. It was decided to interrogate the commander of the returning fleet, but he died before they could speak to him. Whatever had happened, Bernards was paid his full stipend.[26]

After 1742 there were fewer opportunities for private trade on either the outward or homeward voyages, but chances to pursue private trade in Asia had greatly expanded. Whatever the changes introduced in the course of the years, it was always profitable to infringe the set rules and regulations. Observance of the rules was never enforced and there was no systematic checking of private cargoes. If a serious check was carried out, it had usually been preceded by rumours of violation or a betrayal. At the end of the century, the checking and the subsequent punishments meted out were far less severe than they had once been.

---

[25] Cape Town Archives, resolutions C. of P. 9.11.1792 (www.tanap.net).
[26] The Hague, NA, VOC 222, 9.9 and 8.11.1737, 17.6.1738, *DAS* III, no. 6968; 222, 7.10.1751, *DAS* III, no. 7323; 297, 3 and 17.9.1789, *DAS* III, no. 8243.

Earning Money in Asia and a Few Big Earners

Nowhere in this book is there an in-depth description of how commanders in Asia or at the Cape went about pursuing their actual trade and the networks they used. In the description of Kornelis van Dijk we get some insight. In 1758, Commander Jan Bloem traded directly with the Governor of Coromandel. However, for this book the subject has not been thoroughly investigated, because to do so would have required another approach. With some regularity, the *Hoge Regering* in Batavia reported to the Republic that commanders or other crew members had been caught carrying out illegal activities. The *Nederlandsch-Indisch Plakaatboek*, the book in which the decrees of the *Hoge Regering* were published, contains regulations about how much cargo and the sorts of goods that a commander could carry in the hold of his ship on his own account in Asia. The only banned cargoes were the monopoly products: spices, pepper, copper, tin and opium. Generally speaking, most of the goods that were traded were foodstuffs, sugar and timber. Each commander was allowed to conduct business with private citizens, but he could also supply Company posts with wares, ranging from rice to parts of ships. A recent study of Ceylon has shown that the bulk of the bills of exchange which the commanders dispatched from this island were produced by profits from the import of European articles, especially those from trading companies in Amsterdam and Middelburg, but also some from the other Chamber towns.[27]

Consequently it is possible to trace the financial profits from ventures in Asia and at the Cape in the traffic in bills of exchange. This becomes impossible, though, when the aim is to try to trace the profits made on goods which were brought back to the Republic. Such an exercise leads to guesswork about what sorts of goods these were, such as porcelain and textiles. Certainly, the presence of large quantities of porcelain in commanders' houses is tangible evidence of this trade. Similar concrete evidence has been brought to light by the investigation of the wreck of the East Indiaman the *Oosterland*, which sank in Table Bay in 1697. Chinese porcelain was discovered aft and this had been the property of the officers of the ship.[28]

Some commanders spent longer periods in the East because they had been appointed to a shore job, especially that of Superintendent at one of the trading posts. Just as in the Republic, this sort of position offered an opportunity to earn extra income alongside a normal stipend. Some particular positions had the reputation of being more lucrative than others. The most attractive of all was the post of Commodore and Superintendent of the Shipyard in Batavia, but

---

[27] A. van den Belt, *Het VOC-bedrijf op Ceylon. Een voorname vestiging van de Oost-Indische Compagnie in de 18de eeuw* (Zutphen, 2008); Nierstrasz, *In the Shadow*, p. 107.
[28] B. Werz, '*Een bedroefd, en beclaaglijck ongeval'. De wrakken van de VOC-schepen Oosterland en Waddinxveen (1697) in de Tafelbaai* (Zutphen, 2004), pp. 138–43.

there were other opportunities as well. This was illustrated earlier by the career of Roelof Blok. The regulations of 1742 made the position of Commodore and Superintendent of the Shipyard in Batavia an even more plum job. The man who held this position had the right to send eight tons of his own goods to the Republic in every ship of the returning fleet. His deputy could send half this quantity, and the same rule applied for the other Superintendents in the East, including the man in Colombo. If they wanted they could pass this right over to a third party, that is they could sell it.[29]

Unquestionably a commander had the qualifications necessary to be a Superintendent. He was well acquainted with the loading and unloading of ships and he certainly should have been aware that ships needed to be properly maintained and repaired in good time, and he understood the terminology and the materials needed for this. He was also used to being a leader. Various commanders were appointed to such posts. Shortly after his arrival there in 1739, Anthonie Guldeman of the Delft Chamber became Commodore and Superintendent of the Shipyard in Batavia. He advised the *Hoge Regering* authoritatively about whether or not to divide up the space between decks into sections, and about the sale of copper and lead which had been salvaged from ships which were broken up, and he became engrossed in the accepted calculations made by Director Hendrik Decquer in 1689 pertaining to the loading of a ship of the returning fleet. These were set down in a small book entitled *Middelen om uit te vinden de ware ladinge der scheepen na hare grootte* (Means by which to discover the true loading of ships according to their size) and a copy of this was available in Batavia. In 1742 he sent a bill of exchange back home worth *f.* 17,722, a sum which was clearly not solely derived from his monthly salary of *f.* 120. Since the 1730s, Batavia had become an unhealthy place for Europeans because of malaria. Guldeman perished in 1743. His successor, Opmeer, followed him two years later. Their predecessors, Gerbrand Mamus (1730–1732) and Elias Walgaren (1733–1734), had also enjoyed only brief careers. Verleng on the other hand left to go back to the Republic in 1749.

A few of the commanders who occupied the post in Batavia were forced to withdraw against their will; in other words, the *Hoge Regering* dismissed them. The firing of Wessel van Neercassel in 1715 has already been mentioned. Koenraad Mels must have let his work slide, since after almost five years he was put on a transport back to the Republic. He had been guilty of misconduct, but, even worse, he had neglected the maintenance of the ships and had not been present to supervise their being loaded. As a consequence of his negligence, two ships in the returning fleet had foundered and the rest had arrived home in a deplorable state.[30]

---

[29] *Nederlandsch-Indisch Plakaatboek* V, 17.8 and 25.11.1745.
[30] Van Goor, *Generale Missiven* IX, p. 196, X, pp. 393, 588, 733–4 and 1084; *DAS* I, 43–4.

All these former commanders made sure that they were financially secure. After his death as Superintendent in Batavia (1704–1710), each of Jakob Broek's two children received a bill of exchange worth ƒ. 38,400 in 1714 and three years later a supplement to the value of ƒ. 1,896 each. Via his successor Mamus, Mels obtained a bill of exchange worth ƒ. 17,988 in Amsterdam at the end of 1732. When Mamus died, his widow could still expect to receive bills valued at ƒ. 30,417.

Later in the century, Hendrik Booms from Flushing occupied the position of Commodore and Superintendent of the Shipyard (1759–1764) and he had his wife and daughter come out to join him. Not long after him, the post was occupied by Commander Anthonie Vogelzang (1766–1770). In the 1780s, Christiaan Blom managed to make a fortune from this post, all of which was sent to his mother, the widow of Commander Christoffel Blom, and his brother, Barend, a wine merchant, in Amsterdam, via bills of exchange. In total the value of the bills amounted to ƒ. 143,439. His successor, Philip Hendrik de Haard, took charge of the dispatch of the last bills for his predecessor after Blom returned home in 1788. Several other commanders became Superintendent or Deputy-Superintendent as well.

Even in lesser posts, the profits could be just as great. As Superintendent in Ceylon, Paulus Engelaar deposited ƒ. 76,000 with the paymaster. At the end of his career, Olke Andringa of the Enkhuizen Chamber was Superintendent in Colombo. In 1788, the local minister of the Lutheran Church arranged for a bill of exchange for ƒ. 25,000 to be sent to Enkhuizen for Andringa. Andringa had earlier personally made use of bills of exchange in 1770–1772 when he was still a first mate. As commander he had also arranged for bills of exchange at various offices in Asia. Besides Batavia, he had sent them from Bengal and the Cape, where his former colleague Staring helped him out. On top of the bills of exchange mentioned above, the amount involved was more than ƒ. 42,000. They were invariably addressed to the merchant Pancras de Wit and to his wife, both of whom resided in Enkhuizen. His wife did not see her husband very often as Andringa was constantly travelling, and he was still in Ceylon in 1795.[31] In Chapter 3, which discusses the Zealand Chamber, Rijzik and Staring were given as examples of rich commanders after they had each spent some years at the Cape as Superintendent of the Shipyard.

A researcher can never build up a complete picture of the commercial and financial transactions of the Company commander, or of the origins of the profits which were the fruits earned from the occupation of a post overseas such as that of Superintendent. The same problem also has to be faced when investigating similar posts in the Republic. It is just as difficult to find an answer to the question of why one commander and not another happened to be consid-

---

[31] Besides the information about bills of exchange in Wolvers, see *DAS* II, nos. 4174, 4271 and 4352, and II, nos. 7933 and 8009. For Booms and Vogelzang see also *Kroniek Historisch Genootschap* 28 (1872), pp. 98 and 119.

ered for these posts. Such an appointment was not just a matter of ability. But one fact is incontrovertible: many commanders did earn large sums of money as long as they continued to sail and survived. Some of them made very large sums indeed and were, to quote Gaastra, 'men of fortune'. It is also known that after they had given up the sea, many commanders began a second career on land, undertaking such activities as shop-keeping or being a merchant. Wessel van Neercassel, Simon de Groot, Jurriaan Wolberg and even Pieter Angelvorst from Amsterdam are examples of such a switch in occupation. Probably there were many, many more, especially in the second half of the eighteenth century and especially in its closing decades.

13

On Board

The bulk of the fitting out of a ship and the practical preparations for a voyage were made without the direct involvement of the newly appointed commander. Most of these matters were the responsibility of the Superintendent of the Shipyard and his assistants. When the ship made her way from the port to the roads from which she would depart, the ship's officers on board took charge of the reception of the crew and the administration and stowage of the cargo. The commander usually only came on board when the ship was ship-shape and ready to sail. As he had been a ship's officer on many previous occasions he had previously participated in these preparations. After his own appointment and those of his ship's officers by the directors of his Chamber, the commander took no part in the daily preparations for the voyage. He bore no direct responsibility for the recruiting and signing on of the crew. Before a ship set sail there were always a few commanders available at the *Oost-Indisch Huis* in the town, who could take care of the signing on of the crew. These commanders assessed the physical condition of the sailors and the soldiers and asked them questions about their knowledge of seamanship. Not everyone passed these examinations. Commander Verdoes was someone who was always extremely strict in these matters.[1] Usually, the commanders had plenty of time to put their own affairs in order and to organize the financial and commercial side of their private cargo.

In the Roads

Often months would pass between the appointment of a commander and the signing on of his crew before his East Indiaman actually put to sea. Not all preparations could be carried out in the shipyard because there were many hurdles to be cleared between the port and the roads from which she would depart, and these prevented her being fully loaded straightaway. In Zealand, horses had to tow the ships from Middelburg to Fort Rammekens. From Delfshaven and Rotterdam, the passage went via the Old Meuse (*Oude Maas*), Spui and Haringvliet, before the Goereese Gat was reached. The Zuiderzee was so clut-

---

[1] Moree, *Kikkertje lief*, p. 57; Van Gelder, *Naporra's omweg*, pp. 178–9.

tered with large sandbanks and winding channels that it was usually necessary to employ aids to reach the Texel Roads. The wind was not always set fair. The ship's camel, a sort of floating dry dock, was an essential aid in navigating the sandbanks and other shallows of the Zuiderzee, now the IJsselmeer. The worst obstacle of all was Pampus, a shoal at the mouth of the IJ. Ship's camels had been used ever since the end of the seventeenth century. The Navy needed them as well. Their function was to raise the large ships so that they sat higher in the water. In 1780, the Amsterdam camel was worn out, after it had transported ships no fewer than 477 times across the Pampus since 1756. During the eighteenth century, the Chambers of Amsterdam and Enkhuizen probably built three camels each. The transportation of the cargoes, victuals and cannon to the roads was done on lighters, smaller vessels with a shallow draft, whose skippers were under permanent contract to a Chamber. Amsterdam had no less than twenty of them under contract. Around 1750, to load a large East Indiaman required fifteen to eighteen trips by lighter.[2]

The roads hummed with activity. Often several East Indiamen were loaded simultaneously and the last crew members came hurrying aboard. On paper, the overall responsibility for ensuring that matters ran smoothly rested on the shoulders of the Superintendent, but in practice it was his replacement or the master stower, often a retired commander, who bore the real weight of responsibility. In the Texel Roads water barrels were filled with the chalybeate water from the Wezen wells close to Oudeschild. In 1756, for instance, more than 1.8 million litres of water were loaded on board to supply twenty-two departing ships. Often the livestock, destined to be eaten on board, also came from Texel: preferably two sows, three adult pigs, six piglets and nine sheep. Chickens were taken along as well. They were fed with barley and their eggs provided food for invalids.

The commander arrived in the final phase of the preparations. He took over command from the first mate and immediately set the tone and mood on board by his personality and conduct. The very same Verdoes, who was strict when signing on crew members, had once gone too far on the *Drie Papegaaien* in 1752. When he arrived on board he was already blind drunk and within half an hour he had had two experienced sailors flogged for some minor misdemeanour. Just before a ship set sail, a director, who had arrived on the Chamber yacht, came aboard. He inspected the vessel, checked the now complete muster roll and had the relevant clauses of the ship's Article Book read out aloud, and gave the commander his final instructions. This was a ceremonial occasion and was accompanied by the firing of salutes. On one occasion at least it did not go as planned. In 1708, a soldier cut into the director's left cheek with a knife. The culprit was quickly overmastered and executed.

---

[2] The Hague, NA, VOC 308, 23.1.1777; Gawronski, *De equipagie*, pp. 106–8; F.S. Gaastra, '"Een stel cameele"', *Zeemagazijn* 31, no. 3 (2005); G. Boven and A. Hoving, *Scheepskamelen & waterschepen. 'Eene elledige talmerij, doch lofflijk middel'* (Zutphen, 2009).

Before the ship set sail, two pilots, who would later leave her in the Channel, came aboard. The actual departure was determined by weather conditions. If the wind was favourable, occasionally various East Indiamen put to sea one after the other. If a contagious illness was widespread on board, departure was sometimes delayed. In 1771, typhus raged on five ships of the Amsterdam Chamber. Consequently, Commander Jurriaan Verburg and his colleagues had to delay their departure repeatedly. Often, an old, superannuated ship was used as a sort of floating hospital in which the sick were housed.[3]

A Box Brimming with Instructions and Regulations

A commander had a huge amount to think about and there were a great many matters which demanded his attention. Upon his appointment, he had sworn an oath that he would serve the interests of the Company and would carry out all his instructions in a fitting manner.[4] All the instructions and regulations were stuffed in the ship's box which stayed in his cabin. At the very end of the eighteenth century these directions amounted to at least eighty. The list was constantly extended, all additions and addenda coming in printed form. The basis for the list was the Article Book which was drastically revised in 1742. The position of the commander *vis-à-vis* the junior merchant who sailed with him was then greatly reinforced. The Articles prescribed rules for behaviour in the form of a series of numbered items and these had to be obeyed by the ship's company among themselves and in their contact with third parties. The Articles also listed the punishments to be meted out for any violations. The first such book was drawn up very soon after the foundation of the VOC and this was adapted and reviewed in the course of time. In Van Imhoff's day, it was revised in 1742 and eventually contained 121 articles. The crew were expected to know the contents. Sections of it were read out at suitable moments and a copy was nailed to the main mast. The ship had to be scrubbed and cleaned every morning. The ship's chest of every crew member had to be aired once a week. The commander was supposed to keep a sharp eye out to see that, 'the weather and opportunity permitting', common prayers and Bible readings were held every morning and every evening. The rations of victuals had to be shared out fairly. If it should prove necessary to supplement these during the voyage, the commander was allowed to use the ship's money, known as the refreshment money (*ververs-*

---

[3] The Hague, NA, VOC 308, 29.3.1779; Bonke, 'De VOC op de Rede van Texel', in Roeper and Vonk-Uitgeest, *Texel en de VOC*, pp. 17–41; V. Roeper, 'Het Weesewater. Texels drinkwater op de schepen van de VOC', in *ibid.*, pp. 43–51; Van Gelder, *Naporra's omweg*, pp. 183–202; Paesie, *Het VOC-schip Ravesteyn*, p. 177.
[4] The text of the oath is in: The Hague, NA, Archief Van Vredenburch 11, no. 38. I have no idea of what the ship's box looked like. According to an oral report by Dr H. Ketting, the box measured 47 by 28 by 18 cm.

ingspenningen), for this purpose. The amount concerned was proportionate to the size of the crew. The Amsterdam Chamber issued silver ducatoons for this purpose, the Hoorn Chamber Mexican reals.

Besides the Articles there were general rules which governed procedures on board. Various rules and regulations dealt with matters pertaining to food, the treatment of the sick, the maintenance of the ship and the rigging, navigational instruments, the ship's tackle, keeping the log, plus a few other matters such as the use of signalling flags. These prescriptions were invariably recorded in resolutions by the *Heren Zeventien* and could cover matters ranging from special rations for the sick (1760), the calculation of the tides (1792), and the treatment of stowaways (1779) to the chopping of wood for the galley (1737), swinging the lead (1753) and anchoring off Robben Island (1765). Naturally, checking for violations of the rules on private trade goods did not escape their attention. The surgeon, the minister and the carer of the sick were issued with their own instructions, but the commander also had a copy of these in his ship's box.[5]

The commander and the ship's officers were obliged to keep a log (*dagregister*) every day. This record was kept in lined journals and, if the pages happened to be blank, the men were obliged to draw the lines themselves. Information about the weather, the wind, location and course, as well as any extraordinary events, had to be noted per watch. Of great importance in this respect were the meticulously prescribed routes for the outward- and homeward-bound voyages and the memoranda describing the winds and seasons in the various sea areas. After 1754, it was compulsory to mention in the log whether the air pump and the fire hose had been used. The fire hose was used to dampen down the sails and spray the deck clean. In 1753, the *Heren Zeventien* forbade their seafarers to take 'the absolutely useless dogs' with them.[6] Apparently there had been too many of them in the preceding years. Failure to obey the regulations was punished by fines, usually in the form of withholding one or more months' wages.

In the second half of the eighteenth century, a commander had to contend with more regulations than his predecessors. The majority of these rules were of a fairly general nature. Only a few of them concerned specific matters. Their number multiplied rapidly after 1753. Sometimes, the *Heren Zeventien* made several decisions which affected life on board ship and navigation in one year. Most of these rulings had to do with the health of the crew and the treatment of the sick and their rations. Besides these duties, there were regulations on the regular running of the ship, in which the hand of the Amsterdam examiner Jan de Boer can often be recognized.

After the Fourth Anglo-Dutch War, the number of new regulations did not diminish at all. As mentioned earlier, in 1790 the ship's box contained at least eighty documents. Among the ship's papers of Commanders Harmeijer and

---

[5] The Hague, NA, VOC 11.397 (Book on Articles), 1742, and 14.329 (papers in ship's box).
[6] The Hague, NA, VOC 11.528, no. 31.

Plokker, which were captured by the British during the war, were several logs of their previous voyages, as well as those of some other commanders. This was a common custom.[7] All in all, the commander had to assume a multiplicity of tasks and responsibilities. Quite a number of the jobs were delegated to their ship's officers and petty officers. Recalling the experience he had built up on many earlier voyages to the East, the day-to-day life on the ship will not have held many secrets for a commander.

The Commander's Cabin

All officers, including the commander, were accommodated in the stern. In the eighteenth century, the commander was allocated the best of the accommodation: the commander's cabin was situated up on the quarterdeck right at the stern of the ship. It was large, measuring between eight and ten metres across the width of the stern. It measured about four metres in length and was high enough to accommodate an adult man – the average height of a man in the eighteenth century was 166 cm or perhaps a little taller. The stern rose upwards on a slant to the taffrail or counter which was pierced by four windows. In front of the commander's cabin was a bedroom. On the quarterdeck there were other cabins for the ship's officers, the chief surgeon and the minister, plus the wheelhouse. This is the way the accommodation was divided up around 1750. Earlier or later than this, the division was not always precisely the same, and it varied on different sorts of ships. The bulkheads in the commander's cabin were furnished with deep, built-in cupboards and there was a fixed bunk.[8]

Only very sporadically is there any mention of what sorts of personal possessions a commander took with him on the voyages out and home, or had with him during the time he spent in the East. Occasionally remarks were made in passing. The best insight is offered by the inventories of the estates of officers who died on voyages, mentioned in the previous chapter.[9] Besides listing the trade goods, they also record the private belongings of a deceased commander. Few commanders had any large pieces of furniture with them. Probably tables and chairs were part of the furniture provided by the Company. One or two took a small table with them. There was a greater need for extra chairs, usually six in number. Chairs with arms were noted separately. Few commanders had their

---

[7] These ship's papers are to be found in the Prize Papers of the High Court of Admiralty in the National Archives in Kew (HCA 30/712 (1 and 2), 30/720 and 30/721). Dr R. van Gelder drew my attention to them.
[8] Gawronski, *De equipagie*, p. 18; and G. Maat, 'Hoe lang nog? De lichaamslengte van de Nederlander', lecture to HOVO (University of the Third Age students), 15 May 2006, Leiden, pp. 4–5.
[9] The copies of the fifteen inventories of estates of deceased commanders, compiled by Mrs A. Meddens-Van Borselen, form the basis of what follows below.

own beds, although some did take a mattress for the bunk. Of course, they did have their own bedding: lumpy palliasses stuffed with straw or feathers, pillows and various sorts of blankets; and they were seldom without a nightcap. On a ship, free-standing cupboards would not have been practical and mentions of them are rare. Many of the commander's belongings were kept in chests, which were stowed in the built-in cupboards with the sealed chests of silver and gold for the *Hoge Regering* in Batavia. For ordinary crew members, the commander's cabin was forbidden territory. Usually two soldiers stood on guard outside the door.

Every commander had a writing desk, or slope, sometimes made of teak or amboina wood.[10] By standing next to the angled slope, placed on a table or on a stand, he was able to write. Inside, under the lid were small drawers and pigeon-holes, and it was kept locked. In these the commander put away his buttons, buckles, watch and chain, sometimes a snuff box or tooth-pick as well, usually fashioned from silver or gold. These were costly items. He would also have kept his coins inside the writing slope.

Plenty of clothing was taken on the voyage as it was impossible to wash clothes regularly. Underclothes, worn next to the skin, were represented in all sorts and numbers: vests, underpants, silk, wool and cotton (under-) stockings, mules and shoes. Mosquito breeches could also be found. Camisoles, which were long-sleeved vests with slit-pockets, were often worn. Some pieces of clothing were of Asian origin. No inventory failed to mention a bag for the dirty clothes. This was often made of old sailcloth. There was an ample supply of scores of handkerchiefs. Outer clothing was also plentiful, as were wigs, sometimes as many as eight old and/or new, unworn ones.

The commander was not required to dress uniformly every day. When he was fully dressed, over his camisole he wore a frock coat – a long, close-fitting coat – and knee-breeches, fastened at the knee with a buckle, as well as stockings. The fronts of the coats were decorated with gold or silver thread or buttons. The coat, breeches and stockings could be in a whole range of colours: black, brown, red, blue, even yellow. The coat and breeches could be made of Dutch broadcloth or silk or velvet. In the middle of the century, the Company tried to prescribe uniform colours, with blue being the favoured colour for the breeches and coat, with the collar and cuffs also of blue broadcloth. By around 1790, most people did wear dark blue broadcloth, but red and black could still be seen. Green disappeared entirely, because it faded too quickly 'in the burning rays of the sun in these climes'. A hat was also an indispensable part of a commander's outfit, which was considered to be costly. On board the commander walked around in his camisole, which was sometimes embroidered.

---

[10] M. van de Geijn-Verhoeven *et al.*, *Wonen op de Kaap en in Batavia 1602–1795* (Zwolle/The Hague, 2002), pp. 220–1.

On his fifth voyage in 1739, Commander Joris Davidszoon was well supplied. On an earlier voyage he had bought a teak bureau with copper mounts. He had six chairs in his cabin as well as a small, square table and a looking-glass. Besides the furniture, he had all sorts of utensils and these were set out during calm weather in the roads. They included a coffee-grinder and coffee pot plus coffee in a tin caddy, a salver or serving tray, a corkscrew, teapot, glasses, seven porcelain 'small cups and saucers', dice, a sewing-box, pipes, tobacco, a cuspidor and a mortar and pestle. As did his colleagues, he owned a rapier kept in a silver scabbard and with a gilt hilt, attached to his sword belt by a sword knot (*portepee*, in French *porte-epée*). Davidszoon also surrounded himself with other comforts, for instance a dog called Tap and four cages for canaries. With him, entrusted to his care, he also carried letters for the Cape, Batavia and the more distant trading posts. All these were noted down in the inventory of his estate compiled after Davidszoon died a few weeks before he was due to arrive in Table Bay.[11]

Slaves in the Commander's Cabin

There could be big differences in the quantity of belongings commanders took with them, but everybody had most of the items just mentioned on board. It would be rare for there not to be a telescope but books are only sporadically listed in inventories. Parrots and canaries were favourite pets, certainly on the voyage home. It was also a fairly regular occurrence for there to be slaves on board and, after the death of a commander, they were part of his estate. In 1716, Commander Jan Maljaard had three slaves from Madagascar with him, the boys Samson, Januari and Cupido; in 1736 Daniël van Staden had one slave; in 1739 Karel van de Woestijne had the slaves Leander and Lakei from Malabar; in 1751 Jan Tuinman had the slave boy Januari and the slave woman Mina; in 1754 Jozias Ruts had the slave woman Dina and the slaves Adonis and Januari; and in 1792 Jakobus Forster had the slave boys Cupido from Makassar and Welkom from Buton. At the auction held on board, Welkom fetched *f.* 115 and Cupido *f.* 160. Tuinman's two slaves were bought for *f.* 160 and *f.* 170 respectively. These are just a few of the examples which turn up in the lists of the estates of the deceased.

Slaves were brought either from Asia or from the Cape and probably lived at home with the commanders in the Republic. As we saw in Chapter 6, Frederik Schouten did not have another opportunity to take his Bengali slave woman, Johanna, back to Asia, but he did not leave her destitute. From around 1760 it was officially permitted to bring slaves back to the Republic, as long as this was announced beforehand and their voyages back to Asia had been paid for.[12]

---

[11] The Hague, NA, VOC 6096, Sept. 1739; *Nederlandsch-Indisch Plakaatboek* VI, 23.8.1753, and XII, 29.4.1797; *DAS* II, no. 3155.
[12] *Nederlandsch-Indisch Plakaatboek* VII, 15.8.1763.

These slaves were permitted to work only for the commander or the first mate, but were not to perform any sailors' duties. Samson and the others did return to Asia.

In fact, since around 1640 it had become common for high-ranking retiring Company officials to have personal slaves from their foreign households on board to care for their personal needs. In 1713, a regulation was passed that, when slaves left the East, their passage to Europe and back to Asia and their board and lodgings had to be paid in advance. The *Heren Zeventien* considered that they 'were caused daily trouble and inconvenience' because of the slaves who had been brought to Europe and in this manner hoped to make bringing them 'more difficult'. After 1734, the highest-ranking officials were permitted to be accompanied by no less than four slaves. Slaves were so much a part of the daily life of Europeans in Batavia that even those with more humble functions brought a slave along with them. The supervision of the embarkation of slaves was extremely cursory, as was revealed in 1776 and again in 1790. When she left Batavia in 1790, the packet boat *Haasje* had seventeen slaves on board, the majority of them destined for private sale at the Cape. Two of the slaves ran amok and killed the commander and first mate. The later reaction of the *Heren Zeventien* merely touched upon their concern about the fact that 'such excesses and turmoil' could occur with such a number of slaves. When the ship the *Aschat* sank off Makassar in 1776 it was revealed that Commander Jan Paardekoper had a great many unregistered slaves on board. This situation caused the crew great trouble when the ship had to be abandoned, partly because the slaves had been clapped in irons. Paardekoper later had to pay the enormous fine of 3,000 rix-dollars.[13]

Therefore commanders, and probably the ship's officers as well, had to have permission to have slaves, either male or female, with them on the voyage to Asia. These slaves were not noted in the ships' pay books. Where they lived on board and under what conditions is unknown. The evidence available suggests that commanders who lived overseas kept slaves as part of their households. In 1759, the slave woman Astria in Batavia had to pay dearly because she had 'falsely' accused her commander, Pieter Pieterszoon. She was banished for ten years and put in chains. When he died in 1769, Commander Martinus Meytens left two boys from Bengal and a girl from Malabar behind to be sold. In Batavia in 1782, Johannes Snijders owned four slaves and there was also a free Christian

---

[13] *Nederlandsch-Indisch Plakaatboek* IV, 30.10.1713, and VII, 15.8.1763; J.G. Taylor, *The Social World of Batavia. European and Eurasian in Dutch Asia* (Madison, 1983), pp. 29–30; K. van der Tempel, '"Wij hebben amok in ons schip": Aziaten in opstand tijdens drie terugreizen op het einde van de achttiende eeuw', in J.R. Bruijn and E.S. van Eyck van Heslinga (eds), *Muiterij. Oproer en berechting op schepen van de VOC* (Haarlem, 1980), pp. 123–47, see pp. 124–8. For Paardekoper, see The Hague, NA, VOC 3450, fols 2082–5 (OBP 1777). For slavery and the VOC in the seventeenth century, see Markus Vink, '"The World's Oldest Trade": Dutch Slavery and Slave Trade in the Indian Ocean in the Seventeenth Century', *Journal of World History* 14, no. 2 (2003), pp. 131–77.

woman called Pieternel in his house. In the eyes of the seafarers, non-Europeans were trade goods and were transported as manpower. In 1774, the ship's officers of the *Jonge Lieve* were able to take twenty Cape Verdians from the scorched and famine-ridden island of S. Tiago with them as 'stowaways', later to sell them to farmers at the Cape as slaves.[14] Every so often, the government at the Cape permitted commanders of hookers to fetch slaves from Madagascar, and also to send them on to Ceylon.[15]

Social Life on Board

If there were no junior merchant or passengers on board, a commander could be lonely. By the eighteenth century it was rare that a senior merchant, who had been the highest authority on board in the seventeenth century, would be travelling on board. If a commander was too familiar in his relations with his officers and petty officers, this gesture was generally not appreciated. He was expected to maintain a certain distance.[16] He could always retire to his cabin, where he would have been alone unless he had a slave or slaves with him. Sometimes a parrot, a canary or a dog provided company.

It was the custom for a commander to have two cabin boys with him who did not take part in the ordinary work on the ship. Usually, if they were satisfactory, these boys would be recommended to colleagues at the completion of the voyage. They performed all sorts of small jobs for the commander such as copying letters and the logs. If they showed some artistic talent, they also drew land profiles. There was always plenty of writing to be done on board. The commander fed the boys with the leftovers from his own table.[17]

Only sporadically was a commander accompanied by his wife or some other family member.[18] If they wanted to bring relatives they had to ask special permission from the directors and they had to pay for their passage and their board and lodgings. A few commanders took their children with them and planned to settle in Batavia. In fact, the government in Batavia did all in its power to ensure that these commanders were on board at night. They were only permitted to sleep at home in town on Wednesday and Saturday nights. It was a regular occurrence

---

[14] The Hague, NA, VOC 2916 (OBP 1759), fols 1357ff. and 6869, nos. 5340 and 6464; ibid., Aanwinsten (Accessions) 1953, VI, Journaal Wichers, 3.12.1774; Bonke, *De zeven reizen*, pp. 158–9.

[15] For instance, The Hague, NA, VOC 122, 4.9.1739, 221, 19.9.1685 and 11.8.1692, and 222, 9.10.1771.

[16] J.M. Witt, *Master next God? Der nordeuropäische Handelsschiffskapitän vom 17. bis zum 19. Jahrhundert* (Hamburg, 2001), pp. 124–32.

[17] De Moor and Van der Velde, *De Werken van Jacob Haafner* I, p. 102.

[18] See, for example, The Hague, NA, VOC 115, 27.10.1711 (Pieter de Groot), 117, 2.3.1723 (Matthijs Zwaan), 126, 25.8.1750 (David van Elteren), 129, 27.10.1757 (Pieter A. Lindholm) and 297, 13.8.1789 (F.A. Steffers).

for the commander or a ship's officer to marry at the Cape and, if he did so, he was allowed to bring his wife back to the Republic, which is what Jan Siereveld did in 1779. There are some indications that more wives of ship's officers and petty officers accompanied their husbands. In 1726 Maria Meenings managed to smuggle herself aboard the *Berbices*, disguised as a sailor. She was the lover of the elderly commander Jakob Onkruid. When it became generally known that this sailor was a woman, while they were still at sea Onkruid forced his second mate, Frans Vos, to marry her. Afterwards, the pregnant Maria was left behind at the Cape. When it later turned out that Vos had to sail in Asia for a longer period than had been expected, she was sent back to the Republic in 1728. Her petition to be able to take a passage on a ship to join her husband in Batavia was rejected by the authorities at the Cape. Later, after he returned home, she caused Vos a great deal of trouble. The experience of first mate Frederik Godert Wever was completely different. He married on the voyage home on 30 March 1777, at 39°10′ north latitude and 46°17′ longitude, and, upon his return to Amsterdam, he had his marriage registered there as well.[19]

The part that a commander's wife played in shipboard life remains pretty much of a mystery but she certainly did not take part in the daily running of the ship. Occasionally, passengers let something slip in their travel accounts, as in the jottings of the Lammens sisters. They left Middelburg for Batavia in 1736. Their commander was Jan van den Broek, who had his wife with him. When the pilots sailed back from the entrance to the Channel, she was plagued by sea-sickness and wanted to go home to Zealand. She lay on her bunk singing psalms and when 'the weather becoming extremely tempestuous, the wife did nothing but cry out and scream…'. She dared not remain too long in the fresh air because of her 'indisposition'. The Lammens sisters were happy that, during the stop at the Cape, she lodged at a different address, because 'we had had plenty of occasions on board to profit from the company of the good woman', as they noted 'in passing'.[20]

It was normal to have passengers on board. Whatever the situation, there was usually a junior merchant on the ship. On the voyage back to the Republic most of the passengers had been overseas administrative officials of the Company. The commander would meet them for luncheon and dinner, gathered around the large table on the deck under the commander's cabin. The Company provided

---

[19] The Hague, NA, Archief Radermacher 382a, plakkaat (placard) Batavia 1730; Cape Town Archives, resolutions C. of P. 17.2.1728 (www.tanap.net); *DAS* II, no. 2661; R. Dekker and L. van de Pol, *Vrouwen in mannenkleren. De geschiedenis van een tegendraadse traditie in Europa 1500–1800* (Amsterdam, 1989), pp. 46–7; Amsterdam, GA, DTB 749, fol. 508 (30.6.1777); *DAS* II, no. 7970; M.L. Barend-Van Haeften (ed.), *Op reis met de VOC. De openhartige dagboeken van de zusters Lammens en Swellengrebel*, Werken Linschoten Vereeniging XCV (Zutphen, 1996), p. 14.

[20] Barend-Van Haeften, *Op reis met de VOC*, pp. 54–5, 59, 71 and 100. See also The Hague, NA, VOC 221, 3.9.1735.

the green floral cloth which decked the table and was itself covered by another tablecloth during meals. During the 1740s, the Amsterdam Chamber involved six different dealers in napery for the ships which, besides the tablecloth, also consisted of a selection of six table-covers, forty-two napkins, twelve hand-towels and twelve tea-cloths. The table could seat a maximum of twenty-four people.[21] The ship's officers, the minister, if there was one on board, and sometimes the senior surgeon, the carer for the sick and the commander of the soldiers would mess here too. Occasionally the weather conditions and the physical state of fellow diners upset this daily routine. If he expected to have to remain there for a longish interval, the commander sought accommodation on land when he arrived at the Cape. In Cape Town the Superintendent would find him a place to stay, or the commander would know addresses himself.

If relations on board were good the commander would often hold a daily meeting at a set time with his ship's officers. Navigation, the running of the ship and conditions on board would be discussed. Sometimes, their fellow diners would also be informed about these matters. Visits between ships with other colleagues provided entertainment. This was possible when the ships sailed in a convoy and the sea was calm. Under the command of the third mate, the ship's boat would row the commander and perhaps the first mate and some passengers to the other ship. A reciprocal visit would follow. On 19 December 1774, when the *Jonge Lieve* met another Company ship, a passenger noted, '… the ships diverted each other with their favourite music'. Unquestionably, the commander would have drawn the attention of those who sailed with him to the various animals and fish in the sea and the birds that flew overhead, some of which presaged the proximity of land.[22]

The evening meal was late, so the remainder of the evening was short. The system of six watches of four hours each provided a set rhythm for the planning of the day. If the commander did not withdraw to his own quarters, he joined in the conversation or in board games such as goose board. Commander Joris Davidszoon had dice with him and in 1738 Hermanus Blom had a draughts board. Music was not unusual, the violin and flute being the favoured instruments. A number of commanders had an instrument with them. Blom had a *claverchordium*, a clavichord, a rectangular stringed instrument with a keyboard, very suitable for small spaces and easy to transport (see illustration). In Blom's inventory, it is mentioned along with his watch, medicine boxes and writing slope. It seems that Blom personally played the clavichord.[23]

In August 1771, on board the *Aschat* in the Indian Ocean bound for Batavia, it seems that Jan Abel needed some fresh vegetables, so, with the assistance of a passenger, he decided to sow 'some watercress'. They did this in a small wooden

---

[21] Gawronski, *De equipagie*, pp.207–10.
[22] The Hague, NA, Aanwinsten 1953, VI, Journaal Wichers; Barend-Van Haeften, *Op reis met de VOC*, pp. 70–1 and 74; J.R. Bruijn, *Observaties onderweg* (Leiden, 2003), pp. 7–9.
[23] The Hague, NA, VOC 14735; *DAS* II, no. 3097.

box lined with a piece of linen cloth and 'sprinkled it liberally with water'. The small box was hung from a beam in the main cabin. After nine days it was ready to eat.[24]

Among the social happenings of shipboard life was the celebration of the birthday of the Stadholder, who was director-in-chief of the VOC, as was done for instance in 1747, on 8 March. Christmas and the commander's own birthday usually did not pass unnoticed, but the biggest celebrations were reserved for the passing of the Berlenga Islands off the Portuguese coast, and the Equator. On such occasions prayers of thanksgiving were said and alcohol was indulged in more liberally. The Neptune party for crossing the line was quite an event: 'when, as was the custom on ships, people amused themselves by unexpectedly squirting each other sopping wet with the fire hose and sprayed each other with water, which was referred to as christening, on the occasion of crossing the Line, from which nobody who had not yet done so could escape'.[25]

The voyages were always protracted. Approximately eight months was the average. Sometimes they were a little longer, sometimes shorter. The compulsory visits to the Cape were an important interruption, which usually lasted three to five weeks. On the voyage out there was also a very brief visit to the Cape Verde Islands. Apart from these breaks, it was simply a matter of sailing on, with many, many days with nothing but an immensity of water around the ship and nothing happening. All that there was, was the daily routine. The winds were generally very steady, first the north-east trade winds and, after the doldrums around the Equator, the south-west trades, which were followed by prevailing westerly winds. The same pattern was more or less repeated on the voyage home. A *travaat*, a short but violent tropical storm with drenching rain, provided an interruption. Most of the route was in tropical and sub-tropical regions with cool evenings and nights. During the day a tent on the poop offered some protection from the sun. Weather conditions in the Channel, the Bay of Biscay and to the north of Scotland were very different indeed and during this part of the voyage there was often no question of any monotony or routine in the running of the ship. In these seas, the commander had to make quick and bold decisions, as far as possible in consultation with the ship's officers. The violin and the clavichord were silent.

The Ship's Business

The commander bore the final responsibility for everything that happened on his ship, but many matters were delegated to his ship's officers and the petty officers. When the watch was changed, the course, the wind and the estimated speed

---

[24] M. Seffinga, 'Theodorus Bergsma. Het verslag van een reis naar Batavia in 1771', *Jaarboek Fries Scheepvaart Museum en Oudheidkamer* (2002), pp. 54–68.

[25] The Hague, NA, Aanwinsten 1953, VI, Journaal Wichers, 28.12.1774.

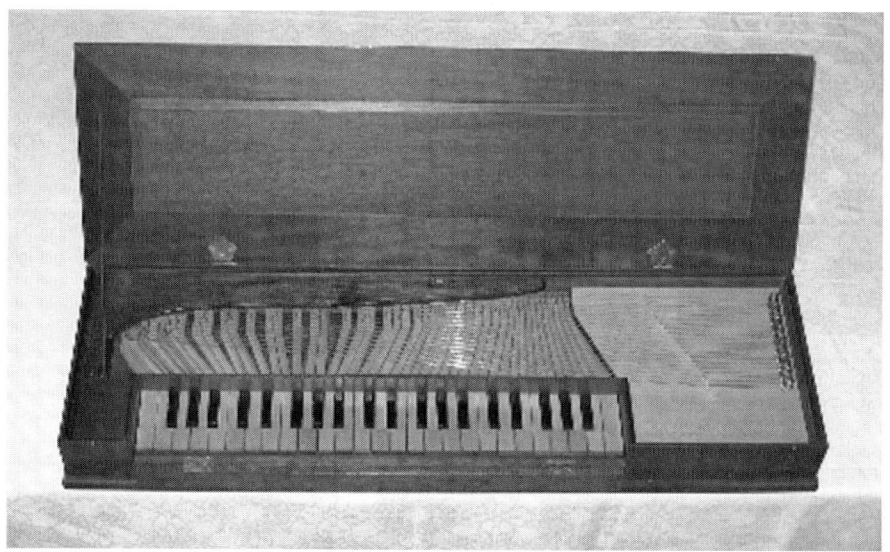

26. Clavichord. The inventory of the estate of the Enkhuizen commander Hermanus Blom, who died on board the *Vis* on the outward-bound voyage in 1738, mentions a clavichord. Blom's musical instrument will have resembled the one illustrated here. It was constructed after an original Northern European example made around 1700. It was suitable for taking on a voyage. It is 100.5 cm long, 30.5 cm wide and, including the lid, 11.3 cm high. The compass of the keyboard is four octaves, including a short octave with broken accidentals, C/E [F#, G#] –c3. The instrument is double-strung with brass strings and is triple-fretted. A clavichord is an instrument which is played individually or only with other clavichords. It produces a soft sound.

were noted, and at noon sightings were taken. The master-at-arms reported on observance of the Articles, the surgeon on the health of the crew and the treatment of the sick.

There was one matter in which the commander did not have the last word, which was expressly mentioned in the 1742 Articles. This concerned the determination of the course of the ship. The commander was obliged to consult the opinion of his ship's officers about this and make a decision in conjunction with them. In the event of any dissension, the ship's council had the last word. This council was composed of the junior merchant or *assistant*, the first and second mates and the chief boatswain, and was presided over by the commander. He also consulted this council on other matters such as punishments. In fact, he had been obliged to do so even prior to 1742.[26] The commander felt the consequences of any failure to comply with these arrangements in his pocket after the completion of the voyage. The imposition of fines or the withholding of monthly stipends was always an easy sanction for the directors to resort to for failure to follow prescribed procedures.

---

[26] The Hague, NA, VOC 221, 8.8.1705 and 11.397, articles 3, 4, 6 and 15.

The commander and the ship's officers each had to make careful annotations of a number of daily matters in their log books, which meant that it was possible to check on them later. When weather conditions permitted, the opening of the gun ports and the hatches had to be seen to on a daily basis, as did the scrubbing of the decks, for which the fire hose could be used. When the ports and hatches could not be opened, in the second half of the eighteenth century the air pump or *ventilator* had to be used, 'in order to freshen the [bad] air' below decks. This air pump had been invented in 1746. It was a closed box-like structure with angled sides and a piece of wood in the box flush with the sides and hinged at the base (see illustration). This light baffle was attached to ropes so that it could be pulled back and forth. Wooden valves on either side alternately let fresh air in. As the air was compressed on the one side, this was expelled into a round ventilation pipe by a similar valve. Those in charge of the ship were not always very familiar with this piece of apparatus, nor were they very fond of it. Especially in the 1770s, various commanders were fined for not using the ventilator.[27] Cooling sails (*koelzeilen*), simple cylinders made of sailcloth (*lugtpijpen*), were also hung up on the main deck (see illustration). The top consisted of a fixed section of turning rings covered with cloth and at the bottom of the cylinder was a lead weight which came out below decks through a hatch.[28] When the weather was very hot, the cooling sails did provide some relief from the heat, but their use was not obligatory. They were also found on slave ships.

Naturally food was a very important matter. One of the papers to be found in the ship's box was the rations instructions and the list of victuals, including specifications of the foodstuffs to which each crew member was entitled. It also included the sorts of victuals which had been loaded before the voyage began. It was the duty of the commander to ensure that his crew received neither too little nor too much to eat. Before arrival at the Cape, in Batavia or back home in the Republic, he had to check, close and hand over the Book on Consumption, kept by the steward, to the Company authorities. For each meal each day how many healthy and how many sick were served had to be recorded. Any shortages which might be discovered had to be made up for by the commander, who invariably did his best to evade all these rules, which only led to the passing of new regulations.[29]

Variety was certainly not lacking in the menu. In 1772 the Superintendent of the Shipyard in Hoorn wanted to get rid of stockfish, that is, dried cod. This

---

[27] The Hague, NA, VOC 222, 3.11.1746, 6.10.1766 and 11.397, art. 13. A demonstration model is kept in the Rijksmuseum in Amsterdam, where there is also a second model: MC 569 and 570. My thanks to Mr A. Hoving. The demonstration model measures 60 by 87 by 34 cm.

[28] The Hague, NA, VOC 162, 23.9.1720, before the cool sail had been introduced. My thanks to Dr H. Ketting.

[29] The Hague, NA, VOC 221, 13.3.1696, 222, 27.10.1757, 25.9 and 12.10.1770, 223, 26.4.1792 and 307, 11.6.1705.

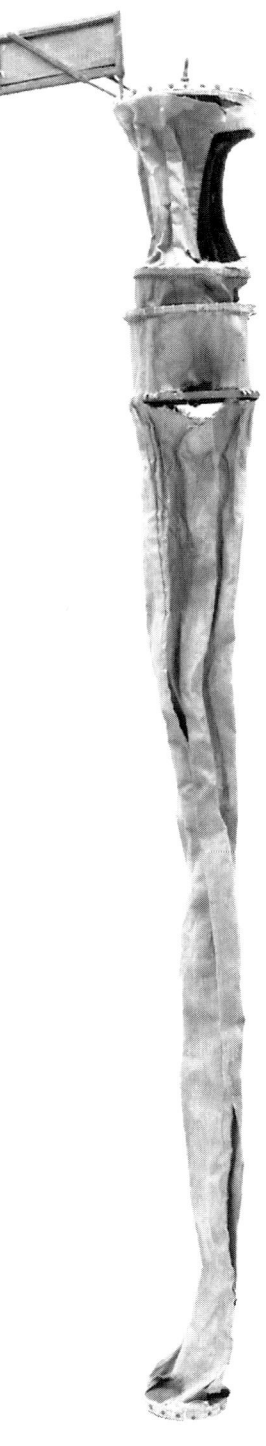

27. Ventilator or air pump. Demonstration model (60 x 87 x 34 cm) for the sort of ventilator that was used on board East Indiamen from 1746. The way the ventilator worked is described in Chapter 13 (see p. 000). It allowed the air below decks to be refreshed. Its use was compulsory in some sea areas.

28. Cooling sail. Presentation model of a cooling sail with a wind vane (95 x 19 x 9 cm). The way the cooling sail worked is described in Chapter 13 (see p. 000). The one illustrated here is a Danish model dating from 1831. When the weather was good the 'air pipe' ensured that there was some relief from the heat. Its use was not compulsory.

fish caused a dreadful stench below decks and required far too much water to make it edible. The *Heren Zeventien* rejected this but in general they were open to advice about how the food could be improved. In the latter part of the eighteenth century, the dreaded scurvy was on the decline. Onions and gherkins were brought on board and were followed slightly later by sauerkraut, which appeared on the menu with great regularity, especially during the 1780s. Sauerkraut with potatoes, which was served on board the *Zeeland* under Joachim Bank in 1786, was a meal rich in vitamin C. Samphire (*Zeekraal, Salicornea europaea*), the leafless, fleshy stalks of plants which were gathered in the salt marshes and mud flats of Zealand, was found only on the menus of the Zealand ships and was considered healthy. A porridge made of buckwheat flour called *Grobbejak* was served from time to time in the 1770s and thereafter. Regular attempts were made to keep the men healthy by providing good food. Before 1744, a commander had to ensure that every morning a mixture of tamarind, sugar, water and wine was poured over the barley porridge, a quantity of 150 centilitres (= *mutsje*) per man.

The quantity and quality of the drinking water was always a matter of concern. Around 1700 attempts were made to desalinate seawater on board, but this failed to offer a solution because of the fire hazard and the huge quantities of firewood it required. Apportioning either too much or too little drinking water was irresponsible. During the 1760s and 1770s, the many cases of sickness meant that large quantities of water were consumed. It was impossible to supplement the water supply at S. Tiago, because the Cape Verde Islands had been afflicted by a severe drought for many years. At least the casks could be filled at the Cape and fresh supplies could be taken on. Because of this situation new attempts were made to use distilling kettles on board in 1770, but nothing more was heard of this experiment.[30]

The commander was naturally affected by what was served at the table in his cabin. Both the noon and the evening meals were served warm and were better and more varied than the food served up in the mess dishes of the crew, for whom set meals were served according to a strict timetable. The discrepancy was even bigger when there were prominent guests on board who brought their own food and drink, over and above paying a hefty sum for board and lodgings. For a long time the commander was responsible, financially, for any extras at the meals. His crew members who messed with him paid him what was known as table money, but in 1742 the Company assumed financial responsibility for the costs of food supplied, which consisted of chickens, French wine, Dutch butter, smoked meat, cumin (Leiden), Gouda and Edam cheese, biscuits, flour, buckwheat flour, plus a small supply of carrots, turnips and onions. At this point table money was abolished. Probably after a lapse of some time, commanders again began to ask for table money from their messmates, or indeed even 'requisitioned' it. After complaints about unreasonable charges, a limit of two months' stipend was set in 1792.[31] One fact is certain: the evening meal especially was a pleasant break in the daily routine.

Funerals were interruptions of an entirely different nature. Sometimes they were frequent, certainly on the last part of the voyage out to the Cape and during epidemics in the roads. In 1775, Johan Wichers, a future member of the *Hoge Regering*, described the funeral of the commander of the soldiers on board the *Jonge Lieve* in the vicinity of Tristan de Cunha as follows:

---

[30] The Hague, NA, VOC 133, 26.3.1770, 134, 15.4.1772, 221, 30.10.1733, and 222, 5.9.1744 and 2.4.1770; Bruijn, *Observaties*, p. 10.

[31] The Hague, NA, VOC 123, 28.3.1742, 221, 7.11.1687, 223, 29.11.1791 and 26.4.1792.

this morning the body of the commander was committed to the sea, lying in a coffin into which holes had been bored, [and] in which small bags of sand and the kit of the deceased had been put, and a flag draped over it, borne by the crew, preceded and followed by a quartermaster who held the slips of the covering jack in their hands, for which every man was paid a bottle of wine.

An ordinary sailor was sewn into his sea blanket and thrown into the sea from the railing. Usually church services were held every week, but this was not always the case. In 1775, on the *Overhout* sailing from the Cape to Batavia, the first service was only held after two months. However, evening prayers were regularly said.[32]

Arrival Overseas

Sailing into Table Bay bore no comparison to putting in at the Cape Verde Islands. At S. Tiago the commander and a few others usually went ashore and, at an audience with the governor, asked for fresh water and supplies. After these had been received, if they were, the ship sailed on as soon as possible. For the more experienced seaman, Cape Town offered something of a homecoming. The landscape of the small town with Table Mountain in the background was a well-known sight. The streets were straight and, around 1750, there were about 200 houses with at the very most two storeys. It was a pleasure for the commander and his guests to be able to enjoy some fresh supplies even before they disembarked. In 1736, Commander Van den Broek lost no time in offering the Lammens sisters two white cabbages, which he helped the ladies to pull apart leaf by leaf. His colleague Gerrit Bijleveld had also been asked by Van den Broek to join in tucking into 'the delicious cabbage with meat'. In the opinion of the sisters, people only realize how invigorating it is to eat fresh foods, 'if they have had to eat from a mess dish for such a long time'.[33] On most occasions the Superintendent of the Shipyard was the first man on board. Probably Staring was not the only one who came to an immediate arrangement with a commander about his private cargo.

There were no inns in Cape Town, which was governed by the VOC, but there were private lodging houses in which the staff could find accommodation for a couple of weeks. For newcomers, the town provided an introduction to a society in which slaves were a prominent part of the population. Besides the Reformed church, after 1780 there was also a Lutheran church. The social customs, clothing and food were heavily influenced by those in the Republic. It was where many commanders and ship's officers found their future spouses. Of course, the members of the crew were already acquainted with carriages and

---

[32] The Hague, NA, Aanwinsten (Accessions) 1953, VI, Journaal Wichers, 7.2 and 28.5.1775; Bonke, *De zeven reizen*, p. 201.
[33] Barend-Van Haeften, *Op reis met de VOC*, pp. 93–4.

farm carts. The sick were disembarked and admitted to hospital. Those who had recovered took their places. Commander Jakob Sombeek from Enkhuizen remained behind in 1734. He had been seriously ill on board the *Lage Polder* for thirteen weeks, 'frequently with amnesia'. A few days before arrival at the Cape, the first mate had died, whereupon the second mate, Jan de Vries, a confidant of one of the Enkhuizen directors, was suddenly promoted to commander.[34]

For everybody on board, Cape Town was a welcome break after the months of sailing. Ships were repaired and fresh supplies taken on. After a series of disasters in the vicinity of Table Bay in the course of the eighteenth century it was forbidden to sail into the anchorage in the southern winter months, that is from the middle of May to the middle of August. In 1794 this prohibition was extended to the period 10 April to 1 September. False Bay was the alternative. All the ship's equipment and supplies that were needed were carried there from the Cape on a hooker.[35] Because the hinterland of the Cape was so well developed agriculturally, this bay was no longer the desolate spot it had once been.

The order to use False Bay during the winter months also applied to homeward-bound ships. On 27 May 1751, Commander Kornelis Vis was not only unable to sail into the bay because of contrary wind; the health conditions on board the *Gouverneur-Generaal* also kept him at sea. He sketched his desperate situation in a letter to the authorities at the Cape:

> twenty-six already dead and more than forty sick, some as stiff from scurvy and dropsical beings, the most ... have become so unmanageable as to make this vessel ungovernable. Moreover, I just recovered, somewhat, from my three months' illness when my lieutenants began to suffer from swollen legs and scurvy. Two ship's officers lie at death's door so that I do not have one who is healthy. If it is to take another eight days, all of us on this ship will be dead. I and my lieutenants are no longer in a state to take the watch.

Vis was ultimately given permission to bring his forlorn ship with his original crew of ninety-one sailors and soldiers into Table Bay and drop anchor.[36]

Arrival in Batavia was different again from arrival at the Cape. It was the end of the voyage. The scenes of tropical flora and fauna and the type of society would have been familiar to the commander from his earlier voyages. Only for his naval colleagues would this all have been new. Even before the Batavia Roads had been reached, the ship would have sailed past a host of small islands, of

---

[34] Information kindly supplied by H. de Vos based on the archive of Dirk Pieterszoon Haak in the Westfries Archief in Hoorn, Letter from Jan de Vries of 2.4.1734; *DAS* II, no. 2926.
[35] A. Biewenga, *De Kaap de Goede Hoop. Een Nederlandse vestigingskolonie 1680–1730* (Amsterdam, 1999), pp. 19–35; M. Barend-Van Haeften and B. Paasman (eds), *De Kaap: Goede Hoop halverwege Indië. Bloemlezing van Kaapteksten uit de Compagniestijd* (Hilversum, 2003), pp. 128–44 and 175–9; De Moor and Van der Velde, *De Werken van Jacob Haafner* I, p. 67. For False Bay, see The Hague, NA, VOC 14.329 and 4393/20.
[36] The Hague, NA, VOC 4183, fol. 1069; Cape Town Archives, Resolutions C. of P. 27.5.1751 (www.tanap.net); *DAS* III, no. 7354.

which Edam was the last. A heavily armed sloop picked up the chests containing the precious metals and money on board as soon as possible. In the days that followed, countless operations to do with the ship's cargo were carried out. Generally there was an extremely strict check to see that everything noted in the ship's papers and lists was on board and was discharged. The Book on Consumption was also thoroughly scrutinized. As soon as the opportunity arose, the ship went to the island of Onrust where it could be overhauled and repaired, Onrust being equipped with a great many shipyard facilities.

From the roads, the view of the city at the mouth of the River Ciliwong was first dominated by the Water Castle, a minor fortification, and after that above all by the Castle, the administrative and military centre of the Company in Asia. It was the seat of the Governor-General and the *Hoge Regering*. It was here that commanders made their reports and received new instructions. To a certain extent the city itself seemed familiar. It had walls, bastions, city gates, canals and streets, laid out in a geometrical pattern, 2,250 by 1,500 metres. Many houses had tiled roofs. The population could attend five different churches, including a Lutheran and a Portuguese church.[37] However, there was one aspect of the city which was an enormous problem: health. In 1762, the English sailor William Spavens spoke of 'a strange and sickly country'. Among the inhabitants of the Pacific Islands, Batavia and its surroundings enjoyed the unenviable reputation of being 'the country which kills'. The explorers Louis Antoine de Bougainville and James Cook and their crews experienced this scourge in 1768 and 1770.[38]

From 1733 Batavia was permanently afflicted with malaria. The building of saltwater fish ponds to the north of the city provided an ideal breeding ground for a species of mosquito which was an important carrier of malaria, and these ponds were situated in a zone that ran two to three kilometres along the coast, and Batavia was located precisely in this zone. Between 1733 and 1738 a veritable malaria epidemic ravaged the city, proving fatal to a great many. When this abated, malaria remained stable in the city, because most of the surviving inhabitants had built up a certain degree of resistance, inseparable from anaemia and a yellowish, enfeebled appearance. In fact the situation worsened in the course of the century because thousands of people who had just arrived in the city, whether they were Chinese, Javanese, slaves or Europeans, fell victim to the malarial mosquito. This mosquito was extremely active during the evening hours in the dry month of August and in the wet months around January and these were months in which the ships from the Republic often arrived. Between 1733 and 1795, approximately 85,000 Company personnel succumbed to malaria. In January 1792, there were no men available to prepare the ships for the voyage

---

[37] Van Gelder, *Naporra's omweg*, pp. 318–21.
[38] N.A.M. Rodger (ed.), *Memoirs of a Seafaring Life. The Narrative of William Spavens, Pensioner on the Naval Chest at Chatham* (Bath, 2000), p. 75; J.C. Beaglehole, *The Exploration of the Pacific* (London, 1966), pp. 218, 28 and 59.

home because of disease.[39] The role of malaria as a major cause of the death of commanders and ship's officers has already been discussed in the first part of this book.

The *Hoge Regering* was the supreme authority in the East, and the commanders also fell under its aegis, but in practical terms most of their dealings were with the Commodore and Superintendent of the Shipyard. Usually he was an extremely busy man whose duties were divided between Batavia and Onrust. The post was often filled by commanders who had recently arrived in Batavia or had participated in the Company's intra-Asian shipping. After 1751, this official was no longer required to check the logs of the ships arriving in Batavia. This task was handed over to the Chief Cartographer, assisted by two of the most experienced commanders who happened to be in the city. Any places which had fallen vacant among the ship's officers were filled by the *Hoge Regering*, and temporary promotions, made during the voyage, were confirmed or overruled.[40]

If they were going to remain in the city for some time, the commander and his officers participated in the local social life, but they could only do this if they had settled all their business affairs first. In 1763, First Mate Kornelis de Vos from Maaslandsluis married a widow with whom he left to become Superintendent at Negapatnam in India, but he was exceptional. Many commanders did not tarry long in the East. They left for the Republic on the same ship on which they had arrived, as soon as all the sections of the return cargo had been loaded and the ship was ready to sail. Others were given a command in intra-Asian shipping and remained longer in the East. They took their instructions from the authorities in Batavia. Sailing instructions, either printed or handwritten, were available for almost all the trade settlements.

The rhythm of the monsoons determined the pattern of the sailings, and two examples show what happened within Asia. After his arrival in Batavia in 1736, First Mate Kornelis Ariënsz Keet sailed first to Padang in Sumatra, back to Batavia, then to Semarang in Java, back to Batavia, from where he set sail for China, back to Batavia and back to China again, then to Semarang and the Eastern Salient of Java (*Java's Oosthoek*) and finally, in June 1739, to China once again, from where he sailed back to the Republic. He arrived home in September 1740, directly from Canton. Keet had made these voyages in four different ships. Shortly after his arrival in Batavia in 1777, Commander Gerrit Bruijn left to sail to the Eastern Salient of Java, came back to Batavia and then made a round-trip voyage to Makassar. After this, he sailed to the Eastern Salient again. He then made a voyage to the Cape and arrived back in Batavia in July 1779, from where he made a voyage to Coromandel in India, followed by a short voyage to Bantam. After this, Bruijn made two voyages to Persia and one to the Eastern Salient.

---

[39] P.H. van der Brug, *Malaria en malaise. De VOC in Batavia in de achttiende eeuw* (Amsterdam, 1994).
[40] The Hague, NA, Archief Nederburgh 28, 10.10.1768; *Nederlandsch-Indisch Plakaatboek* VI, 10.6.1751.

He always sailed on the *Hoorn* but he returned to the Republic on another ship in 1784 after also having completed a short voyage to Cheribon in Java. Years earlier, as a ship's officer and commander he had also been to Malacca, Bengal, Persia and several Javanese ports. When he arrived home in 1785 at the age of forty-five, Bruijn had made twelve voyages to Asia, having sailed on his maiden voyage in 1758. He had spent two long periods sailing in Asian waters: fifty-two months from 1770 to 1773 and eighty-seven months from 1777 to 1784. When he returned to Monnickendam, a whole new life awaited him.[41]

During these voyages and the time they spent in Batavia, many commanders earned the money from their private commercial transactions to buy bills of exchange. Some commanders were tempted into actions which did not pass muster in the eyes of the *Hoge Regering*. Examples of this kind of behaviour are the actions of men such as Tobias Uilenburg and Wessel van Neercassel, who have been mentioned earlier. During its short-lived existence, the *Académie de Marine* profited from the fines which were imposed for all manner of violations.

To a lesser degree, Galle in Ceylon was also the terminus for ships from the Republic. All sorts of administrative and shipping facilities were available on this island. It was 'always very lively and cheerful', according to a description dating from 1756. No malaria raged there. Some of the East Indiamen took on their return cargoes at Galle, leaving to sail directly for the Republic without sailing to Batavia.[42]

Going Home

The months of November, December and January were usually the period in which most Company ships returned home from Batavia, and from Galle, Bengal and China as well. The intention was to sail to the Cape as far as it was possible as a fleet. All ships were obliged to sail in convoy as soon as they left the Cape. The route which was to be taken was meticulously laid down in the sailing instructions. On the voyage home, ships were required to take one and a half sets of new sails and a set of patched ones.[43] The *Hoge Regering* always appointed the commodore or admiral of the return fleet, usually either a retiring member of the *Hoge Regering* or the Superintendent, or a commander with many years' service overseas. Instructions were given about the formation in which the ships were to sail.

Before he sailed, a commander had to make sure that he had wound up all his own private business interests. The ready money he had earned had to be handed

---

[41] See Chapter 2. The Hague, NA, VOC 11.346; M. Peters, *In steen geschreven. Leven en sterven van VOC-dienaren op de Kust van Coromandel in India* (Amsterdam, 2002), p. 193; Jacobs, *Merchant in Asia*, pp. 5 and 245.
[42] Wagenaar, *Galle*, ch. 5.
[43] s'Jacob, *Generale Missiven* XIII, 357.

in to the paymaster in return for a bill of exchange. If he happened to have been there for a longer period, he might have done this already. He was permitted to take a fairly large quantity of cash in his own cargo.[44] Unfortunately, there are no inventories available of estates of deceased commanders who died on the way home, as there were for the voyage out. The crew of an East Indiaman was smaller than on the outward voyage, on average only about 100 men. From 1742 the commander had been personally responsible for the bookkeeping.[45] For a while, on the voyage to the Cape, tropical foodstuffs dominated the menu. On board were all kinds of tropical and later Cape fauna, including ostriches, monkeys, parrots and penguins. As the century progressed, it became increasingly difficult to find sufficient European seamen and soldiers to man the East Indiamen. Moors (Muslim Indians), who had their own separate list of victuals, had already been in service for a long time on the intra-Asian routes and now it became necessary to recruit Asians for the return voyage as well. Most of the sailors were Javanese or Chinese. Many of the commanders and ship's officers had already sailed with them in the East. In the 1780s and 1790s almost without exception there were teams of Asians on board. In the Republic they were kept apart and sent back to Asia as soon as it was possible to do so. In 1785, it was said of the Chinese that they 'have been very satisfactory in all sections, as long as they were not required to climb'.[46]

Upon arrival at the Cape, the pattern of the outward-bound voyage was picked up again. On various occasions a commander was left behind there to become Superintendent, or a retired Superintendent was appointed commander of a ship headed to the Republic or took passage on such a ship to take him home. Jakob Rijzik is one example. For many of the crew, the stay at the Cape was an opportunity to sell the slaves they had bought in Asia. After departing from either Table Bay or False Bay, the ships sailed in convoy formation. Each commander had been allotted his appointed place and was subject to the authority of the commodore or admiral. In the Great Council (*Brede Raad*), which was composed of all the commanders and presided over by the commodore or admiral, discussions were held and first mates could be asked for advice about such matters as determining the course or position. The island of St Helena could only be called at in cases of dire necessity. A signal letter set out in great detail which rules and regulations the commanders had to observe. In 1771, Frederik Kelger handed over to the Amsterdam Chamber a list of the names of colleagues who had 'wilfully' sailed past him when he was the commodore. Commander Gerrit Berg sailed past his commodore, Commander Christiaan Rebel, no less than three times in 1775. When he arrived home this infringement cost him a fine of

---

[44] See the discussion in Chapter 12.
[45] The Hague, NA, VOC 222, 28.3.1742.
[46] The Hague, NA, VOC 11.346; Haarlem, Rijksarchief in Noord-Holland, Archief Pilotage 13, 9.8.1785; Dillo, *De nadagen*, pp. 104–9 and 163; Van Gelder, *Het Oost-Indisch avontuur*, p. 210.

f. 36, which was given to the poor. Simon de Graaf did not escape so easily in 1761. He lost the whole of the stipend he had earned since the Cape and had to forgo half of his bonus. However, Jochem Outjes got off scot-free when he had a seventeen-gun salute fired in honour of his birthday on 6 May 1751. The general rule was to be thrifty with cannon balls.[47]

At the approach to the Channel, or after passing the Shetland Islands, tension heightened as people wondered if and when the cruising warships would be spotted. This period was also covered by instructions, and sanctions were prescribed for not obeying the orders. The next important event was picking up the pilots. Pilot boats lay off Beachy Head on the English south coast, but only until 20 September, after which they moved to Dover. Sometimes they lay too far to the west, off the Lizard.[48] When the commander arrived in the roads of Walcheren, Goeree or Texel, his voyage was not yet finished. The dropping of the anchor, the greetings, discharging the cargo, sailing on to the port, all were covered by a plethora of procedures, which were the result of the unceasing efforts of the Company to combat smuggling and fraudulent deficiencies in ships' cargoes. Outjes, for example, was caught red-handed smuggling in 1755.

One or more of the directors of the Chamber were present in the roads in the Chamber yacht. They did not come aboard but had the commander come to their yacht to greet them and to hold an initial conference. Only after this had been completed did they sail to the ship to welcome the crew and proceed to the ship's cabin to hear a detailed report about the state of the ship, the victuals and the condition of the crew. The numbers of the dead and the sick were highly relevant to the Book on Consumption. When this had been completed, it was followed by a thorough interrogation about unauthorized goods. The commander had to hand over all the ship's papers, including his log, and the letters from the Cape and Batavia plus any private mail. He also handed over stowaways, if there were any on board. He was required to hand in the keys to the hatches. Only when all this had been done could the passengers and the sick be taken ashore and as quickly as possible. The ship's officers and seamen who were no longer needed or 'who had earned large stipends' were also given permission to disembark. The strongest crew members had to remain behind to help discharge the cargo. Finally the commander himself went ashore. In 1762 Christiaan Blom took leave of his people with tears in his eyes. One crew member wrote: 'We climbed aloft to give three cheers because of our affection for our commander.' Not all of Blom's colleagues will have shared his emotion.[49]

---

[47] The Hague, NA, VOC 222, 4.4.1761 (*DAS* III, no. 7575), and 308, 27.5.1771 and 27.6.1776 (*DAS* III, nos. 7945 and 7946); Barend–Van Haeften, *Op reis met de VOC*, p. 48.
[48] The Hague, NA, VOC 11.343.
[49] The Hague, NA, VOC 222, 24.11.1741; Archief Van Vredenburch 15. For Blom, see J.A.H. (= Jan Ambrosius Hoorn), *Mijne lotgevallen ter zee en bedrijven op Batavia in dienst der (voormalige) O.I. Comp.* (Groningen, 1819), p. 62. P. Moree kindly drew my attention to this publication.

The voyage for the commander was only finally completed after the ship was in port, the holds had been unloaded and the ship's papers had been inspected. He could then expect his final settlement. There was also an investigation into whether he had followed all the rules and regulations or whether he had to pay a fine or forgo bonuses. Various examples of this have been given in the previous chapters. Sometimes the submission of an appeal helped. The commander had to answer for the ship's money. In 1749, Simon de Groot had bought extra food for his crew on St Helena, paying for it out of his own pocket. The money was promptly repaid to him.[50]

---

[50] The Hague, NA, VOC 221, 2.10.1686, and 308, 30.10.1749; *DAS* III, no. 7308.

14

Their Ships

What concerned the directors of the Company most was that a commander sailed his ship and her cargo safely to their intended destination. How he achieved the goal was a minor matter. In each Chamber the appointment of a commander was the result of an allocation system in which each of the directors took his turn. This was not to guarantee that the best available man was appointed, although there were some built-in safety checks which would help to ensure that the choice was a good one. Undoubtedly some conscientious directors did take their duty seriously. In Amsterdam and Zealand especially, these gentlemen were busy with work for the Company on an almost daily basis. The loss of a ship was a personal blow, because its effects were felt in many parts of the business. If the disaster was the fault of one of the men whom he had patronized, it undermined the position of the director concerned in the eyes of his colleagues.

Nevertheless, there were at least some guarantees of professional competence. First and foremost, the candidate for a commander's post had to pass an examination for each of his promotions through the three ranks of ship's officers. After 1751, he also had to pass an examination the first time he was promoted to the post of commander. This sort of examination system existed nowhere else in the shipping world at the beginning of the eighteenth century. In 1743 the Amsterdam Chamber had taken the lead in expanding these examinations to include both a theoretical and a practical element. From this distance in time, it is very difficult to ascertain anything about the predictability of these examinations. Besides the examinations themselves, another check was the practice of circulating the nomination to the other Chambers for their comments. In Jakob Welgevaren's case, the objection raised was ignored, but the Sautijn affair illustrates that the directors in the Amsterdam Chamber did not invariably approve of every candidate. Keizer's appointment in 1719 was temporarily blocked. Finally, there was the steadily expanding list of rules and regulations on which a commander could fall back in almost any situation if he was uncertain about what he should do. The practice of checking the contents of the ship's logs introduced in 1743 gave the examiners some insight into how far the regulations were obeyed. These checks made it possible to uncover failure to use the ventilator or the fire hose or failure to join the obligatory convoy. The same sanctions applied to the use of the navigation instruments, but what checks were there on the condition of the ships?

Problems with the Ships and the Commanders

In the two decades from 1720 to 1740, the Company had to cope with more losses of ships than had ever occurred before. Ships sank at all sorts of places along the fixed sailing routes, not only near land but also on the high seas, for example, between Batavia and the Cape. Between 1721 and 1730, the majority of the disasters occurred on the voyage out (24), but in the 1730s more ships were lost on the voyage home (21). The year 1722, when no fewer than fourteen ships were lost, was a particularly bad year.

These losses signalled that it was time to stop and take a look at the reliability of the ships and the quality of the people in charge of their navigation. On 15 June 1722, the loss of seven ships on the voyage out in the face of a north-west gale in Table Bay could be dismissed as a regrettable consequence of an act of God. The ships which lay at anchor were in no condition to ride out the heavy seas by rising and falling with the waves because they were pulled underwater by their forecastles. This sort of explanation did not apply to the other losses. In 1697, the *Heren Zeventien* laid down the measurements for the three classes of East Indiamen and those for a fluyt. These measurements were already being tampered with in 1714, and in the 1720s this happened again on several occasions. The directors of the Chambers were too ready to allow their shipwrights to follow their own ideas about how a ship should be constructed – an attitude which did not put safety first. In 1737, there was another disaster in Table Bay: eight ships were sunk in one night.[1] In 1740 six ships were lost. This provoked some action. The following year, the *Heren Zeventien* did not mince words when they said that when they lay at anchor, their ships were not in a suitable condition to weather a storm and that the widening of their waists created an enormous risk of falling prey to heavy seas. They dared to be so outspoken because people in Batavia had also made complaints about the ships. Hampered by their unwieldy construction, the ships were considered to be sluggish compared to those of other companies. In the course of the discussion, Van Imhoff, who had returned from Batavia shortly before, turned ship design, along with a great many other matters, on its head.[2]

---

[1] This matter will be examined in more detail in Chapter 15.
[2] DAS I, 44–46; A.J. Hoving and A.A. Lemmers, *In tekening gebracht. De achttiende-eeuwse scheepsbouwers en hun ontwerpmethoden* (Amsterdam, 2001), p. 46; J. de Hullu, 'Over den Chinaschen handel der Oost-Indische Compagnie in de eerste dertig jaren van de 18^e eeuw', *Bijdragen Taal-, Land- en Volkenkunde van Nederlandsch-Indië* 73 (1917), pp. 32–154, see p. 140.

Table 14.1 Losses of ships in the period 1721–1740

	Outward	Homeward		Outward	Homeward
1721	1	–	1731	–	–
1722	7	7	1732	1	1
1723	1	–	1733	1	–
1724	3	–	1734	–	1
1725	4	–	1735	2	–
1726	2	3	1736	3	–
1727	2	–	1737	–	8
1728	3	–	1738	–	3
1729	1	–	1739	–	2
1730	–	–	1740	2	6
	24	10		9	21

In other words, it was years before the subject of the quality of the ships was seriously discussed. After all, not all the ships were in bad shape. Between 1714 and 1737 the ship *Meijenburg* of the Zealand Chamber made ten round-trip voyages and had sailed to Batavia on her eleventh voyage just as quickly as she had done in 1714, earning a bonus for the commanders and their crews. The *Mijnden* of the Amsterdam Chamber made her maiden voyage in 1709 and sailed for the East for the ninth time in 1728. After that, both ships also served a number of years in the intra-Asian trade before they were broken up in Batavia.[3]

It was the same story with any investigation into the professionalism of the commanders and the ship's officers. Initially, their professional abilities were never doubted and, indeed, in 1728 the *Heren Zeventien* decided to give priority to long-standing rather than new candidates for such posts. It was also thought to be a good idea to try to keep a returned commander and his crew together as far as possible and to have them sail again on the same ship. Such efforts were increasingly frustrated in the 1730s because there was a shortage of good commanders and ship's officers. The major culprit was the malaria epidemic in Batavia, because many a career was abruptly cut short in that city.

Another fairly ineffectual order given to commanders was that they should pay closer attention to the condition of the planks of the hull than they had been in the habit of doing. After arrival in the East, the ship's carpenters had to carry out a stricter check of the hull to search for any signs of weakness. As a precaution it was also laid down that in extraordinarily strong winds, the cables should already be made fast to the anchors and the riggings should be trimmed with extra care.[4]

The veritable flood of tidings of disaster, especially after 1736, made a great impression in the Republic. In 1740, when the extension of the charter of the

---

[3] DAS II, 2092, 2227, 2757 and 3101.
[4] The Hague, NA, VOC 118, 12.8.1728 and 10.3.1729, and 221, 16.8.1728.

29. Gustaaf Willem, Baron Van Imhoff (1705–1750). A native of Leer in East Friesland (Germany), Van Imhoff sailed for Batavia with the rank of junior merchant in 1725. He enjoyed a lightning Company career overseas in trade and in the administrative apparatus. In 1736 he was appointed Governor of Ceylon. In 1741 he wrote down his *Consideratiën*, his concepts for the improvement of Company policy. The following year he left to return to Batavia as Governor-General. His plans for the ships and the way they were run, especially those for commanders and the ship's officers, set many changes in motion. Here he poses in all his glory in a print by Pieter Tanjé from 1745.

Company came up for discussion, the province of Holland set down express conditions for renewal. One was that the construction of the ships had to be reformed and the skills of the sea-going personnel had to be improved.

Succumbing to this pressure, in 1741 the *Heren Zeventien* ordered their six shipwrights to present ideas for improved design of ships because, as they said: 'The current poor state of the Company fleet is widely known.' The chief shipwrights proposed extending the length in proportion to the beam but this suggestion was swept from the table when Van Imhoff championed yet another way of tackling the problem. The future Governor-General had been impressed by English insights and practices in shipbuilding which had already been in use in the dockyard of the Admiralty of Amsterdam for a number of years. He urged the *Heren Zeventien* to introduce these practices in the Company, and they did so in 1742, still unaware that in the early spring of that year another six East Indiamen had been lost. The Amsterdam Chamber was the first to make a move when it purchased a brand new warship from the Admiralty, the *Herstelder*, on which Van Imhoff sailed for Batavia in October 1742. Thereafter, not only was the length–beam proportion of Company ships altered but their draught was also changed and reduced. The bow of the ship was made more rounded and the stern sharper. The well-known, flattish stern frame was also made more rounded. Because fewer heavy construction methods were used, the ships became lighter.

The Amsterdam Chamber was the real pioneer in all these changes. It asked the advice of five commanders as 'men with an understanding of the sea': Jan Reebok, Kornelis Oterlijk, Jan van Thiel, Jan de Boer and Jean Belleveau. The first two were retired commanders while the other three were still at sea. They were all positive about the innovations. The Zealand Chamber was cooler in its reaction, as were the four retired commanders whom it asked for advice. All of them had sailed for the last time in the 1720s: Kornelis Braams, Joost Nose, Pieter van Genechten and Michiel Landsheer, who had later been appointed Superintendent in Middelburg. The commanders were not consulted any further about this matter, but the shipwrights were extremely disturbed and put up stiff resistance to the changes. The 1742 regulations on construction were not uniformly implemented. The chief shipwright of the Rotterdam Chamber especially persisted in going his own way and used his own idiosyncratic proportions for his ships. The official measurements were adjusted somewhat in 1749.[5]

Eventually, the innovations unquestionably contributed to the safety of the shipping and the voyages out were certainly much safer. Between 1743 and 1779 only nine ships were lost. Of the ten ships which were still lost on the homeward-bound voyage between 1743 and 1748, nine had been built following older designs. After this episode, the return voyage was also blighted by far fewer shipping disasters, even though the number that did occur was always higher than

---

[5] The Hague, NA, VOC 7237; I.M. Brunt, 'De veranderingen in het charter van de VOC schepen 1740–1742' (MA thesis, Leiden University, 1997); *DAS* I, 46–7; Hoving and Lemmers, *In tekening gebracht*, pp. 48–50.

the number on the voyage out. Between 1749 and 1779, twenty-eight ships in total were lost.

In 1742, a number of other matters affecting the leadership on the ships were thoroughly investigated, though the attention paid to many of them was only short-lived.[6] A campaign was launched with the purpose of improving the status and the standards of knowledge of the commander and the ship's officers. These goals were to be achieved by the introduction of a system of ranks borrowed from the Navy, the appointment of naval officers, and different, specially adjusted, rewards. The routine of the policy of appointment was suddenly interrupted by the imposition of greater demands for experience among candidates. Commanders in the East were ordered to inspect their ships and pay a great deal more attention to doing so, so that any signs of severe rotting could be reported earlier. At the same time, it was made easier for commanders in the East to earn more money to 'put by' for their old age. Finally, in 1766, the Zealand Chamber was the last to introduce an examination for commanders, an innovation which Amsterdam had made fifteen years earlier.

The administrative attention paid to the quality of the ship and her commander bore fruit in the 1750s and 1760s. The safety and the dependability of shipping increased considerably. The length of the voyage was reduced by shortening the actual time spent at sea. The stop at the Cape remained unchanged: on average it was a little less than four weeks outward-bound and a good four to five weeks on the voyage home. Only the mooring time for the Ceylon ships dropped, from an average of five to about three weeks. In the period 1720–1749, there were only two years in which there were no losses of ships. In the subsequent period up to 1779 there were twelve. In these years, it was usual for more than fifty ships to sail back and forth between the Republic and Asia. Around 1770, the largest ships especially – those measuring 150 feet – still proved completely satisfactory.[7] Therefore the conclusion has to be drawn that the professionalism of the commander and his officers was also of a high standard. The standard of navigation will be examined in Chapter 15.

Table 14.2 Average duration of voyages between the Republic and Batavia/ Ceylon

	To Batavia	To Ceylon	From Batavia	From Ceylon
1720–1749	248 days	266 days	245 days	230 days
1750–1779	236 days	225 days	222 days	205 days

[6] See Chapter 10.
[7] DAS I, 69, 74, 85 and 89.

The Commanders of the Zealand Chamber as Champions of a Different East Indiaman

Indications that the Company often made use of the specific expertise of its commanders and ship's officers are few and far between. In the period around 1730, when the heated debate was raging about the quality of the East Indiamen, their opinion was not explicitly asked. This step was taken only in 1741/1742, when the Zealand Chamber sounded out commanders who had long been retired, but the Amsterdam Chamber turned to those who were still active. Perhaps Jean Belleveau could thank his appointment on the *Herstelder* to his contacts with Van Imhoff. Probably from around this time, the practical ideas of those who lived in the shipping world found their way more easily up to the administrative level. It was at precisely this time that the Amsterdam Chamber appointed two examiners for officers, one for the theory and one for the practical side of things. The latter was invariably a retired commander, and he will have had practical tips more readily at hand, supplied by his former colleagues, than a director would have had earlier. Jan de Marre put forward suggestions for improvements to the sea charts, and Jan de Boer later succeeded in having regulations laid down for practical matters such as use of sea anchors. One thing is certain. Around 1745 sailing to Asia was safer and quicker than it had been in the preceding decades. The next drastic innovations would only be introduced around 1790.

During the 1770s, the professional knowledge and skill of the seafaring officers were appreciated much more conspicuously in the Zealand Chamber than they were in the other Chambers. Why was this so? In the 1760s, various master shipwrights in the Company shipyards were individually preoccupied with the problem of how to improve the safety of the existing East Indiamen. The father and son Willem Udemans in Middelburg put forward a plan in 1763 in which they proposed to cover the open space between the forecastle and the stern, the waist (*kuil*), thereby creating three continuous decks. These so-called three-deckers had two enormous advantages. Unquestionably they were safer in a severe gale and 'fearsomely heavy seas', because sea water no longer streamed directly into the waist. Moreover, there was more room available for the crew on the second deck. During this period, this factor was very important on the voyage out, because it was necessary to transport so many people out to the East. On the voyage home there was more space for cargo. Nothing else had to be changed on the ship itself. The Udemans had thought of everything, including a better place for storing the ship's boat, the supply of fresh air below decks and another sort of gun port. The construction of a three-decker would cost only 2,000 guilders more than that of a waist-deck ship. Although this proposal was revolutionary for the VOC, it was a matter of course for the other East India companies. In England the East India Company had begun to sail with three-deckers in 1748, and its example was speedily followed by the Swedish Company.[8]

Outside Zealand, the Udemans' ideas won no support. As a trial, the *Heren Zeventien* gave permission for Middelburg to finish constructing the *Pallas*, which had already been laid down, as a three-decker. *Pallas* proved to be an excellent ship and the Zealand Chamber even built four more three-deckers, but the other Chambers did not follow its lead. In 1773, the Zealand Chamber even received instructions to stop building any more three-deckers for the time being. Uniformity in the Company fleet had to prevail. This ushered in a period for the Company in which it sought all sorts of advice and recommendations. It is interesting to look at who the Amsterdam Chamber asked for advice: three rear-admirals, one vice-admiral and an Admiralty captain. None of these naval gentlemen had ever had any experience of Company ships let alone three-deckers in the storm-swept Indian Ocean. Of them, only Captain Willem van Braam had any right to have his voice heard as he had sailed for some years for the VOC and had made the voyage home on the *Pallas* in 1769–1770. The flag officers were negatively inclined and even Van Braam was critical. It was difficult to defend the three-decker against an enemy, and there was too little fresh air below decks, they observed. However, Van Braam did concede that it offered more protection against the danger of water streaming in than a ship with an open waist.[9]

The Zealand Chamber tackled the matter in a different way. Here Director Daniël Radermacher[10] was the driving force behind the three-decker concept of the Udemans. He had various commanders, ship's officers and chief surgeons write down their experiences. He already had a report by Commander Jakob Boekhout in his possession, and Boekhout was certainly a man qualified to speak. From 1764 to 1768, he had taken part in the first two voyages of the *Pallas*, both of them round-trips to China, which was always a hazardous voyage. Boekhout could not praise the ship highly enough, saying that the designers had proved all the advantages which they had claimed for their ship. Without a moment's hesitation, he opted for a three-decker rather than a traditional East Indiaman.

Radermacher went to a great deal of trouble to find his informants. His commanders, especially Jan Siereveld who had served under Boekhout as third

---

[8] J. Sutton, *Lords of the East. The East India Company and its Ships* (London, 1981), pp. 51–2.
[9] The account of the three-deckers is based on B. Loeve, 'De driedekker: drie decennia discussie. De invoering van een nieuw scheepstype bij de VOC, 1763–1793' (MA thesis, Leiden University, 2001), and *DAS* I, 47–50. For the reports, see The Hague, NA, VOC 11356. For the voyages cited, see *DAS* II, nos. 3917, 3975, 4101, 4156 and 4196, and III, nos. 7627, 7752, 7796 and 7862.
[10] See Chapter 9.

and second mate on the *Pallas* and after that had sailed once again on ships with open waists, wrote lengthy reports. In this matter, Siereveld unquestionably had 'hands-on' experience. He must have been a cultivated man and he set out point by point five aspects for which a three-decker was criticized by outsiders: draught, instability (crankiness), supply of fresh air, manoeuvrability and defensibility. He organized his arguments for and against and finally opted for the three-decker. A letter sent by Kornelis de Roo from Rochefort on 12 December 1772 implicitly confirmed the advantages of a closed waist. This commander had been caught in a squall in his open-waist ship, the *Bleiswijk*, and had taken on an enormous quantity of water. The masts had been lost and all together there had been over 100 men injured or killed. Two years later, in 1774, Stavorinus said that he had had to weather a severe cyclone in the *Ouwerkerk*: 'however the splendid ship behaved herself excellently. Had the *Ouwekerk* been a ship with an open waist there would not have been the least chance that we could have kept our rigging, if indeed nothing worse had befallen us.'

However, neither these reports, nor the answers to a competition held in 1777 about which type of ship was better, convinced the Chambers that it would be a good idea to change over to the three-decker. Nevertheless, in 1780 the *Heren Zeventien* did decide that the Zealand Chamber could again build three-deckers. Radermacher had finally managed to achieve this goal with the support of such men as Boekhout, Siereveld and Stavorinus. But it was only in 1793 that the Amsterdam Chamber changed tack and also commenced building these ships. Criticism from Canton about the lamentable sailing qualities of the Dutch ships in comparison with the English copper-bottomed three-deckers had made this decision easier.

Another interesting aspect of the discussion about three-deckers demonstrates that, in this period, in contrast to their confrères in other Chambers, the directors in Zealand relied on the professional knowledge and experience of their commanders. The following example shows that their professionalism was recognized and valued.

In the second half of the eighteenth century, a great many learned societies were founded in the Republic. Their driving force was the desire to find answers to all manner of problems by applying scientific methods. Initially their memberships were confined to the social and intellectual elite. Membership was by nomination. In Zealand and Amsterdam, the number of directors of the VOC and the Admiralty who participated in these activities quickly rose. The *Zeeuwsch Genootschap* was founded in Flushing in 1769 and in no time at all Radermacher had been appointed one of its directors. The Middelburg branch followed in 1784. High-ranking military officers also lost no time in becoming members of these sorts of societies and in Zealand these included naval officers who had earlier sailed for the Company or had been temporarily in its service. Vis, Haringman and Stavorinus are examples of such men. They acted as members of the jury in competitions to do with sailing matters set by the society. There is no doubt that Stavorinus was a valued member, because on two occasions after

30. East Indiaman, the *Gerechtigheid*. In 1742 innovations were introduced in the construction of East Indiamen. Each Chamber had models of the three classes of ships: respectively 150, 136 and 120 feet in length. The model illustrated is of the *Gerechtigheid* measuring 136 feet, built in Enkhuizen in 1742/1743. On the stern frame is the date 1761, by which time the ship had already been in the East for two years, where she was sold in 1763. Of special interest is the fact that the deck above the commander's quarters can be removed to reveal the way it was arranged, complete with the table, wine bottle and pipe-smoking figures.

his death in 1788 one of the members read out passages from his book *Reizen* (Voyages).[11]

Following the example of the societies at home, in 1778 Jakobus Radermacher, a cousin of Daniël, took the initiative to found the *Bataviaasch Genootschap van Kunsten and Wetenschappen* (Batavia Society for the Arts and Sciences) in Batavia. Membership was open to a wide range of people. The only barrier was a financial, not a social one: the annual contribution was 11 rix-dollars. In 1779, six commanders and a first mate applied for membership, asking to join the

---

[11] Davids, *Zeewezen en wetenschap*, pp. 320, 360–4; W.W. Mijnhardt, 'Wetenschapsbevordering onder het Ancien Régime: het Zeeuwsch Genootschap der Wetenschappen 1765–1794', *Koninklijk Zeeuwsch Genootschap der Wetenschappen* (1985), pp. 1–94, see pp. 19–22 and 45–6; Ten Bokkel Huinink, 'Een vergeten Zeeuws zeekapitein', in Bruijn *et al.*, *Marinekapiteins*, pp. 145–55.

other ninety-six members. Among them were some, like George Jakob Meyer, who had lived in Batavia for years and had retired from a life at sea. In 1782 the death of Josua de Wolf van Ieperen was recorded in the *Verhandelingen* (Transactions), which were published annually, as a loss for the society. After having made a number of voyages, he had settled in Batavia in 1776. The membership of commanders is an indication of their social recognition in the white colonial world.[12]

Ships Lost without Trace

In principle, the loss of his ship was a blot on his escutcheon for a commander. Nevertheless, ships were lost, because the unsinkable ship has never been invented. Nature, mistakes in design and during construction, not to mention errors in navigation, have always caused the loss of ships. In the previous chapter, it was made plain that the Company board generally held a commander accountable for the loss of his ship, albeit not in every case. An investigation into the cause of the loss could sometimes take place only after long delays, and the same was true of the imposition of any punishment of the commander and ship's officers. However, there was one category of shipping disaster which could never be investigated, the disappearance without trace of a ship with all hands in the Indian Ocean.

On their voyage home on the way to the Cape many a ship disappeared on the high seas. This was what Daniël Radermacher was talking about in 1776 when he spoke of Company ships 'from which no tidings were ever heard or nobody survived; to all appearances the majority were swallowed up by the swirling seas in the south and sank'.[13] Alongside the names of sixty-two of the 107 ships which were lost on the voyage home, *Dutch Asiatic Shipping* reports nothing more than 'lost between Batavia [or Ceylon, Bengal, China] and the Cape', 'lost after departure', occasionally with the mention of the degree of latitude, or the place, Mauritius. Five left from Ceylon, four from Bengal, one from China and all the rest, fifty-two, had sailed from Batavia.

Nowadays, in shipping the phenomenon of 'freak' or 'rogue' waves is recognized. These are waves which tower above the others, two to three times higher (sometimes more than 20 or even 25 metres), resembling a wall and preceded by a deep trough. Satellite observations have shown that such freak waves occur in all seas, even in calm water, though naturally they are more prevalent during bad or stormy weather. They come without any warning. Even today the disap-

---

[12] J.P.M. Groot, 'Van de Grote Rivier naar het Koningsplein. Het Bataviaasch Genootschap van Kunsten en Wetenschappen 1778–1867' (PhD thesis, Leiden University, 2006), pp. 46–8 and 66–72; on page 68 the author gives other numbers than those mentioned in the *Verhandelingen*.
[13] The Hague, NA, VOC 11356.

31. The wreck of the *Woestduin* in 1779. The Middelburg maritime artist Engel Hoogerheyden made four drawings of the stranding and subsequent sinking of the *Woestduin* of the Amsterdam Chamber, but under charter to the Zealand Chamber, on the Rassen (sandbanks) off Westkapelle. She had a Hollander, not a native Zealander, on board as pilot. Arend Fokke (1755–1812) and Matthias de Sallieth made copper-plate engravings of the four drawings. Drawing number three shown here shows the sinking of the ship and flag between ten and twelve at night on 24 July 1779. The coast of the island of Walcheren can be seen in the background.

pearance of many ships is blamed on them. In the area of sea to the east and south-east of southern Africa, where the Agulhas Current flows out in a south-easterly direction, these freak waves occur at what is called the 100-fathom line, when there is a south-west gale. However, it is not necessary to attribute all the losses of VOC ships to freak waves. In the months of December to April, the sea area to the east and north-east of Madagascar is frequently hit by tropical cyclones, especially in the period from January to March.[14]

It would have been possible not to sail in the cyclone season but the trading system of the Company in the Netherlands dictated otherwise. The six Chambers could not hold their auctions of Asian wares too late in the autumn. October, or at the very latest the beginning of November, was the practical limit because then merchants could still transport the goods they bought to their final destinations before frost set in. So, various factors determined that December–January was the most suitable time for departure from Batavia, but not much later. Hence, on their way home the ships generally found themselves in the middle of a cyclone. They carried barometers which would have given them some sort of warning on board, but only from around 1790. The majority of the ships were spared the cyclone or were able to weather it, but not the ninety-two mentioned above. On

---

[14] *Science News Online* 170, no. 21 (18 November 2006), pp. 328ff.

the basis of the dates of departure from Batavia, Ceylon, Bengal and China, it is possible to determine with a fair degree of certainty that these ships were lost in an area of the sea made perilous by cyclones, especially in the vicinity of the island of Mauritius. This estimate is based on an average speed of three nautical miles per hour at the most. Some could also have disappeared in the area of the freak waves. Apart from a group of five ships which left Batavia together on 10 December 1739, and all of which were lost, most of the East Indiamen which disappeared had sailed for the Cape alone or in the company of one other ship.[15] Any investigation into the cause of the loss was not feasible, nor indeed was the apportioning of any blame.

Reaction of the *Hoge Regering* to the Shipping Disasters

Ships also disappeared without trace on other parts of the route out or back. The loss of these ships was usually caused by an unintentional collision with a cliff or rock or by running aground. In most of these cases, there were survivors and clues to assist in an investigation into who was to blame.

In its investigation of shipping disasters, the Company acted cautiously. The ship and her cargo were the mainspring. If the ship was outward bound, the authorities were most interested in the fate of the chests containing precious metals. If there was any chance at all it would be useful, divers were employed to search underwater in the wreck for the chests and to bring these up. The place where they were stowed on the ship was known, the commander's cabin. This happened, for example, in 1753 when the *Bredenhof* shattered to pieces on a reef off a small island group between Mozambique and Madagascar (latitude 19°15' south). She was on her way to Ceylon and was carrying *f*. 300,000 in bar silver and 5,000 gold ducatoons on board. A search party from the Cape was organized and divers and their equipment were taken along. All was in vain. The wreck was not found despite the descriptions given by the survivors. It was only in 1986 that divers were able to trace the silver bars to their resting place. If outgoing ships were lost in the North Sea or the Channel, the Company preferred to employ English divers in its salvage attempts. These were not always successful. The precious metals aboard the *Buren*, which sank in a storm on the Noorderhaaks, a shallow near Texel, in 1729, could not be raised. All that was salvaged was a cannon and some cable.[16]

---

[15] Captain S. Sybesma (Rtd) provided me with meteorological information and research data compiled by the former Koninklijke Nedlloyd (Royal Dutch Lloyd) in Rotterdam and made the calculations. See also Gaastra, *De geschiedenis*, pp. 151–4.

[16] The Hague, NA, VOC 4197 (OBP 1755), fols 1564–9, 4200 (OBP 1756), fols 1007–18 and 7263, 23.10.1752; Schooneveld-Oosterling, *Generale Missiven* XII, p. 612; *DAS* II, no. 3582. For the *Buren*, see Jörg, *Porselein als handelswaar*, p. 19, and *DAS* II, no. 2782.

32. A diver at work. Hired by the VOC, the Englishman John Lethbridge made various dives to wrecked ships. After having salvaged several objects from the *Slot ter Hoge* in 1725, the Company presented him with a small silver chalice which he had personally brought to the surface. It is not known if the chalice is still extant. This picture on the chalice was published in a nineteenth-century publication which also mentioned the location (degrees and minutes) of the place where the wreck was found, which helped modern salvagers to find the wreck.

On a fairly regular basis, the authorities in Batavia were confronted with ships which had got into difficulties on the far-flung intra-Asia trade routes. If they had survived the disaster, commanders and ship's officers were not let off lightly in the investigations into the causes of the problem. How thoroughly the Superintendent in Batavia and other 'experienced men of the sea' set about their work is demonstrated by the investigation into the *Sloten* which ran aground no fewer than three times under Willem Houthuizen in 1755. She was bound for China but immediately after leaving Batavia on 7 July she ran aground near Boompjes Island, a coral island off Java. This was blamed on 'poor setting of the course' and carelessness during the stowing of the cargo. Eventually she was able to be pulled off with the help of a kedge anchor. After this, a boat was sent to precede her to sound the depths but, despite this precaution, the *Sloten* ran aground again; this time she was stuck fast and it was four days before she was refloated, and only after the cannon and the water barrels had been thrown overboard. Once again the kedge anchor offered the greatest assistance. However, on 24 July, the ship became stuck fast in the mud off the coast of South Sumatra. Assistance had to be called in and despite all efforts it was 30 August before the *Sloten* could be pulled free. After these events, Houthuizen's promising career was in ruins. The report of the investigation was unforgiving. As well as trusting in 'Divine Providence', a commander, the monitors observed, was expected to ensure conscientiously and prudently that 'the keel entrusted to him was never put in peril as a consequence of rashness'. But this was what had happened and Houthuizen was found responsible for the three incidents.[17]

The *Rijnsburg* capsized in the South China Sea in 1772 because in heavy seas water had come in through the gun ports which had not been secured, and she fetched up on the coast. The few survivors told their story in Canton. The VOC factory there ordered some Chinese divers to make attempts in several consecutive years to salvage some of the cargo, but all was in vain. Another ship was purchased locally to replace the *Rijnsburg*, something which had never happened before. The Company officials in Canton bought a slightly larger ship built in Bombay in 1769, from the Governor of Macao. She was named the *Herstelder* and she proved a good buy. The hull planking which was joined by rabbets and not caulked guaranteed that she was absolutely watertight. The English East India Company purchased its first Asian vessel in 1777, eight years later. These teak ships were more durable than their European counterparts.[18]

Jan Montagne was actually made financially responsible for the loss of his ship. In 1789, the Enkhuizen commander lost the newly constructed *Belvliet* in the Bay of Bengal. The judge in Batavia declared him to be an incompetent 'subject', but the matter did not stop there. The Company assessed the loss at *f.* 450,000. Montagne was required to pay two-thirds of this sum and his second-in-command the rest. However, in 1793, the authorities in Batavia informed the people at home in the Republic that the bailiff could not collect any payments from Montagne. He had declared bankruptcy and was living off the bread of charity provided by considerate friends.[19]

---

[17] The Hague, NA, VOC 2845 (OBP 1756), fols 347–9; *DAS* III, no. 7466; Schooneveld-Oosterling, *Generale Missiven* XII, pp. 494, 508 and 612.
[18] *DAS* I, 49 and 95; Van Dyke, *The Canton Trade*, pp. 87 and 145.
[19] The Hague, NA, VOC 3869 (OBP 1791), fols 2508, 3947 (OBP 1793), fols 1898 and 3949 (OBP 1793), fol. 1899; *DAS* II, no. 4563.

15

Striking Differences in Personalities

In the previous chapters, a long line of commanders has passed in review. It has been possible to catch some glimpses of their careers, origins, lives ashore and on board, but the personalities of these men often remain unfathomable. Sometimes, to the joy of the historian, a contemporary happened to noted that a certain commander was pleasant, irascible, a tippler or melancholic. Grasping on to these sorts of remarks, the historian can try to use them to fashion a man of flesh and blood, but in this attempted reconstruction of the commander all sorts of other facts have to be combined to get a well-rounded picture.

Nevertheless, a reconstruction can never be more than an attempt to probe a man's personality. If a commander was a difficult person, a trait which caused him problems with his ship's officers, his other crew members or those in authority on shore, there is a good chance that some sort of report of this might have been deposited in the Company archive. In such a case the researcher has some firm basis for an opinion. Unfortunately, for the vast majority of commanders there is no evidence for what sort of men they were in the performance of their duties or ashore. In this chapter, something will be said about those commanders for whom it is possible to find some more data. Alas, the muse of History still guards the answer to the question of how representative they actually were of their group.

'Humane Heads of Ships'

Why Kornelis Keet jumped overboard into the Indian Ocean on the night of 14 June 1742, on his maiden voyage as commander, has to remain shrouded in mystery. This man from Rotterdam was then forty-five years old and had been married for eighteen years. He left behind a widow and three young children. Was he depressed because he thought he might have to spend as long in the tropics as he had done on his previous voyage? On 22 March 1776, Asmus Hendrik Sterrenberg tried to commit suicide in the same way off La Rochelle, but he was rescued by alert crew members. A sailor who was a good swimmer jumped in after him and, despite his resistance, was able to grab him. No time had been lost in launching the ship's boat and so it proved possible to bring him back on board. There on his ship, the desperate commander shouted at his men not to obey any order given by an officer. He was confined to his commander's cabin and three days later was taken ashore. The ship continued on the way home to Amsterdam under the command of the first mate. Apparently Sterrenberg had been having problems with navigation as his ship had run completely off course. Five years later, at his own request, the Amsterdam Chamber granted him a weekly pension of ƒ. 10.[1]

Luckily there were other commanders who really enjoyed their work. Christiaan Blom was extremely popular with his men. His farewell in the Texel Roads in 1762 has already been mentioned. Perhaps one factor in his popularity was that it was well known that he never touched 'any strong drink, liqueurs or red wine'.

A few crew members committed what they thought of their commanders to paper. Jakob Haafner, who later worked in India, served under a number of commanders, mostly as a cabin boy, a job which ensured that he was very well acquainted with the moods of his superiors. In the period around 1770, he was very happy with Andries Hansen and Kornelis Bos, both of the Amsterdam Chamber. He categorized Bos among the 'reasonable and humane ship's commanders … who were so thin on the ground'. This commander got on extremely well with his cabin boy: 'no father could have treated his son better'. Haafner had much the same to say about the retired commander and Superintendent at the Cape, Rijzik. A chief surgeon from Geneva had had experience of Rauwenhof as commander in 1753/1754 and he described this former naval officer as 'a young man, vigorous and very proper in the dispatch of all his duties'.[2]

In their travel account of 1736, the two Lammens sisters from Zealand paint a picture of the good atmosphere which prevailed among all the ranks on board. They were very happy with their commander, Van den Broek from Flushing, and his ship's officers. During the voyage the commander had maintained friendly contact with his colleague Gerrit Bijleveld from Zierikzee. The latter was immediately invited to a meal when fresh vegetables arrived in Table Bay, as mentioned earlier. Even before that, weather conditions permitting, the two commanders had looked each other up on various occasions for a 'neighbourly chat'. If a sheep was slaughtered on one commander's ship, the other was given half of it. It was essential that it be eaten quickly because the meat soon went off in the heat. On one occasion, Bijleveld sent a small suckling pig as a present and two flying fishes especially for the sisters. On 28 May, when a third colleague from Zealand,

---

[1] The Hague, NA, VOC 308, 1.2.1781, 4259, 5137 and 14192, no. 3228; Davids, *Zeewezen en wetenschap*, p. 218.
[2] Hoorn, *Mijne lotgevallen ter zee*, p. 54; De Moor and Van der Velde, *De Werken van Jacob Haafner* I, pp. 67, 72–3, 92 and 101.

Adriaan Cats, turned up, the scene resembled 'the Saturday club' in the middle of the ocean.³

However, reports of a good atmosphere on board and humane commanders are few and far between. It is as well to remember though that it is not generally the custom to make remarks about what is usual or good, as we see in the modern media every day. What is deviant or wrong is far more likely to attract attention. Consequently, the behaviour of unpleasant or cruel commanders has been recorded far more often and various examples of such men are not lacking.

Brutal and Drunken Commanders

Tensions were unavoidable in a society consisting of several hundred people who were cooped up together on a ship for months on end. Conflict was especially prevalent in periods of intense heat, when the ships were becalmed or the voyage was proceeding at a snail's pace. At such times, a sultry atmosphere could seethe, literally and figuratively. In 1766, Commander Klaas Roem of the Amsterdam Chamber had neither the courage nor the capability to stand up to his officers who spent their time antagonizing each other. For instance, during his watch the first mate was found in the arms of the junior merchant's daughter. Everything conspired to build up tension and ruin the atmosphere.⁴

Roem acted ineffectually but matters were far worse when it was the behaviour of the commander himself which was the source of the problem. During the 1730s, Kornelis van der Hoeven from Enkhuizen lived on board like an animal and his conduct was especially bestial. It was useless to complain, as was mentioned in Chapter 1. Much the same accusation could be levelled against Commander Jan Schellinger from Amsterdam, and his conduct eventually led to the loss of his ship the *Hertog van Brunswijk* off the west coast of Ceylon in 1769. Schellinger's officers were afraid of him, which turned out to be a fatal mistake. For years the commander had built up a notorious reputation in the shipping world as a coarse, brutal and reckless man, 'out of whose mouth in the exercise of his function nearly as many hideous curses as words issued'. When his ship stranded on 31 August the blame could be laid squarely on the fact that in the running of his ship he would neither listen to nor accept the advice of others. His ship's officers saw that they were approaching land, Schellinger being confined to his cabin 'indisposed', but he would not allow them to adjust the position or change course. It was absolutely unnecessary, Schellinger knew, since after all he had been in this area twice already. In view of their previous experiences with him, the officers did not dare to oppose their commander. The investigation report later recorded that the commander was a domineering, intractable, obsti-

---

³ Barend-Van Haeften, *Op reis met de VOC*, pp. 38–9, 69, 71, 73, 77 and 83; *DAS* II, nos. 3025, 3026 and 3027.
⁴ Barend-Van Haeften, *Op reis met de VOC*, pp. 52–4; *DAS* II, no. 3959.

33. The quarterdeck of the *Stavenisse*. The Lutheran minister Jan Brandes (1743–1808) made drawings and watercolours wherever he happened to be, including on board. Born in Bodegraven, he sailed to Batavia with his wife on board the Holland under Commander Benjamin van der Spek in 1778. He remained there as minister until 1785. In 1785 he made the voyage to the Cape via Ceylon on the *Stavenisse*. He returned to the Republic in 1787, but soon left to make his home in Sweden. M. de Bruijn and R. Raben have produced an extensively documented publication of Brandes' watercolours. This watercolour shows the quarterdeck of the *Stavenisse*, where the officers had their quarters. The large double helm, the steward, the bird cages and chests all catch the eye. The deck is protected from the sun by a sailcloth.

nate and surly man. Schellinger was dead by then, having died a week after the ship ran aground. Despite these facts, his first and second mates were dismissed. They should have realized that, 'because of the illness from which he was then suffering', their commander 'was *non compos mentis*'. The commander's personality was no excuse for their failure to intervene.[5]

Bastiaan Verdoes from Katwijk was a very experienced sailor. He had no equal in his ability to sense the coming of a sudden storm, but he was addicted to drink. In the previous chapter there is an account of how he arrived on board in

---

[5] The Hague, NA, VOC 3263, fols 723–4; Van Gelder, *Naporra's omweg*, p. 226; DAS II, no. 3972.

the Texel Roads in 1752 blind drunk. Quite apart from his alcoholism, Verdoes was a brutal, crude, loutish man. A senior merchant from Mechelen who was on board a Prussian ship from Emden on his way to Asia reported how obtusely Verdoes behaved on the Cape Verde Islands. The senior merchant's ship was already lying at anchor there when Verdoes arrived. His own commander immediately sent the Dutch ship some fresh meat and fruit, as a gesture of collegiality. On his arrival, Verdoes had not even bothered to salute the Prussian ship. He is supposed not to have recognized the Prussian ensign and to have taken it for that of the German Emperor, who 'was not worth several charges of gunpowder'. Verdoes also did not bother with the customary return gift, which prompted the man from Mechelen to add sarcastically, 'but one has to pardon a nation where courtesies barely exist and the people are distinguished by manners which scarcely pass muster'.

Verdoes regularly quarrelled with his officers and had constant problems with them. He had his first mate, Nauwman, shut up in his cabin for weeks on end. In 1754, in Surat he again embarked blind drunk and proceeded to give the wrong orders for weighing the anchors. Consequently, it proved impossible to raise them and a great deal of confusion ensued. Verdoes continued his drinking and finally slept off his hangover in the beakhead, the crew's lavatories. The next morning, having slept it off, he immediately made his apologies to the boatswain and the second mate, who had been most involved in the incident, after which the ship was finally able to sail. The directors did not think that this sort of behaviour was any reason to keep him from getting a new command or to demote him. Likewise, when his ship was paid off in 1777, Hillert Volkers was tipsy and his officers were interrogated about this, but even so two years later Volkers was given a new command.[6]

There is only one sole source for the story recounted below, but it is generally considered reliable. Jakob Haafner's tale of Commander Willem Koelbier is gruesome. Haafner depicts this Rotterdam man as a savage, sadistic brute, traits he showed as soon as he was on board and had complete command. In 1773 Haafner served under Koelbier on a protracted voyage from Chinsura in Bengal to Negapatnam in the far south-east of India. This commander had an especially foul reputation and as a result had trouble finding a full complement of crew. Sailors who were available in Chinsura feigned illness when men were being recruited for Koelbier's ship.

Against his best intentions, Haafner was again appointed cabin boy, a post which brought him into intimate contact with the commander. Scared out of his wits by his superior and his notorious floggings, his predecessor had jumped overboard at the beginning of the voyage. Koelbier also drove three others to their deaths and, in describing these incidents, Haafner does not hesitate to

---

[6] The Hague, NA, VOC 308, 15.7.1776; Van Gelder, *Naporra's omweg*, pp. 206, 236–7, 294–8, 304, 360–1 and 447; *DAS* II, no. 4341, and III, no. 7948; I am grateful to M. Alcide for the French quotation.

use the word 'murder'. This commander loved flogging, thrashing and starving his victims to death. Haafner compares him to a tiger and he was personally continually subjected to this sort of ill treatment. On one occasion he was hit on the back of his head with a piece of wood. Koelbier was unable to tolerate anything which had not been done precisely as he wanted it. He also had a suspicious nature. Badly injured, with an open wound on his back, Haafner escaped his tormentor in Negapatnam. The local authorities did deal with a written complaint signed by many of the crew, but quickly covered the matter up. Later, when he was writing down this story in Amsterdam, what still upset Haafner the most was that, not very far away, since 1791 Koelbier had been Superintendent of the Shipyard and Inspector for the Rotterdam Chamber.[7] It is not unreasonable to surmise that a crew or its individual members could in practice be sacrificed to the whims of a commander. There was also the case, described earlier, of Onkruid pressuring his third mate into marrying his cast-off mistress.

The Company was not interested in how its commanders conducted themselves on board. Investigations were set in motion and punishments followed only when ships foundered or ran aground and cargoes were lost as a consequence. The information just recounted about the behaviour of individual commanders is therefore not based on documents in the Company archives, but has been gleaned from comments of the very few contemporaries who recorded their experiences.

Authors and Victims of Tensions

Haafner's writings are the only source about the strained relationships on Roem's ship but there were cases of other seriously disturbed relationships which did reach the ears of the authorities and which a researcher can find in the Company archives. Such cases occurred throughout the whole of the eighteenth century and were only to be expected. The circumstances in which tensions could build up did not change. The ships were not any bigger or the length of the voyage any shorter and the hierarchy remained precisely the same. A number of individual cases will be described below, beginning with two in which the commander was the author of the trouble, followed by others in which he was the victim.

In comparison with such colleagues as Verdoes and Koelbier, Frederik Wielard of the Rotterdam Chamber was mild-mannered, but on his maiden voyage in 1756 he was confronted with all manner of problems. He had the second mate confined to quarters with a guard on the door for some weeks, which was not an unusual measure. He regularly humiliated the young bookkeeper. He had a soldier, not the bookkeeper, take care of such work as writing up the reports of meetings of the ship's council, and he gave the soldier permission to sleep in

---

[7] De Moor and Van der Velde, *De Werken van Jacob Haafner* I, pp.145–60 and 166–7.

the cabin. Wielard was convinced that the bookkeeper had not yet mastered his work properly: 'You are a bloody fool of a boy who hasn't got the sense to even write the muster roll', he exclaimed, throwing the roll at his feet. He pushed him and, in full view of bystanders, he kicked him down a companionway. During the ship's council he sat, 'with his usual gravity as lord of the ship in the chairman's seat, that great shrine on board ... in which the small ship's tyrants imagine themselves more awesome and redoubtable than is a monarch on his seat of justice'. In Batavia officers and others testified against Wielard, who was fined twelve months' stipend for abusing his power. His suspension was lifted and his further career did not suffer at all. Not long after he returned home, he was given his next command and made four voyages in rapid succession. Kornelis Pietersen was let off even more lightly in 1765. The crew of the *Huis Om* thought that he had kept them short of rations and submitted a complaint to the Amsterdam Chamber. Pietersen was fined a month's stipend.[8]

Occasionally the governments in Batavia and Cape Town did pay considerable attention to complaints about misconduct, as was shown earlier. On the voyage out in 1722, Jan Geerse and his second and third mates had behaved in an unseemly fashion and had maltreated the first mate. Geerse was declared 'incompetent' and dismissed from the service of the Company. In 1743, Batavia took severe measures against two first mates who were then shipped off to the Republic as 'useless boarders'. Frederik Schouten of the Amsterdam Chamber was also punished for the same reason the following year.[9]

Conversely, on more than one occasion commanders personally became the target of aggression by one or more members of the crew. The reasons for this treatment are usually unknown. Joris van der Wijn was murdered by a sailor on the way home in 1704. In 1712 in Cape Town Jakob van der Anker was attacked with a dagger by his first mate; the man was drunk. Apparently Van der Anker had stirred up problems with his second-in-command. 'Mutual embitterment' had also led to the transfer of another of his first mates in Cape Town in 1708. On 11 December 1750, discontent brewed among the crew of the *Sloterdijk* about their rations. They claimed they had to eat too much unhusked rice (*padie*). The boatswain and the boatswain's mate (*schieman*) were asked by the crew to present their complaint to Commander Herman Zoet, but at this point matters went awry. The boatswain's mate was tipsy, at least according to the commander, but not the boatswain, and spoke to the commander about the matter with the greatest disrespect. He happened to have a plate of rice with him. A quarrel erupted and Zoet punched the boatswain's mate in the face. This

---

[8] The Hague, NA, VOC 9458, criminele rol 16.3.1758 (Dr H. Ketting provided me with this source) and 2916 (OBP 1759), fol. 1346; *DAS* I, nos. 3675 and 3795, and III, no. 7556; for Pietersen, see VOC 308, 12.9 and 19.12.1785, and *DAS* III, no. 7682.

[9] The Hague, NA, VOC 1968, fols 1267ff. and 2659, fol. 1240; Schooneveld-Oosterling, *Generale Missiven* XI, pp. 203 and 461; *DAS* II, no. 2447.

turned into a fight which went on until the boatswain's mate was overpowered by the other crew members.[10]

On the voyage out, on the quarterdeck, Commander Isaak van den Berg was reviled as 'scum and a scoundrel', incapable of carrying out his duties, by his first mate in the presence of all the guests on board. The commander was then punched in the chest and threatened with being thrashed 'against the rail'. The first mate was confined to his quarters, but he was so popular among the crew that after a while they refused to carry out their duties. In 1773, Abraham van der Weide 'had a dispute about some trivial matter' in Cape Town with his colleague Karel Philip Kassel whereupon the two men 'attacked each other with their daggers unsheathed'. Van der Weide was wounded and died two days later. In desperation, Kassel fled on board a French warship which happened to be lying in the bay, thereby evading any judicial consequences of his action, and, after a whole series of petitions submitted over a number of years, he was acquitted in 1783. Jan Frederik Raatjes was openly insulted by the chief surgeon, when the latter accused the commander of treating those on board who were ill badly.[11]

All these were cases of problems of conduct and discipline involving the commander which were discussed in the ship's council and by the authorities and so were reported on paper. Both parties would have been heard in a ship's council. When such cases had to be heard, the council was chaired not by the commander but by another of its members.

'A Horrible Man': Jan Hokkeling

At home in Rotterdam Jan Hokkeling caused trouble and pain and his conduct did not change on board the ships on which he sailed. He was involved with various women, made promises of marriage and begot children. His mother disowned him. He was promoted to first mate in 1722, but six years later, on the voyage home on the *Loenderveen*, he still had not made any further progress. His commander, Matthijs Zwaan, was not a person who radiated authority and the presence of his wife aft caused practical complications derived from the stowing of her baggage. The *assistant* was not happy with this and conspired with Hokkeling about the matter. The first mate was a real toper. Sometimes he awoke so fuddled that 'his eyes were not open before he had already begun to swig again'.

---

[10] The Hague, NA, VOC 307, 10.11.1704 (*DAS* III, no. 6101), 4069, fol. 775 (*DAS* III, no. 6268) and 10950 (*DAS* III, no. 7345).

[11] The Hague, NA, VOC 4291, fols 1–3, and *DAS* III, no. 8030 (Raatjes) and 10965 and 4238, fols 355–62 with *DAS* III, no. 7683 (Van den Berg). For Kassel, see The Hague, NA, VOC 222, 16.10.1777, 25.3.1778 and 20.11.1783, and 308, 27.5, 26.8.1773 and 11.7.1774; Cape Town Archives, resolutions C. of P., 31.1.1773 (www.tanap.net); *DAS* III, nos. 7869 and 7870.

34. The surgeon's cabin. Drawings of cabins and other accommodation are very rare. Brandes drew the cabin of the chief surgeon on the port side of the *Stavenisse*. This ship was of the highest class and was built by the Zealand Chamber in 1772. She was broken up in Batavia in 1792. This cabin probably measured three square metres. The perspective of the bunk is incorrect. In the corner above the cupboard are the surgeon's instructions and ship's logs of the Zealand Chamber.

He preferred to have someone with him when he was on watch because then he could drink and sleep. Commander Zwaan had no control over him because Hokkeling simply ignored his orders. With the help of a generous supply of alcohol, the first mate had made many friends on the quarterdeck and the second mate also joined the group, which meant that there was now a majority on the ship's council which could outvote the commander. Zwaan's authority was completely undermined, which meant he had to stand helplessly by as Hokkeling and others ridiculed him when the chief surgeon treated him for kidney stones. In a drunken fit, the second mate divested himself of almost all his clothes and stood before the commander's wife, who was sitting doing her embroidery, virtually naked. Hokkeling repeatedly threatened Zwaan with physical violence and showered him with verbal abuse. The Cape offered the severely tried commander a way out. Hokkeling and his henchmen were tried and found guilty of various breaches of the Articles. It was demanded that they be dismissed from Company service and set on a transport ship to the Republic. However, it was necessary to move quickly as the returning fleet was on the point of sailing and there was no time to investigate the matter thoroughly. Consequently the authorities at the Cape did no more than fine Hokkeling three months' stipend and put him and the second mate on other ships.

In modern terms, Hokkeling got off lightly. The directors did not consider this sort of conduct a reason to get rid of him. Quite the reverse in fact, since Hokkeling was appointed as a commander in 1729. Nothing is known of what happened on his maiden voyage, but there is plenty of information about his second command. On 6 July 1733, he sailed on the *Alsem* which set sail with two other ships of the Amsterdam Chamber. It proved to be a momentous voyage, which was to end for him as commander at the Cape. Hokkeling breached the rules on no fewer than four points. In the early morning of 8 August, the *Blijdorp*, one of the three ships, ran aground on the African coast north of the Cape Verde Islands. The trio of ships were hopelessly off course, for which Hokkeling as commodore bore the main responsibility. The other two ships did not bother to heave to and help those who had been shipwrecked or to salvage the chests of precious metals, but just sailed on. One of the ship's officers said that there certainly had been opportunities to help and no one in 'all good conscience' could deny this. Hokkeling and his colleague, Adriaan van der Graaf, had not paid any attention to their ship's officers on their ships and had sailed on.

On the *Alsem*, the first mate also indulged in excessive bouts of drinking which lasted for some time. This was a problem with which Hokkeling must have been personally familiar. The first mate no longer performed his duties satisfactorily and often could not even stand up, much less take a reliable sighting. Consequently the ship's council demoted him to sailor, but the man then walked around ranting and raving. Hokkeling had him clapped in irons and put him on the poop deck in the open air without any protection from the sun, wind or rain. The former second-in-command sat like this for weeks. This punishment was too much for everybody on board, except Hokkeling. His reaction to requests that the former first mate be better treated was: 'Let the blackguard lie there, he doesn't deserve any better.' A few hours before he died, the first mate was finally laid in the cabin.

In the meantime, the commander and various passengers on a Portuguese ship had also experienced Hokkeling's conduct. When the Portuguese ship approached, for a while the *Alsem* treated her as an enemy. It did not take long to clear up this mistake, but when they came aboard, Hokkeling treated his Portuguese colleague and his retinue as if they were indeed hostile. He had them all clapped in irons and had the Portuguese officer badly maltreated in order to force him to speak 'low German'. It was thought that he could do so but just did not want to. Nobody on either of the ships could understand one another. Later, Hokkeling claimed in his defence that his Portuguese colleague had behaved badly. In the month before the ship arrived at the Cape, the health of the crew deteriorated. On repeated occasions, the chief surgeon asked for extra means to treat the sick but Hokkeling refused these requests point blank.

In the meantime, the report of the loss of the *Blijdorp* had reached the Cape. The government decided to hold an inquiry after the arrival of the two ships. Hokkeling and his colleague, Van der Graaf, made statements which contradicted those of their officers. Besides their accusations, Hokkeling also had to put forward a defence of his conduct towards his first mate, the men from the Portuguese ship and the many sick on board his ship. The investigation resulted in both commanders being dismissed from their posts. They were then put on a transport to Batavia with their dossiers. Hokkeling died on 11 May 1734, halfway through the voyage, thereby escaping the death penalty. Their behaviour in relation to the *Blijdorp* was taken extremely seriously. Van der Graaf was condemned to death in 1735 but two years later this sentence was commuted to a declaration of 'incompetence' and a complete, perpetual banishment from the East. There would have been no extenuating circumstances for Hokkeling as commodore to escape punishment and, moreover, he would have also had to answer charges about his treatment of the sick and of his first mate. The commotion in connection with the Portuguese ship was not included in the range of charges. Thus, a truly horrible man by his death escaped judgement.[12]

No New Command after the Loss of a Ship?

In the shipping between the Republic and Asia, the greatest concern of the directors was that a commander brought his ship safely to her destination with her cargo intact and undamaged. Just as their predecessors had done, the new directors again and again laid down all sorts of rules and regulations, kept together in the ship's box in the commander's cabin. When this was handed in after the completion of a voyage, they had these checked by the examiners. If anything was amiss on any point the punishments were a fine and deductions from the stipend and sometimes a temporary suspension or a declaration of incompetence. What happened professionally between commander, officers and passengers during a voyage was immaterial. Examples of misconduct by commanders have been given above which had no detrimental influence on their future careers with the Company. Nevertheless, there is an impression that the authorities overseas were more alert to such matters than those in the Republic.

As far as the directors were concerned, matters were only really serious when they heard of unauthorized private trade in a foreign port or the smuggling into the Republic of non-authorized goods. When such transgressions occurred, usually the commander concerned was never given another command. He also lost his job, as he had gambled away his ship. At least in most cases that is what

---

[12] The Hague, NA, VOC 2323 (Kaap), 2329, fol. 2001, 2396, fol. 1988, 4109, fols 1055–74 and 5981, fol. 1; Van Goor, *Generale Missiven* IX, p. 593, and X, p. 45; *DAS* II, nos. 2781 and 2921–3, III, nos. 6732 and 6799. See also R. van Gelder, 'De stranding van de Blijdorp, 1733. Lotgevallen van een bemanning', *Tijdschrift voor Zeegeschiedenis* 21 (2002), pp. 24–33.

happened. Haye Blauwhuis was found not guilty of the stranding of the *Blijdorp* in 1733. When he returned to the Republic after many hardships and wanderings, his first mate and his colleague Hokkeling had already been found responsible for the incident. Blauwhuis was once more declared 'admissible', but he never sailed again. On 21 May 1737, on one stormy night eight East Indiamen sank simultaneously in Table Bay. There was no question of apportioning blame. The commanders involved, including Jan van Heemstee and Ary van Veurden of the Delft Chamber who have been mentioned earlier, were given new commands.[13]

Every commander who lost his ship or ran her aground could expect to face an investigation and report, usually followed by a declaration of incompetence. Of course, he was spared this fate if he had gone down with his ship, as had happened on *'t Vliegend Hart* and the *Anna Catharina* in the Wielingen in 1735, or on various East Indiamen on the route from Batavia to the Cape. A total of 171 Company ships were lost in the eighteenth century, sixty-four during the voyage out and 107 on the way back to the Republic. Therefore, 2 per cent of the ships on voyages out and 4.5 per cent of those on voyages home never reached their destination. Besides these, the VOC lost forty-one ships through enemy action during the War of the Spanish Succession, the Fourth Anglo-Dutch War and in the Wars of the French Revolution from 1793 to 1795.[14] Below are a few examples of commanders who were held to be guilty of or responsible for losing their ships and were never reinstated in their former posts.

Such a commander was not technically dismissed because he was no longer employed after his return from a voyage. After all, commanders had applied for one posting on a specific ship. The directors simply designated a commander who had failed in their eyes 'incompetent' and he could not be reappointed. Adriaan de Ruiter and his officers received their marching orders in this way after he had run the *Voetboog* aground on the Brazilian coast near Pernambuco in 1700. After consultation with his staff, he had not made the obligatory stop at the Cape on his way home. At least three commanders never re-entered Company service because they had lost their ships to the French: Jan de Rooy of the *Hogestelt* in 1706, Jan Munkhoven of the *Domburg* in the same year, and Jakob Zalm of the *Kievit* in the Indian Ocean in 1709. Zalm's officers claimed that the capture could have been avoided if the commander had altered course in time. In the ensuing fight, he had shown no leadership and had acted in a cowardly fashion. He had even deserted the quarterdeck.

In the declaration of De Rooy as incompetent, the report of his officers had been decisive. The directors were implacable if a commander did not follow the advice of his staff. As a consequence of this neglect, Willem Dekker had let the *Loosdrecht* run aground on the Isle of Wight in 1719. Far worse was the nonchalance of the staff of the *Slot ter Hoge* under Willem de Smit. This ship foundered

---

[13] Van Gelder, 'De stranding', pp. 30–1; *DAS* II, nos. 2977–8, and III, nos. 6991–3, 6998–7000, 7002 and 7003.
[14] *DAS* I, 75 and 91.

off Maio, one of the Cape Verde Islands, in 1732. Gerbrand Swaag was given no thanks for the forfeiting of the *Watervliet* near Calais in 1742. Half a century later, shortly after her departure, the heavily damaged *Berkhout* had to be laid up in Dover. This spelled the end of Christiaan Martens' career with the VOC.[15]

The Middelburg commander, Jan Steyns, of the Zealand Chamber, faced a significantly worse fate. On the evening of 9 June 1727, his new ship, the *Zeewijk*, was wrecked on a submerged rock near the Houtman Abrolhos at a latitude of 29° south, off the west coast of Australia. Of the 208 members of her crew, eighty-two eventually survived the disastrous voyage. The shipwrecked men were able to reach a small islet which lay close by. They managed to launch the ship's boat to go to seek help in Batavia, but the boat never reached its destination. Finally, after four months, those who had remained behind succeeded in building a new boat from pieces of the wreckage and wood from the vegetation on the island, under the direction of the ship's carpenter. They called her the *Sloepje*. On 26 March 1728, Steyns and the rest set off on a voyage of 1,700 nautical miles to the Sunda Strait and Batavia. A month later, the eighty-two on board – with ten undamaged chests of precious metals – arrived there alive. Of course, there was an investigation into the cause of the disaster and what had happened afterwards. Steyns was held responsible. He was said not to have taken sufficient precautions when approaching the Australian coast, having not obeyed instructions and having forged the log. Historians have questioned this verdict. For Steyns, the harsh reality was to have to hear, eighteen months after the shipwreck, a demand that he be held up to public ridicule and sentenced to fifteen years' hard labour on the chain gang. The actual sentence was somewhat milder: perpetual banishment from the chartered territory of the Company, payment of the costs of the trial and forfeiture of all his possessions. Shortly afterwards, Steyns was shipped off back to the Republic and disappeared from history.[16]

A younger brother of the later admiral Jan Hendrik van Kinsbergen saw his VOC career in ruins within a month of his departure. Jan Hermanus had had experience as a lieutenant in the Navy. In 1769 he and a colleague successfully applied to the Amsterdam Chamber for posts and he got a position as commander and his colleague was appointed first mate. A later inquiry report was merciless in its criticism of both men. Both were declared guilty of the loss of the *Leimuiden* on a reef near Boa Vista, in the Cape Verde Islands. After

---

[15] Respectively the following voyage numbers in *DAS* II and III and archive numbers in the VOC-archief: no. 6034 and 113, 17.2.1702, no. 1992 and 221, 28.10.1706, no. 2006 and 114, 23.2.1707, no. 2041 and 221, 30.3.1711, no. 2372 and 221, 21.7.1719, no. 2877 and 221, 26.8.1733, no. 3248 and 222, 22.8.1742 and no. 4724 and 223, 13 and 17.11.1792.

[16] Coolhaas, *Generale Missiven* VIII, pp. 178–80; Van Goor, *Generale Missiven* IX, p. 57; *DAS* II, no. 2680. See also H. Edwards, *The Wreck on the Half Moon Reef* (Adelaide, 1970); and J.P. Sigmond and L.H. Zuiderbaan, *Dutch Discoveries of Australia. Shipwrecks, Treasures and Early Voyages off the West Coast* (Adelaide, 1979), pp. 119–32.

the report, Van Kinsbergen left immediately for Berbice in South America to become a planter. Probably his only consolation was that he was compensated ƒ. 200 for the gold watch which he had exchanged with a priest on the island for food for his crew. Of the thirty-seven gold bars on board, the Company in the end retrieved sixteen.[17]

The Company also wielded suspension and demotion as punishments. In 1725, on the voyage out Jan Bot ran aground on the Isle of Wight in the *Nieuwvliet*, without suffering any really serious consequences. Nevertheless, after his return to the Republic in 1726 Bot was 'suspended' for six years and in fact only sailed again as a commander in 1733. This was not the fate of Jakob Welgevaren. In Chapter 9, we saw that the Amsterdam Chamber wavered about his competence. Despite these reservations, the Delft Chamber appointed him commander. Less than a fortnight after she had sailed under Welgevaren's command in 1758, the *Erfprins* foundered and was a total loss. Welgevaren was not declared incompetent, but was demoted to second mate and was only allowed to sail again in that rank four years later. In 1776, the Zealand Chamber demoted Commander Jan Frederik Schuts to first mate. Six years later he was given another ship.

Pieter van der Weert was given a curious punishment when the *Vrouwe Elisabeth* ran aground in the Weemsbrug Shallows to the east of the Isle of Wight in 1773. At the time he was on watch. The ship was quickly pulled off and continued her voyage but the English help needed to pull her free cost ƒ. 2,225. Van der Weert had to pay this out of his own pocket, but nevertheless he was given a bonus. However, he was demoted to the rank of first mate for two voyages and in 1779 he was required to retake his commander's examination in the presence of three directors of the Rotterdam Chamber. He went down with his ship, the *Bredenhof*, in the Indian Ocean on the voyage home in 1785.[18]

It has already been said with reference to the great disaster in Table Bay in 1737 that the loss of his ship and her cargo did not invariably mean that a commander was declared incapable. Jan Almees, Jakob Hoogstad and Willem Vroom all eventually escaped this judgement. In February 1736, they all lost their ships, by the Zuiderhaaks, a sandbank off the coast of North Holland near Den Helder, and on the Goodwin Sands off the cost of Kent. Almees had set sail with twelve other ships, but had made the wrong decision to return to

---

[17] The Hague, NA, VOC 308, 1.10.1770; and R.B. Prud'homme van Reine, *Jan Hendrik van Kinsbergen 1735–1819. Admiraal en filantroop* (Amsterdam, 1990), pp. 51–3. In the 1990s divers brought up the rest of the bars. In March 2000, one of them was presented to the Koninklijk Penningkabinet (Royal Numismatic Collection). It would have been the only bar of Company gold in a museum collection but a few days after the presentation it was stolen and melted down.

[18] Respectively the following voyage and archive numbers in the VOC-archief: *DAS* II, nos. 2615, 2920, III, no. 6668, and 118, 28.2.1727, nos. 3739, 3835 and 222, 10.10.1759 and 7.10.1763, *DAS* II, no. 4392, III, no. 7919 and 222, 22.3.1776; for Van der Weert, *DAS* II, no. 4349, and III, nos. 7849, 8132, and 181, 31.3.1773, 134, 7.10.1773, 222, 7.4.1774, 308, 4.2.1779, and Archief Van der Heim 93, 29.1.1779.

Texel during a sudden storm. His pilot did not succeed in getting the *Hillegom* within the buoys that marked protected anchorage. Hoogstad and Vroom did manage to make it to safety and chose to put to sea again a few days later. From the outset, they steered a wrong course and hence ran onto the Goodwin Sands, instead of sailing into the Channel. Everything pointed to the 'complete ignorance of the officers or else to negligence'. Great doubts were entertained about Hoogstad's expertise. The sounding line should have been used more effectively and more frequently. A 1737 report confirmed this supposition. It was compiled by the Amsterdam examiner and five of the most senior experienced commanders. The reports also noted that fortunately Almees' and Hoogstad's ships had no cash on board and that carried on Vroom's ship was rescued. The three did not resign themselves to their painful disqualification. In the end, a year later, the blame was laid squarely on the shoulders of the pilots. All three commanders were again declared 'competent'. Only Hoogstad did not rejoin the Company. He became the owner of herring boats in his home port of Vlaardingen.[19]

After the stranding of the *Amsterdam* off Hastings in 1749, Willem Klump from Latvia was soon at sea again. Neither he nor his officers were blamed for the loss of the brand new ship. Jan Kelder was a commander who was not so lucky. Near the completion of his second voyage, the *Horstendaal* stranded within sight of home between Callantsoog and Huisduinen. Kelder was exonerated of any blame. In less than a year, in 1743, he had a new command, the newly built *Hollandia*. Among his passengers was one of Van Imhoff's younger brothers. Ten days out of Texel, the ship foundered near the Scilly Isles. She went down with all hands. The sea around the Scillies is made treacherous by submerged rocks and at that time the waters had not yet been properly charted. Another, somewhat later, example is Gottlieb Mulder. In 1785, on her way home the *Brederode* sank off Cape Agulhos, the southernmost tip of Africa. Just as with Kelder, Mulder went down with his ship. In 1788, the *Admiraal de Suffren*, the largest ship of the Company, disappeared on her way from China to the Cape without leaving a trace.[20]

Naturally, a mutiny among the European crew members or the running amok of their Asian counterparts or of slaves tarnished the reputation of a commander, but these were rare occurrences. Ten cases which occurred between 1750 and 1790 have been studied in more depth. For nearly all the commanders concerned, the outbreak of a mutiny or disruption on board signalled the end

---

[19] DAS II, nos. 3016, 3019 and 3021. See also Moree, 'Een Vlaardinger'; and Chapter 8.
[20] For Klump, see Marsden, *De laatste reis*, pp. 76–7 and 213–15, and DAS II, nos. 3437 and 3514; for Kelder, see The Hague, NA, VOC 124, 25.2.1743, and DAS II, nos. 3275 and 3514; R. Cowan, Z. Cowan and P. Marsden, 'The Dutch East-Indiaman *Hollandia* Wrecked on the Isles of Scilly in 1743', *International Journal of Nautical Archaeology and Underwater Exploration* 4 (1975), pp. 267–300, see pp. 268, 274 and 277; for Mulder, see The Hague, NA, VOC 308, 29.5.1786, and DAS II, no. 4543, and III, nos. 8136 and 8218.

of their career with the Company. A few of them were allowed to retain their position on the voyage home.²¹

No Longer Admissible

Of course, there were other commanders who were never again entrusted with a command. It has to be remembered that a crime such as being caught smuggling by the authorities was a mortal sin in the eyes of the authorities, both in the Republic and in Batavia. Some examples of those who were judged unfit for employment have already been given: Uilenberg in 1714, Van Neercassel in 1715, Outjes in 1755 and Rauwenhoff a year later, all of them from the Amsterdam Chamber. After it was discovered in 1733 that, on his voyage home from China, he had stored a large amount of tea and porcelain in a warehouse at the Cape and had later sold these commodities for *f*. 4,500, Pieter Verley never managed to redeem himself. He also forfeited all his goods. In 1741, the authorities in Batavia arrested Gillis Oudemans from Maassluis on the charge of trading in pepper and tin on his own account. Oudemans had served many years as a commander in the intra-Asian trade. Denial was of no use. He was deported back to the Republic from the East and declared incompetent. He probably died during the voyage home in 1742.²²

Flourishing trade always gladdened the hearts of the directors. In the direct China trade, problems would sometimes flare up in Canton between commanders and supercargoes, and the Company usually sided with the supercargo. Waiting for the monsoon meant that a long period of time often had to be spent there between arrival and departure. In 1762 Hendrik Winkelman was judged no longer suitable to be a commander because he had sold victuals intended to provision his ship in China. Later, in 1791 the same action meant that Pieter Stokbroo was faced with the sanction that he would never be sent to China again. This simultaneously also spelled the end of his career with the VOC.²³

Occasionally, there were truly sad cases of commanders who no longer needed to apply for a new position, such as that of Hilverduin. In 1721, after five voyages for the Amsterdam Chamber, Regenboog was dismissed on account of 'thoughtlessness' (*ijlhoofdigheid*). The same Chamber was also implacable in its attitude toward Hendrik Worms who had been ill the whole of the voyage home from Bengal in 1765 and confined to his bunk. At the first opportunity, the director who inspected his ship, the *Oranjezaal*, in Texel had the half-dead Worms disem-

---

[21] Bruijn and Van Eyck van Heslinga, *Muiterij*.
[22] For Verley, see The Hague, NA, VOC 5958, and *DAS* III, no. 6869; for Oudemans, see The Hague, NA, VOC 221, 9.9.1734; Van Goor, *Generale Missiven* X, pp. 213 and 737.
[23] The Hague, NA, VOC 222, 17.3.1762, 223, 15.8.1791 and 299, 22.8.1791; *DAS* III, nos. 7596 and 8278. A survey of all China voyages can be found in Liu Yong, *The Dutch East India Company's Tea Trade with China, 1757–1781* (Leiden, 2007), appendix 2 (1758–1793).

barked. It did not take long to discover that confusion had reigned during the voyage and everything had been neglected. The Chamber immediately decreed that Worms, who took a year to recover, could never again sail as a commander. In 1773, he tried to re-apply for service and submitted a petition to this end, but it was rejected. Finally, in 1779, he was found fit to sail, but as second mate. The examiners of the Chamber, Steenstra and Pietersen, judged him 'a skilled, alert and vigilant seaman'. The directors accepted this report and, after more than thirteen years, Worms could serve again, but he was never again a commander.[24]

When the Rotterdam Chamber re-appointed him in 1778, Pieter van Prooien, who was mentioned in Chapter 9, was already a man with a reputation. At the end of 1780 he was assigned another ship, but then fate struck. On the third day of the New Year, the *Vrouwe Katharina Wilhelmina* was captured and taken as a prize by two British warships off Beachy Head. This happened very shortly after the outbreak of the Fourth Anglo-Dutch War. Van Prooien lost everything, including his trade goods. The crew was speedily released but Van Prooien later lodged a complaint with his Chamber claiming that he had now been plunged into 'dire poverty' and was unable to pay any creditor 'anything, let alone the whole sum'. Shortly afterwards, he had a stroke and lost his power of speech. He hoped for compensation and for a new appointment should he recover, but he never sailed again. Karel Magnus Poulin was another who had a sad end to his career. He was caught in the harbour at Portsmouth 'attempting to perpetrate a scandalous deed'. He was arrested and later tried at the Cape. Society was hard and merciless towards homosexuals. Poulin died soon after at the Cape.[25]

In 1778, as he was inspecting one of the recently arrived East Indiamen, a director of the Amsterdam Chamber was thrown into consternation by the tremendous filthiness on board the ship the *Loo*. The whole ship stank and he was overwhelmed by a stream of complaints about Commander Stoffel Kok and his first mate. This was the end of Kok's career with the VOC; and only a few years earlier he had acted as commodore of the returning fleet. He and his first mate were suspended for three years and were paid nothing. The reason for their conduct was excessive addiction to alcohol.[26]

One case which never reached the directors but was heard by the Judicial Council at the Cape concerned the conduct of Hans Christiaansz de Rotte from Flensburg. De Rotte was in charge of the *Ter Meijen*, one of the hookers which were used at the Cape for transporting all manner of things. He was not a commander but held a rank equivalent to that of first mate, and such men

---

[24] The Hague, NA, VOC 222, 11.10.1765, 22.3.1766, 8.10.1773 and 20.4.1779; *Kroniek Historisch Genootschap* 28 (1872), pp. 115–16; Lequin, *Het personeel* I, p. 61, and II, p. 257; *DAS* III, no. 7679.

[25] For Van Prooien, see The Hague, NA, VOC 137, 18.5.1782, and *DAS* II, no. 4390; and for Poulin, see *DAS* II, no. 4329 and Cape Town Archives, resolutions C. of P., 6.7.1779 (www.tanap.net).

[26] The Hague, NA, VOC 308, 15.10.1778 and 1.3.1779.

were often promoted to commander. De Rotte smoked opium or *amfioen*, which inevitably affected his conduct on board. Initially his behaviour could be tolerated, but later it deteriorated. He thrashed his slave boy so badly that he died and De Rotte had the naked body thrown into the sea. He ordered the quartermaster to take the sightings, which the latter refused to do as this was the duty of an officer or of De Rotte himself. He often ordered floggings and rescinded orders when they had been half carried out. He gave the impression that he 'did not know where he was'. He is also said to have tried to seduce a member of the crew to 'commit the sin of sodomy'. On one occasion loud screams for help were heard from De Rotte's cabin and he was found with one hand in the quartermaster's hair while the other grasped a knife. The threatened man was released, after which a piece of opium as large as a nutmeg was found in the cabin. Rotte's mouth was full of 'something which caused him to spit brown saliva'. Moreover, he removed something brown from his mouth which he lost no time in tossing into the sea. De Rotte was tried at the Cape.[27]

This chapter has presented a very colourful series of ships' commanders who caused scandals or found themselves in difficulties. The reaction of the directors in the Republic and of the *Hoge Regering* in Batavia to the events which occurred was often decisive for the future careers and lives of these men. The examples cover a period of nearly a century and are taken from a total of more than 1,200 commanders. Together they made around 5,300 voyages out and home. Most of the examples are recorded in the archives of the Company, which is how we know about them. However, there is no evidence of problems like these affecting the majority of the commanders.

---

[27] The Hague, NA, VOC 10953; Cape Town Archives, resolutions C. of P., 7.8.1753 (www.tanap.net). Dr H. Ketting drew my attention to this source. For promotion from person in charge to commander, see The Hague, NA, VOC 222, 1.10.1778.

16

Professionals in a Conservative Company

The discovery of an octant at the beginning of the 1970s in the wreck of the *Hollandia*, which foundered off the Scilly Isles in 1743, is a tangible reminder of the standard of the art of navigation. The first mention of the octant, an instrument used to measure the altitude of a heavenly body, was in 1731 and this find raises the question of whether the most up-to-date instruments were made available to VOC commanders, and whether in their own day they were among the most modern seafarers. Were the *Heren Zeventien* aware of the most recent innovations in shipping and navigation and did they take steps to ensure that the most modern technology was used in their business?

Contemporaries only very sporadically made any comments about this in print. In his two travel accounts which were published posthumously in 1793 and 1797, Stavorinus was critical. In his account of his final voyage home in 1777–1778 he denounced the practice of following the sailing instructions without any deviation. On 26 April 1778, when they were in the waters around Ascension Island, five commanders who had sailed from Cape Town together on 3 April decided to follow what seemed to them to be the most efficient course rather than sticking to that stipulated. Leendert van Koopstad, Wopke Popta, Jan Och, Olke Hendrik Andringa and Stavorinus, who sailed for three different Chambers, falsified their logs until 8 May and noted down the obligatory courses, ones which they did not actually follow. Stavorinus claimed that their route was far shorter. The examiners did not pick it up and all the bonuses and perks were paid. Interestingly, other commanders who had sailed from Table Bay a month earlier had an even swifter passage home. Cornelius de Jong, who was a naval officer, was critical of the speed of the Company ships and questioned their officers' skill in determining their position at sea. When he convoyed them from the Cape to the Dutch Republic in 1794, De Jong wrote later in his published travel accounts, they followed him unthinkingly.[1]

---

[1] Wilcocke, *Voyages to the East Indies* III, pp. 465–8; *DAS* III, nos. 8000, 8002 and 8007–9, and the shorter voyages nos. 7999, 8001 and 8003–5; J.R. Bruijn and C. van Baalen, *Van zeeman tot residentieburger. Cornelius de Jong van Rodenburgh (1762–1838)* (Hilversum, 1996), p. 26.

Knowledge and Experience of Navigation

Almost without exception, authors over the last century have drawn a negative picture of the knowledge and experience of the art of navigation in Dutch seamanship in the eighteenth century, reserving their severest criticism for the VOC. In 1963 and 1965, the Englishman C.R. Boxer made extensive use of the writings of Stavorinus and others to present a picture of commanders who were weighed down by bureaucratic instructions and were thwarted in their attempts to introduce any innovations. The famous scholar of the history of navigation in the 1930s and 1940s, Ernst Crone, unfairly claimed that the theoretical knowledge of the ship's officers was poor and they also failed when they had to apply their theoretical knowledge in practice. His main point of criticism was the determination of position (*plaatsbepaling*) in which he said that 'the Dutch navigator lagged behind'.[2] Later authors, among them C.A. Davids in 1982 and 1986, A.R.T. Jonkers in 2000 and W.F.J. Mörzer Bruyns in 2003, have been kinder.[3] This book sides with the latter group, but not without taking the opportunity to make some critical comments.

The commanders and ship's officers of the Company found their way to Asia and back with the aid of all sorts of sea charts, navigational instruments and textbooks on navigation. In their logs they noted, as far as possible on a daily basis, their estimated position at sea, which course was being steered and how much estimated distance had been covered (*verheid*). Estimation of the latitude was confirmed by taking sightings of the altitude of the sun, usually at noon. Observations were also made of the stars. Sightings to determine latitude generally began after leaving the Channel. In the first part of the eighteenth century, the instruments most likely to have been used to determine the altitude of heavenly bodies were quadrants and back-staffs or Davis quadrants. At that time it was still impossible to determine longitude precisely and this was attempted by calculating the course and the distance covered from the last known observed position, in essence dead reckoning. Occasionally, the calculations could be verified by calling at a port or sightings of well-known geographical features such as capes and islands, among them St Helena and Ascension in the Atlantic or St Paul and Amsterdam in the Indian Ocean. The sky and the water could also contain clues. For instance, the *trombas* (*Ecklonia buccinalis*) was a species of

---

[2] C.R. Boxer, 'The Dutch East-Indiamen: Their Sailors, Their Navigators, and Life on Board, 1602–1795', *Mariner's Mirror* 49 (1963), pp. 81–104; C.R. Boxer, *The Dutch Seaborne Empire 1600–1800* (London, 1965), pp. 107–8; and C.R. Boxer, 'The Maritime Twilight of the V.O.C., 1780–95. Some Sources and Problems', *Tijdschrift voor Zeegeschiedenis* 1 (1982), pp. 114–23; Crone, *Cornelis Douwes*, p. 35.

[3] C.A. Davids, 'Commentaar op het artikel van C.R. Boxer', *Tijdschrift voor Zeegeschiedenis* 1 (1982), pp. 124–31; Davids, *Zeewezen en wetenschap*; A.R.T. Jonkers, *North by Northwest. Seafaring, Science, and the Earth's Magnetic Field (1600–1800)* (Göttingen, 2000), PhD thesis, Free University, Amsterdam, 2000; Mörzer Bruyns, *Het schip recht door zee*.

seaweed which heralded the proximity of the Cape. The colour of the water would change or the swell would alter from longer to shorter waves, and the presence of land birds was also a clue to the approach of land.[4] Experience in the recognition of such signs was extremely important. Company ships which sailed together as a fleet, which was the invariable practice from the Cape back to the Republic, regularly compared their positions with each other and using an average position calculated a better one. There were various types of compasses available but the deviation in the indication of true north, the variation, still had to be determined. The speed of the ships was measured by using a hand log, but if the wind was hard and the seas rough sailors had to rely on pure guesswork, and estimates were unreliable. It is known that with a following wind the great three-masters could sail within 60 degrees of the wind and that the tiller and, not long after, the steering-wheel helped to keep the ship pretty much on course.[5]

Towards the middle of the eighteenth century, new possibilities which allowed a better determination of latitude appeared. The octant, an invention of the Englishman John Hadley in 1731, allowed determination of latitude under all sorts of weather conditions and in all manner of swells, even when the ship was pitching heavily or the weather was foggy; something which could not be done with the earlier instruments. The octant was an instrument which measured angles in an arc of one-eighth of a circle with a scale of 90°. It ensured the measurements were quicker and more accurate. The octant was quickly embraced by the international shipping world and could be used to measure the altitude of the sun or the stars. There was an octant on a Dutch warship on her way to the West Indies in 1737 and on a VOC ship in 1742. The Company had purchased three in 1741 and one had been put on the *Herstelder* and one on the *Anna* under Christiaan Blom. As mentioned earlier, another octant was recovered from the wreck of the *Hollandia* which had been under Kelder's command. In 1747, the *Heren Zeventien* decreed that from that time each ship had to be equipped with an octant with its instructions for use. In 1762, the first mate was also assigned his own octant. The second mate had to wait for this honour until 1780. The inventory of his estate reveals that Commander Martinus Meytens had an octant in Batavia in 1769. His estate also included two sets of mathematical instruments, an astrolabe and a terrestrial globe. Cornelis Douwes again drew attention to one existing method for determining 'latitude at a time other than midday'. This method consisted of taking two altitude measurements of the sun, one before and one after the meridian, noting the lapse of time between the two measurements. This method was published in 1754 but only began to be used regularly in the 1760s because by then the octant had proved satisfactory.[6]

---

[4] Bruijn, *Observaties*, pp. 7–9.
[5] Davids, *Zeewezen en wetenschap*, pp. 165–77; Mörzer Bruyns, *Het schip recht door zee*, pp. 15–17; Crone, *Cornelis Douwes*, pp. 33–42; a survey in Jonkers, *North by Northwest*, pp. 202–56.
[6] Davids, *Zeewezen en wetenschap*, pp. 175–6 and 228–36; Mörzer Bruyns, *Het schip recht*

Finally, in the second half of the eighteenth century it became possible to measure longitude at sea. In theory there were two methods for doing this, but the practical application of both of them was only possible after John Harrison invented a seaworthy chronometer. This allowed comparison of the time at the location of the ship to be compared to the time at some fixed location. The difference indicated longitude. The fairly general adoption of the chronometer began abroad not much before 1780. The other method was to determine the longitude by lunar observation and then comparing that to previously calculated tables of the altitude of the moon which were compiled in 1760 and published in the new *Nautical Almanac* from 1766.⁷ Although the octant was inadequate for taking these new sightings, by then the new sextant had come into use. It allowed measurement of angles up to 120 degrees and was also more accurate. It began to become standard issue around 1770. These innovations were largely British and French in origin. A sextant was a very expensive instrument. The type the Company bought in 1788 cost 150 guilders.

Information about these new methods only gradually began to appear in Dutch books for ship's officers, in the 1780s. Both the instruments and the tables were very expensive. Although the Navy did already experiment with them, better information became available in the Republic in 1788 when, in imitation of the British and French publications, an *Almanach ten dienste der zeelieden* (The Sailor's Almanac), which contained the essential astronomical information, was published. Nevertheless, determination of longitude using lunar observation was only used sporadically before 1795 on board both Company and Navy ships. In the Republic people certainly kept their eye on international developments but tended to be cautious and were not quick to make use of their practical applications. A few naval captains, among them Jan Olphert Vaillant, were quickly and acutely aware of the implications of these new developments and wrote urging for their introduction. Their writings created an impression, and then reinforced it, that the Republic was lagging behind.⁸

Unquestionably, the Company had hastened to embrace the use of the octant and had added it to the *Generale Lijst* (General List). It took rather longer, until 1788 in fact, to introduce the chronometer and the sextant. Calculation of longitude was still done by using variation, the angle between true and magnetic north on the compass. It became easier to make these calculations with the arrival of the large pelorus and azimuth compasses in 1747. Compass roses and needles were also improved. The men behind these improvements, which they invented themselves, were De Marre and Martens, examiners of the Amsterdam Chamber. After crossing the Equator, before which a zone had been plotted out

---

door zee, pp. 20–1, 64–6 and 91–4. Meytens' inventory in The Hague, NA, VOC 6464, 12.5.1769.

⁷ For the struggle to find the best method for determining longitude, see D. Sobel, *Longitude* (New York, 1995).

⁸ Dörr, *De kundige kapitein*, pp. 115–17.

on a chart, known as the *wagenweg* (cart track), it was essential to use variation. The compass roses were regularly adjusted. Both men also produced steering compasses with much less deviation.[9]

Around a decade earlier, the Zealand Chamber had run tests for making a better determination of position by using an apparatus which measured the speed of the ship, which meant that the distance covered could be fixed. The device could also be used to measure current which would give an improved reading of the course kept. If their ideas proved to be sufficiently accurate, both inventors could expect a reward of a maximum of *f.* 12,000. These apparatuses were tested on the outward- and homeward-bound voyages of the *Westkapelle* and the *Huis te Rensburg* between 1731 and 1735, but eventually it turned out that they did not offer enough improvement to make them worth using, or for the inventors to reap the monetary reward.[10]

The complaint made by Commander George Christiansz Hartz about his first mate and the latter's resistance in Table Bay in 1765 offers a glimpse of navigation in practice. Hartz criticized his second-in-command claiming that not only 'had he on various occasions made very grave mistakes in the noon reckoning of the meridian, but even in the computing of the azimuths and sightings of the horizon'; but after that the commander knew for certain that this was caused either by 'ignorance or by enormous carelessness'. The first mate sprang to his own defence claiming that these were not mistakes 'in the determination of the latitude or in the sightings, only in the calculation of the meridian, which could happen to even the greatest mathematician'.[11]

The Company directors finally got around to revising the navigational equipment on their ships around 1740 and during the years that followed, precisely the period in which the design and the construction of their ships were the centre of attention. A whole range of matters was subject to critical scrutiny. Initially the chief instigator of these changes was Van Imhoff. The appointment of two experienced examiners in Amsterdam in 1743 and 1745 was not a coincidence. Both men were immediately given plenty of scope to put forward their ideas about what should be improved. One extremely important part of their work is discussed later in this chapter. After this period, reforms relating to official policy about navigation ground to a halt. The examiners, such as Jan de Boer around 1770, only tackled certain aspects of the work of the commanders and ship's officers. Decisions about the construction and introduction of the three-decker, which was a generally accepted type of ship internationally for sailing to Asia, were either postponed or not taken at all. It was only at the

---

[9] Davids, *Zeewezen en wetenschap*, pp. 178–208; Mörzer Bruyns, *Het schip recht door zee*, pp. 21–8 and 45–8; Jonker, *North by Northwest*, pp. 185–6. An overview of the required equipment is in Gawronski, *De equipagie*, pp. 225–51.

[10] Davids, *Zeewezen en wetenschap*, pp. 138–41; *DAS* II, nos. 2861 and 2958, and III, nos. 6862 and 6957.

[11] Cape Town Archives, resolutions C. of P., 11.6.1765 (www.tanap.net); *DAS* II, no. 3864.

end of the 1780s that a new period dawned in which genuine changes affecting both the ships and navigation were introduced.[12] A decision was finally made about the three-decker; packet boats were introduced into service; and finally the Company adopted an entirely new sort of ship, the pink. New innovations in navigation were also given a chance. Examples were given earlier and further examples follow.

Commanders and their Navigational Instruments

To assist them in their navigation, commanders and their officers had at their disposal instruments which were set down in the *Generale Lijst* and issued for the voyage by the *Heren Zeventien* according to ancient custom. Occasionally, if the examiners put forward some proposals, this list was adjusted and new inventions were accepted. However, after 1675 it was over half a century, in 1731, before any new, admittedly not very drastic, alteration was made to the *Generale Lijst*. De Marre and Martens saw to it that the revision which took place in 1747 was far more significant. The octant made its appearance, as did the compasses, noted above, in their modified form. Their price and number were always noted on the list and the commander had to sign when he received the chest of instruments, which was brought on board shortly before departure. After arrival in the East, the chest was taken ashore and only returned on board just before the ship was due to sail on the return voyage. Each Chamber had its own instruments bought from regular suppliers. The list was accompanied by instructions about how everything should be treated. For example, the steel needles of the compasses were not to be allowed to rust. Should this happen, they had to be replaced. The charts should be kept in tin cylinders and annotations could be made only in red chalk or pencil. Use of ink was absolutely forbidden.[13]

The *Generale Lijst* of 1747 was never revised but it was adjusted on certain points, for instance, the number of octants available. In 1788, one of the three octants had to make way for a sextant. A copy of the *Almanach ten dienste der zeelieden*, in which the standard meridian was given as that of Tenerife in the Canary Islands, was always aboard. Furthermore, from that time a 'large sea watch/chronometer' worth $f.$ 112 was part of the standard equipment. This means of measuring time had been introduced by the small Danish *Asiatisk Compagnie* four years earlier. The VOC was always insistent that on account of variation the compasses had to be constantly adjusted. Navigators were not to wait until a compass showed that it was 5 degrees out. Adjustment had to be made after it deviated only a quarter of a degree. On the voyage to Asia, even a quarter of a degree made a big difference. In the Channel, it was always essential

---

[12] Dillo, *De nadagen*, ch. 8.
[13] The Hague, NA, VOC 221, 28.3.1731, 308, 2.5.1746 and 14.329 (1747); Schilder and Mörzer Bruyns, 'Navigatie' III, pp. 191–225; Gawronski, *De equipagie*, pp. 225–31.

to allow for a large degree of deviation. Even an experienced commander such as David Brouwer sailed into the 'wrong channel', that is, into the Bristol Channel, in 1724, and Samuel Wanjon made the same mistake again in 1753. The same almost happened to Maarten Hakker in 1771 because he had not adjusted the compasses in time. Failure to make the adjustments cost commanders fines.[14]

Research into ship's logs, such as that carried out by Davids for his 1986 study, reveals that on Company ships, both those sailing to and from Asia and those engaged in the intra-Asian trade, the noon meridian was always taken and, after 1760, the latitude at some other time of the day as well. Davids' study also shows that there was an increasing tendency to make the first observation of the sun in the North Sea directly after departure. Davids has also calculated how large the error of deviation in latitudes was. Erroneous estimation was not much higher than 3 degrees, even on the long route to the Cape of Good Hope. This is certainly a long way short of the margin of 10 degrees which is sometimes mentioned in the literature. When this is compared to the state of affairs in the third quarter of the eighteenth century there was a considerable improvement in accuracy.[15]

The *Generale Lijst* indicated which instruments were available for use on board and sometimes this information is confirmed by finds in wrecks. The *pleinschaal*, a sort of slide rule, with five scales, had been on the list since 1731. One was found on the wreck of the *Hollandia* which went down in 1743. On board there was also at least one octant, which had been specially purchased in 1741. Also found in the wreck was a fragment of a cross-staff. Thanks to its very greatly improved sights, this instrument was still in use in 1791. The lid of a tin chart cylinder was brought up from the wreck of the *Vliegend Hart* (1728), as were a great many other items: two complete *pleinschalen* and segments of a third, eighteen pairs of compasses or parts of these, sections of two cross-staffs, and a few leads from sounding lines, one of which weighed 10 kilos.[16] Navigational instruments are sometimes found among the possessions of commanders who died during the voyage. Despite the fact that the Company provided the equipment, apparently some commanders also felt the need to have their own personal instruments. The inventories of their estates bear witness to the devotion of

---

[14] The Hague, NA, VOC 117, 16.10.1724, 134, 10.10.1771, 222, 13.4.1772, 308, 9.8.1753 and 14.329 (various orders); Davids, *Zeewezen en wetenschap*, pp. 189–90. See also E. Gøbel, 'The Danish Asiatic Company's Voyages to China, 1732–1833', *Scandinavian Economic History Review* XXVII (1979), pp. 1–23, see p. 9.

[15] Davids, *Zeewezen en Wetenschap*, pp. 166, 234–8 and 241–3.

[16] W.F.J. Mörzer Bruyns, 'Navigatie-instrumenten van de zeebodem 16^e tot 19^e eeuw', *Tijdschrift voor Geschiedenis Geneeskunde, Natuurwetenschappen, Wiskunde en Techniek* 10 (1987), pp. 263–82; W.F.J. Mörzer Bruyns and A.J. van der Horst, 'Navigational Equipment from 't Vliegend Hart (1735)', *International Journal of Nautical Archaeology* 35 (2006), pp. 319–25.

their owners to their profession. The purchases made by officers in Pieter Holm's shop, as described in Chapter 10, likewise confirm this supposition.[17]

In 1716, Commander Maljaard had a cross-staff and a book of sea charts, but when the inventory was being compiled the junior merchant present remarked that this was the property of the Company. In 1739, Van de Woestijne had a cross-staff with five transoms, a *pleinschaal*, four rulers, four pairs of compasses and a binnacle, the wooden housing in which a mariner's compass could be hung. The first octant is mentioned among the items in Ruis' estate in 1759. In the same year Elsevier owned a cylinder with charts. Much later, in 1792, Forster's octant fetched *f*. 13 at auction in Batavia. All the lists mention a telescope. An astrolabe, such as that owned by Meytens in 1769, and other obsolete instruments were things of the past.

After 1747, commanders always had a Company octant at their disposal on board but this privilege did not apply to the ship's officers. The VOC only purchased these in greater quantity later. Before a second octant was provided in 1762, Holm had already sold nine to third mates, petty officers and other crew members. Three of these men sailed for the Amsterdam Chamber and two for Hoorn; the Chambers which employed the others are not mentioned. Holm had sold the first examples to Company mariners as early as 1754. The following two years he sold three, almost one after the other. The ship's officers who sailed to the West Indies also showed an interest in octants.

It is clear that the commander and officers were equipped according to the requirements and the possibilities available at their time, but they were never the first to have these pieces of equipment in the world of international shipping. The examples quoted validate this claim, as does the recent literature. This raises the question of where the story of antiquated navigation techniques of the VOC in the final decades of the eighteenth century originated.

Stagnation in Charting the Sea

During the 1730s great anxiety reigned about the precariousness of shipping. The measures to improve the situation which were taken in the 1740s brought some improvement. However, shipping disasters were caused not only by the quality of the ships. The standard of navigation was another very important factor. In a memorandum which he wrote in 1741, Martens, then a reader in navigation in Amsterdam, put his finger on the principal weaknesses and he managed to win the support of a few of the Amsterdam directors. No sooner had he been appointed examiner, at the same time as De Marre, than a whole

---

[17] For the inventories of estates of deceased commanders, see Chapter 12, note 10. For the purchasers of instruments, see Mörzer Bruyns, *Schip recht door zee*, pp. 94 and 165–71. Davids, in *Zeewezen en wetenschap*, describes how the instruments were used (pp. 117, 156–7, 220, 275 and 395).

series of innovations was set in motion. The *Generale Lijst* of 1747 was the result.[18]

A few matters also changed in relation to the sea charts. De Marre was able to convince the directors that the existing charts of the waters where the Company operated and the sailing instructions (rutters) for this area should be published. This became Volume 6 of the *Nieuwe groote lichtende Zee-Fakkel* (New, Enlarged Luminous Sea Torch), published by the firm Van Keulen. This volume appeared in 1753 and the *Heren Zeventien* immediately dispatched several copies to Batavia, with some of those to be forwarded to other settlements. Before this, commanders had only been provided with manuscript charts. On arrival, they were required to be scrupulous in handing in these 'parchment charts'. For instance, in 1736 Gerrit Klinkhamer returned ten too few and had to pay more than *f.* 24.

Commanders and the ship's officers were now admonished to note down any improvements carefully and to send these back to the Republic.[19] Greater attention was also paid to hydrographic measurements of Asian coasts. Nevertheless, the later editions of Volume 6 of the *Zee-Fakkel* showed no signs of revision, an important oversight. In his work, De Marre had absorbed the latest British and French geographical findings, but after his efforts this work stagnated. No great effort was made to ensure that the manuscript charts of particular waters which were being handed out along with the *Zee-Fakkel* had been brought up to date properly. After a great period of prosperity in the 1740s and 1750s, the cartography business in Batavia slipped into a gradual decline. The closure of the *Académie de Marine*, the dismissal of the instructor in mathematics and navigation attached to it, and the neglect of the cartography office were other nails in the coffin.[20]

After the publication of the *Zee-Fakkel*, the VOC did not trouble to make any further annotations to its charts, additions which could have recorded the great progress which French and English hydrographers had made in charting the Indian Ocean and other Asian waters. The pioneer publication in this field in France was D'Après de Mannevilette's *Routier des côtes des Indes orientales et de la Chine* in 1745. Like De Marre, D'Après de Mannevilette had been a sailor and he knew many of the areas he described from his personal experience of sailing them. He also combed countless ship's logs for additional accurate information. Most importantly, his atlas was constantly kept up to date. Many inaccuracies and mistakes in the Dutch maps of Pieter Goos and Johannes van Keulen,

---

[18] W.F.J. Mörzer Bruyns, *Konst der stuurlieden. Stuurmanskunst en maritieme cartografie in acht portretten, 1540–2000* (Amsterdam/Zutphen, 2001), p. 57; Davids, *Zeewezen en wetenschappen*, p. 350.

[19] *Nederlandsch-Indisch Plakaatboek* VI, 6.3 and 6.4.1753; D. de Vries et al. (eds), *The Van Keulen Cartography Amsterdam 1680–1885* (Alphen aan den Rijn, 2005), p. 137; DAS III, no. 6964.

[20] Schooneveld-Oosterling, *Generale Missiven* XII, pp. 176 and 383.

which the French Company had often used earlier, were corrected. The outline of islands such as Madagascar and the Maldives was reliably reproduced for the first time, and the coastline of eastern Africa was sometimes adjusted by as many as 15 to 60 nautical miles. The west coast of Australia was moved further east and the islands of Java and Sumatra were given different positions on the chart. The position of the Sunda Strait was also altered. When he sailed into this strait in 1766, Commander Meytens had run onto submerged rocks which projected further out from the coast than had been marked on his chart. It was possible to free the *Vredelust* but she had to undergo very extensive repairs on Onrust. In 1771, the *Aschat* under Commander Jan Abel hit an uncharted submerged rock off the south coast of Java: 'God knows how many ships which sailed past here in the east monsoon have foundered on this submerged rock', wrote one of the passengers on board. Abroad, hydrographic work pressed on. Encouraged by the directors of the various companies, many new charts were produced, but the VOC turned its back on progress. It even paid no attention when a much shorter route to Ceylon was recorded on a chart in 1767. Shortly afterwards, the English East India Company lost no time in adopting the hydrographic work of Alexander Dalrymple.[21]

In light of this attitude, it is not surprising that the data collected about the Indian Ocean by James Cook and other explorers never or only much later appeared on the Company charts. In 1774, as the south coast of Java loomed up and looked different from the way it appeared on the chart, Stavorinus was angry that he had not been given an accurate map. A situation like this was absolutely unnecessary. Remarkably, the cartographers of the Chambers of Amsterdam and Zealand did include the superior French and British cartographic information in their charts – for instance, about the waters around Britain.[22]

Innovations in Navigation around 1790

Experiences such as those recorded by Stavorinus, reports that as early as the 1770s lunar observation was being used on some ships of the English East India Company, and critical opinions expressed by such men as Vaillant and De Jong have given rise to the idea that the VOC held fast to obsolete methods of navigation.[23] The impression which emerges is that innovations were not introduced

---

[21] Ph. Haudrère, *La Compagnie Française des Indes au XVIIIe siècle (1719–1795)* (Paris, 1989), pp. 573 and 661–9; Ph. Haudrère, 'The 'Compagnie des Indes' and Maritime Matters', in J.R. Bruijn and F.S. Gaastra (eds), *Ships, Sailors and Spices. East India Companies and Their Shipping in the 16th, 17th and 18th Centuries* (Amsterdam, 1993), pp. 81–97; Sutton, *Lords of the East*, p. 108. For Meytens, see The Hague, NA, VOC 3250, fol. 462; for Abel, see Seffinga, 'Theodorus Bergsma', p. 62.

[22] Schilder and Mörzer Bruyns, 'Navigatie' III, pp. 198–207; Wilcocke, *Voyages to the East Indies* II, pp. 111–12.

[23] Sutton, *Lords of the East*, p. 106; Davids, *Zeewezen en wetenschap*, p. 192.

quickly enough. We have seen that the new possibilities for determining longitude and latitude were known to the VOC and permission was given for these to be adopted in stages. Nevertheless, many of the charts of the territory of the Company were hopelessly out of date, and not all the sailing routes were as efficient as they might have been. However, it should also be noted that it took the English quite a while to master the method of lunar observation. Certainly Dutch commanders and their contemporaries were not haunted by any idea that their techniques of navigation were imperfect. The idea that they might have been lagging somewhat behind the latest and best practices had more to do with the sometimes tardy introduction of new techniques, especially combined with the almost inevitable faults found in the voyages themselves by Company authorities.

As early as the seventeenth century the Company had begun to issue instructions or *zeilage-orders* to its commanders. In these the routes which had to be sailed were described in ever greater detail, with the troughs and shoals which could be met and the dangers which might loom noted. There were the tried and tested instructions to sail to Java in May and those for the autumn. The commanders were also provided with instructions which explained the patterns of the monsoon winds. In 1783 the Company issued an explicit order that 'at all times' they had to sail through the Sunda Strait. The directive was revolutionary in comparison to its predecessors. The last of these dated from 1768 and was largely concerned with the changes in variation and in adjusting compasses. The 1783 order was brief, only eight pages, short on details and unquestionably explicit. The complicated crossing of the Equator was not even mentioned so it might in fact be considered to have been a break with the past. However, in 1785 and again in 1789, the Company remained resolute about the use of its own charts; but in 1789 there was at least a discussion among the Chambers about the question of whether or not it was really advisable to follow the sailing instructions as strictly as had formerly been done. This applied especially to the direct route to China. The Amsterdam Chamber voiced its faith in the expertise of its commanders and officers and wanted to allow them some leeway, but a few of the smaller Chambers insisted that a set course was essential. As a result, no decision was made to leave the plotting of the course free, but deviations, if they could be supported by argumentation, were permitted. This discussion also demonstrates that, generally speaking, people were satisfied with the 1783 sailing instructions.[24]

The VOC could not be called a pioneer in innovations in navigation, and indeed to have played such a role would have been risky for a business with such far-flung shipping. Finally, around 1790, the Company did take a number of measures which signalled its approval of the full introduction of approved

---

[24] The Hague, NA, VOC 199, April and 3.11.1789 (with appendices), 223, 25.4.1785; Loeve, 'De driedekker', ch. IV.

techniques and instruments. This series of measures was rounded off in 1793 with the introduction of a tougher examination for officers and newly appointed commanders in the use of octants and sextants, determination of latitude apart from the sighting taken at noon, using the chronometer, and fixing longitude by lunar observation. By that time, guidelines had already been issued to the effect that observations using the sextant had to be noted in the ship's log. In 1788, the Company purchased the *Almanach* for the first time. In fact it bought forty-eight copies. This move was accompanied by the introduction of the first two sextants, which were very expensive, as we have already seen. In the same year, the first commanders were issued with chronometers, which their Danish colleagues had had since 1784. These were silver watches with a second hand, at *f*. 80 or more per watch, intended to be used to determine longitude at sea. They were supplied by Frederik Louis Dupuis, watchmaker of Amsterdam. These purchases represented a substantial investment in instruments, and various commanders heartily embraced all these new methods to determine their position at sea. Willem Smalt is just one example. He sailed on the packet boat the *Luchtbol* in 1793. Another was Gerard Ewout Overbeek who commanded the *Castor* in 1794. There is evidence that the directors were occupied with the introduction of modern methods of determining longitude almost to the end of the life of the Company in the resolutions of the *Heren Zeventien* of 2 May 1795. Even though the Batavian Republic had been established, the directors were concerned with the fact that longitude could not be determined on the *Drechterland*, because the instruments and books required to do this had not been dispatched to the Cape. Despite this, Kornelis van Eps had arrived in Texel from the Cape on 2 August 1794, in the normal sailing time of around 110 days.[25]

A Closer Look at the Route to China

The passage of VOC ships between the Republic and Asia was not as fast as that of the other East India companies. It is difficult to make a properly balanced assessment because each company had its own usages, or there is simply not enough detailed information. However, shipping to China does offer a good opportunity to compare the VOC with its competitors. In the eighteenth century each East India company sent ships to Canton to fetch tea. There was no monopoly on this trade and there was also the opportunity to buy up other goods such as porcelain and silk. In the volume of its China trade the VOC was second only to the English East India Company. This trade underwent spectacular developments, especially in the second half of the eighteenth century. In the period around 1775 often as many as four VOC ships took part. The

---

[25] Davids, 'Commentaar', pp. 124–31; De Vries *et al.*, *The Van Keulen Cartography*, pp. 156–8; Mörzer Bruyns, *Het schip recht door zee*, p. 28; *DAS* II, nos. 4775 and 4749, and III, no. 8359. For the *Drechterland*, see The Hague, NA, VOC 209, 2.5.1795.

Swedish and Danish East India Companies were also active on this route and together their ships made nearly as many voyages as those of the VOC. The time they took to sail home provides a good basis for comparison. Leaving out a call at the Cape, an average voyage home lasted 189 days. If the stop in Table Bay was included, this rose to 203 days. On average, on a slightly shorter route, the VOC ships needed 225 days.

This discrepancy of almost three weeks raises some questions. Were the Scandinavian ships much better or was their navigation superior? Furthermore, the Danes and Swedes lost fewer ships. There is no unequivocal answer. The VOC generally put its newest vessels on this route and therefore these ships were sailing directly to Canton on their first or second voyages. They were among the largest ships on the route and certainly they had more cargo capacity than the Scandinavian ships. Perhaps this made them cumbersome and hence slower. When it was appointing its commanders, the Company did not pay particular attention to their experience of China, but navigation in the South China Sea and making the best use of the monsoons made great demands on their expertise. By far the greatest majority of commanders made only one voyage to Canton in that capacity. The directors of the two Scandinavian companies had other ideas about this matter. They had their ships sail to China – after all the main interest of both companies – with the same commanders and the same crews for years on end. This strategy allowed them to bring the tea to Copenhagen and Gothenburg increasingly earlier in the year, in June and July. This was helped by ensuring they left Canton in good time.[26] In contrast, the VOC received its tea at ever later dates, between July and September, because its ships were not made ready for the voyage home promptly enough and consequently they faced much worse weather conditions on the voyage.

Apart from the less efficient handling of shipping and the tardy arrival of the tea on the market, the negative result of the comparison between the VOC and the Scandinavian companies is also explicable in the light of the differences in their policies of appointment of commanders. What does such a comparison turn up? There were three VOC commanders who made four consecutive voyages to Canton: Kornelis Kuiper, Jan Och and Wopke Popta, all of them appointed by the Amsterdam Chamber, who sailed this route in the 1760s and 1770s. Och and Popta always sailed with each other and conspired in the falsifying of the log books mentioned by Stavorinus. With the exception of one voyage, these three commanders always returned in July and on average they made the voyage more quickly than their Scandinavian counterparts did. Their third voyage lasted only 180, 183 and 191 days respectively. The same more or less holds true for the few other commanders who made the voyage two or three times. Kornelis Pietersen was another of these China specialists. His five voyages home, the last two of

---

[26] T. Veltschow, 'Voyages of the Danish Asiatic Company to India and China 1772–1792', *Scandinavian Economic History Review* XX (1972), pp. 133–52, see pp. 144–7; Gøbel, 'The Danish Asiatic Company's Voyages', pp. 13 and 17–19.

them from Canton, were all shorter than average.[27] Probably his appointment as examiner in practical seamanship by the Amsterdam Chamber in 1779 was a very good choice. Experience on a route was important and it often translated into swifter and safer voyages. Hence, there was not much wrong with the navigational qualities of the commanders, even when these are compared to those of their foreign colleagues.

Towards another Type of Commander: The 1780s and 1790s

In the 1760s a deluge of new regulations began to pour forth. The commanders had to work with them and were aware that their obedience to them could always be checked. Their freedom of movement was constantly being restricted. There was some let up only in the slavish following of the prescribed routes, a matter which has already been discussed. The issuing of rules never stopped and sometimes it was extreme. For instance, in 1783 it was peremptorily ordered that all departing ships had to carry oil on board which could be poured on heavy seas to moderate the swell. This rule had already been obligatory on the voyage home for some time. In 1784, the title of commander was changed to that of captain. The first mate became a captain-lieutenant, the second mate could call himself lieutenant and the third mate sub-lieutenant. Without any further ado the old ranking system, which had caused such a fuss in 1742, was abolished.

By the 1780s, trying to recruit among the Company's own men produced fewer and fewer men who were suitable officer material. As mentioned earlier, the various Chambers had to rely on a rising number of foreigners. The situation forced the Company to look for candidates for the higher echelons of command outside its own men. The sailors it found were often those who had had plenty of experience in other branches of marine business. Wietse de Boer had already made five voyages as first mate and eight as master in other branches of the merchant navy when he was appointed captain by the VOC in 1789. Some men stepped over to the Company after they had already been to the East at least once on a chartered merchant ship. Andries Laurens Kanters had been at sea since he was a boy and had visited the West Indies and later Batavia and Ceylon as first mate when he became a captain in 1789. Uilke Barends from Heerenveen in the province of Friesland had a similar background. Dirk Peek, who came from the north of Germany, already had thirty-one years' experience

---

[27] A survey of the voyages (1763–1793) is in Liu Yong, *The Dutch East India Tea Trade*, pp. 179–203; Davids, *Zeewezen en wetenschap*, pp. 205 and 399; *DAS* I, 99–103; *DAS* III, nos. 7620, 7681, 7753 and 7831 (Kuiper), 7780, 7859, 7931 and 8008 (Och), 7779, 7858, 7929 and 8007 (Popta); see also nos. 7930, 7982 and 8053 (Johan van Voorst) and nos. 7652, 7703, 7739, 7803 and 7880.

35. The *Vrijburg*. This porcelain plate decorated in polychrome with a drawing of the Zealand ship the Vrijburg bears the text Chpist Schooneman oppr stuerman opt schip *Vrijburg* ter reede Wanrho in China int jaar 1756 (Christian Schoneman first mate on the ship the Vrijburg in the roads at Wanrho in China in the year 1756). Christian Schoneman came from the Danish island of Lolland and began to sail for the Admiralty in Zealand in 1747 and soon afterwards joined the Zealand Chamber. He sailed to Batavia as first mate in 1754. In 1756 he sailed to Canton on the Vrijburg but died shortly afterwards, just before he arrived back in Batavia. The plate eventually arrived in Zealand.

at sea in 1789.[28] As we saw earlier, Klaas Keuken came from the whaling fleet. Not all who applied were signed on, indiscriminately. Some were turned down.

The chartering of fully fitted-out and manned private merchantmen was an emergency measure adopted during the Fourth Anglo-Dutch War, but after the war was over this sort of ship did not disappear, which sometimes had unexpected consequences. The Company was required to insure these ships. In 1782

---

[28] The Hague, NA, VOC 223, 10.12.1790, 297, 2.4, 30.7 and 17.9.1789, and 298, 1.7.1790.

for a voyage to Batavia the premium was 14 per cent of the total value of the ship and its cargo but by 1784 half that rate was sufficient. Up to the 1780s the ships had never been insured. The authorities in Batavia had always assumed that the stowing of the cargo was the unalterable responsibility of the ship's officers; after all they possessed the requisite expertise. Proper stowage was very complicated work because all sorts of matters had to be thought of depending on the composition of the cargo. In 1787 six commanders of chartered ships asked to be excused from this responsibility. They argued that they were unacquainted with the weights and volumes of Asian products, let alone the interactions of all sorts of fragrant spices with each other. They preferred to leave the drawing up of a stowage plan to others who were better versed in and more experienced with the products. Jan Koenraad Haverkamp put the problem into words in 1790: 'I have never had the opportunity to stow a Company ship and I need the help of somebody who has handled such matters more on several occasions.'[29]

A steadily growing number of officers came from outside the Company and obviously their familiarity with shipping to Asia fell short of that of colleagues who had spent their whole career in the service of the Company. In 1789, the Zealand Chamber complained that it could not find officers who were suitable for promotion to captain. In the winter of 1790–1791, when three of its ships got into difficulties and foundered shortly after they had sailed from Texel Roads, the Amsterdam Chamber wondered if there was something lacking in knowledge of navigating the North Sea. The ships involved were three small ones which the Chamber had purchased. Shortly after setting out, the *Valk* under George Gottlieb Hebner sailed well off course and ended up in Glückstadt at the mouth of the Elbe in northern Germany. The ship was only able to sail from there four months later, but shortly afterwards, on 23 February 1791, she came to grief on a sandbank off Yarmouth in England. Hebner had fallen overboard and drowned just before this happened. Most of the crew were rescued but the *Valk* continued to drift around helplessly for some days. On 26 November 1790, the *Negotie* under Herman Driesman ran aground off Texel and was battered to pieces. Five days after the *Valk* was lost, the hooker the *Zaanstroom* ran aground off Pointe de Barfleur in Normandy. Moreover, on 23 January 1791 the *Meerwijk* under Jan Jobst Droop had collided with a British ship in the Downs roadstead, between the North and South Foreland in the Channel. Repairing the damage took a considerable time.[30]

In May 1791 the Amsterdam Chamber came up with a proposal to have a packet boat cruise in the North Sea during the summer months carrying on

---

[29] The Hague, NA, VOC 3743 (OBP 1788), fol. 1171, 3766 (OBP 1789), fols 220–2, and 3826 (OBP 1790), fols 3711–12; D. van Hogendorp, *Stukken raakende den tegenwoordigen toestand der Bataafsche bezittingen in Oost-Indië en den handel op dezelve* (The Hague/Delft, 1801), pp. 131–2 and 269–70.

[30] The Hague, NA, VOC 298, 4.11.1790, and 299, 20.1, 3.2, 28.2, 7.3, 14.3, 23.6 and 30.6.1791; *DAS* II, nos. 4682, 4686, 4687 and 4692.

board officers who happened to be ashore waiting for new appointments. The small ship would perform all sorts of manoeuvres in the vicinity of shoals and currents. Initially the plan was judged too expensive but eventually, in 1793, Amsterdam was allowed to put it to the test. The Company thought up more measures which would ensure that it employed 'skilled and vigilant' men. Extra bonuses were introduced and the stipends were raised because the new policy of carrying the freight of private merchants meant that the trading opportunities of captains and lieutenants were more restricted. Consequently the latter complained that their earnings were too low. In the end the recognition rights and permitted trade goods of the officers were reduced in exchange for a bonus according to the amount of cargo space ceded. A captain received the sum of *f.* 370 per cubic foot, which meant that on a round-trip voyage to the Indies he would receive a sum of more than *f.* 1,000, and a captain-lieutenant would receive *f.* 450. The monthly stipend was then raised to *f.* 80, *f.* 100, or *f.* 125 according to whether it was a first, second or third voyage. The officers also received proportionally higher stipends. By that time, because it had become easier for naval officers to join the Company in 1792, there was no longer any question of a shortage of officers. The nub of the problem was professional skills. The Zealand Chamber was still complaining about this in 1794. The situation as far as the recruitment of the ordinary crew members was concerned steadily deteriorated. Out of sheer necessity, the Chambers had to be satisfied with every man or boy from whatever background.[31]

A sombre view of the future must have already taken root among the directors of the Zealand Chamber in 1786, if the name of a ship they bought is anything to go by. The ship in question was the hooker the *Surseance* (*Suspension of Payment*). Despite their apparent gloom, they still had new ideas about a cheaper but very practicable type of ship. In 1786, the Zealand Chamber had bought a pink, a ship which had won the approval of Udemans, the head of the shipyard. However, it was another eight years, in 1794, before the use of this sort of ship became widespread. The Chambers of Delft and Hoorn had been particularly awkward about this matter. In 1788, a packet-boat service had been introduced for the transport of people and the mail. These small, fast ships with copper-bottomed hulls maintained the connection with the East. Finally after years of discussions about the pros and cons of the matter, in 1794 it was decided that all ships, not just the packet boats, would have their hulls sheathed with copper plates. This reduced the amount of marine growth on the hull and increased the speed. The great decisiveness of the VOC in the 1790s is conspicuous, just as is the resoluteness it displayed about both its officers and its ships. To a very important degree, this was attributable to what was known as the Holland-Zeeland State Commission (*Hollands-Zeeuwse staatscommissie*) which had begun to intervene in the running of the Company in 1790. As the

[31] Dillo, *De nadagen*, 138–40.

Company was mired in enormous financial problems by this time, it could do nothing but accept this paternalistic meddling by the government.[32]

In the meantime, the shipping business showed no signs of flagging and absorbed all the changes and innovations. New captains, captain-lieutenants and lieutenants continued to be appointed. The names of all the naval officers, as the Company referred to them by this time, who were serving in eastern seas or in land jobs were listed in the annual *Naamboekje* (Name Booklet) published by the *Hoge Regering* in Batavia. According to the 1790 booklet, in March of the previous year there had been sixty-six captains, fifty-five captain-lieutenants, fifty lieutenants and 103 sub-lieutenants, a total of 274 men. The logs of ships were still conscientiously checked and reports continued to be made. One such report was about the losses of the *Valk* and the *Zaanstroom*, discussed on 30 June 1791, which acquitted the officers on both ships of any blame. In 1794, Kikkert and De Hartog,[33] examiners of the Amsterdam Chamber, went through the logs of five East Indiamen with a fine-toothed comb and confirmed that they had kept to their sailing instructions satisfactorily, had taken part in the convoy with an escort of two warships in an orderly fashion and had obeyed the regulations about turning over the gunpowder so that it would be evenly dry, the use of the fire hose and other matters. Only one captain was denied his bonus, because he had not observed the determination of longitude properly. Both examiners examined at length the logs of the *Leiden* under Teunis Groen and the *Drechterland* under Kornelis van Eps, which had come in on 2 August 1794, the last two East Indiamen ever to reach the Republic directly.[34] After this, the war forced various captains to seek refuge in neutral foreign harbours. Other ships were captured and taken as prizes, first by the French and later by the British. In June 1795, the *Surseance* and seven other ships were taken as prizes by the British off St Helena. On her way to Britain, this ominously named ship foundered. Her last captain, Diedrich Wiese, a man from Bremen, survived and, after the end of the period of the French occupation of the Netherlands, he fulfilled a number of administrative functions in such places as Delft.

---

[32] Dillo, *De nadagen*, pp. 71, 164, 166–96; Moree, 'Met vriend die God geleide'; *DAS* II, no. 4557, and III, no. 8386.

[33] See K. Zandvliet, 'Adriaen de Lelies portret van de VOC-examinator Hendrik de Hartog, 1790', *Bulletin Rijksmuseum* 47, no. 1 (1999), pp. 45–52.

[34] The Hague, NA, VOC 299, 30.6.1791, and 302, 28.5 and 25.9.1794; *Naamboekje* 1790, 38–49; *DAS* III, nos. 8354 and 8359; Van Eyck van Heslinga, *Van Compagnie*, pp. 41–9.

17

The English East India Company and Other Companies: Dutch Commanders in a Broader Perspective

Although there were great similarities, there were great differences as well among the commanders of the five European East India Companies which dominated shipping to Asia for long stretches during the eighteenth century. This comparison concentrates on these five, leaving out a few of the more ephemeral Companies. Whether employed by the English, French, Danish, Swedish or Dutch Company, and whether called *commander*, *captain*, *capitaine*, *kaptajn*, or *capitaine*, all of these men formed an elite group in the world of shipping. Sailing to Asia was always imbued with a special atmosphere, compounded of long voyages, priceless cargoes and high earnings. In all five businesses, the majority of the ships' commanders were recruited from within their own circles. Men worked their way up through the ranks to achieve the highest position, but their social origins and the framework in which they reached the top could be very different in the five Companies.

It goes without saying that earning money was an essential facet of working as a commander and of course all the Companies paid their commanders a monthly stipend. In the English East India Company (EIC) the monthly stipend was £10 or *f.* 120, and this sum was supplemented by various bonuses and the income to be made from transporting passengers. However, in all the Companies the main part of a commander's income was derived from their own trade in commodities. The large sums which a commander had to pay out to obtain his command had to be earned back many times over. The regulations governing such activities were very similar but, whereas the VOC allotted a number of chests, the EIC allocated certain proportions of the ship's tonnage.

All commanders were issued with rutters and sailing instructions by their superiors. The principal destinations in Asia ranged from offices or factories scattered along the Indian coast, to Canton and Batavia. For the most part, the routes on the voyages out and back home did mirror each other, but there were some differences. It was only in the second half of the eighteenth century that ships other than those of the Dutch Company called in at Table Bay. The other

Companies preferred to put in at St Helena on the voyage home, but some also called at Ascension Island which offered the crews food in the form of pigeons and tortoises, but no drinking water. The English ships and those of the French, Danish and Swedish Companies put in at Cadiz to take on silver for the voyage to Asia.

The English East India Company

It is likely that the commanders of the English East India Company who made multiple voyages made real fortunes. Unquestionably, command on one of its ships was worth a great deal of money to the holder of the post. Towards the end of the eighteenth century, between £8,000 and £10,000 was being paid for the privilege, in other words £. 10,000 or more. At least this was the arrangement for a maiden voyage on a particular ship, but it was not continued in subsequent seasons. Earlier in the century, the sums had been substantially lower. Jean Sutton estimates that the commander had already recouped his investment after two or at the most three voyages.

Once they had been appointed, the commanders were perfectly aware that it was up to them how many voyages they made because a command was held in perpetuity. This difference was because the English Company had a completely different system of ship procurement. The EIC in London did not own any ships but chartered them from very powerful ship owners in Blackwall on the Thames, who constructed ships specifically for the Asian routes. These ship's husbands, or the principal managing owners, controlled everything tightly in their own hands, particularly in the middle of the century, and regulated all the sailings as well as the appointing of commanders and other ship's officers. Nevertheless, the EIC had to give its consent to the appointment of a commander. In fact it could be said that some of the men appointed had actually been commanders from their cradles, if they happened to have been born into such East India shipping families as the Larkins and Wordsworths, which produced some of the best of them. Destined for a command from birth, they entered the service at an early age as midshipmen and served as mates until considered fit for a command. The Company was at the mercy of these groups and had to pay any price they cared to name. As a consequence, freight rates paid by the Company were always high, and reached their zenith around 1750. Nowhere else did an East India Company have to pay so much for its transport. Parliament and the Navy were worried about the situation and began to ask questions. Too many East Indiamen were being constructed and chartered, but freight rates remained high. However, it was only in 1783 that more competition in chartering was allowed, and it was 1796 before the system known as the 'hereditary bottoms', and with it the perpetual post of commander, was abolished. It has to be said that in the period 1700–1740, in the VOC system, in which the Company was both the builder and owner of its own ships, transport costs were very much the same as those of the EIC, but after 1740 the expenses faced by the EIC were higher than those the VOC had to contend with.[1]

An EIC commander was dependent on and bound to the Thames-side ship owners, which meant that money and the maintenance of good relations with this world were crucial if he was to receive a command. If a man had been given command of an East Indiaman during a voyage because of the death of a commander, this post was usually confirmed and continued after a financial settlement with any heirs. This system of appointments was only altered in 1796. Sometimes a sailor did climb up through the ranks to become a ship's officer, but the majority of these men were from the higher echelons of society or, as someone said in 1792, 'They were one and all gentlemen by education and family'. The men who were appointed commanders were expected to have made at least four voyages to Asia as a ship's officer, and without exception they were all Englishmen or Scots. There were no foreigners. In the second half of the eighteenth century there was a growing tendency to address East India captains as commanders, but in British historiography they have earned the nickname 'Lords of the East', or they have been described as 'those aristocrats of the world's mercantile marine'. After 1774, many of them were members of an exclusive professional association known as the Society of East India Commanders, which ran a welfare fund, represented the interests of the members, and also served as a monthly dining club which met at the Jerusalem Coffee House in London. The subscription fee was £50. Those who had a successful career often dreamed of later becoming a Blackwall ship owner.[2]

All the activities of the EIC and the other Companies were concentrated in one central place. Arriving and departing ships were loaded, unloaded and repaired in Deptford. January to March was the usual sailing period. The ships were armed and could carry from twelve to forty cannon. Although three-deckers were introduced early, in 1748, the EIC was relatively late in coppering its ships. The Royal Navy introduced this technique in 1761 and by 1782 all naval vessels were copper-bottomed, but, even at that stage, hardly any East Indiamen had coppered hulls. By 1790, when the VOC was still debating the issue, this situation had changed and a great many of the ships had been coppered.

The EIC issued regulations which governed the private trade of its crews. As time passed, the total amount of cargo space designated for this purpose

---

[1] J.R. Bruijn, 'Productivity, Profitability, and Costs of Private and Corporate Dutch Ship Owning in the Seventeenth and Eighteenth Centuries', in J.D. Tracy (ed.), *The Rise of Merchant Empires. Long-Distance Trade in the Early Modern World 1350–1750* (Cambridge, 1990), pp. 174–94, see pp. 189–91.

[2] Sutton, *Lords of the East*, pp. 53–64 and 77; H.V. Bowen, 'Privilege and Profit: Commanders of East Indiamen as Private Traders, Entrepreneurs and Smugglers, 1760–1813', *International Journal of Maritime History* XIX, no. 2 (2007), pp. 43–88, see pp. 44–5. For the names and careers of EIC officers, see A. Farrington, *A Biographical Index of East India Company Maritime Service Officers 1600–1834*, 2 vols (London, 1999).

increased sharply. At the beginning of the century, the allowance was still only 5 tons out and 3 tons home. By 1750 these allowances had been raised to 25 and 15 tons respectively. By the end of the century these amounts had quadrupled, which meant that approximately 12 per cent of the value of the return goods was in private hands by 1790. A commander had more or less half this private space for his own purposes.

On the voyage out, a multitude of assorted goods were loaded because the EIC relied on its crews to provide for the personal requirements of its personnel overseas. In fact, the goods they took with them differed very little from those taken and traded by their VOC colleagues, except that the cheese was from Cheshire. When they sailed on to Canton, the commanders were eager to be able to have several thousand pounds in silver with them which could be exchanged there for gold. On arrival in London, the Asian wares were auctioned off, as was the case with the other Companies, and the money raised from the sale of his goods went to the commander. However, everybody did their utmost to avoid these auctions of private goods, in the hope of earning more from direct sales. Tea was often offloaded in the Channel. An incident which occurred in 1783 gives a glimpse of how this was done. A cutter came alongside and asked: 'Well, Captain, how is tea?' There was some haggling about the price and then all the private tea was loaded onto the cutter. The battle against the import of non-authorized private goods also caused the EIC some headaches. There are vivid descriptions of how contraband goods were taken off even in Deptford. As in the VOC, being caught committing a serious breach of the rules meant suspension, not instant dismissal. In 1788, the rights of EIC merchants in the transportation of their commodities to and from Asia were expanded. The restrictions were lifted first on the voyage out, later on the voyage home. The VOC followed this example. The activities of the merchant Van Hoboken described in Chapter 5 illustrate this.[3]

Many commanders worked as genuine entrepreneurs who acted safely, responsibly and efficiently because of their own great interest in their ships. However, Bowen indicates that the command of a ship was not always 'an easy path to riches'. There were also men who failed. A few impoverished commanders petitioned the directors of the EIC for some relief from severe financial hardship, giving details of ill fortune, poor health, infirmity or unemployment, but these were very much a minority.[4]

The French *Compagnie des Indes*

Like the EIC, the *Compagnie des Indes* did not have foreigners among its ship's officers, in fact seven out of ten of them were Bretons, from St Malo in partic-

---

[3] Sutton, *Lords of the East*, pp. 65–75; Bowen, '"So Alarming an Evil"'.
[4] Bowen, 'Privilege and Profit', p. 80.

ular. The headquarters of the Company were in Lorient and the majority of its officers were recruited from a close network of well-to-do families with connections in trade and shipping. Very few came from naval families. Nevertheless, Company officers and their naval colleagues regularly transferred between services, either on a temporary or permanent basis. A trainee officer in Lorient was instructed ashore, after which he was given practical experience at sea for a period of time, for which he had to pay himself. Only after he had a few voyages behind him could he expect an appointment as a ship's officer. This training was greatly sought after. A captain personally looked for six to ten boys who wanted to make a voyage, so in fact the result was a fairly cohesive closed circle of officers with reciprocal links to each other, a completely different situation from that which prevailed in the VOC. There was also a full system of promotion. Captains were on average forty-two when they were given their first command. Thirty-eight was young. Unquestionably, the theoretical knowledge of the French ship's officers was greater than that of their VOC counterparts.[5]

In Lorient, the monthly stipend of a captain of the *Compagnie des Indes* was 200 *livres tournois* or about *f*. 170 (one *livre* = 17 *stuivers*). Besides this regular payment, he was also entitled to some small bonuses. His most important source of income was his possession of what was known as a *port-permis*, authorized private cargo but expressed in monetary terms. In 1739, it became possible for a captain to deposit around 17,000 *livres* with the paymaster in Lorient. This sum of money was used by the local authorities in Asia to buy the goods that he wanted to trade on his own behalf. When everything had been finalized after his return, the captain was paid the proceeds of the auction. The same system was available to the officers but the sums were lower in proportion to their ranks. An examination of the finances of eleven captains in the years 1756–1770 shows that their average earnings per voyage amounted to 33,000 *livres*. The biggest hurdle was depositing the initial sum in Lorient because most of the captains had to borrow this hefty amount in the local mercantile community. The usual rate of interest was excessively high, as much as one-third of the sum borrowed. Under these circumstances, not every captain became a rich man, but most of them made a reasonable profit. Many naval officers transferred to the Company simply to seek their fortune. Considering their training, professional knowledge and service, the Company captains thought themselves the social equals of their naval colleagues.[6]

Apart from the *port-permis*, the *Compagnie des Indes* did not allow *pacotille*, the transportation of genuinely private goods, unless freightage was paid. Unsurprisingly, this rule was more honoured in the breach than the observance despite attempts to stem these infringements with a whole series of regulations and prohibitions. If there had been no payment, this trade was contraband and the

---

[5] Haudrère, *La Compagnie Française des Indes*, pp. 539–52.
[6] Haudrère, *La Compagnie française*, pp. 565–71 and 616.

thoroughness of the checking to uncover it depended on the strictness of the personnel ashore, as did any chance of arrest. In no way different from their counterparts in the Republic and England, the captains and their officers did their best to land their goods before they put in to Lorient or some other port. The coastal dwellers of southern Brittany were very familiar with these practices.

The *Dansk-Asiatisk Compagnie* and the *Svenska Ostindiska Kompani*

Very little information can be gleaned from the available literature about the commanders of the ships of the *Dansk-Asiatisk Compagnie*. There is no question that these men built up a wealth of experience on particular routes, such as that to China. Danish captains knew Canton well because they visited it on average nine times in the course of their career as ship's officer and captain. After 1772 not a single Company ship was lost. The *Svenska Ostindiska Kompani* had sent ships to Asia from Gothenburg from 1731. As in Denmark, England and France, the majority of the Swedish officer corps were probably recruited from the upper echelons of society, including the nobility. There was a training course on board for cadets, in which four to six boys could participate at one time. The captains and ship's officers were appointed from the ranks of the Company and it was a rare occurrence indeed for a boatswain or quartermaster to rise through the ranks. Temporary or permanent exchanges of officers between the Navy and the Company were normal. Because, like their Danish colleagues, Swedish captains almost invariably sailed the same routes, they were very familiar with particular sea routes, especially the one to Canton. Except for a few losses in the initial period, shipping disasters were rare. By the middle of the century, the three-decker was already established as the favourite type of ship.[7]

A captain in the service of the *Svenska Ostindiska Kompani* earned a monthly stipend of 100 silver dollars or about ƒ. 132, twice as much as his colleagues in the Swedish merchant navy. A first mate received 80 dollars (1 silver dollar = about ƒ. 1.32). Besides this fixed income, just as in the VOC and EIC, there was an opportunity to take along free private freight, the quantity restricted to a number of chests with set measurements. The Danish Company also followed this system. This *pacotille* was abolished in Sweden in 1748 and its place was taken by 'privilege money', the amount of which depended on the rank held. For a voyage just to Canton, the captain received 8,000 dollars, and this rose to 12,000 dollars for a voyage to both Surat and Canton. For the same voyages, a first mate got payments of 5,000 and 8,000 dollars respectively. The literature does not supply any answer to the question of whether the system, which was

---

[7] E. Göbel, 'The Danish Asiatic Company's Voyages'; C. Koninckx, *The First and Second Charters of the Swedish East India Company (1731–1766)* (Kortrijk, 1980), pp. 303–17. See also two articles by Göbel and Koninckx in Bruijn and Gaastra, *Ships, Sailors and Spices*, pp. 99–120 and pp. 121–39, respectively.

very like that devised by the VOC in 1742, was continued after 1766. It seems that after that year the *pacotille* was once again permitted. One fact is certain: a Swedish captain was in a position to earn large sums of money.[8]

VOC Commanders in Comparison

When the VOC commander is compared to his colleagues in other Companies there are a few differences which immediately stand out. The most conspicuous is that he worked for a decentralized business which consisted of six Chambers, permitted to work independently in how they administered the policies laid down by the *Heren Zeventien*. Furthermore, the commanders of VOC East Indiamen were almost without exception men who had climbed up through the ranks. These commanders had also spent time among the crew and petty officers and had learned all there was to know about the sailing of a ship in practice. Many came from humble backgrounds and had been able to make a big leap socially as a consequence of their career in the VOC. They were men who had forged their own careers by relying on their own initiative and personal qualities, though occasionally given a helping hand by circumstances. This system had probably prevailed since the very beginning of the Company. The few naval officers who sailed for the Company at various times do not change this general picture.

The VOC commanders and their officers were well acquainted with the practical side of seafaring from a very early age but they had to rely on their own initiative to learn about the theoretical background to navigation, the way the instruments worked and the contents of the textbooks. They paid their own instruction fees when they attended a cramming college like that run by Pieter Holm. The *Zeemanscollege* in Amsterdam and the similar institution in Rotterdam were exceptions rather than the rule. Unquestionably, their French and Swedish colleagues were far more privileged in their training since they were able to enjoy systematic instruction.

In the five Companies, there were no conspicuous differences in the stipends, perks and bonuses which were paid out by the authorities, and these payments were earned for the same sorts of activities. It is far more difficult to try to discover just how much a commander of an East Indiaman could actually earn. It is impossible to attempt to assess the cost of purchasing commodities for private trading at one end of the voyage against what such goods would actually fetch at the other end. This would need different sources and research. All that it is possible to say is that large sums were involved. The amount which a commander in the Republic or in London was willing and able to put on the table to obtain a command is an indication that the English commander could

---

[8] Koninckx, *The First and Second Charters*, pp. 320–9.

36. The Reverend Jan Brandes' cockatoo. Jan Brandes surrounded himself constantly with cockatoos and parakeets. He drew this cockatoo from Ambon, whose name was Beka, on 30 October 1784. Beka was white with some reddish highlights and could speak and whistle like a human being. Later Brandes enjoyed the company of this cockatoo for many years in Sweden. Crew members often brought birds and other animals from the East home with them.

expect to earn far more money than his Dutch colleague. The sums involved in private trade in Lorient and Gothenburg foster the suspicion that earnings there as well were higher than in the Republic. It was only when a commander was lucky enough to be appointed to a post overseas such as Superintendent of the Shipyard, especially in Batavia or Cape Town, but also elsewhere in the East, that he could hope to see more generous financial rewards and higher sums were entered on the bills of exchange sent back to the Republic. Roelof Blok is an exception because he made his career in the administrative hierarchy overseas.

In the literature about the other Companies, there is no mention of a high death rate among the captains, which was certainly a significant factor in the VOC for many years. Arrival in Batavia, and spending a longer period of time there, proved fatal to many commanders and ship's officers. They succumbed to the rampant malaria. Aware of this scourge, foreigners avoided the administrative and commercial hub of the VOC, and preferred to call at small islands in the Sunda Strait to take on fresh water, on their way to or coming back from Canton.

Despite his somewhat limited and more superficial knowledge of navigation, the VOC commander compared well with his foreign colleagues. He possessed a wealth of experience in navigation and all sorts of other matters to do with ships and the sea. Perhaps socially he might have felt a little at a loss, and he was not surrounded by a bevy of five or six boys whom he could train and patronize. His counterparts were more stylish and they were better born, but as time went by he too at least had a uniform. It was not his fault that he did not sail the China route regularly and acquire a more thorough knowledge of the South China Sea. The blame for this omission lay with the directors who considered that shipping to Batavia had the highest priority. In a fifteen-year period (1779–1793), twelve ships were lost on the way to Canton, whereas the numbers lost by the other Companies were far fewer or even none at all. Stavorinus gave vent to the frustration generated by antiquated sea charts but it was as late as 1788 before D'Après de Mannevilette's chart book became standard issue on board Dutch East Indiamen.[9]

When the information about the other Companies summarized above is mulled over, it casts considerably more light on the initiative taken by Van Imhoff in 1742 to raise the prestige and the standard of the Company commanders. Van Imhoff was a man of intelligence and he was qualified to make comparisons. He thought that the effort made by the VOC to attract naval officers was a move in the right direction, as was the introduction of a new system of ranks with a thoroughly revised scale of payments. In its own day, the *Académie de Marine* was an absolute innovation. The establishment of this training college in Batavia was an expensive and controversial project but it soon produced its first officers.

---

[9] Bruijn and Gaastra, *Ships, Sailors and Spices*, pp. 195–7.

However, the death of the man behind it spelled a speedy end to an interesting and very promising project.

In the 1750s, the VOC and its directors returned to the routine which had prevailed before the momentous years of the 1740s. The Van Imhoff episode had brought useful and durable improvements in such matters as the construction of ships, better navigational instruments, more accurate sea charts and higher earnings for the commanders and their officers, but it did little to improve their training or revise the ranking system. In comparison with their foreign colleagues, their social status remained the same.

The opportunity to sail in the better three-deckers, which were certainly considered safer, came to them only much later. Once more they found themselves sailing in the century-and-a-half-old wake of the routine in the East Indian shipping. It was only towards the end of the 1780s that they were again suddenly confronted with a whole wave of changes and improvements, as they had been in the 1740s. These innovations did not have a lasting impact since the VOC was liquidated fairly soon after the French invasion in 1795. Certainly the Company commander did profit from the fact that he could finally call himself captain, and his first mate was now a captain-lieutenant, but the old pattern of career-building had virtually disappeared. Most of his new colleagues had begun their lives at sea in another branch of shipping. After 1780, the tried and trusted East Indiaman was increasingly replaced by other sorts of ships, which were often either chartered or bought outright. They were no longer all built by the Company in Company yards. It was a real improvement that a new French book of sea charts and the chronometer were now available on board. The private trading commodities of the commander and ship's officers had now been elbowed out by the freight belonging to private merchants. This loss was compensated with a sum of money. Taken as a whole, all these were enormous changes over which the commander had no control. He was not alone. A few years later his colleagues in the EIC also had to deal with an enormous number of radical changes, as we have seen.

For nearly two centuries, with great regularity commanders and their ship's officers worked to ensure that the ships of the VOC reached their destinations safely. In a quest to find out more about these men, this book has found some answers, at least for the eighteenth century.

Conclusion: Commanders in Retrospect

Almost every commander who ever served with the VOC had begun his career as ship's boy, deckhand, sailor or gunner's mate. At least this was certainly the picture in the eighteenth century and there is no reason to think it would have been otherwise in the seventeenth. All the clues which can be obtained from studying the careers of commanders around 1700 and from delving into their social origins point in that direction. There is nothing which hints at any drastic changes occurring in the preceding decades. Their parents belonged either to what was called the *smalle burgerij* (lower middle class) – which included small craftsmen and shopkeepers, skippers of small boats, and lower-ranking administrative officials – or to the masses, the lowest group (*grauw*), which was composed of craftsmen and workers with low skill levels and ordinary seamen. Their fathers had often been seamen themselves. During the first four decades of the eighteenth century there were groups of families in the Chamber towns whose members, connected by all sorts of degrees of kinship, went to sea with the Company they knew and trusted. There were striking examples of such families in the Pomps, the Bents, the Van der Poels and the Brouwers in Enkhuizen, Hoorn, Delfshaven and Rotterdam. These families produced many commanders. For a number of years the post of commander usually went to men who lived in the town in which the Chamber had its seat or came from the area in the immediate vicinity. Three towns on the island of Walcheren in Zealand produced many of the commanders of the Zealand Chamber.

As time passed, gradual shifts emerged in this pattern. Foreigners who had become permanent members of the seafaring personnel of the VOC now began to rise to the highest ranks more frequently. They had often lived in the Chamber towns for years and had been completely assimilated. Naval officers also began to show some interest in working for the Company, if only for a year or two. Towards the end of the century, the VOC appointed increasing numbers of ship's officers and commanders, both Dutchmen and foreigners, who had been recruited from other branches of the shipping industry. There is no straightforward explanation for what happened. In almost all the Chamber towns population numbers had plunged dramatically, which meant that the potential for recruiting seafaring personnel also declined. Gradually the names of well-known seafaring families disappeared from the Company registers. The families of most commanders and ship's officers consisted of only one or two children and some of these would have died young. Many crew members died at sea or during the time they had to spend in Batavia and in other places overseas. In the 1730s and 1740s in particular, and also later, malaria wrought havoc in Batavia, killing huge numbers of people including commanders. The shrinking of the traditional source of officers was aggravated by a growing demand for men who were officer material because in precisely this same period there was a marked upsurge in shipping activity undertaken by the VOC. Under these circumstances, it is not surprising that the social and geographical backgrounds of the commanders changed as well. By the end of the century, a candidate for a commander's post would have been unrecognizable to a Company director of 1700. When a man applied, the prescription that a commander had to profess the Reformed religion was being increasingly circumvented. With the passing of time, all obstacles to Lutherans and even Roman Catholics becoming commanders were removed.

As a general rule, a commander had risen above the social background into which he had been born. In the town in which he lived he was a member of the bourgeoisie, composed of wealthy shopkeepers, successful craftsmen and small-scale entrepreneurs. Occasionally he could even count himself as one of the upper middle class (*grote burgerij*) of rich merchants, ship owners and high-ranking municipal officials. Only a very few ever managed to qualify to enter the ranks of the gentry, among them the glass-blower's son Roelof Blok and Jakob Goosen Hoogstad and Frank Verzijde from Vlaardingen. Adriaan Pool became burgomaster of Bovenkarpsel, a smallish town in the northern part of the province of Holland.

Most of the commanders managed to accumulate some capital and many of them lived off their investments after they had retired from the sea. They put their money into loans, bonds and real estate, including country estates and houses. Only sporadically did any of them ever invest in maritime commerce by buying shares in ships or fishing boats. Salomon Reynders did become a director of the *Middelburgse Commercie Compagnie*. Jan van Heemstee and Huig Goedhart's widow ran distilleries in Rotterdam and Delfshaven. Jakob Welgevaren had money in a pottery producing Delftware and is a very rare example of a retired commander who invested in industry. Also in Delft, Kornelis van Kolster became a slum landlord. A number of retired commanders launched second careers as shopkeepers or merchants. There are examples of such enterprises in Amsterdam.

A rise in social status was indissolubly linked to certain external signs and symbols. Commanders paid a much higher licence fee or tax to get married, have a child christened or for a funeral than they might have done in their earlier years. Their estimated annual income was the basis on which these fees were calculated, hence their rise up the social ladder became visible when they married for a second time or moved to a better address in the town. A few retired commanders went to live in manor houses or on country estates, among them Jakob Rijzik in Rockanje, Johan Splinter Stavorinus outside West-Souburg near Flushing, Jean Belleveau in Hillegersberg and Justinus van Gennep near Leerdam. Unquestionably, in the case of many commanders it is definitely possible to detect a process of gentrification. Of course, there were always the exceptions like poor Adriaan van Katersveld in Delft.

One tangible sign of social recognition was occasional appointment as one of the minor officials in the town. In Hoorn, Gerrit Kuit and Jan Peereboom were appointed *boongangers*, which meant that they could vote for candidates for municipal offices. One very sought-after job was that of Superintendent of one of the six Chambers, which held the promise of very attractive compensation. Maarten van der Meer and Jakob Bruijn occupied this post in Delfshaven and Enkhuizen respectively. Willem Koelbier was appointed in Rotterdam. It was not an invariable custom to appoint a retired commander to this job but such men did occupy the post regularly.

A position as Superintendent at one of the Company trading posts overseas offered good opportunities to earn very large sums of money. The chances of very tangible financial rewards were especially good in Batavia or at the Cape. Certainly commanders were well qualified for the job but such an appointment signalled a rupture in their sea-going lives, usually for a number of years, unless their tenure was prematurely interrupted by their death. Men such as Hugo Damiaan Staring and Jakobus Verleng succeeded in markedly improving their financial status. Olke Andringa did very well for himself in Ceylon.

The ordinary fixed stipend of a VOC commander was much higher than that earned by anybody else who sailed for a living. Until 1742, on an annual basis a commander earned *f.* 1,000 on average for a round-trip voyage, and after 1742 this sum was doubled or could sometimes be even higher. Because ships spent less time in Batavia as the century wore on, and hence the people on them went home more quickly, a commander had far more chances than before to apply for a new ship. Over time, the Company was able to create a sort of regular shipping service, which had a number of advantages for a commander. An extensive system of bonuses enlarged his chances of making extra money, but the directors wielded not only rewards but also punishments to ensure that their commanders obeyed all the rules as far as this was possible.

Over and above these generous earnings, a commander enjoyed a real opportunity to make very large sums of money from his trade in private goods. There had always been legitimate opportunities to do this and these were expanded in 1742. Usually a commander would borrow the money he needed to buy commodities for trade from suppliers in his home port. He repaid the money plus the agreed interest to business partners of his suppliers after he had made his sales at the Cape or in the East. What he had left over was remitted home in the form of bills of exchange. As the century progressed, the traffic in bills of exchange increased, as did the sums that were sent. Five-figure amounts (*f.* 10,000 or more) were not uncommon. Financially a sailor who had climbed up through the ranks to become a commander and had made one or more voyages in this capacity, and most importantly had survived his sojourn in the tropics, could be satisfied that he was a successful man. At home in his town or village he became a local worthy, although he was not as conspicuous in larger societies such as Amsterdam as he was in a village like Katwijk or on an island like Texel.

In the eighteenth century, in almost all the towns in which the Company had a Chamber, the local economy was heavily dependent on its economic activities. Hundreds of the men in the town worked in the Company business on shore while hundreds of others embarked for the East. In the early days this embarkation occurred three times a year but later there were more departures spread over the year. The numbers of those who came home were always smaller than those who sailed. Often those who went were away for years on end. Even the better-off commanders' families went to pick up monthly letters at the *Oost-Indisch Huis*. The majority of the commanders, including the foreigners, were married, home-loving men. There was little mobility between the Chambers and what little there was was most frequent between Rotterdam and Delft/Delfshaven. Amsterdam was the only city with a diversified economic structure, which meant that it was less dependent on the prosperity of the Company.

There was a fixed career pattern for ship's officers and commanders and this was surrounded by a framework of examinations which had to be sat for every promotion. At the time of his first appointment a commander was aged between thirty and forty, on average thirty-four to thirty-five. The Amsterdam Chamber invariably took the lead in issuing and implementing new regulations. The number of these regulations grew throughout the century. There was a thorough shake-up of the rules around 1742 when Baron Van Imhoff was appointed Governor-General. He was a man brimming with new, innovative ideas which touched upon many areas. The construction of ships did not escape his critical observation, nor did the recruiting and training of future officers, which was turned upside-down at his insistence. Various changes were introduced in the payment and rewarding of seafaring personnel. Private trade was always the area in which the most opportunities were offered. Although an institution like the *Académie de Marine* in Batavia was ephemeral, various other regulations which came from Van Imhoff's reforms lasted much longer.

A man was only appointed commander if a director put his name forward to his colleagues. The directors took turns to make such nominations. The candidate had to pay for his post as commander but, generally speaking, the Company could boast that it employed competent men. A system of examinations, which was expanded in 1793, guaranteed that an aspiring commander was well grounded in a basic knowledge of practical and theoretical nautical matters. He acquired these skills from practice during earlier voyages and by teaching himself. Until deep into its history, the 'training' for a commander took place entirely within the Company's own shipping business. Independent learning on board and schooling in small private nautical colleges like that run by Pieter Holm ensured that basic knowledge and expertise had been properly inculcated. Various commanders owned their own navigational instruments, even though it was the duty of the Company to see that all ships were provided with the prescribed instruments and sea charts as part of their standard equipment.

Shipping disasters often give rise to the impression that there is something amiss with the shipping company involved and the VOC did not escape such suspicions. Usually the situation was not dire, with the exception of the years 1730–1740. A huge number of voyages passed uneventfully, which indicates that the ships were competently run. The voyages were long and the position of the commander in the midst of an environment composed of very divergent characters was not always easy. Conversely, brutal commanders could influence the atmosphere on board for the worse. Refuge was sometimes sought in drink. There were tales of dreadful commanders like Jan Hokkeling or Willem Koelbier, but they are offset by plenty of stories of good relations on the quarterdeck. The Lammens sisters and Jakob Haafner are among the people who recounted positive tales of travel on VOC ships. Some insight into the private life of a commander on board is offered by the inventories of the estates of commanders who died during their voyages. The presence of slaves inside and in the vicinity of the commander's cabin during a voyage to the East comes as a surprise.

The Company commanders had no reason to feel inferior to their foreign colleagues, either in their professional expertise or in their experience at sea and life on board ship. Commanders who had made ten or even more voyages to Asia were not an exception, but the VOC failed to exploit the specialized knowledge which such men had built up or would have been able to acquire. The China route was a prime example of this. Foreign companies certainly did make use of such expertise. According to the standards of the time, the navigational instruments on board Company ships were adequate, even though the VOC could not be called a pioneer in the introduction of new techniques. This somewhat aloof policy towards innovations is understandable in such an enormous business as the VOC, although such an important innovation as the octant was introduced on board relatively quickly. New instruments, like the sextant and the chronometer, were often very expensive. It was well into the eighteenth century before commanders were supplied with reliable, improved charts of Asian waters.

Broadly speaking, the course of the careers of the men in charge of the ships of the other East India Companies did not diverge greatly from that of their counterparts in the VOC, even though there was probably a big difference in their social origins. Certainly, the system of ship-owning and the appointment of commanders in the EIC did not fit the pattern in the other Companies. Commanders in the EIC had to pay very large sums for their appointments, but once they had their posts they were in a position to earn a great deal and become very rich.

Great changes affected the shipping business of the VOC after 1780. The tried and tested East Indiaman became the centre of a controversy and the VOC chartered ordinary merchantmen or just bought such ships outright. The stream of officers from its own ranks tended to dry up, which opened the door wider to foreigners. The commander was now called a captain. The freight system was altered to allow private merchants greater opportunities to ship their own cargoes. The commander was obliged to give up the space allocated to him for his own trade goods in exchange for substantial financial compensation. The Rotterdam merchant Anthonie van Hoboken is a good example of how the commercial world welcomed these changes. Working with Captains Smalt and Rogge, he seized these new opportunities with enthusiasm. On the eve of the Batavian Revolution in 1795, the Company ships and the men in charge of them certainly were not lagging behind the times. In fact they could have been called reasonably modern.

Bibliography

Aarsbog, S.W., *Med Mars og Merkur. En analyse av norsk deltakelse i VOC basert på skipssoldbøker 1633–179* (Trondheim, 2003)

Akveld, L.M., 'Noordzeevisserij', *Maritieme Geschiedenis der Nederlanden* III, (Bussum, 1977), pp. 318–44

Akveld, L.M. et al. (eds), *Vier eeuwen varen. Kapiteins, kapers, kooplieden en geleerden* (Bussum, 1973)

Akveld, L.M. et al. (eds), *In het kielzog. Maritiem-historische studies aangeboden aan Jaap. R. Bruijn bij zijn vertrek als hoogleraar zeegeschiedenis aan de Universiteit Leiden* (Amsterdam, 2003)

Alphen, M.A. van, 'The Female Side of Dutch Shipping: Financial Bonds of Seamen Ashore in the 17th and 18th Centuries', in J.R. Bruijn and W.F.J. Mörzer Bruyns (eds), *Anglo-Dutch Mercantile Marine Relations 1700–1850* (Amsterdam/Leiden, 1991, pp. 125–32

Arkenbout, G.C. and A.A. Arkenbout, *Arkenbout op zee. Leden van een bekende familie op Voorne-Putten in dienst van de Verenigde Oost-Indische Compagnie en de Nederlandse marine, 1721–1834* (Bernisse, 2001)

Barend-van Haeften, M.L. (ed.), *Op reis met de VOC. De openhartige dagboeken van de zusters Lammens en Swellengrebel*, Werken Linschoten Vereeniging XCV (Zutphen, 1996)

Barend-van Haeften, M. and B. Paasman (eds), *De Kaap: Goede Hoop halverwege Indië. Bloemlezing van Kaapteksten uit de Compagniestijd* (Hilversum, 2003)

Beaglehole, J.C., *The Exploration of the Pacific* (London, 1966)

Beers, J.K. and C. Bakker, *Westfriezen naar de Oost. De kamers der VOC te Hoorn en Enkhuizen en hun recruteringsgebied, 1700–1800* (Hoorn, 1990)

Beijerinck, Fr. and M.G. de Boer, *Het dagboek van Jacob Bicker Raije 1732–1772* (Amsterdam, no date)

Belt, A. van den, *Het VOC-bedrijf op Ceylon. Een voorname vestiging van de Oost-Indische Compagnie in de 18de eeuw* (Zutphen, 2008)

Beyers, C., *Die Kaapse Patriotte gedurende die laaste kwart van die agtiende eeu en die voortlewing van hul denkbeelden* (Pretoria, 1967)

Biewenga, A., *De Kaap de Goede Hoop. Een Nederlandse vestigingskolonie. 1680–1730* (Amsterdam, 1999)

Bijl, M. van der, *Idee en interest. Voorgeschiedenis, verloop en achtergronden van de politieke twisten in Zeeland en vooral in Middelburg tussen 1702 en 1715* (Groningen, 1981)

Boetzelaer van Asperen, C.W. and Th. van Dubbeldam, *De Protestantsche kerk in Nederlandsch-Indië. Haar ontwikkeling van 1602–1939* (The Hague, 1947)

Bokkel Huinink, J. ten, 'Een vergeten Zeeuwse zeekapitein: Johan Splinter Stavorinus (1739–1788)', in J.R. Bruijn et al. (eds), *Marinekapiteins*, pp. 145–56

Bonke, H., *De zeven reizen van de Jonge Lieve. Biografie van een VOC-schip, 1760–1781* (Nijmegen, 1999)

Bonke, H., 'De Verenigde Oost-Indische Compagnie op de rede van Texel', in V. Roeper and I. Vonk-Uitgeest (eds), *Texel en de VOC*, pp. 18–41

Bonke, H. and K. Bossaers, *Heren investeren. De bewindhebbers van de West-Friese Kamers van de VOC* (Enkhuizen, 2002)

Boon, P., *Een dijk van een kaart* (Hoorn, 1991)

Boon, P.A., *Bouwers van de zee: zeevarenden van het Westfriese platteland, c. 1680–1720* (The Hague, 1996)

Boon, P.A., 'Kerk en schip.Westfriese zeelieden omstreeks 1700 en hun godsdienstige achtergrond', in L. Akveld et al. (eds), *In het kielzog*, pp. 317–29

Booy, E.P. de and J. Engels, *Van erfenis tot studiebeurs. De Fundatie van de vrijvrouwe van Renswoude te Delft. Opleiding van wezen tot de 'vrije kunsten' in de 18de en 19de eeuw. De fundatiehuizen. De bursalen in deze eeuw* (Delft, 1985)

Bos, S., *'Uyt liefde tot malcander'. Onderlinge hulpverlening binnen de Noord-Nederlandse gilden in internationaal perspectief (1570–1820)* (Amsterdam, 1998)

Bossaers, K.W.J.M., *'Van kintsbeen aan ten staatkunde opgewassen'. Bestuur en bestuurders van het Noorderkwartier in de achttiende eeuw* (The Hague, 1996)

Boven, G. and A. Hoving, *Scheepskamelen & waterschepen. 'Eene ellendige talmerij, doch lofflijk middel'* (Zutphen, 2009)

Bowen, H.V., '"So Alarming an Evil": Smuggling, Pilfering and the English East India Company, 1750–1810', *International Journal of Maritime History* XIV, no. 1 (2002), pp. 1–31

Bowen, H.V., 'Privilege and Profit: Commanders of East Indiamen as Private Traders, Entrepreneurs and Smugglers, 1760–1813', *International Journal of Maritime History* XIX, no. 2 (2007), pp. 43–88

Boxer, C.R., 'The Dutch East-Indiamen: Their Sailors, Their Navigators, and Life on Board, 1602–1795', *Mariner's Mirror* 49 (1963), pp. 81–104

Boxer, C.R., *The Dutch Seaborne Empire 1600–1800* (London, 1965)

Boxer, C.R., 'The Maritime Twilight of the V.O.C., 1780–95. Some Sources and Problems', *Tijdschrift voor Zeegeschiedenis* 1 (1982), pp. 114–23

Brakel, J.P. van, 'Katwijkse koopvaardijkapiteins', *Rijnland. Tijdschrift voor sociale geografie en streekgeschiedenis van Leiden en omstreken* VI (1969), issue 23–24, 84 1–859, nos. 23, 35, 42, 87 and 107, not 53

Brug, P.H. van der, *Malaria en malaise. De VOC in Batavia in de achttiende eeuw* (Amsterdam, 1994)

Bruijn, I.D.R., *Ship's Surgeons of the Dutch East India Company. Commerce and the Progress of Medicine in the Eighteenth Century* (Leiden, 2009)

Bruijn, J.R., *De admiraliteit van Amsterdam in rustige jaren 1713–1751. Regenten en financiën, schepen en zeevarenden* (Amsterdam, 1970)

Bruijn, J.R., 'Zeevarenden', *Maritieme Geschiedenis der Nederlanden* III (Bussum, 1977), pp. 147–90

Bruijn, J.R., 'Productivity, Profitabilty, and Costs of Private and Corporate Dutch Ship Owning in the Seventeenth and Eighteenth Centuries', in J.D. Tracy (ed.), *The Rise of Merchant Empires. Long-Distance Trade in the Early Modern World 1350–1750* (Cambridge, 1990), pp. 174–94

Bruijn, J.R., *The Dutch Navy of the Seventeenth and Eighteenth Centuries* (Columbia, SC, 1993)

Bruijn, J.R., *Varend Verleden. De Nederlandse oorlogsvloot in de zeventiende en achttiende eeuw* (Amsterdam, 1998)
Bruijn, J.R., 'Commandanten van Oost-Indiëvaarders in de achttiende eeuw', *Tijdschrift voor Zeegeschiedenis* 20, no. 1 (2000), pp. 4–13
Bruijn, J.R., *Observaties onderweg* (Leiden, 2003)
Bruijn, J.R., 'Seafarers in Early Modern and Modern Times: Change and Continuity', *International Journal of Maritime History* XVII, no. 1 (2005), pp. 1–16
Bruijn, J.R. and J. Lucassen (eds), *Op de schepen der Oost-Indische Compagnie. Vijf artikelen van J. de Hullu* (Groningen, 1980)
Bruijn, J.R. and P.F. Poortvliet, 'De officieren van de admiraliteit (1714–1795): hun carrières, bemanningen en schepen', in J.R. Bruijn et al. (eds), *Marinekapiteins*, pp. 17–33
Bruijn, J.R., and C. van Baalen, *Van zeeman tot residentieburger. Cornelius de Jong van Rodenburgh (1762–1838)* (Hilversum, 1996)
Bruijn, J.R., F.S. Gaastra and I. Schöffer (eds), *Dutch-Asiatic Shipping in the 17th and 18th Centuries*, Rijks Geschiedkundige Publicatiën, Grote Serie 165–167, 3 vols (The Hague, 1979–1987 [abbreviated as *DAS*]
Bruijn, J.R., A.C. Meijer and A.P. van Vliet (eds), *Marinekapiteins uit de achttiende eeuw. Een Zeeuws elftal* (The Hague/Middelburg, 2000)
Brunt, I.M., 'De veranderingen in het charter van de VOC schepen 1740–1742' (MA thesis, Leiden University, 1997)
Buisman, J., *Duizend jaar weer, wind en water in de Lage landen* 5 (1675–1750) (Franeker, 2006)
Chijs, J.A. van der (ed.), see *Nederlandsch-Indisch Plakaatboek*
Chijs, J.A. van der (ed.), see *Realia*
Coolhaas, W.Ph. (ed.), see *Generale Missiven*, vols VI–VIII
Cowan, R., Z. Cowan and P. Marsden, 'The Dutch East-Indiaman *Hollandia* Wrecked on the Isles of Scilly in 1743', *International Journal of Nautical Archaeology and Underwater Exploration* 4 (1975), pp. 267–300
Crone, E., 'Pieter Holm en zijn zeevaartschool', reprinted from *De Zee* (1930), pp. 5–20
Crone, E., *Cornelis Douwes 1712–1773. Zijn leven en zijn werk met inleidende hoofdstukken over navigatie en zeevaart-onderwijs in de 17de en 18de eeuw* (Haarlem, 1941)
Davids, C.A. 'Commentaar op het artikel van C.R. Boxer', *Tijdschrift voor Zeegeschiedenis* 1 (1982), pp. 124–31
Davids, C.A., *Zeewezen en wetenschap. De wetenschap en de ontwikkeling van de navigatietechniek in Nederland tussen 1585 en 1815* (Amsterdam, 1986)
Davids, C.A., 'Het navigatie-onderwijs aan personeel van de VOC, in P. van Mil and M. Scharloo (eds), *De VOC in de kaart gekeken*, pp. 65–74
Dekker, P., 'Drei Hooger Befehlshaber auf niederlandändischer Ostindienfahrt im 18. Jahrhundert', *Nordfriesisches Jahrbuch* 7 (1971), pp. 56–61
Dekker, P., 'De walvisvaarders uit noordelijk Noord-Holland van 1770–1783', *West-Frieslands Oud en Nieuw* 40 (1973), pp. 51–2
Dekker, P. 'Zwischen Amsterdam und Batavia. Der Aufstieg des gebürtigen Sylters Nickels Petersen vom Schiffsjungen zum Kommandeur in niederländischen Seediensten', *Nordfriesisches Jahrbuch*, Neue Folge 10 (1974), pp. 133–42

Dekker, P., 'De pilotage te Petten in de 18ᵉ eeuw', *West-Frieslands Oud en Nieuw* 42 (1975), pp. 36–71

Dekker, P., 'Der "Admiral" Nis de Bombell (1706–1772). Ein Nordfriese in niederländischen Seediensten', *Nordfriesisches Jahrbuch*, Neue Folge 13 (1977), pp. 107–33

Dekker, P., 'De financiële toestand van de bewoners langs het Marsdiep gedurende de tweede helft van de 18e eeuw', *West Frieslands Oud en Nieuw* 48 (1981), pp. 154–5

Dekker, R. and L. van de Pol, *Vrouwen in mannenkleren. De geschiedenis van een tegendraadse traditie in Europa 1500–1800* (Amsterdam, 1989)

Delahaye, V., 'De Vlaeminck en de Zeeuw; 30.000 mensen overzee', in J. Parmentier (ed.), *Uitgevaren voor de Kamer Zeeland*, pp. 47–87

Dillo, I.G., *De nadagen van de Verenigde Oostindische Compagnie 1783–1795* (Amsterdam, 1992)

Doe, E. van der and A. Wiggers, 'Varen voor de kamer Zeeland van de V.O.C. Enige opmerkingen over zeevarenden aan boord van de Zeeuwse schepen in de achttiende eeuw', *Zeeuws Tijdschrift* 37, no. 6 (1987), pp. 209–21

Dörr, S., *De kundige kapitein. Brieven en bescheiden betrekking hebbende op Jan Olphert Vaillant kapitein-ter-zee (1751–1800)* (Zutphen, 1988)

Dutch-Asiatic Shipping, abbreviated as *DAS*, see Bruijn, Gaastra and Schöffer

Edwards, H., *The Wreck on the Half Moon Reef* (Adelaide, 1970)

Elias, J.E., *De vroedschap van Amsterdam* (Amsterdam, 1903–5)

Enthoven, V., '"Veel vertier. De Verenigde Oostindische Compagnie in Zeeland, een economische reus op Walcheren"', *Archief Koninklijk Zeeuwsch Genootschap der Wetenschappen* (1989), pp. 49–127

Eyck van Heslinga, E.S. van, *Van Compagnie naar koopvaardij. De scheepvaartverbinding van de Bataafse Republiek met de koloniën in Azië 1795–1806* (Amsterdam, 1988)

Farrington, A., *A Biographical Index of East India Company Maritime Service Officers 1600–1834*, 2 vols (London, 1999)

Feijst, G. van der, *Geschiedenis van Schiedam* (Schiedam, 1975)

Francke, J., *'Utiliteyt voor de gemeene saake'. De Zeeuwse commissievaart en haar achterban tijdens de Negenjarige Oorlog, 1688–1697* (Middelburg, 2001)

Frijhoff, W. and M. Prak (eds), *Geschiedenis van Amsterdam. Centrum van de wereld 1578–1650*, II, 1 (Amsterdam, 2004)

Frijhoff, W. and M. Prak (eds), *Geschiedenis van Amsterdam 1650–1813. Zelfbewuste stadstaat*, II, 2 (Amsterdam, 2005)

Gaastra, F.S., 'Friesland en de VOC', in P.H. Breuker and A. Janse (eds), *Negen eeuwen Friesland-Holland. Geschiedenis van een haat-liefde verhouding* (Zutphen, 1997), pp. 184–96

Gaastra, F.S., *The Dutch East India Company. Expansion and Decline* (Zutphen, 2002)

Gaastra, F.S., *Particuliere geldstromen binnen het VOC-bedrijf 1640–1795*, Van Gelder-lezing (Leiden, 2002)

Gaastra, F.S., '"Een stel cameele"', *Zeemagazijn* 31, no. 3 (2005)

Gaastra, F.S., 'Zeeuwen in de VOC in de tweede helft van de achttiende eeuw', in J. Parmentier (ed.), *Noord-Zuid in Oost-Indisch perspectief* (Zutphen, 2005), pp. 99–116

Gawronski, J., *De Equipagie van de Hollandia en de Amsterdam. VOC-bedrijvigheid in 18de-eeuws Amsterdam* (Amsterdam, 1996)
Gawronski, J., 'Vals plat en de VOC. Opgravingen op Oostenburg, Amsterdam', in Akveld et al. (eds), *In het kielzog*, pp. 163–73
Geijn-Verhoeven, M. van de et al., *Wonen op de Kaap en in Batavia 1602–1795* (Zwolle/The Hague, 2002)
Gelder, R. van, 'Van Saksen naar Batavia. Gottfried Preller 1726–1735', in P. van Zonneveld (ed.), *Naar de Oost! Verhalen over vier eeuwen reizen naar Indië* (Amsterdam, 1996), pp. 17–43
Gelder, R. van, *Het Oost-Indisch avontuur. Duitsers in dienst van de VOC* (Nijmegen, 1997)
Gelder, R. van, 'De stranding van de Blijdorp, 1733. Lotgevallen van een bemanning', *Tijdschrift voor Zeegeschiedenis* 21 (2002), pp. 24–33
Gelder, R. van, *Naporra's omweg. Het leven van een VOC-matroos (1731–1793)* (Amsterdam/Antwerp, 2003)
Gelder, R. van and L. Wagenaar, *Sporen van de Compagnie. De VOC in Nederland* (Amsterdam, 1988)
Genabeek, J. van, *Met vereende kracht risico's verzacht. De plaats van onderlinge hulp binnen de negentiende-eeuwse particuliere regelingen van sociale zekerheid* (Amsterdam, 1999)
Generale Missiven van Gouverneurs-Generaal en Raden aan Heren XVII der Verenigde Oostindische Compagnie VI (1698–1713), VII (1713–1725) en VIII (1725–1729), IX (1729–1743), X (1737–1743), XI (1743–1750), XII (1750–1755), XIII (1756–1761), Rijks Geschiedkundige Publicatiën, Grote Serie 159, 164, 193, 205, 250, 232, 257 and 258 (The Hague, 1976, 1979, 1985, 1988, 1997, 2004 and 2007)
Gøbel, E., 'The Danish Asiatic Company's Voyages to China, 1732–1833', *Scandinavian Economic History Review* XXVII (1979), pp. 1–23
Göbel, E., 'Danes in the Service of the Dutch East India Company in the Seventeenth Century', *International Journal of Maritime History* XVI (June 2004), pp. 77–93
Goor, J. van (ed.), *Generale Missiven*, vols IX and X
Goor, J. van, *Jan Kompenie as Schoolmaster. Dutch Education in Ceylon 1690–1795* (Groningen, 1978)
Grimm, P. (ed.), *Heeren in zaken. De kamer Rotterdam van de Verenigde Oostindische Compagnie* (Zutphen, 1994)
Groot, J.P.M., *Van de Grote Rivier naar het Koningsplein. Het Bataviaasch Genootschap van Kunsten en Wetenschappen 1778–1867* (PhD diss., Leiden University, 2006)
Groot, S.J. de, 'De "Groote Christelycke Zee-vaert" en "de God-vreezende Zeeman", hun meer dan driehonderdjarige rol als toeverlaat voor de zeevarenden', *Mededelingen Nederlandse Vereniging Zeegeschiedenis* 34 (1977), pp. 5–18
Haan, F. de, 'De "Academie de Marine" te Batavia, 1743–1755', *Tijdschrift Indische Taal-, Land- en Volkenkunde* XXXVIII (1895), pp. 551–621
Habermehl, N.D.B., 'De Kweekschool voor de Zeevaart vanaf de oprichting in 1785 tot de vernietiging in 1811. Een Amsterdams antwoord op het kwantitatieve en kwalitatieve tekort aan zeevarenden', *Mededelingen Nederlandse Vereniging voor Zeegeschiedenis* 42 (1981), pp. 5–40

Haks, D., *Huwelijk en gezin in Holland in de 17de en 18de eeuw. Processtukken en moralisten over aspecten van het laat 17de- en 18de-eeuwse gezinsleven* (Assen, 1982)

Hart, S., *Geschrift en getal Een keuze uit de demografisch-, economisch- en sociaalhistorische studiën op grond van Amsterdamse en Zaanse archivalia, 1600–1800* (Dordrecht, 1976)

Hart, S., 'De rederij', *Maritieme Geschiedenis der Nederlanden* II (Bussum, 1977), pp. 106-25

Haudrère, Ph., *La Compagnie Française des Indes au XVIIIe siècle (1719–1795)* (Paris, 1989)

Haudrère, Ph., 'The "Compagnie des Indes" and Maritime Matters', in J.R. Bruijn and F.S. Gaastra (eds), *Ships, Sailors and Spices. East India Companies and Their Shipping in the 16th, 17th and 18th Centuries* (Amsterdam, 1993), pp. 81-97

Heeres, J.E., 'De "Consideratiën" van Van Imhoff', *Bijdragen Taal-, Land- en Volkenkunde van Nederlandsch-Indië* 66 (1912), pp. 441-621

Heijden, M. van der, 'Achterblijvers. Rotterdamse vrouwen en de VOC (1602–1750)', in M. van der Heijden and P. van de Laar (eds), *Rotterdammers en de VOC*, pp. 181-212

Heijden, M. van der and D. van den Heuvel, 'Sailors' Families and the Urban Institutional Framework in Early Modern Holland', *History of the Family* 12 (2007), pp. 296-309

Heijden, M. van der and P. van de Laar (eds), *Rotterdammers en de VOC. Handelscompagnie, stad en burgers (1600–1800)* (Amsterdam, 2002)

Heijer, H. den, *De geoctrooieerde compagnie. De VOC en de WIC als voorlopers van de naamloze vennootschap* (Deventer, 2005)

Heuvel, Danielle van den, *'Bij uytlandigheijt van haar man'. Echtgenotes van VOC-zeelieden, aangemonsterd voor de kamer Enkhuizen (1700–1750)* (Amsterdam, 2005)

Heuven, D.B. van, 'Nautisch onderwijs op Java in vervlogen dagen', *Marineblad* 63 (1953), pp. 544-52

Hogendorp, D. van, *Stukken raakende den tegenwoordigen toestand der Bataafsche bezittingen in Oost-Indië en de handel op dezelve* (The Hague/Delft, 1801)

Hoorn, Jan Ambrosius (J.A.H.), *Mijne lotgevallen ter zee en bedrijven op Batavia in dienst der (voormalige) O.I. Compagnie* (Groningen, 1819)

Houtzager, H.L. et al. (eds), *Delft en de Oostindische Compagnie* (Amsterdam, 1987)

Hoving, A.J. and A.A. Lemmers, *In tekening gebracht. De achttiende-eeuwse scheepsbouwers en hun ontwerpmethoden* (Amsterdam, 2001)

Hoynck van Papendrecht, A., *Gedenkboek A. van Hoboken & Co. 1774 –1924* (Rotterdam, 1924)

Hullu, J. de, 'Over den Chinaschen handel der Oost-Indische Compagnie in de eerste jaren dertig van de 18^e eeuw', *Bijdragen Taal-, Land- en Volkenkunde van Nederlandsch-Indië* 73 (1917), pp. 32-154

Jacob, H.K. s', see *Generale Missiven* XIII

Jacobs, E.M., *Merchant in Asia. The Trade of the Dutch East India Company during the Eighteenth Century* (Leiden, 2006)

Jansen, W.M. and P.A. de Wilde, 'Het probleem van de schaarste aan zeevarenden in de 18^e eeuw' (MA thesis, Leiden University, 1970)

Jas, J. et al., *Het Peperhuis te Enkhuizen* (Zwolle, 1996)

Jonge, J.C. de, *Geschiedenis van het Nederlandsche zeewezen* IV (Haarlem, 1861)

Jonkers, A.R.T., *North by Northwest. Seafaring, Science, and the Earth's Magnetic Field (1600–1800)* (Göttingen, 2000)

Jörg, C.J.A., *Porselein als handelswaar. De porseleinhandel als onderdeel van de Chinahandel van V.O.C. 1729–1794* (Groningen, 1978)

Kalff, S., 'Een zee-officier van de O.-I. Compagnie', *Onze Vloot* 1 (1925), pp. 4–8

Knevel, P., 'Een kwestie van overleven. De kunst van het samenleven', in T. de Nijs and E. Beukers (eds), G*eschiedenis van Holland*, pp. 217–54

Knoppers, J.V.Th., 'De vaart in Europa', *Maritieme Geschiedenis der Nederlanden* III, pp. 226–61

Kok, J., '"t Weldaadig stormtuig". Sociaal-politieke initiatieven in Hoorn, 1770–1850', in R.P. Zijp et al. (eds), *Barre tijden*, pp. 58–73

Koninckx, C., *The First and Second Charters of the Swedish East India Company (1731–1766)* (Kortrijk, 1980)

Kooijmans, L., *Onder regenten. De elite in een Hollandse stad. Hoorn 1700–1780* (Amsterdam, 1985)

Kranenburg, H.A.H., *De zeevisscherij van Holland in den tijd der Republiek* (Amsterdam, 1946)

Kroes, J., 'Chinees porselein met Nederlandse familiewapens', *Genealogie* 3, vol. 1 (1997), pp. 4–7

Krom, N.J., *Gouverneur Generaal Gustaaf Willem van Imhof* (Amsterdam, 1941)

Kroniek Historisch Genootschap, vol. 28 (1872)

Kuijpers, E., *Migrantenstad. Immigratie en sociale verhoudingen in 17^e-eeuws Amsterdam* (Hilversum, 2005)

Laar, P. van de, 'Rotterdam. De koopstad en de VOC', in M. van der Heijden and P. van de Laar (eds), *Rotterdammers*, pp. 30–55

Landheer, T., *Oranje of Napoleon? De wisselvallige levensloop van Christiaan Antonij Ver Huell 1760–1832* (Utrecht, 2006)

Leest, S. van der, 'Jacob Pieter van Braam (1737–1803). De jaren 1787–1803, de nadagen in de carrière van een achttiende-eeuwse marineofficier' (MA thesis, Leiden University, 2005)

Leeuwen, M.H.D., *De rijke Republiek: gilden, assuradeurs en armenzorg 1500–1800* (The Hague/Amsterdam, 2000)

Lequin, F., 'Het personeel van de Verenigde Oost-Indische Compagnie in Azië in de achttiende eeuw, meer in het bijzonder in de vestiging Bengalen' (PhD, Leiden University, 1982)

Lesger, C.M., *Hoorn als stedelijk knooppunt. Stedensystemen tijdens de late middeleeuwen en vroegmoderne tijd* (Hilversum, 1990)

Leuftink, A.E., *Harde heelmeesters. Zeelieden en hun dokters in de 18e eeuw* (Zutphen, 1991)

Loeve, B., 'Een matroos uit Colijnsplaat: Cornelis Vis (1714–1789)', in J.R. Bruijn et al. (eds), *Marinekapiteins*, pp. 94–110

Loeve, B., 'De driedekker: drie decennia discussie. De invoering van een nieuw scheepstype bij de VOC, 1763–1793' (MA thesis, Leiden University, 2001)

Lottum, J. van and J. Lucassen, 'Six Cross-Sections of the Dutch Maritime Labour Market: A Preliminary Reconstruction and its Implications (1610–1850)', in R. Gorski (ed.), *Maritime Labour: Contributions to the History of Work at Sea, 1500–2000* (Amsterdam, 2007), pp. 13–42

Lucassen, J., 'Holland, een open gewest. Immigratie en bevolkingsontwikkeling', in T. de Nijs and E. Beukers (eds), *Geschiedenis van Holland*, pp. 80–216

Maat, G., 'Hoe lang nog? De lichaamslengte van de Nederlander', lecture to HOVO (University of Third Age students), 15 May 2006, Leiden

Malsen, H. van, 'Briefwisseling van den gouverneur-generaal Gustaaf Willem baron Van Imhoff met den advocaat fiscaal der Amsterdamsche admiraliteit mr. Jacob Boreel Janszoon (1738–1750)', *Bijdragen en Mededelingen Historisch Genootschap* 50 (1929), pp. 321–426

Marion, O. van, 'Vechtlust of verliefdheid? Dichterlijke verbeeldingen van Jacoba van Beieren', *Tydkrifvir Nederlands en Afrikaans* 5, vol. 2 (1998)

Marsden, P., *De laatste reis van de 'Amsterdam'* (Bussum, 1974)

Meilink-Roelofsz, M.A.P., 'Johan Splinter Stavorinus (1739–1788)', in L.M. Akveld et al. (eds), *Vier eeuwen varen*, pp. 176–96

Mentink, G.J. and A.M. van der Woude, *De demografische ontwikkeling te Rotterdam en Cool in de 17e en 18e eeuw* (Rotterdam, 1965)

Messchaert-Heering, S., *Van koopmansstraat tot Nieuwmarktspijp* (Enkhuizen, 2001)

Messing, F., *Lief, je bent zo ver van mij ... Over schipper Govert van Oudekerke en zijn vrouw Mathilde omstreeks 1660* (Amsterdam, 2004)

Middelburgse Courant, 4 and 10 October 1771

Mijnhardt, W.W., 'Wetenschapsbevordering onder het Ancien Régime: het Zeeuwsch Genootschap der Wetenschappen 1765–1794', *Koninklijk Zeeuwsch Genootschap der Wetenschappen* (1985), pp. 1–94

Mil, P. van and M. Scharloo (eds), *De VOC in de kaart gekeken. Cartografie en navigatie van de Verenigde Oostindische Compagnie 1602–1799* (The Hague, 1988)

Mollema, J.C., *Een muiterij in de achttiende eeuw. Het aflopen van het Oost-Indische Compagnieschip Nijenborg in 1763* (Haarlem, 1933)

Moor, J.A. de and P.G.E.I.J. van der Velde (eds), *De Werken van Jacob Haafner*, I, Werken Linschoten-Vereeniging XCI (Zutphen, 1982)

Moree, P., 'Jacob Hoogstad (1702–1776). Een Vlaardinger in dienst van de Verenigde Oostindische Compagnie', *Historisch Jaarboek Vlaardingen* (1988), pp. 77–87

Moree, P., *'Met vriend die God geleide'. Het Nederlands-Aziatisch postvervoer ten tijde van de Verenigde Oost-Indische Compagnie* (Zutphen, 1998)

Moree, P., 'Reders en vroedschapsleden in Vlaardingen in het jaar 1750', *Netwerk, Jaarboek Visserijmuseum* (2000), pp. 21–9

Moree, P., 'Gezagvoerders op VOC-schepen van de Kamer Rotterdam in de achttiende eeuw', in M. van der Heijden and P. van de Laar (eds), *Rotterdammers*, pp. 136–60

Moree, P., *Kikkertje lief. Brieven van Aagje Luijtsen geschreven aan haar man Harmanus Kikkert, stuurman in dienst van de VOC* (Texel, 2003)

Mörzer Bruyns, W.F.J., 'Navigatie-instrumenten van de zeebodem 16^e tot 19^e eeuw', *Tijdschrift voor Geschiedenis Geneeskunde, Natuurwetenschappen, Wiskunde en Techniek* 10 (1987), pp. 263–82

Mörzer Bruyns, W.F.J., *Konst der stuurlieden. Stuurmanskunst en maritieme cartografie in acht portretten, 1540–2000* (Amsterdam/Zutphen, 2001)

Mörzer Bruyns, W.F.J., *Schip recht door zee. De octant in de Republiek in de achttiende eeuw* (Amsterdam, 2003)

Mörzer Bruyns, W.F.J. and A.J. van der Horst, 'Navigational equipment from 't

Vliegend Hart (1735)', *International Journal of Nautical Archaeology* 35 (2006), pp. 319–25

Nederlandsch-Indisch Plakaatboek (ed. J.A. van der Chijs), III (1678–1709), IV (1709–1743), V (1743–1750), VI (1750–1754), VII (1755–1764), VIII (1765–1775), X (1776–1787), XI (1787–1795) and XII (1795–1801) (Batavia/The Hague, 1886–1894)

Nieborg, J.P., *Indië en de zee. De opleiding tot zeeman in Nederlands-Indië 1743–1962* (Amsterdam, 1989)

Niemeyer, Th., 'Een strijdbare zeekapitein: Evert Blonkebijle Corneliszoon (1696–1769)', in J.R. Bruijn et al. (eds), *Marinekapiteins*, pp. 65–82

Nierstrasz, C., 'In the Shadow of the Company. The VOC (Dutch East India Company) and its Servants in the Period of its Decline (1740–1796)' (PhD diss., Leiden University, 2008)

Nijs, T. de and E. Beukers (eds), *Geschiedenis van Holland*, II (1572 to 1795) (Hilversum, 2002)

Noordegraaf, L., *Daglonen in Alkmaar 1500–1800* (Oostvoorne, 1980)

Okkema, J.C., 'Het College van Commissarissen van de Weth', *De Stad Delft, cultuur en maatschappij van 1667 tot 1813* (Delft, 1981), pp. 69–70

Oldewelt, W.F.H. (ed.), *Kohier van de personeele Quotisatie te Amsterdam over het jaar 1742*, 2 vols (Amsterdam, 1945)

Oldewelt, W.F.H., 'De beroepsstructuur van de bevolking der Hollandse stemhebbende steden volgens de kohieren van de Familiegelden van 1674, 1715 en 1742', *Economisch-Historisch Jaarboek* 25 (1951), pp. 167–248

Oosterwijk, B., *Koning van de koopvaart. Anthony van Hoboken (1756–1850)* (Rotterdam, 1983)

Overvoorde, J.C. and P. de Roo de la Faille (eds), *De gebouwen van de Oost-Indische Compagnie en van de West-Indische Compagnie in Nederland* (Utrecht, 1928)

Paesie, R., *Het VOC-schip Ravesteyn. De laatste reis van een Zeeuwse Oostindiëvaarder* (Amsterdam, 1999)

Parmentier, J. (ed.), *Uitgevaren voor de Kamer Zeeland* (Zutphen, 2006)

Peters, M., *In steen geschreven. Leven en sterven van VOC-dienaren op de Kust van Coromandel in India* (Amsterdam, 2002)

Pol, A., '"Tot gerieff van India". Geldexport door de VOC en de muntproduktie in Nederland 1720–1740', *Jaarboek voor Munt- en Penningkunde* 72 (1985)

Priester, P., *Geschiedenis van de Zeeuwse landbouw circa 1600–1910*, A.A.G. Bijdragen 37, (Wageningen, 1998)

Prins, Y., 'Van scheepsjongen tot admiraal van de retourvloot. Het leven van VOC-dienaar Roelof Blok (1712–1776)', *Jaarboek Centraal Bureau voor Genealogie*, vol. 52 (The Hague, 1998), pp.156–99

Prud'homme van Reine, R.B., *Jan Hendrik van Kinsbergen 1735–1819. Admiraal en filantroop* (Amsterdam, 1990)

Prud'homme van Reine, R.B., 'Dirk Muller: portret van een VOC-kapitein', *Zeemagazijn* 28, no. 4 (2002), p. 4

Realia. Register op de generale resolutiën van het Kasteel van Batavia, 1632–1805, 3 vols (ed. J.A. van der Chijs) (Batavia/The Hague, 1882–5)

Reij, C., 'De geslaagde Texelse VOC-schipper: Arie Lambertsz Kikkert, 1746–1807', in V. Roeper and I. Vonk-Uitgeest (eds), *Texel en de VOC*, pp. 65–85

Reinders Folmer-Van Prooijen, C., *Van goederenhandel naar slavenhandel. De Middelburgse Commercie Compagnie 1720–1755* (Middelburg, 2000)
Rodger, N.A.M. (ed.), *Memoirs of a Seafaring Life. The Narrative of William Spavens, Pensioner on the Naval Chest at Chatham* (Bath, 2000)
Roeper, V., 'De schipbreuk van de Negotie. Een scheepsramp bij Texel in 1790', in V. Roeper and I. Vonk-Uitgeest (eds), *Texel en de VOC*, pp. 123–35
Roeper, V., 'Het Weesewater. Texels drinkwater op de schepen van de VOC', in V. Roeper and I. Vonk-Uitgeest (eds), *Texel en de VOC*, pp. 43–51
Roeper, V. and I. Vonk-Uitgeest (eds), *Texel en de VOC. Schepen op de Rede, Texelaars in de Oost* (Texel, 2002)
Roos, D., *Zeeuwen en de VOC* (Middelburg, 1987)
Schilder, G. and W.F.J. Mörzer Bruyns, 'Navigatie', *Maritieme Geschiedenis der Nederlanden* III (Bussum, 1977), pp. 191–225
Schmidt, A., *Overleven na de dood. Weduwen in Leiden in de Gouden Eeuw* (Amsterdam, 2001)
Schokkenbroek, J.C.A., 'Versteend verleden. Chinese portretbeeldjes in de collectie van het Nederlands Scheepvaartmuseum Amsterdam', *Vormen uit Vuur* 203 (2008/4), pp. 2–13
Schooneveld-Oosterling, J.E. (ed.), *Generale Missiven* XI and XII
Schoor, A. van der, *Stad in aanwas. Geschiedenis van Rotterdam tot 1813* (Zwolle, 1999)
Schouwenburg, K.L. van, 'Het personeel op de schepen van de kamer Delft der VOC in de eerst helft der 18e eeuw', *Tijdschrift voor Zeegeschiedenis* 7 (1988), pp. 76–93, and 8 (1989), pp. 179–86
Schutte, G.J., *De Nederlandse Patriotten en de koloniën. Een onderzoek naar hun denkbeelden en optreden, 1770–1800* (Groningen, 1974)
Schuyleman, L.S., 'Jan Siereveld, de "manhafte" schipper der V.O.C. en zijn nageslacht', *Van Zeeuwse Stam* 65 and 66 (1989), pp. 115–17 and 182–9
Seffinga, M., 'Theodorus Bergsma. Het verslag van een reis naar Batavia in 1771', *Jaarboek Fries Scheepvaart Museum en Oudheidkamer* (2002), pp. 54–66
Seffinga, M.J., 'Het ivoren "Bloemenschip" van Jan de With – 1746', *Jaarboek Fries Scheepvaart Museum en Oudheidkamer* (2004), pp. 65–8
Sigmond, J.P., *Nederlandse zeehavens tussen 1500 en 1800* (Amsterdam, 1989)
Sigmond, J.P. and L.H. Zuiderbaan, *Dutch Discoveries of Australia. Shipwrecks, Treasures and Early Voyages off the West Coast* (Adelaide, 1979)
Sobel, D., *Longitude* (New York, 1995)
Stapel, F.W. (ed.), *De Beschryvinge van de Oostindische Compagnie* I, Rijks Geschiedkundige Publicatiën, Grote Serie 63 (The Hague, 1927)
Staring, A., *Damiaan Hugo Staring. Een zeeman uit de achttiende eeuw 1736–1783* (Zutphen, 1948)
Sutton, J., *Lords of the East. The East India Company and its Ships (1600–1874)* (London, 2000)
Tartwijk, B. van, et al. (eds), *Hoorn en de zee* (Hoorn, 2002)
Taylor, J.G., *The Social World of Batavia. European and Eurasian in Dutch Asia* (Madison, WI, 1983)
Tempel, K. van der, '"Wij hebben amok in ons schip: Aziaten in opstand tijdens drie terugreizen op het einde van de achttiende eeuw"', in J.R. Bruijn and E.S. van

Eyck van Heslinga (eds), *Muiterij. Oproer en berechting op schepen van de VOC* (Haarlem, 1980), pp. 123–47

Tikoff, V.K., 'Saint Elmo's Orphans. Navigation, Education and Training at the Royal School of San Telmo in Seville during the Eighteenth Century', *International Journal of Maritime History* XX, no. 1 (2008), pp. 1–32

Tramper, A., 'Vlissings varend verleden: "uijt het weeshuijs na Oostindiën gevaren voor den armen"', *Den Spiege* 20, vol. 3 (2002), pp. 13–17

Van Dyke, P.A., *The Canton Trade. Life and Enterprise on the China Coast, 1700–1845* (Hong Kong, 2007)

Veltschow, T., 'Voyages of the Danish Asiatic Company to India and China 1772–1792', *Scandinavian Economic History Review* XX (1972), pp. 133–52

Verbeek, J.R., 'Kapitein Jacob Pieter van Braam. Commandant van het eerste landseskader in Indië 1783–1786' (MA thesis, Leiden University, 1981)

Verbout-Wamsteeker, A., 'Navigatieopleidingen aan de Fundaties van Renswoude 1756– 1795', *Tijdschrift voor Zeegeschiedenis* 17 (1998), pp. 37–55

Verburg, A., 'De Vlaardingse notarissen vóór 1811 en hun archieven', *Historisch Jaarboek Vlaardingen* (2004), pp. 36–61

Verhees-Van Meer, J.Th.H., *De Zeeuwse kaapvaart tijdens de Spaanse Successieoorlog 1702–1713* (Middelburg, 1986)

Vink, M., '"The World's Oldest Trade": Dutch Slavery and Slave Trade in the Indian Ocean in the Seventeenth Century', *Journal of World History* 14, no. 2 (2003), pp. 131–77

VOC-Glossarium. Verklaringen van termen, verzameld uit de Rijks geschiedkundige Publicatiën die betrekking hebben op de Verenigde Oost-Indische Compagnie, Institute for Dutch History (The Hague, 2000)

Vonk-Uitgeest, I., 'Schipper in poolijs en tropenzon. Simon Jansz Vaartjes, 1753–1795', in V. Roeper and I. Vonk-Uitgeest (eds), *Texel en de VOC*, pp. 95–121

Vonk-Uitgeest, I., 'Texelse opvarenden in dienst van de VOC', in V. Roeper and I. Vonk-Uitgeest (eds), *Texel en de VOC*, pp. 149–204

Voort, J.P. van de, *De Westindische plantages van 1720 tot 1795. Financiën en handel* (Eindhoven, 1973)

Vries, D. de et al. (eds), *The Van Keulen Cartography Amsterdam 1680–1885* (Alphen aan den Rijn, 2005)

Vries, J. de and A. van der Woude, *The First Modern Economy. Success, Failure, and Perseverance of the Dutch Economy, 1500–1815* (Cambridge, 1997)

Vries, P.J. de, *De plattegronden van Enkhuizen. Van ganzenveer tot cd-rom* (Enkhuizen, 2004)

Vries, R. de, 'Crisis en sociale politiek in Enkhuizen, 1650–1850', in R.P. Zijp et al. (eds), *Barre tijden*, pp. 36–57

Vries, R.J. de, *Enkhuizen 1650–1850, bloei en achteruitgang van een Zuiderzeestad* (Amsterdam, 1987)

Wagenaar, L., *Galle, VOC-vestiging in Ceylon. Beschrijving van een koloniale samenleving aan de vooravond van de Singalese opstand tegen het Nederlandse gezag, 1760* (Amsterdam, 1994)

Warnsinck, J.C.M., *De Kweekschool voor de Zeevaart en de Stuurmanskunst 1785–1935* (Amsterdam, 1935)

Werz, B., 'Een bedroefd, en beclaaglijck ongeval'. De wrakken van de VOC-schepen Oosterland en Waddinxveen (1697) in de Tafelbaai (Zutphen, 2004)
Wiel, K. van der, Op zoek naar een biografisch portret van het verleden (Hilversum, 2003)
Wijsenbeek-Olthuis, Th., Achter de gevels van Delft. Bezit en bestaan van rijk en arm in een periode van achteruitgang (1700–1800) (Hilversum, 1987)
Wilcocke, S.H. (trans. and ed.), Voyages to the East-Indies by the Late John Splinter Stavorinus, Esq., Rear Admiral in the Service of the States-General, 3 vols (London, 1798; reprinted 1969)
Willemsen, R., Enkhuizen tijdens de Republiek. Een economisch-historisch onderzoek naar stad en samenleving van de 16^e tot de 19^e eeuw (Hilversum, 1988)
Wingen, T. van, 'Van konstabelsmaat tot gevierd kapitein: Maarten Haringman (1715–1784)', in J.R. Bruijn et al. (eds), Marinekapiteins, pp. 111–18
Witt, J.M., Master next God? Der nordeuropäische Handelsschiffskapitän vom 17. bis zum 19. Jahrhundert (Hamburg, 2001)
Wolf-Smoes, D. de, 'De Enkhuizer haringvisserij en de rol van het stadsbestuur tijdens de oorlogen in de periode 1670–1720' (MA thesis, Leiden University, 1998)
Wolvers, G., 'Het wisselverkeer van het maritieme personeel van de Verenigde Oostindische Compagnie vanuit Azië naar Nederland in de 18^e eeuw' (MA thesis, Leiden University, 1988)
Worp, J.A., Geschiedenis van den Amsterdamschen Schouwburg 1496–1772 (met aanvulling tot 1872) (Amsterdam, 1920)
Yong, Liu, The Dutch East India Company's Tea Trade with China, 1757–1781 (Leiden, 2007)
Zeilemaker, M., Op zoek naar het historisch interieur (Hilversum, 2005)
Zijp, R.P. et al. (eds), Barre tijden. Crisis en sociale politiek rondom de Zuiderzee, 1650–1850 (Zutphen, 1989)

Index of Names

The Index refers to names in the text and illustrations, not in the annotation. Years of life, when available, have been mentioned only of commanders and directors.

Aart, Arie van der   218
Abel, Jan   235, 291
Adonis   231
Alkmaar, Pieter   199
Almees, Jan   277–8
Andriessen, Pieter   200
Andriessen, Willem Jakob (1755– after 1795)   103, 220
Andringa, Olke Hendrik   223, 282, 312
Angelvorst, Pieter (1735–1777)   117, 205, 217, 224
Anias, Abraham   174
Anker, Jakob van der   270
Antje,   115
Arkenbout, Jacobus Ariesz (1766–1834) frontispiece, 32, 37–8
Astria   232

Baane, Jan Kornelis (1762–1823)   88, 153–4
Bakker, Pieter   167
Bank, Joachim   239
Banken, Jacobus van (–1777)   100
Barends, Uilke (1757–1810)   138, 295
Beer, Nikolaas de (1706–1774)   144
Beieren, Jacoba van   120, 122
Belleveau, Jean (–1759)   95, 97–8, 141, 143, 177, 253, 255, 311
Belleveau, Jean Daniël (1728–1754)   95, 97
Bellon, Isaak Louis de (c.1740–after 1794)   53, 149
Ben, Barend Jansz (1699–1727)   47–8
Ben, Hendrik Jurriaansz (c.1665–1752)   47–8
Ben, Jan Jurriaansz (1669–1718)   47–8
Bent, Arend Dirksz (1684–1726)   47
Bent, Daniël Arendsz (1685–after 1723)   47
Bent, Daniël Dirksz (1683–1722)   46–7
Bent, Daniël Jakobsz (1688–1722)   47
Bent, Dirk Daniëlsz (c.1658–1709)   47
Bent, Meinoutje   47
Berg, Gerrit   246
Berg, Isaak van den   271
Berg, Jacobus van den (1727–1819)   82–4

Bernards, Jakob   220
Bijleveld, Gerrit   241, 265
Blauwhuis, Haye   275
Bloem, Jan   221
Blok, Anthonie   33
Blok, Roelof (1712–1776)   31–3, 38, 49, 50, 88, 161–2, 222, 308, 311
Blom, Barend   223
Blom, Christiaan   179, 223, 247, 265, 284
Blom, Christoffel (–1745)   116, 177, 223
Blom, Hermanus (–1738)   235, 237
Blonkebijle, Evert (1696–1769)   70–1
Boekhout, Jakob   256–7
Boer, Adriaan van den   168
Boer, Jan (Gerritsz) de (–1778)   120, 123–4, 135, 148, 190, 200–1, 228, 253, 255, 286
Boer, Kornelis de (c.1700–1736)   19, 20
Boer, Wietse de   295
Bogaard, Barend (1698–1727)   94
Bogaard, Jacobus (1672–1743)   94
Bok, Pieter de   46
Bonekamp, Gijsbert (c.1708–1751)   94, 97
Booms, Hendrik   223
Booms, Steven (1734–1795)   32, 35–6, 38–9
Boon, A.   146–7
Boreel, Jakob   142–4
Borselen, Frank van   122
Bos, Kornelis   265
Bosch, Kornelis   218
Bot, Jan   277
Bot, Lambert   189, 191
Bougainville, Louis Antoine de   243
Bowen, H.V.   303
Boxer, C.R.   283
Braam, Jakob Pieter van (1737–1803)   150, 180–1
Braam, Willem van (1732–1807)   150, 256
Braams, Kornelis   253
Brandes, Jan   80, 267, 307
Brattem, Jakob van,   99

Brattem, Kornelis van (1732–1781) 99–102, 204–5
Brattem, Teunis van (1739–1769) 99–102, 204–5
Breems, Kornelis den (1703–1738) 128
Breems, Maarten den (1712–1747) 128, 199
Breen, Jan Huigen van 77
Breen, Maria van 77
Broek, Jakob 223
Broek, Jan van den (c.1695–1740) 234, 241, 265
Brouwer, Arie (1685-na 1746) 94
Brouwer, Barend (1684–1746) 94
Brouwer, David 288
Brouwer, Gilles 191
Brouwer, Jakob (1680–1765) 92, 94, 97
Bruijn, Dr. Gerrit 33–4
Bruijn, Gerrit (1740–c.1807) 35, 45, 51, 244–5
Bruijn, Jakob (1737–1807) 32–6, 38, 45, 78, 312
Bruijn, Jan 35
Bruijn, Nikolaas 34
Brunel, Thomas 200
Buteux, Pieter 163, 166

Cats, Adriaan 266
Cau, Bonifacius 61
Cederborg, Swerus Magnus 126
Chef, Anthonie (–1725) 219
Citters, van 163
Clemens, Johan Carl 126
Cook, James 243, 291
Cornets de Groot, Hugo 165
Crasser, A. en J. 98
Crasser, Andries 99
Crone, E. 283
Cupido I 231
Cupido II 231

Dalen, Pieter van 200
Dalrymple, Alexander 291
Dam, Jakobus van 106
Davids, C.A. 283, 288
Davidszoon, Joris 231, 235
Decquer, Hendrik 222
Dekker Willem 275
Dijk, Kornelis van 57, 191, 220–1
Dijkhuizen, Maria van 28
Dina 231
Doen, Sijtje 52
Dol, Dirk (c.1695–1738) 20, 22–3
Dol, Hero (c.1669–1721) 20, 22
Douwes, Cornelis (1712–1773) 185–6, 284
Driesman, Herman 297

Drillinger, Jan Everwijn (1748–1807) 32, 36–7, 39, 57, 59
Droge, Pieter ten 199
Droop, Jan Jobst 297
Dupuis, Frederik Louis 293

Eikels, Pieter 218–9
Elsevier, Reinier Jan 210–11, 289
Elteren, David van (1707–1753) 119
Engelaar, Paulus 223
Engelsman, Ype (1692–1730) 20, 25–6, 38
Eps, Kornelis van (1759–before 1810) 71, 293, 299
Evertsz, Elder 197

Falck, Jan Werner 149
Ferrero, A. 61
Ferret, Willem (1742–1775) 8
Fierman, Matthijs (1726–1770) 131
Fletcher, Thomas 192
Fokke, Arend 260
Forster, Jacobus 231, 289
Franke, Hendrik Andries 148
Fransz, Arie 198
Fret, Kornelis 219

Gaal, Thomas 138
Gaastra, F.S. 73, 224
Gas, Georg Philip (1760–1808) 82, 84
Geerse, Jan 167, 270
Genechten, Pieter van 253
Gennep, Justinus van (1744–1801) 67–8, 163, 166, 311
Gietermaker, Claes Hendriksz 174, 184
Goedhart, Huig (1698–1733) 77, 311
Goedhart, Teunis (1701–1738) 77
Goedhoen, Klaas 26–9, 38
Goos, Pieter 290
Graaf, Adriaan de (–1765) 44–5
Graaf, Adriaan van der 273–4
Graaf, Simon de 247
Gracht, Gerrit van der (1714–1778) 45–6
Grindet, Hermanus (1680–1740) 62
Groen, Teunis 299
Groot, Simon de (1688–1750) 108, 209, 224, 248
Guldeman, Anthonie 222

Haafner, Jakob 65–6, 265, 268–9, 314
Haak, Dirk (1685–1747) 24, 160–1, 164
Haard, Hendrik Otto de (1734–1771) 149
Haard, Philip Hendrik de 223
Hadley, John 284
Hakker, Maarten (1715–1784) 131, 198, 288
Hansen, Andries 265
Hansen, Hans 198

INDEX OF NAMES

Haringman, Maarten (1715–1784)   61, 63, 70–1, 73, 96, 220, 257
Harmeyer, Gerrit (1718–1784)   85–7, 203, 205, 228
Harmeyer, Koenraad   87
Harrison, John   285
Hart, Abraham van der (1700–1737)   128
Hart, Simon   119
Hartog, Hendrik de (1751–1838)   299
Hartz, George Christiaansz   286
Haverkamp, Jan Koenraad   297
Hebner, George Gottlieb (–1791)   297
Heemskerk, Jan Kristoffel van (1721– after 1778)   83–4
Heemstee, Jan van (1705–1776)   77–8, 90, 275, 311
Heijpe, Reinier (c.1680–1725)   62
Heim, Jakob van der (1727–1793)   46, 160, 164–5, 168–9, 175
Helena   68
Hilverduin, Hendrik   170–1, 279
Hoboken, Anthonie van   73, 103–4, 208, 315
Hoedt, P.H. de   103
Hoek, Stoffel   79
Hoeven, Kornelis van (1690–1741)   24–5, 164, 266
Hokkeling, Jan (c. 1692–1734)   92, 94, 101, 271–5, 314
Holm, Pieter (1696–1776)   184–5, 289, 306, 312
Honsdorp, George Christiaan   183
Hoogerheyden, Engel   65, 260
Hoogland, Willem   185
Hoogstad, Jakob Goosen (1702–1776)   129, 277–8, 311
Houthuizen, Willem   262–3
Houting, Nikolaas (1706–1772)   179–80

Ieperen, Josua de Wolf van   259
Imhoff, Gustaaf Willem, baron van   46, 95, 97, 141–5, 149, 158, 176, 179, 181–3, 190, 206, 212–13, 215, 227, 250, 252–3, 255, 278, 286, 308–9, 313
Ingelse, Maarten   59

Jansz., Haye   167
Januari I   231
Januari II   231
Januari III   231
Jellesz, Pieter   199
Johanna   115, 231
Jong, Cornelius de   282, 291
Jonkers, A.R.T.   283
Juel, Eschel   116

Kaiser, Nanning   142

Kakelaar, Jan (c. 1715–1754)   59
Kanters, Andries Laurens (1762–1794)   295
Kassel, Karel Philip   271
Katersveld, Adriaan van (1723–1793)   86, 88, 312
Keet, Kornelis Ariënsz   244, 264
Keizer, Isaak de   217
Keizer, Jan Pietersz   164, 167–8, 175, 249
Keizer, Michiel de (1697–1746)   77
Kelder, Jan   278, 284
Kelger, Frederik (1722–1775)   117, 194, 196, 205, 246
Kemp, Willem   191
Ketel, Jakob   43
Keuken Jr, Klaas Klaasz (c. 1752–1808)   137, 139, 296
Keulen, firm Van   290
Keulen, Johannes van   123, 290
Kikkert, Albert Albertsz (1738–1771)   132
Kikkert, Albert Lambertsz (1737–1782)   132
Kikkert, Arie (1746–1807)   124, 132, 135–6, 217, 299
Kikkert, Harmanus (1749–1806)   132–6
Kikkert, Klaas Harmanusz   134
Kikkert, Lambert (–1783)   132, 134
Kikkert, Lammert Harmanusz   134
Kinckel, Hendrik August, baron van (1747–1821)   60, 180
Kinsbergen, Jan Hendrik van   276
Kinsbergen, Jan Hermanus (1742–1790)   276–7
Klerk, Johan de   115
Klinkhamer, Gerrit (1692–1767)   290
Klump, Willem (1715–before 1770)   202, 204, 278
Koelbier, Willem (1736–1799)   93, 98, 268–9, 312, 314
Koen, Joost   200
Koetsier, Pieter   107
Kok, Laurens (–1756)   102
Kok, Stoffel   200, 280
Kolster, Kornelis van (c.1685–1735)   82, 86, 311
Koopstad, Leendert van (c.1734–1780)   53, 282
Kornelisz, Kornelis   201
Kort, Johannes de (1748–1780)   82–3, 186
Koster, Jan   218
Krielaard, Jan (–1738)   94
Kroon, Paulus   220
Krootjes, Lukas   199
Kuiper, Kornelis   294
Kuit, Gerrit Jansz (1696–1755)   48, 51, 312

Laarbeek, Gilles van   71

Lakei 231
Lammens, sisters 234, 241, 265, 314
Landsheer, Michiel 253
Lang, Jan Frederik 217
Lans, Kornelis (c.1690–1733) 94–5
Lanschot, Gerrit van (–1715) 119
Larkins 301
Leander 231
Lesger, C. 109
Lethbridge, John 262
Leus, Willem de (1674–1728) 211
Linde, Huibert van der (1716– after 1777) 129–30
Lokeman, Jan (–1708) 81,85
Lond, Christiaan 187
Loosen, Jan van 24
Loosen, Joosje van 24
Loosen, Pieter van (1690–1743) 24, 38
Loot, Gerrit 167
Lovelt, Dirk 191
Lub, Reinder 30
Lubken, Jan Koenraad 219
Luijtsen, Aagje 132–4

Maljaard, Jan 210, 231, 289
Mamus, Gerbrand 222–3
Mannevilette, D'Apres de 290, 308
Marijnissen, Anthonie 211
Marre, Jan de (1696–1763) 120–4, 135, 174, 185, 255, 285, 287, 289–90
Martens, Christiaan 276
Martens, Martinus 122–3, 182, 185, 285, 287, 289
Mathias- Pous, Bonifacius (1744–1797) 160
Mathias, Johan Constantijn (1691–1765) 160, 165
Meenings, Maria 234
Meer, Ary van der 79
Meer, Maarten van der (1710–1770) 78–9, 312
Mels, Koenraad 222–3
Mensburg, Jan van 32
Mensburg, Willem van (1704–1776) 20–1, 30, 32, 148, 162, 178
Meurer, Frederik Alexander (1750–1811) 151
Meyer, George Jakob 259
Meyer, Jan Balthus 200
Meytens, Martinus (1730–1769) 232, 284, 289, 291
Mina 231
Minne, Jan (1683–1764) 49, 160–1, 164
Molenaar, Wiggert 57
Molensteen, Jurriaan 119
Montagne, Jan 263
Moree, P. 132
Morgans 168

Mörzer Bruyns, W.F.J. 283
Mulder, Gottlieb 278
Mulder, Jan 170
Muller, Dirk (1758–1834) 125–6
Munkhoven, Jan 275
Munts, Johan Willem 183

Nauwman, Jan Zacharias (- after 1791?) 146, 148–9, 268
Nauwman, Mrs 147
Neercassel, Floris van 112
Neercassel, Wessel van (1671–1759) 111–12, 119, 222–3, 245, 279
Nieuwpoort, Willem van der 183
Nimwegen, Dirk Wolter van (1712–1750) 142–4, 179
Nimwegen, Pieter Hendrik van 143
Nose, Joost 253

Och, Jan 282, 284
Ongewassen, Jan 217
Onkruid, Jakob (1661–1729) 118–19, 170, 219, 234, 269
Opmeer, Hendrik (1702–1745) 108, 119, 143, 222
Oterlijk, Kornelis 253
Otter, Jan den 168
Oudemans, Gilles (1692–1742) 279
Outjes, Jochem (c. 1707–1767) 118, 124, 218–19, 247, 279
Overbeek, Gerard Ewout 293
Overraad, Kornelis van (–1709) 194, 196

Paardekoper, Jan 180, 232
Pater, Lucas 121
Pauluszn, Paulus 182
Peek, Dirk 295
Peereboom, François 53
Peereboom, Jan (1709–1782) 51–3, 60, 312
Peereboom, Jan 51
Peereboom, Reinier 52–3
Philippi, Jan Lodewijk (1724–1754) 148–9
Pieternel 233
Pietersen, Kornelis (–1793) 270, 280, 294
Pietersz, Kornelis (1727–1780) 72
Pieterszoon, Pieter 232
Pijpen, Jan van der 168
Plas, Johan van der (1762/3– after 1795) 57, 59, 89
Plokker, Dirk Kornelisz (1742–) 229
Poel, Dirk van der (1709–1741) 77
Poel, Hendrik van der 76
Poel, Jakob van der (–c.1730) 76–7
Poel, Koenraad (I) (1704–1743) 76, 204
Poel, Koenraad (II) (1715–1744) 76–7
Pols, Jakob 199

INDEX OF NAMES

Pomp, Dirk (1704–1741)   20–1, 24, 26, 30, 209
Pomp, Jan (–1741)   20
Pomp, Jeltje   20
Pomp, Simon (1701–1737)   20, 30
Pool, Adriaan (1709–1759)   23–4, 38
Pool, Sieuwert (1684–1732)   164
Poortvliet, P.F.   58–9
Popman, Meinoutje   25
Popta, Wopke (1734–1800)   196, 282, 294
Poulin, Karel Magnus (–1779)   280
Pous   163
Prooien, Pieter van (c.1735–)   169, 280

Quack, Kornelis (1707–1757)   92, 97, 178, 194
Quinkhard, J.M.   121

Raatjes, Jan Frederik   271
Radermacher, Daniël (1722–1803)   73, 160, 163, 166, 168, 256–9
Radermacher, Jacobus   258
Radermacher, Samuel (1693–1761)   160, 165, 168
Ramas, Grietje   20
Ramas, Jan (1700–1737)   20
Ramas, Maarten   20
Ramas, Suzanna   21
Rauwenhof, Paulus (1730–1764)   149, 169, 182–3, 218, 265, 279
Rebel, Christiaan   246
Reebok, Jan   253
Regenboog, Jakob (1669–1727)   85, 107, 279
Renswoude, Baroness of   82
Reynders, Salomon (1708–1770)   60, 70–1, 73, 89, 311
Rheede, Ficco van   144
Rijzik, Jakob (1723–after 1792)   64–7, 127, 148, 217, 223, 246, 265, 311
Roem, Klaas   266, 269
Rogge, Arnoldus (1758–1802)   102–4, 208, 315
Roo, Kornelis de (-1773)   257
Rooy, Jan de (1672–1724)   275
Rossum, Lodewijk Willem van (1763–)   170
Rotte, Hans Christiaan de (1722–1754)   280–1
Rozeboom, Lukas (–1741)   45
Ruis, Pieter   210–11, 289
Ruiter, Adriaan de   275
Russeplukker, Jan (1685–1762)   19, 20, 25, 32, 92, 134
Ruts, Jozias   211, 231
Ruurdsz, Harmen   201
Ruyter, vader De   132

Sallieth, Matthias de   65, 260
Samson   231–2
Sautijn, Willem   164, 167–8, 249
Schaap, Bregje   19, 20, 25, 38, 134
Schaap, Michiel   19
Scharf, Pieter (1684–1743)   211
Scheler, Gerrit (–1802)   54, 126
Schellinger, Volkert (1708–1746)   52
Schellinger, Jan (1724–1769)   266–7
Schilde, Dirk van der (1710–1781)   94, 98, 178
Schkopp, Johann Alexander   115
Schoneman, Christiaan   295
Schoning, Marten   198
Schouten, Frederik (1705–1773)   108, 115–16, 119, 203, 231, 270
Schuller, Rebecca, see Nauwman, Mrs
Schut, Bartholomeus (–1788)   85, 98, 203
Schuts, Jan Frederik   277
Siberg, Johannes   187
Siereveld, Jan   68, 234, 257
Sluiter, Karel (–1721)   72
Smalt, Willem (1760–1819)   102–4, 208, 293, 315
Smit, Willem de (–1732)   62, 275
Snijders, Johannes (–1782)   232
Sombeek, Jakob (–1767)   162, 242
Spavens, William   243
Spek, Benjamin van der (1737–1787)   46, 199
Spek, Jan   185
Staden, Daniël van (1687–1738)   44–5, 51, 209, 231
Staring, Damiaan Hugo (1736–1783)   64, 67–8, 151–2, 211, 223, 241, 312
Stavorinus, Jan   69–70
Stavorinus, Johan Splinter (1739–1788)   69–73, 89, 163, 179–80, 199, 257, 282–3, 291, 294, 308, 311
Steenstra, Pybo   83, 123, 184, 280
Steffers, Anthonius Franciscus   126
Sterrenberg, Asmus Hendrik   264–5
Stevens, Kornelis   201
Steyns, Jan   276
Stocke, Gerard (–1736)   62
Stokbroo, Pieter   279
Stuiver, Klaas   43
Swaag, Gerbrand   276
Sutton, J.   301
Symons, William   57

Tanje, Pieter   252
Tarncke, Jochem Aldertsz (–1760)   28–9, 202
Thiel, Jan van   253
Timmerman, Adriaan Kornelis (1674–1726)   107

Titsingh, Guillelmus   186
True, Jens *see* With, Jan de
Tuinman, Jan   231
Turfkloot, Arie (1671– after 1714)   194, 196

Udemans Jnr. Willem   255–6, 298
Udemans Snr. Willem   255–6, 298
Uilenberg, Tobias (1673–)   111, 245, 279

Vaartjes, Simon Jansz (1753–1795)   137, 139, 170
Vaillant, Jan Olphert   285, 291
Varkenvisser, Dirk Dirksz (1758–1805)   130
Varkenvisser, Dirk Reinsz (1753–1783)   130
Veerden, Christiaan van   153
Velde, Kornelis van der (1700–1742)   128
Verburg, Jurriaan (1735– after 1795)   200, 227
Verdoes, Bastiaan (1702–1757)   130–1, 182, 225–6, 267–9
Verkerk, Pieter (1738–1778)   46, 86, 94
Verleng, Jacobus (1704–1753)   107–8, 119, 141, 177, 222, 312
Verley, Pieter (1687–1736)   118, 279
Verschuur, Frans   217
Verschuur, Paulus   169
Verzijde, Frank (1683–1736)   128–9, 311
Veth, Dirk de (1689–1741)   44–5, 199
Veurden, Ary van (c.1702–1774)   81, 86, 275
Vis, Kornelis (1714–1789)   60, 62–3, 70–1, 73, 165, 242, 257
Visser, Pieter   201
Vivaldi, Anthonio   122
Vlaming, Evertje   167
Vogelzang, Anthonie   223
Volkers, Hillert   268
Vos, Frans   234
Vos, Gerrit Reindertsz   191
Vos, Kornelis de (1732–1769)   244
Vos, Melchior de (1652–before 1710)   85–6
Vredenburch, Adriaan van (1680–1759)   160
Vredenburch, Gerard Adriaansz van (1710–1784)   88, 160, 164, 169
Vries, Erasmus de (–1768)   102
Vries, Isaac de   167
Vries, Jakob de   200
Vries, Jan de   242
Vries, Klaas de   174, 184
Vroom, Willem   277–8
Vrucht, Willem   64

Wagtels, Dirk (1728–1779)   63–4
Wal, Johannes van der   83
Walgaren, Elias   222
Wanjon, Samuel   288
Warius, Pieter   174
Weert, Pieter van der (–1785)   277
Weide, Abraham van der (–1773)   271
Weiland, Philip Frederik   206
Welgevaren, Jakob (1725–1787)   85–6, 98, 169, 249, 277, 311
Welkom   231
Wesseling, Evert (1740–1808)   72
Westerman, Adam   95
Westlye, Ivar Gjode *see* Wesseling
Westphaal, Jochem   57
Westvaal, David   185
Wever, Frederik Godert (1733–)   175, 234
Wichers, Johan   240
Wiebe, Jakob (c.1704–1766)   116, 119, 196, 205
Wielard, Frederik   269–70
Wiese, Diedrich (1768–1820)   259
Wijmeren, Anthonie van   57
Wijn, Joris van der   270
Wijs, Willem de (c.1690–1756)   177
Wilcocke, S.H.   69
Willem IV   143
Willem V   67, 129, 135, 150
Winkelman, Hendrik   279
Wit, Adriaan de   77
Wit, Barend de   129
Wit, Kornelis Leendertsz de (1749–1796 or 1804)   79
Wit, Leendert de   78
Wit, Pancras de   36, 223
With, Jan de (1715–1781)   96, 110, 116–17, 119
Woestijne, Karel van de   231, 289
Wolberg, Jurriaan   85, 108, 224
Wordsworths   301
Worms, Hendrik   278–80

Zalm, Jakob   275
Zeeridder, Klaas (–1732)   52
Zegert, Jan Frederik   191
Zoet, Herman   270
Zummack, Christiaan   73
Zwaan, Matthijs (1690–1738)   271–2
Zwijndregt, Pieter van   79

Index of Ship Names

Admiraal De Ruyter   170
Admiraal de Suffren   278
Afrikaan   57
Alsem   273
Amsterdam   202, 204, 278
Anna   284
Anna Catherina   275
Aschat   232, 291

Bartha Petronella   163
Belvliet   263
Berbices   234
Berkhout   276
Bleiswijk   257
Blijdorp   101, 273–5
Blitterswijk   57
Boekenrode   189
Bredenhof   261, 277
Bredenrode   189, 278
Broeders Lust   139
Buren   261

Castor   293
Castricum   192

Delft   57
Domburg   275
Drechterland   293, 299
Drie Papegaaien 226

Edam 141
Eendracht   141
Enkhuizer Maagd   57
Erfprins   277

Faam   219

Geertruid   25
Gerechtigheid   258
Gouverneur-Generaal   242

Haamstede   220
Haasje   232
Handellust   197
Heesburg   120
Herstelder   95, 141–2, 149, 181, 253, 255, 284

Herstelder   263
Hertog van Brunswijk   266
Hillegom   208, 278
Hofvliet   205
Hofwegen   137
Hogestelt   275
Holland   80
Hollandia   176, 278, 282, 284. 288
Hoorn   245
Horstendaal   278
Huis Om   270
Huis te Krooswijk   165
Huis te Rensburg   286

Ida   161

Jonge Hellingman   168
Jonge Lieve   233, 235, 240
Juffrouw Johanna Barbara   78
Juno   68

Kasteel van Medemblik   52
Kievit   275
Kronenburg   185

Lage Polder   242
Leiden   299
Leimuiden   276
Lekkerland   190
Loenderveen   271
Loo   280
Loosdrecht   275
Luchtbol   293
Luchtenburg   209

Meerlust   211
Meerwijk   297
Meijenburg   251
Mijnden   251

Nagelboom   57
Negotie   135, 297
Nieuwvliet   277
Nijenburg   43

Oosterland   221
Oosthuizen   54

Oranjezaal   279
Ouwerkerk   163, 257
Overhout   241

Padmos   101
Pallas   256–7
Pasgeld   106

Rendier   104
Rijnhuizen   191
Rijnsburg   263
Rust en Werk   169

Schelde   57
Sloepje   276
Slot ter Hoge   62, 208, 262, 275
Sloten   262
Sloterdijk   270
Stavenisse   267, 272
Stralen   219
Surseance   73, 298–9

Ter Meijen   280

Valk   297, 299
Vis   237
Vliegend Hart   208, 275, 288
Voetboog   275
Voorberg   34
Vredelust   291
Vreeburg   79
Vrijburg   66, 296
Vrouwe Elisabeth   277
Vrouwe Katharina Wilhelmina   280

Waakzaamheid   49, 50
Watervliet   276
Westkapelle   286
Woestduin   260

Zaanstroom   297, 299
Zeeland   239
Zeewijk   208, 276